CONTEMPORARY ART

FROM CRESCENT MOON PUBLISHING

The Art of Andy Goldsworthy: Complete Works: Special Edition
by William Malpas

The Art of Andy Goldsworthy
by William Malpas

Andy Goldsworthy: Touching Nature
by William Malpas

Andy Goldsworthy In Close-Up
by William Malpas

Richard Long: The Art of Walking
by William Malpas

The Art of Richard Long: Complete Works: Special Edition
by William Malpas

Constantin Brancusi: Sculpting the Essence of Things
by James Pearson

Alison Wilding: The Embrace of Sculpture
by Susan Quinnell

Eric Gill: Nuptials of God
by Anthony Hoyland

The Erotic Object: Sexuality in Sculpture
From Prehistory to the Present Day
by Susan Quinnell

Minimal Art and Artists in the 1960s and After
by Laura Garrard

Land Art, Earthworks, Installations, Environments, Sculpture
by William Malpas

Land Art: A Complete Guide to Landscape, Environmental,
Earthworks, Nature, Sculpture and Installation Art
by William Malpas

Richard Long In Close-Up
by William Malpas

Land Art In Close-Up
by William Malpas

Installation Art In Close-Up
by William Malpas

Colourfield Painting: Minimal, Cool, Hard Edge, Serial
and Post-Painterly Abstract Art From the Sixties to the Present
by Laura Garrard

Mark Rothko: The Art of Transcendence
by Julia Davis

Land Art In Close-Up

Land Art In Close-Up

William Malpas

CRESCENT MOON

CRESCENT MOON PUBLISHING
P.O. Box 393
Maidstone
Kent, ME14 5XU
United Kingdom

First published 2001. Second edition 2007.
© William Malpas 2001, 2007.

Printed and bound in Great Britain.
Set in Garamond 9 on 14pt.
Designed by Radiance Graphics.

The right of William Malpas to be identified as the author of *Land Art In Close-Up* has been asserted generally in accordance with sections 77 and 78 of the Copyright, Designs and Patents Act 1988.

British Library Cataloguing in Publication data

Malpas, William
Land Art: In Close-Up. 2nd ed. (Art In Close-Up Series)
1. Earthworks (Art)
2. Conceptual Art
3. Art, Modern – 20th century
I. Title

709.04076

ISBN 9781861712367 (Pbk)

CONTENTS

ACKNOWLEDGEMENTS

Thanks to Anthony d'Offay Gallery, London; Sperone Westwater, New York; Verlag der Buchhandlung Walther König, Köln; Thames & Hudson, London; Coracle Press, London; Karsten Schubert, London; Konrad Fischer Galerie, Düsseldorf; Hayward Gallery, London; MW Press, Noordwijk, Holland; Musée d'Art Moderne de la Ville de Paris; Center for Contemporary Arts, Santa Fe, New Mexico; Phaidon Press, London; Tate Gallery, London; Tate Publishing.

Illustrations: all works by Richard Long are in the collection of the artist, and © the artist, unless otherwise stated.

Thanks to the copyright holders of the illustrations:
Tate Gallery, St Ives. Tate Modern, London. Museum of Modern Art, New York. Skystone Foundation. Chinati Foundation, Texas. Sculpture At Goodwood. Her Majesty's Stationery Office. Kunstsammlung Nordrhein-Westfalen, Düsseldorf (Walter Klein). Galeria Mário Sequeira, Braga, Portugal. Musée d'Art Moderne de la Ville de Paris. Saatchi Collection, London. Chris Drury. Andy Goldsworthy. Hamish Fulton. David Nash.

For poetry quotations: University of California Press, Berkeley. Routledge, London. Methuen, London. Faber & Faber, London.

ABBREVIATIONS

ROBERT SMITHSON

RS   *Selected Writings*

RICHARD LONG

IC 1/2   *Richard Long: In Conversation*, Parts 1 & 2
OW   *Old World New World*
WC   *Walking in Circles*
SF   *An Interview with Richard Long*, 1994
RC   *An Interview with Richard Long*, by R. Cork
RL   iRichard Long, *1986*

ANDY GOLDSWORTHY

AG   *Andy Goldsworthy*
S   *Andy Goldsworthy: Stone*
HE   *Hand to Earth: Andy Goldsworthy, Sculpture, 1976-1990*

INTRODUCTION

For the land artist, the whole planet is an artist's studio. The land artist ranges over the whole globe. A desert, a beach, a field, a forest becomes a studio, a place of creative activity. The landscape itself is crucial in land art. That's obvious. Or is it? This means the very texture and colour and shape and dampness and springiness and strength and size of moss, for instance. Or a stone. Or a crevice in a rock formation. The way the light falls on a patch of grass, the little bits of dead, yellowish grass on top of the newer, green grass. Pine cones, closed-up. Flowers turning sunward in the late afternoon. These are the things land artists deal with in making art. These are the actualities that artists employ when they create artworks. To fully appreciate land art, then, one has to look really closely, to grasp the details, as well as the overall conception. This is true of small sculptures, as well as the larger American earthworks.

For David Nash, land art is about getting as close as possible to nature: the land artist does not paint nature, at a distance, with a paintbrush or watercolour block in front of her/him. The sketchpad or easel is a wall between artist and world. The land artist, rather, dives in, 'gets right in there', as Nash says. The land artist does not use oil or pastel or ink to 'represent' nature. Rather, s/he works directly with nature, getting her/ his fingers dirty with mud, snow, sheep shit, stone, ferns, wood. It is exactly the same with poetry. Poets have long written of nature in close-up, of the tiny details that go to make up an accurate description of the natural world. Land art can be seen as the sculptural equivalent, in one sense, of nature poetry, so that Heizer, Long, Fulton, Nash, de Maria, Holt and Aycock are the inheritors of Wordsworth, Basho, Petrarch, Frost, Shakespeare, Dickinson, Neruda, Rilke and Pushkin. The nature poem itself is a piece of land art, a work evoking or representing or describing or situated in particular places. ('The sculpture that I do,' says David Nash, 'is appropriate to a particular place and it stays in that place. It is made from and for that place').[1]

'Land art' is a term that includes a wide variety of artistic forms, like the term 'garden'. Gardens are not a single form with a single set of characteristics. Gardens can be so various that some critics have suggested that the word 'garden' is as broad and vague as words such as 'art'.[2] (Gardens can be very small or very large; they can be flat or terraced; they can be organized around a 'natural' plan or a strict geometric plan; they can be 'wild' or 'tamed'; they can be enclosed or open; they can contain lakes, ponds, streams, fountains, statues, trees, lawns, shrubs, rocks, walls, fences, benches, flowers, stones, follies, ruins, grottoes, temples, paths and many kinds of environmental art. A Japanese garden, with its stones and sand raked into patterns, is quite different from an English kitchen garden. Gardens can be vast displays of state and regal power, such as the garden as Versailles, or modest attempts at cultivating food in a backyard. Gardens have been made for many reasons: in the pursuit of decoration, finance, medicine, religion, contemplation, play, sport, and food. Isamu Noguchi thinks of gardens as 'sculpturing of space: a beginning, and a groping to another level of sculptural experience and use: a total sculpture space experience beyond individual sculptures. A man may enter such a space: it is in scale with him; it is real' (1968).

If there can be 'found art', can there be 'found gardens'? Perhaps an artist, working in the Conceptual and environmental art mode, could simply claim any piece of land as their 'found garden', just as artists such as Marcel Duchamp and Robert Rauschenberg took found objects and exhibited them as art. When does a garden start becoming a garden? Is a blade of grass a garden? Is two plants on a window ledge a garden? Or five plants, or ten plants, clustered together in pots? Is an overgrown path a garden? Or an allotment dedicated to growing tomatoes and runner beans? Is a patch of grass behind an abandoned petrol station a garden? Is a municipal park, consisting only of children's swings and slides on grass a garden? Is a farmer's field a garden? And when does a garden stop being a garden? Is a garden of a hundred years ago that can barely be seen amidst piles of refuse still a garden? How much of the human touch is required to make a piece of land a garden? If sand raked into a pattern can be a garden for the

Japanese, is any piece of raked sand a garden? Are the patterns made in the sand by the receding tide a garden?

Environmental or land or garden art can include American earthworks (such as those by Michael Heizer and Walter de Maria); ephemeral interventions in the environment (such as those by Andy Goldsworthy, Christo and Michael Singer); architectural installations (such as those by Alice Aycock, Mary Miss and Nancy Holt); land art as performance art (Richard Long, Hamish Fulton, Christo); land art that involves landscaping and garden art (such as Alan Sonfist, Robert Irwin and Ian Hamilton Finlay); and sculpture or art parks.

Land art gains much of its power from particular places. Most land artists, for instance, work away from built-up areas. Some, like Michael Heizer and Walter de Maria, work in what are regarded as 'exotic' locations – deserts and mountains. The 'glamour' of the locations aids the sculptures. Some land art is over-powered by the Romantic settings. Some of Richard Long's stone circles, for instance, look feeble in their desert or snowscape locations. Land art in its grander moments echoes the gestures of High Romanticism – the Blakean, Wordsworthian, Goethean, Turnerian gestures – which have become so familiar in Western art. 'The Romantics' awe in the face of nature is hard to revive in a culture as estranged from nature as ours' remarked Robert Hughes, 'but, enfolded in distance and immensity, such works of land-art [by Heizer and de Maria] are saturated in nostalgia for it' (1991, 386).

The 'Land Art Sublime' (*pace* Robert Rosenblum's coining of the term 'Abstract Sublime' to describe Barnett Newman's and Mark Rothko's paintings) might include the snow and stone circles made in the wildernesses of Scotland, Nepal and Peru of Richard Long; the stone circles of Nancy Holt; Christo's islands surrounded with pink polypropylene; and of course Smithson's *Spiral Jetty*. The nature poet uses the same emotional/ cultural stuff as the land artist: the human relationship with nature. Whatever the poet writes about or the land artist sculpts, it is the *feeling* for nature that is important, the relation between self and nature, that is employed by both poet and land artist. As Clement Greenberg, the foremost critic of postwar art in America, wrote: '[a]rt is a matter strictly of experience, not of principles', a statement which chimes with the views of land artists, for whom experience is primary.[3]

Brancusi, Long, Woodrow, Houshiary and many sculptors have spoken of the importance of materials in their work, how they learn from their materials, and 'follow' their materials. Tony Cragg speaks of 'works in which I learnt from the materials'.[4] A stone is not merely a stone for land artists: it has its own essence, its own form and presence.

> Nothing could convince Brancusi that a rock was only a fragment of inert matter; like his Carpathian ancestors, like all neolithic men, he sensed a presence in the rock, a power, an "intention" that one can only call "sacred." [5]

The land artist has a special, fetishistic relation with her/ his materials: they are not simply bits of matter to be wielded in a particular way. They are treated with respect. Goldsworthy and Laib collect leaves, berries, pollen, honey and other natural elements and weave sensuous artifacts that are ephemeral and intricate.

Much (but not all) of land art is very expensive. That is, it is expensive moving tons of earth around. Taking a motorbike out into the desert and drawing lines with it is one thing (as Michael Heizer had done in *Circular Surface Displacement* [1968], north of Las Vegas), but making a 40 mile 18 foot high fence (Christo) is another. Much of land art requires patrons, sponsors, coordination with galleries, lawyers, public administrators, helpers and industry. The costliness of land art may explain why much of it is American.[6] Land art requires investment with no immediate return. Patrons are crucial to land art. In American earthworks the key patrons were the Dia Art Foundation, Robert C. Scull and Virginia Dwan, director of the Dwan Galery between 1966 and 1971.

Richard Long perhaps speaks for many British sculptors when he writes of his aversion to American earthwork art:

> In the Sixties there was a feeling that art need not be a production line of more objects to fill the world. My interest was in a more thoughtful view of art and nature, making art both visible and invisible, using ideas, walking, stones, tracks, water, time, etc, in a flexible way... It was the antithesis of so-called American "Land Art," where an artist needed money to be an artist, to buy real estate to claim possession of the land, and to wield machinery. True capitalist art.[7]

Although Long (and others) may despise the amounts of money spent by the American earthwork artists, isn't he also part of '[t]rue capitalist art'? Doesn't he also live off his art? Doesn't he just wander around the planet on his sacred 'walks', putting a few stones into a pile, and taking a photo of his (slight) efforts? Isn't Richard Long (and Andy Goldsworthy, David Nash, Shirazeh Houshiary, Rachel Whiteread, Richard Wentworth, Bill Woodrow, Helen Chadwick, Alison Wilding, Hamish Fulton, Richard Deacon) also a part of the 'capitalist' art world? Don't Long's artworks sell for lots of money, a lot more money than the materials cost? Isn't Long being hypocritical when he criticizes the bombastic aspects of American land art when he himself benefits from the hugely over-priced art gallery system, where even mundane art it seems (such as artists' prints) are sold for 'silly prices'?

It's easy to view Christo's wrapped buildings or de Maria's $500,000 *Vertical Earth Kilometer* as expensive, pointless art. This sort of land art may be '[t]rue capitalist art', an art of excessive cost and excessive waste, but then, art has been full of idiot amounts of money for ages. What about Christo's wrappings? They cost a bomb, for sure, but, as Christo says, he pays for it himself, with money made from selling smaller works. Christo's *Running Fence* cost $2.5 million; *The Umbrellas* in Japan and California, cost $26,000,000. Christo says his art 'has to do with things that are very simple'[8] This definition can also apply to other land artists; they, too, transform ordinary things.

When these transformations of the ordinary cost so much, and require 200 rock climbers, as Christo's covering of the Reichstag in Berlin needed, then commentators wonder about the 'importance' of such artistic productions. There is something right and homely about Andy Goldsworthy and his couple of stonewallers building a wall in the Northern wildernesses of Britain. They toil away in true grimy, stalwart, Eric Gill-like craftsman style. But there's something cynical and obscene, perhaps, about Michael Heizer or Walter de Maria carving great gashes in the American desert, or Christo making artworks that cost 26 million dollars yet only last for two weeks. Surely that money would be better spent on a hospital? Or on feeding Third World countries? Surely artworks that cost millions of dollars but only 'benefit' a (relatively) tiny amount of people are wasteful? Isn't famine relief a better alternative? Perhaps one could make famine relief/ earthquake relief/ medical supply/ housing, and other 'charity' and 'aid' projects, an art event? Perhaps if Christo spent $26 million on providing food for the needy instead of wrapping a building in Berlin in a bit of plastic, people would not be so angry? When artists spend such vast amounts of money on art, it's no wonder people find this obscene. But then, if spending millions of dollars on art were outlawed, we'd have no Hollywood, no movie industry, no television. These are the hypocrisies and ambiguities that surround art. How can one 'justify' a $26,000,000 Christo wrapping? Or a typical Hollywood feature film (cost: $30 million, with a typical advertizing budget of $2-10 million)?

If Christo's artworks cost a lot, this is chickenfeed to scientific and military experiments, which cost billions of dollars. The Large Hadron Collider, for instance, will cost $1.5 billion. Just one nuclear submarine costs the same amount. In the mid-1980s 1,000,000 dollars per minute were spent on the arms industry (1982 figures). That's $16,500 per second. Cheap, eh?

Land art is related to, or a part of, Conceptual art. For much land art exists only in photographs, memories, words, various texts which are not the land art itself. Works that can be seen and those that are hidden or 'invisible' have the same importance for the artist. One of the hallmarks of the 'ideal Conceptual work', as Mel Bochner says, is 'an exact linguistic correlative, that is, it could be described and experienced in its data and it could be infinitely repeatable'.[9] Land art is often Conceptual art: Christo's *Running Fence*, de Maria's *The New York Earth Room* and Robert Morris's steam pieces exist now only as photographs, memories and criticism. Many sculptors have spoken of the importance of the *making* of the sculpture, its actual construction, with real (and sometimes organic, living) materials. As Barry Flanagan put it: '[m]y work isn't centred in experience. The making of it is itself the experience'.[10] In some artists, the material employed also has a symbolic or added meaning, as in Joseph Beuys' *Fettecke* or 'fat corner', a sculpture with powerful autobiographical and semiotic associations. Beuys emphasized process, evolution, change: his sculpture, he said, was not 'fixed and finished. Processes continue in most of them: chemical reactions, fermentations, colour changes, decay, drying up. Everything is in a *state of change*'.[11]

The texts of land artists also draw on poetry, on concrete or 'visual poetry', or typewriter art. Long, for instance, prints his laconic texts in circles (*Full Moon Circle of Ground*, Dartmoor, 1983), in concentric circles (*Three Moors, Three Circles,* Liskeard to Porlock, 1982), in vertical lines, as in trendy style magazines (*The Isle of Wight as Six Walks*, 1982), and in curved swathes of text (*A Moved Line in Japan*, 1983).

Laid over Long's walks is the grid of the map: the maps in Conceptual art constitute a new landscape of the soul, as Robert Smithson wrote in 1968:

> A cartography of uninhabitable places seems to be developing – complete with decoy diagrams, abstract grid systems made of stone and tape (Carl Andre and Sol LeWitt), and electronic "mosaic" photomaps from NASA. (1968, 26)

In land art photographs, the viewer is not offered a *range* of viewpoints of a work, although land artists clearly take more than one shot of each work they make. No artist takes just *one* photo out of a 36 exposure 35mm film, or one frame out of a twelve shot 120mm format film. No, an artist, like an photographer, takes a range of shots, at different, bracketed exposures, from different viewpoints (much as the trendy advertizing film director of today shoots twelve hours of footage for just one thirty second advert). 12 Each land artist, then, must select this or that viewpoint, behind this bush or next to that tree. The land artist is therefore also a photographer, selecting views, reframing their works, making choices about lighting, angles, lenses, film stock, and so on. The land artist will make decisions about exactly *when* to photograph their work. Some works are ephemeral, and last only moments, so the photograph must be taken immediately. Other works, such as the stone circles of Nancy Holt, last longer. The land artist as photographer can therefore wait for a certain combination of sunlight and clouds. This is particularly crucial in cloudy places like Britain, where lighting can vary so dramatically over a few minutes. As anyone who has been on Dartmoor or the Peak District will know, the sunlight can burst through the clouds at one moment, then a moment later there'll be dark, sombre clouds, looking as if it's going to rain. A moment later, it *will* rain, and afterwards, facing away from the sun, you might see a rainbow. Much of the world's weather is this changeable, so every land art photograph is a highly selective and subjective view of a particular place.

Land artists must also oversee the journey of the films they've shot from development through printing to framing. As anyone who has taken a photo will know, all manner of details can affect how one reads a photograph: how it is printed, light, dark, soft, hard, cropped, full frame, more red, more blue, burnt in, dodged, touched up, glossy or matt paper, and so on. The size of the photo affects it very much, as does the frame. Go into any framer's shop and one'll see a plethora of different types of frame. All these things the viewer might take in at one glance in a gallery, but the artist has to make decisions all the time about all these matters, and many more. Land artists/ sculptors, then, must be accomplished photographers. Their work must be high standard, for it is exhibited in 'high art' locations, such as the city gallery, or glossy coffee table art books.

In land art, the commentary, the written records, the obsessive documentation, is just as important as the artwork itself. Often, it *is* the artwork. The land artist's life becomes part of the artwork. Jan Dibbets said that documenting the work wasn't important: 'I've done lots of works without taking photographs'.13 Meticulously, land artists record their activities ('walk this morning; made a snow sculpture; it wasn't successful; back home for lunch'). Ultimately, *any* activity can be land art. Going to the shops can be a piece of art. You might drop a stone on the path as you go, or perhaps not. Either way, you've just made a work of art. Is, then, walking to Josie Smith's corner shop in Taunton Street for a pint of milk and twenty cigs a fully accomplished and thoroughly authentic work of art? Where does authenticity end and artifice begin? Or, rather, where does life end and art begin? Clearly, they are a continuum in land art.

The relation between outdoor and indoor works, between stone circles in some remote zone and a stone circle in a Western gallery, is resolved simply in land art by being regarded by the artist as a continuum. For the land artist both indoor and outdoor works are one, i.e., part of the same thing. But the viewer might see them as separate, because the viewer can't see the outdoor pieces (some land artists like to keep the locations secret). The viewer only knows the outdoor pieces from the photographs. So it's often an odd relationship with land art for the viewer. For the land artist, it's great, because the big photos and text pieces relate to her/ his own experiences, of working in the wilderness. S/he knows the work inside out: *s/he lived it*. The viewer, though, gets a different experience: s/he sees words in capitals, odd phrases, titles, dates, measurements, photographs, a bit of earth on the floor. So people love land art not because they love the little words and the photographs. They love it, perhaps, because of *what it suggests*. Land art persuades people to look outwards, away from cities, towards the landscape, towards stones and water and all the rest of it. Perhaps that's why people love land art, and nature poetry, and all things to do with nature, from gardening to walking the dog. The *work itself* isn't present in the text or photos. The work isn't 'in' the gallery. No, the work is *elsewhere*, and it is to that *elsewhere place* that people want to go. Land art creates *desire* in people, as the work of J.M.W Turner or Aleksandr Blok creates desire – for travel, for other places. Land artists speak of aiming to feel refreshed and renewed after making a work. It's the experience, perhaps, that viewers wish to gain from land art, from all art. Land art, whether by Heizer, Aycock, Holt, Long, Nash or Christo, is part of a postmodern trend in self-reflexivity, the *mise-en-abyme* commentary so familiar now. Art about (the artist's) life.

Sometimes it's odd to see land art in a gallery, for the mound of soil, the cairn of stones, the slate circle, demands the viewer to look outwards, to nature, to the wildernesses from whence this art comes. Long's stone circles are familiar now, having seen them in galleries and museums, but one is always aware of the place of their origin, and how odd they look.[14] Those sticks and stones are tiny parts of nature, bits extracted, chopped up, rearranged, as all art is nature chopped up and reformed according to the artist's æsthetics. Land art creates an ambiguous continuity with the world of nature that exists outside the gallery. Sometimes this ambiguity works against the art on show in the gallery space.

The indoor-outdoor dialectic much concerned Robert Smithson, who said 'I don't think you're freer artistically in the desert than you are inside a room'.15 One of the problems land art must address is the age-old relation between the 'real world' and art, between objects as they are in the everyday world, and objects as they are represented in art. Land art makes the viewer look again at nature: not just at the beauty of it, but at the multitudinous variety of forms in nature. Land art/ sculpture is a poetry of natural forms, in which notions of 'representation' are sidestepped, because it uses things 'as themselves' (the use of photography, though, sees a swift return of confusions over the politics of representation). An object such as the snowball in Andy Goldsworthy's *Snowballs in Summer* (1989) is not plastic masquerading as a snowball, but a real snowball. Similarly, the twigs and stalks and needles and pebbles folded into the snowballs are real. What's amazing is the actuality of nature: the variety of forms; the way the branches twist, for instance. Land artists would have the viewer look closely at nature again. By using 'real' objects, land artists aim to demolish notions of representation and mediation. Instead of a picture of snow, you get snow itself; rather than paint pebbles, or sculpt them in bronze, land artists use real pebbles. Of course, there are problems with using objects as objects – Duchamp with his ready-mades confronted this problem. The problem is partly one of context: for, placed in a museum, so obviously as items to be studied, the natural forms become art. The objects may not be on pedestals, but they are perceived as art objects. If you're looking at land art in a book or a gallery, you are already anchored in a gallery/ art/ æsthetic mode of viewing.

Ephemeral, land art aims for an eternity in one place: the soul. As Lawrence Weiner, the Conceptual/ Process artist who exhibited 'statements' (text on a wall), said: '[o]nce you know about a work of mine, you own it. There's no way I can climb into somebody's head and remove it.'16 Thus, much of land art exists in that socio-cultural space which is actually inside people's heads. Thus, anyone can 'own' land art: simply by thinking about it.

Crucial in land art is the concept and reality of change, for these works in wood, snow, ice, leaves, water, slate, grass, and so on, do not stay. They are not 'permanent', in the way that, say, bronze, marble, steel or stone can be. The soil in de Maria's *Earth Room* dries out and alters; Morris's steam works are blown away by the wind; Christo's plastic wraps stay on for two weeks. Some land artists enjoy the impermanence of (their) art, and exploit it. As politicians know, words such as 'permanent' are difficult to define, and even more difficult to maintain. Artists with a large vision of life know that nothing on Earth will be truly 'permanent'. After all, 'civilized' humanity is only 10,000 years old, or three million (depending on how one measures 'civilized'). And the planet itself will not last forever: millions more years, but not forever.

Some environmental/ action/ conceptual artworks had a built-in imperm-anence, such as Allan Kaprow's *Fluids*, large structures made from blocks of ice, which were left to melt. In "Natural Phenomena as Public Monu-ments" (1968), land artist Alan Sonfist suggested building 'museums of air' in cities, which would 'recapture the smells of earth, trees and vegetation different seasons and at different historical times, so that people would be able to experience what has been lost' (1978). Sonfist also suggested monumentalizing the natural world with sounds: '[c]ontinuous loops of natural sounds at the natural level of volume can be placed on historic sites' (ibid.).

The circle, one of the primæval symbols of eternity, cycles, time, rebirth, and so on, is employed throughout the work of land art. Circles in land art are made from slate, timber, snow or by walking in a circle; they seem to be gentler, more eco-friendly kinds of 'sculpture'. The circle shape itself speaks of organic forms, and, in some religions, speaks of the 'feminine' and the Goddess. Not a few sculptors and land artists have made the circle crucial to their works: Alison Wilding, Richard Deacon, Stephen Cox, Mary Miss, Anish Kapoor, Peter Randall-Page, Robert Morris and Dennis Oppenheim.

Some artists have produced stone circles which look very much like Stonehenge, such as Nancy Holt's monumental *Stone Enclosure: Rock Rings*. These Minimal sculptures are ambivalently related to ancient monu-ments, however, as Samuel Wagstaff remarks of Tony Smith's works: '[t]hey are related to early cultures intentionally or through sympathy – menhirs, earth mounds, cairns... [and] to this culture with equal sympathy – smokestacks, gas tanks, dump trucks, poured concrete ramps.'[17]

The land artists, then, consciously or slyly invoke ancient, prehistoric monuments. Heizer, Smithson, Morris and Holt make references to ancient earthworks, and some land artists work in landscapes rich in megaliths (such as Richard Long in the South-West of Britain). There are over nine hundred stone circles in the British Isles, a fact which surprised Richard Long when I told him.[18] Long too makes connections with prehistoric art in terms of manufacture: the cave paintings at Lascaux, Long says, were made by people's hands on the rock. Long has made references to some of the key sacred/ religious/ prehistoric sites of Britain: to Silbury Hill, the largest humanmade mound in Europe, so the textbooks say; to the ithyphallic Cerne Giant in Dorset; to Glastonbury Tor, mecca for hippies, occultists and New Age travellers; to Windmill Hill, and so on. Long even put a picture of himself with a rucksack in Africa right next to one of the famous ancient hill figures of England, the so-called 'Long Man of Wilmington', 231 foot tall, in Sussex. This is one of those prehistoric sites that some see as being an alien, or St Paul, or King Harold. Richard Long ironically compares himself with another 'Long' Man.

Land artists' stone circles often recall prehistoric stone circles. While they may deny it verbally, Nancy Holt's *Stone Enclosure*, Robert Morris's *Observatory* and Richard Long's circle sculptures evoke the great circles of Britain: the Rollright Stones in Oxfordshire, Boscawen-Ûn and the Merry Maidens in West Penwith, Cornwall, Castlerigg in Cumberland, Stanton Drew in Somerset (a huge and little-known set of circles, and the nearest large circle to Richard Long's home in Bristol), and of course the mother of all stone circles, Avebury.

The land artists benefit from the allusions to ancient monuments, because the atmosphere and magic of prehistoric stones rubs off on their own work. In stressing the importance of megaliths, the land artists not-so-subtly imply a continuity between themselves and these prehistoric relics. The æsthetic continuity that's emphasized also implies religious affinities. Thus, the land artist is the postwar equivalent of the priests and hieratic sects who created Stonehenge, the lines in Peru, the Pyramids, and Australian aborigine 'songlines'. A spirituality is affirmed in land art, which only a few land artists actually speak about. But this religious feeling is definitely there, definitely a part of the discourse of Heizer, Smithson, Fulton, Morris and Holt.

Land art is a huge area of cultural activity, with many practitioners. Instead of including a single work by many artists, I have concentrated on some of the key land artists, such as Smithson, de Maria, Heizer, Christo, Long and Goldsworthy.

ROBERT SMITHSON: *SPIRAL JETTY*

Robert Smithson was the chief mouthpiece of American earth/ site æsthetics, and is probably the most important theoretician among all land artists. Smithson's theoretical statements were published in three essays. In "The Crystal Land" Smithson recounts a trip he made to a quarry with Donald Judd, the key Minimal artist. Smithson evokes the decayed nature of the quarry, those aspects of entropy which would feature in his own work ('cracked broken shattered earth, of fragmentation, corrosion, decomposition, disintegration, rock crisis, debris slides, mud flow avalanche').[1] In the second article, "Entropy and the New Monuments" (1966), Smithson discussed the important Minimal show *Primary Structures* at the Jewish Museum. Smithson's themes were entropy in nature and art; he used the science of crystals and minerals as paradigms of the new art. Smithson had collected crystals and rocks as a child. Crystallography, for Smithson, offered 'a way of dealing with nature without falling into the old trap of the biological metaphor' (R. Hobbs, 12). No wonder, then, that when Smithson saw Judd's pink plastic boxes he compared them to 'giant crystals from another planet'.[2] The dissolution of crystals also provided Smithson with another analogy for his theory of natural entropy. The third piece, "A Sedimentation of the Mind: Earth Projects" (1968), concerned notions of time and place. Rather than sculptors such as Anthony Caro and his ilk, who still clung to the old-fashioned ideas of beauty, Smithson spoke of artists such as Walter de Maria, Carl Andre, Michael Heizer, Dennis Oppenheim, Tony Smith and Douglas Huebler (*Writings*, 85). Smithson was also interested in science fiction: the poetic elements of his art thus form a continuum: between the industrial wastelands he visited for his 'non-site' sculptures and the desolate planets of science fiction; between chaos theory in the New Physics and its exploration in postmodern science fiction; between the forms of crystals and Minimal sculptures, and so on. Smithson's exaltation of lonely postindustrial sites was echoed in the speculative fictions of writers who evoked post- or near-Holocaust worlds.

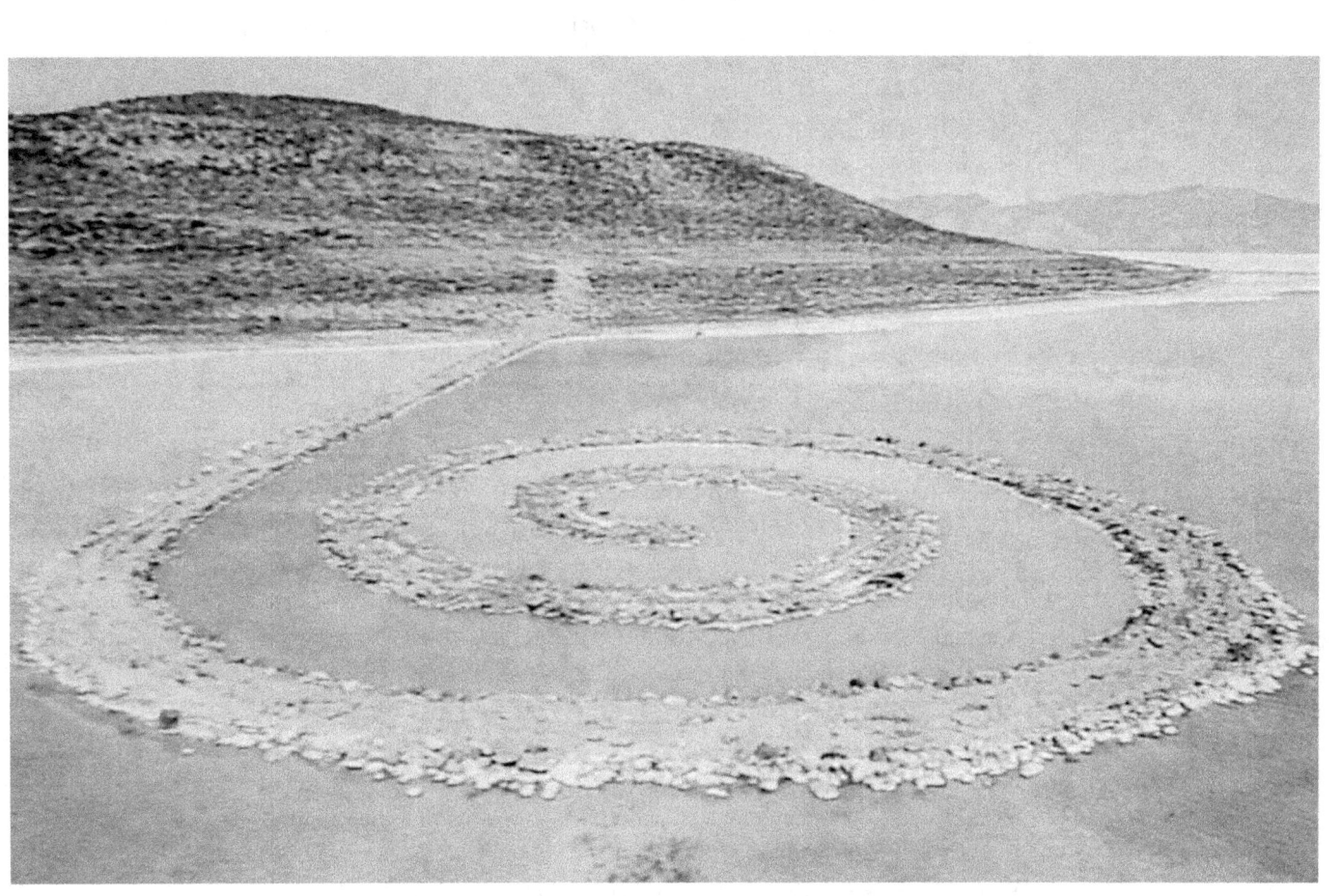

J.G. Ballard, for example, wrote of post-industrial desert lands and run-down townscapes (in *The Drought*, *Vermilion Sands*, *High-Rise* and *Low-Flying Aircraft*). In the essay "Tour of the Monuments of Passaic", itself a sci-fi sort of title, Smithson wrote about 'great pipes, sand boxes, bridges with wooden sidewalks, all standing for the irreversibility of eternity. Under the dead light of the Passaic afternoon, the desert becomes a man of infinite disintegration and forgetfulness' (*Writings*, 56). This sort of imagery is echoed in William Burroughs, J.G. Ballard, Tom Disch and other speculative fiction writers.

Robert Smithson's famous *Spiral Jetty* is a 'monumental' earthwork, though the use of the spiral motif has connotations with the ancient symbols of the Goddess.[3] Of his *Spiral Jetty*, Smithson wrote:

> As I looked at the site, it reverberated out to the horizons only to suggest an immobile cyclone while flickering light made the entire landscape appear to quake. A dormant earthquake spread into an immense roundness. From that gyrating space emerged the possibility of the Spiral Jetty. No idea, no concepts, no systems, no structures, no abstractions could hold themselves together in the actuality of that phenomenological evidence. [4]

Smithson was impressed by the characteristics of the Great Salt Lake site, the pinkish mud, the faintly violet water surrounded by limestone hills, and the 'crushing light' of the sun. He had been reading about salt lakes in Bolivia, where bacteria turned the water red to match the colour of the flamingos. Smithson found out that the Utah salt lakes were also red and pink due to algæ and mineral waste. Smithson and his wife, Nancy Holt, surveyed the area and chose a lake at Rozel Point in Utah, which had a number of cracks in the mud under the shallow water. Smithson began building it in April 1970, excavating 6,650 tons. *Spiral Jetty* was made from rocks, water, mud and precipitated salt crystals. It was 1,500 ft long and 15 ft wide. Smithson was aided by Virginia Dwan and the Ace Gallery of Vancouver. As with many other projects of the time a film was made of the construction of *Spiral Jetty*. Smithson related the work to spiral nebulæ, to salt crystals and microscopic organisms. Smithson thought in terms of eons of time, and mused on how entropy would overtake the site.[5]

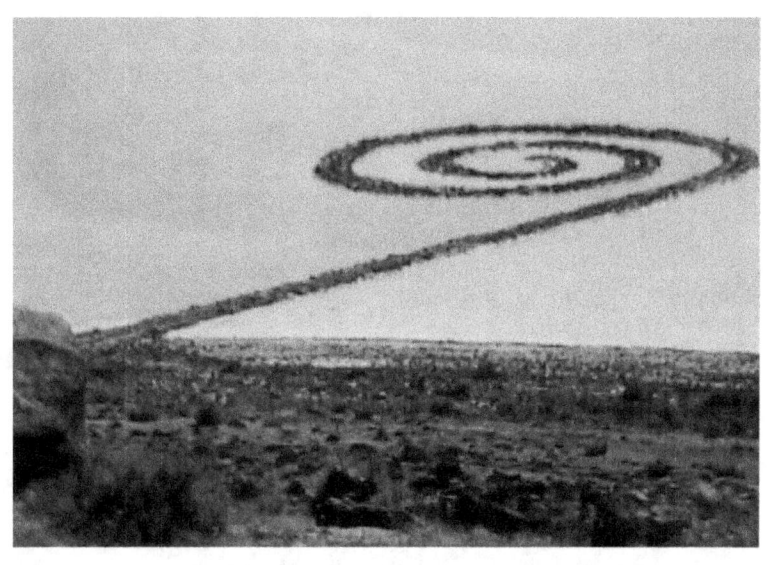

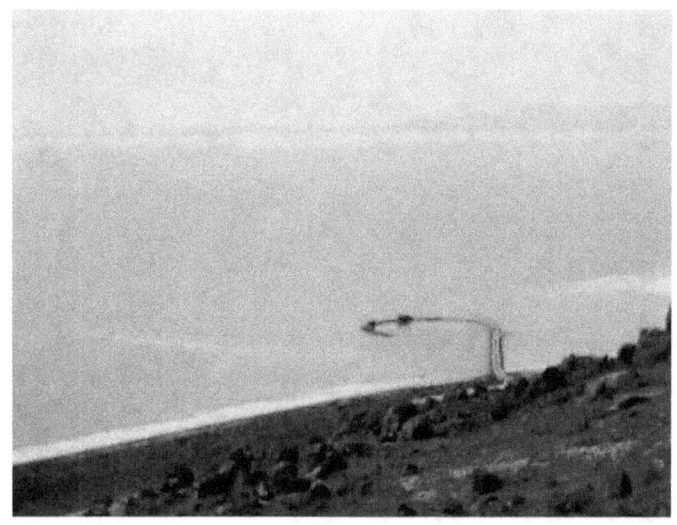

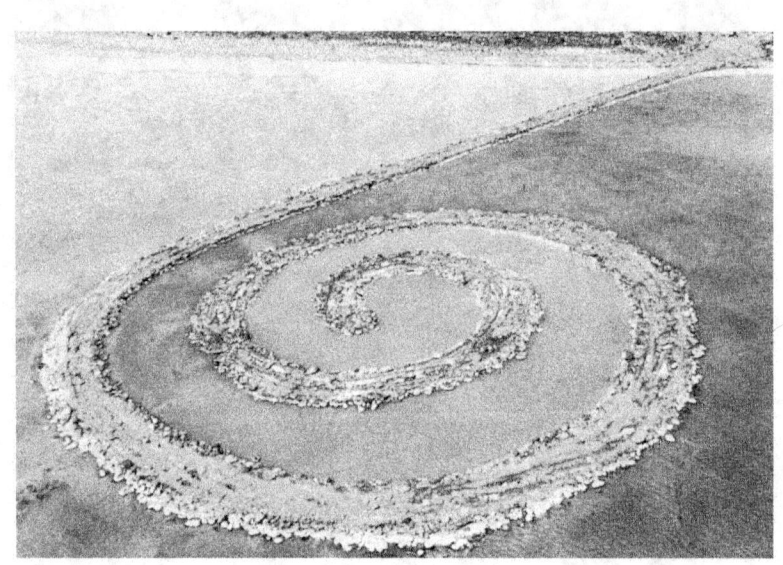

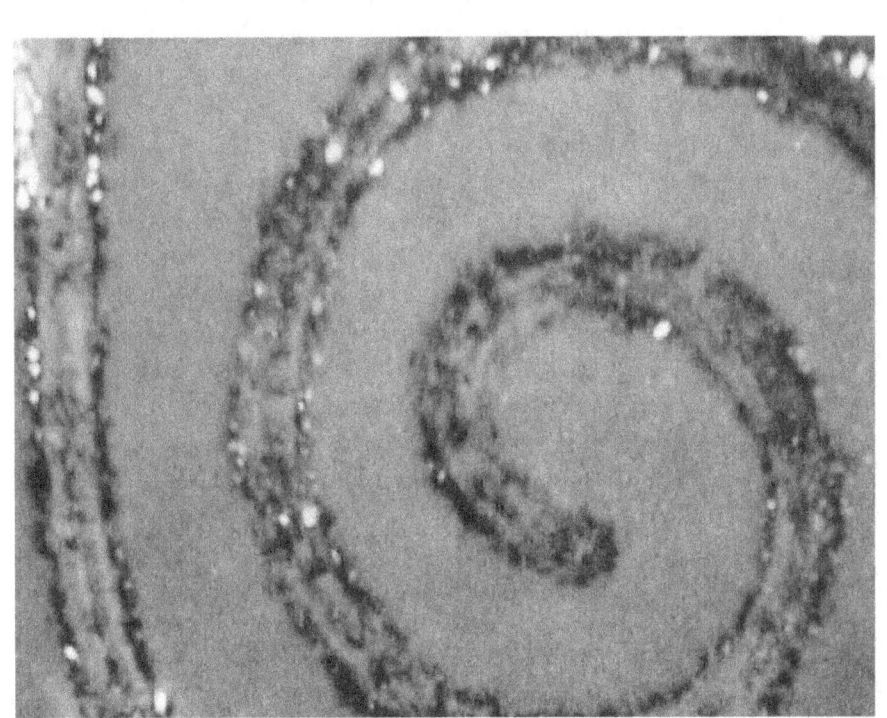

ROBERT SMITHSON: *SPIRAL JETTY*

Robert Smithson used one of the primary forms of land art, the circle, in many works, combining it with ideas taken from science (such as *Gyrostasis*, which, said Smithson, 'refers to a branch of physics that deals with rotating bodies').[1] Smithson was not adverse to religious feelings about art: when he visited the site of his *Spiral Jetty*, in the Utah salt flats, he experienced a feeling of 'a rotary that enclosed itself in an immense roundness' (ib., 111). The two elements - rational, mathematical, scientific precision and intuitive, emotional, religious feeling - are two of the chief characteristics of land art. On the one hand, land artists talk about measurements, practical details, materials, maps and spatial data. On the other hand, they hint at religious awe, spiritual feelings, prehistoric art and the influx of the numinous into modern art.

Smithson also identified his *Spiral Jetty* with a mythic whirlpool that sprang up from a tunnel connected to the Pacific Ocean. His *Spiral Jetty* was an 'immobile cyclone', it spiralled inwards from the outside: the track leaves the shore and twists round and round to the centre. *Spiral Jetty* was also linked with notions of decay in nature. In "A Sedimentation of the Mind: Earth Projects" Smithson had written '[e]very object, if it is art, is charged with the rush of time, even though it is static' (ib., 90). Ironically, Smithson's *Spiral Jetty* was itself subject to natural entropy: the water level rose and *Spiral Jetty* was submerged under water. It was ironic too that Smithson died in a plane crash while he was flying over and inspecting a site in Texas.

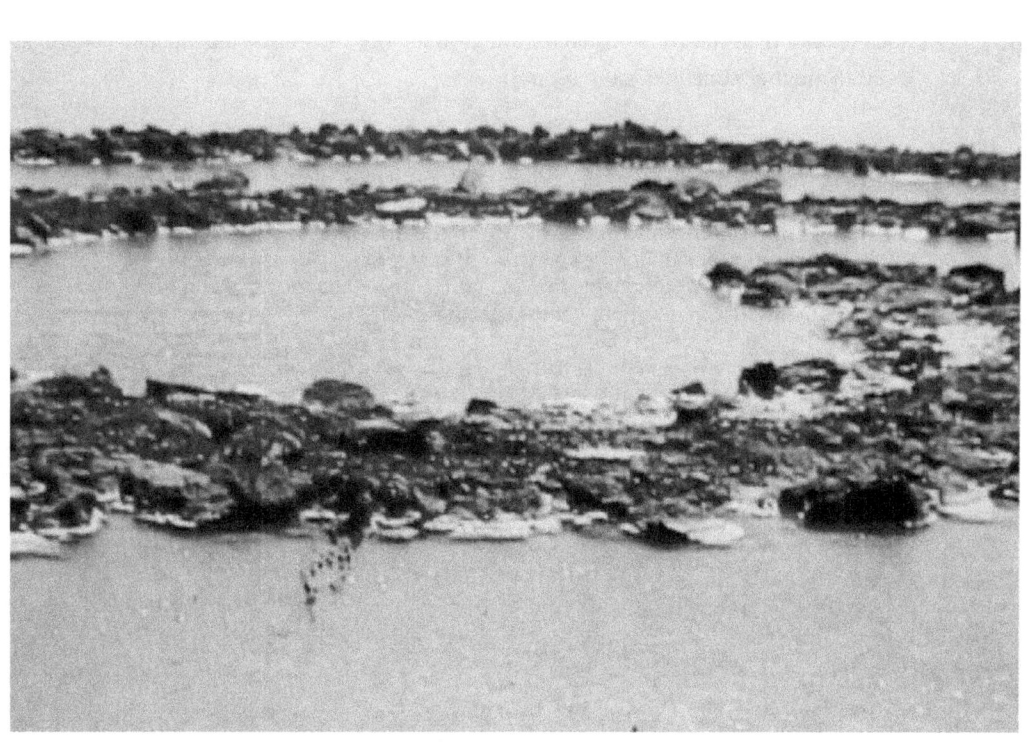

ROBERT SMITHSON: *NON-SITE WORKS*

Robert Smithson's theory of the 'non-site' was based on 'absence, a very ponderous, weighty absence'.[1] Smithson proposed a theory of a dialectic between absence and presence, in which the 'non-site' and 'site' are both interacting. In the 'non-site' work, presence and absence are there simultaneously. 'The land or ground from the Site is placed in the art (Non-Site) rather than the art is placed on the ground. The Non-Site is a container within another container – the room'.[2]

> In a sense my nonsites are rooms within rooms. Recovery from the outer fringes brings one back to the central point... The scale between indoors and outdoors, and how the two are impossible to bridge... What you are really confronted with in a non-site is the absence of the site. It is a contraction rather than an expansion of scale. One is confronted with a very ponderous, weighty absence... There is this dialectic between inner and outer, closed and open, center and peripheral.[3]

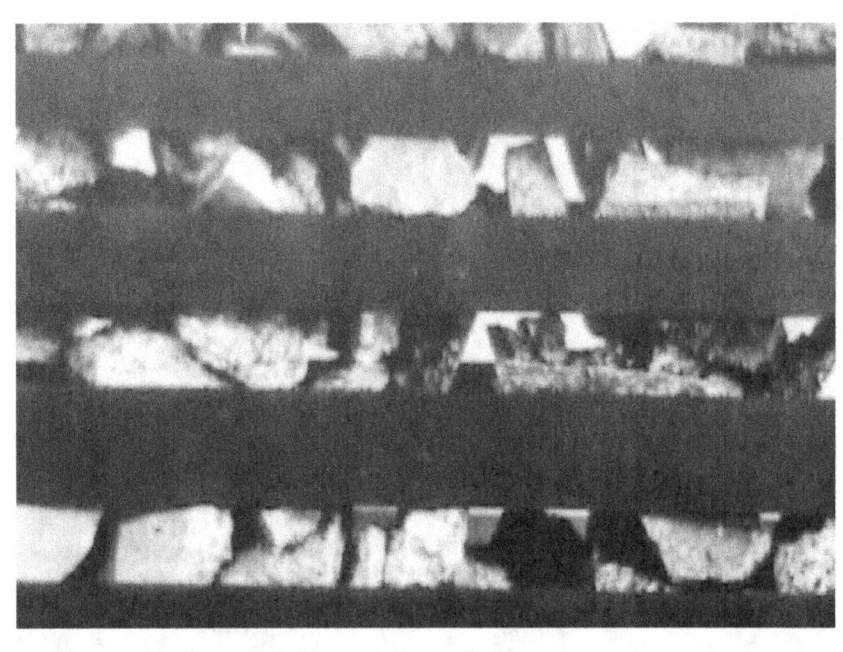

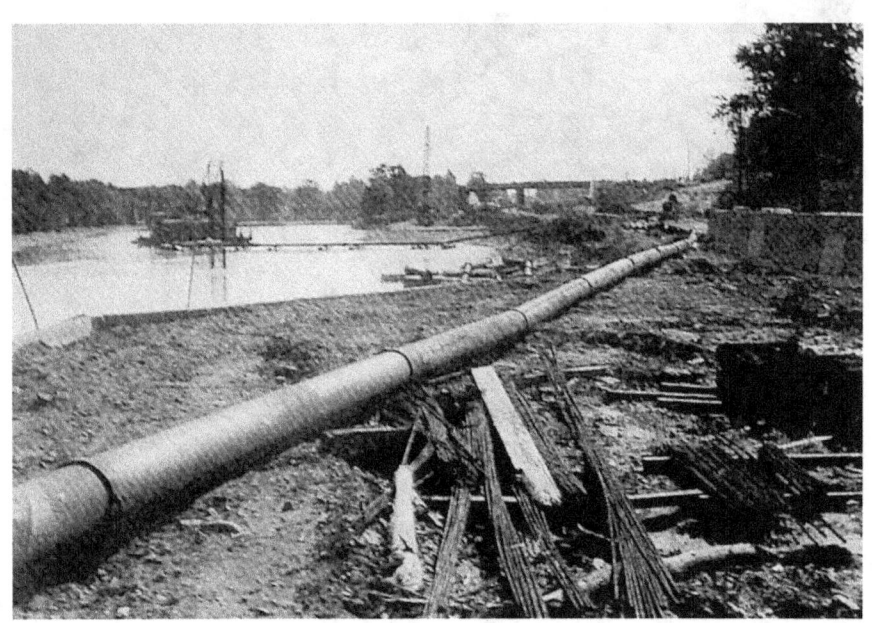

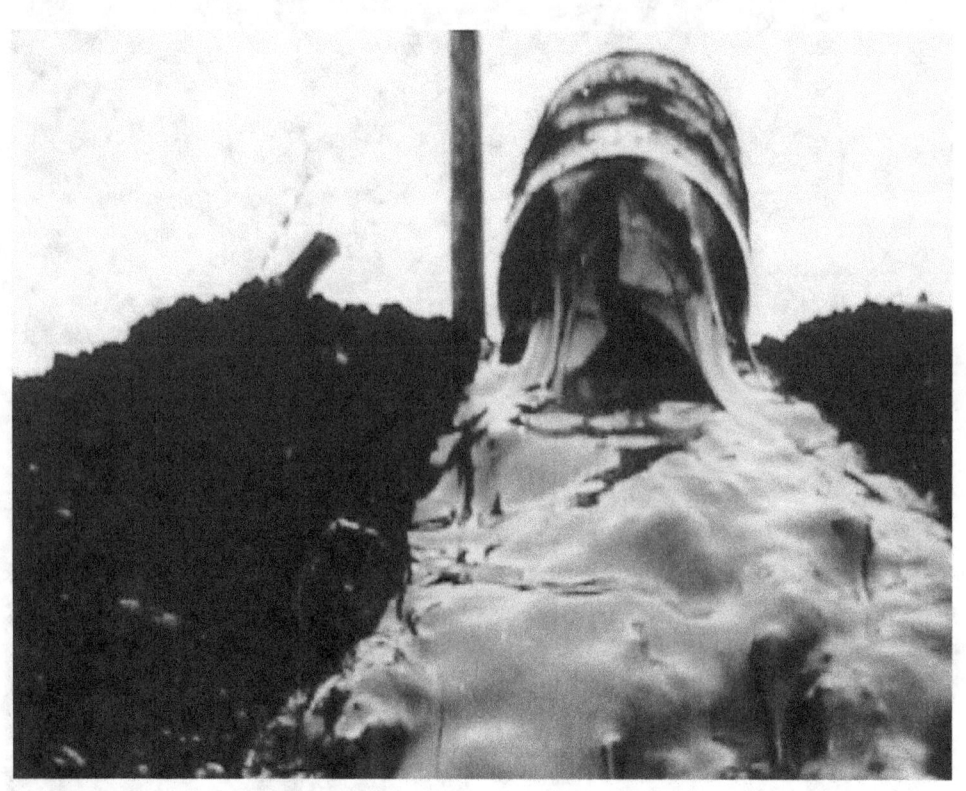

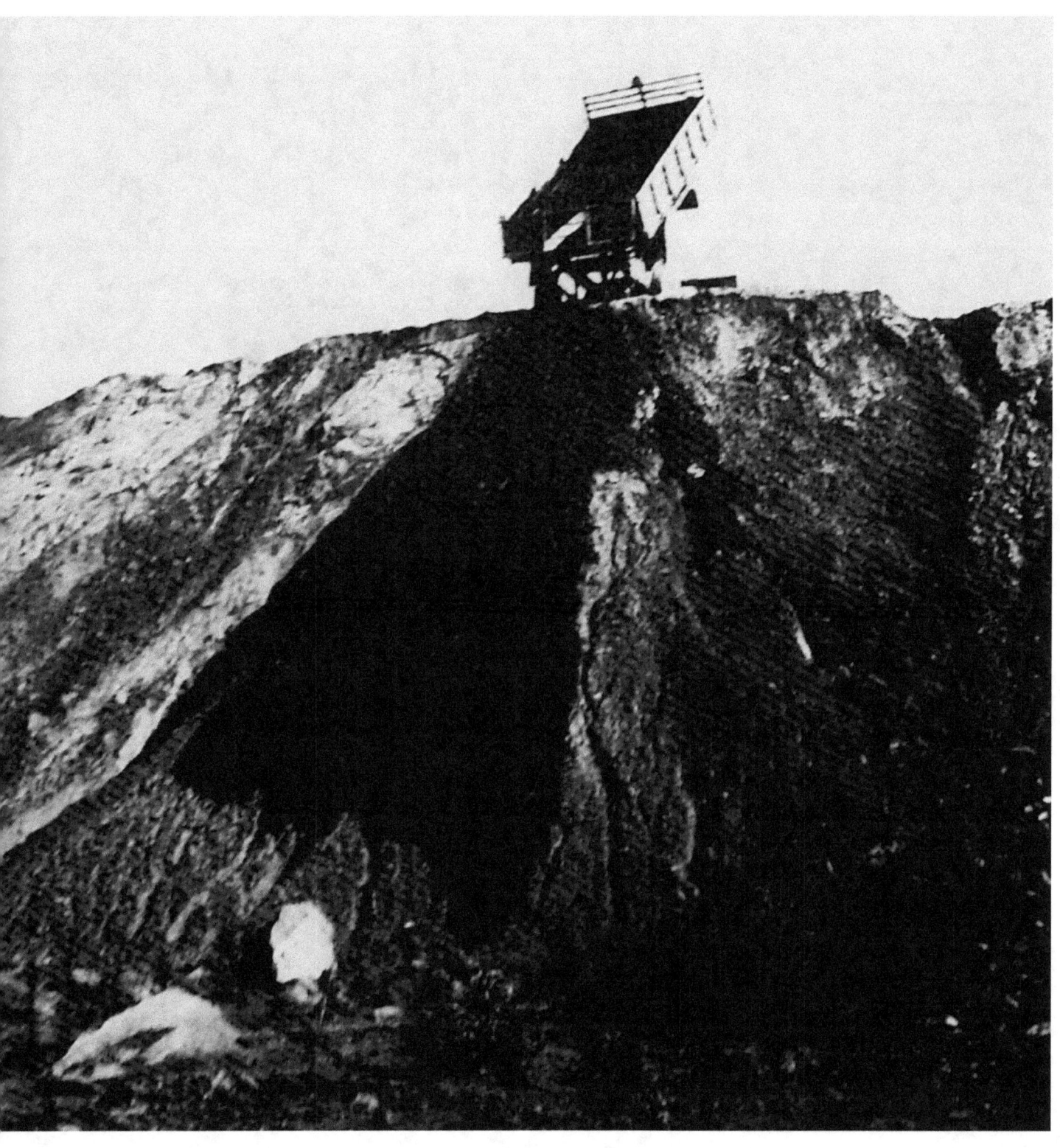

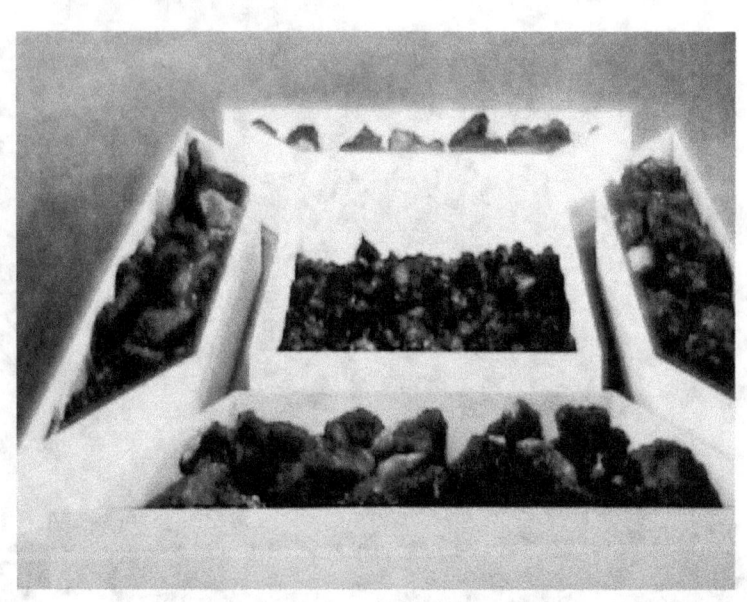

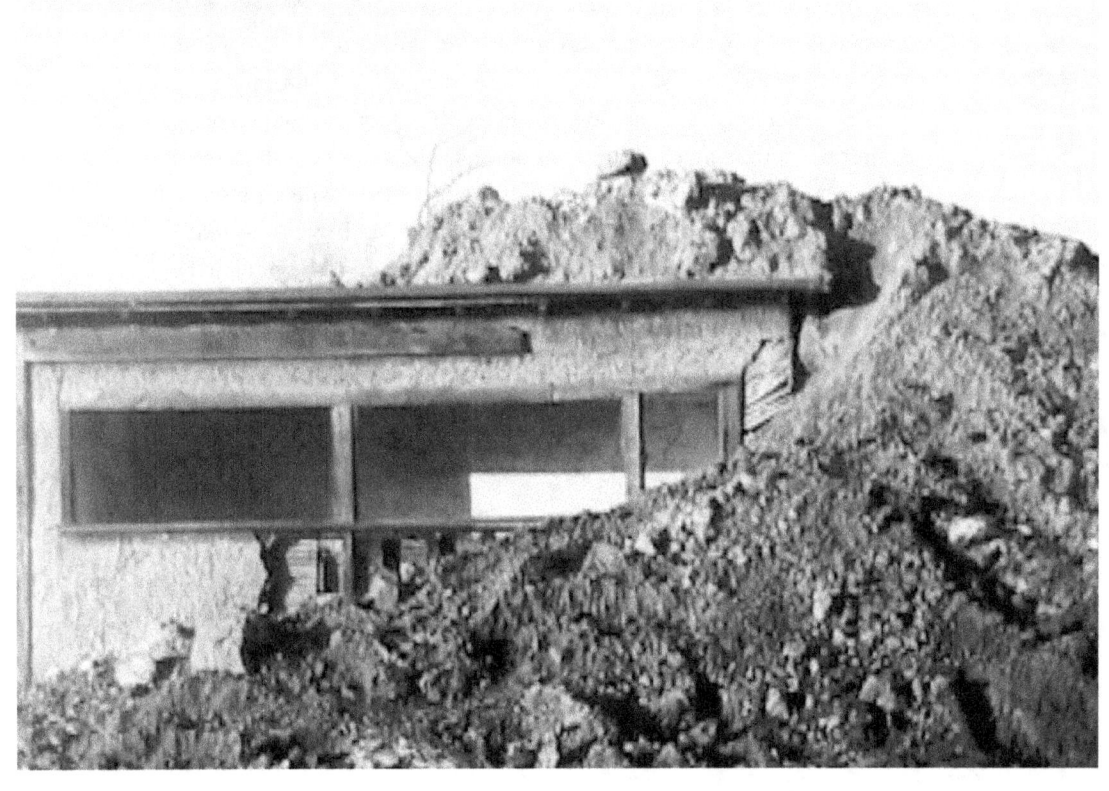

ROBERT SMITHSON: *MIRROR DISPLACEMENTS*

The 'non-site' works were permanent, gallery works. Robert Smithson's *Mirror Displacements* (1968) consisted of putting some mirrors in various settings and taking photographs of them before moving them somewhere else. *Mirror Displacements* was documented in Smithson's *Artforum* article "Incidents of Mirror Travel in the Yucatan" (1969). Sometimes Smithson put soil on top of the mirrors, to dirty them up, to sabotage 'the perfect reflections of the sky'. Smithson liked dirt, gravel, sand, sludge and sediment – indeterminate, malleable substances. Land artists often sabotaged the clinical nature of much of art – putting soil or grass or slate or horses in the clean, white gallery space. Of his Italian horse piece, where he stabled horses in a gallery, Jannis Kounellis said the aim was to increase awareness of the 'basic nature of a gallery, of its bourgeois origin', its economic and ideological aspects.[1]

1. C. Robins, 1984, 82.

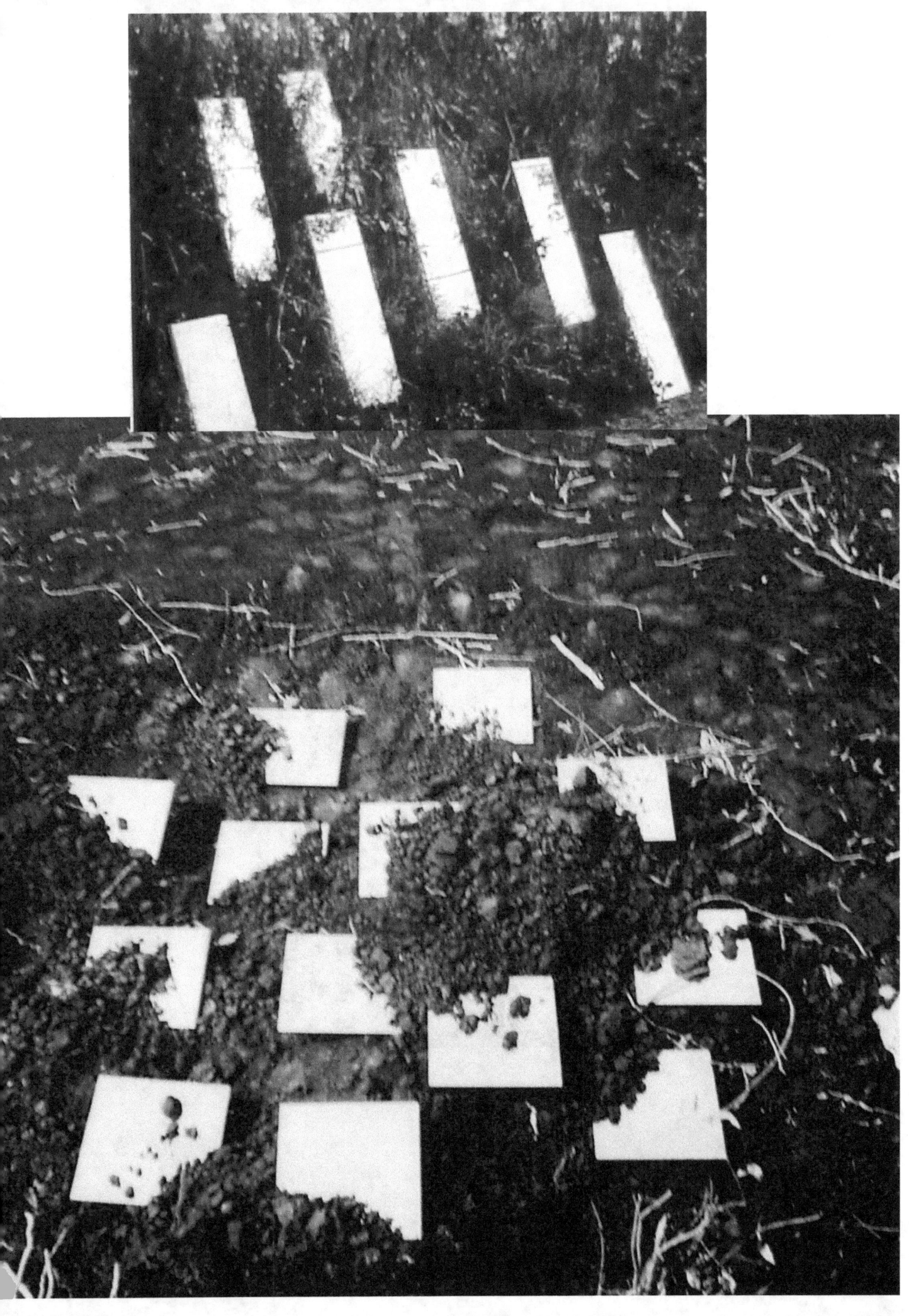

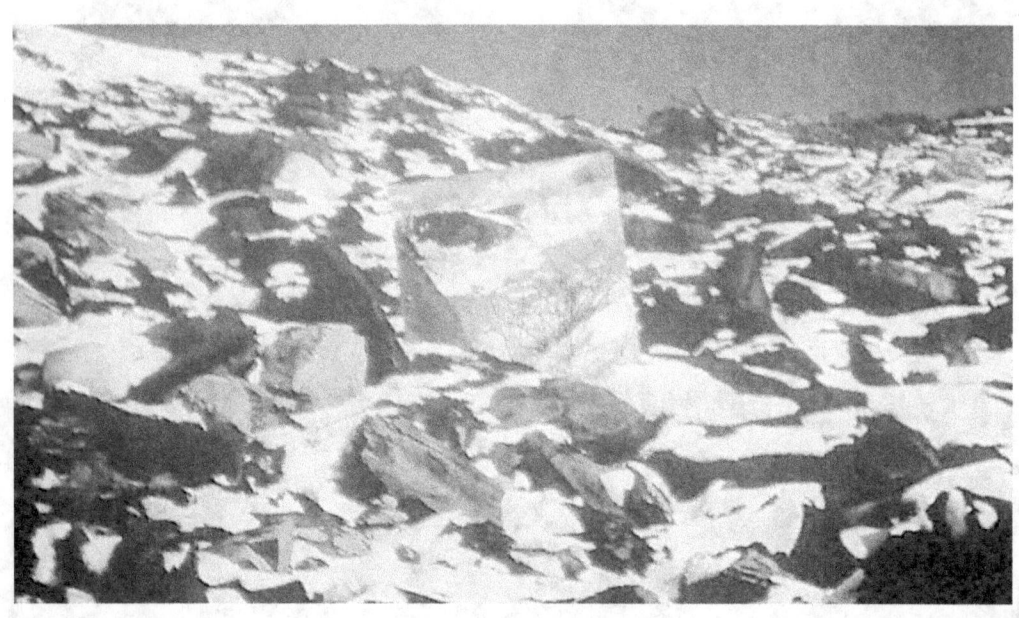

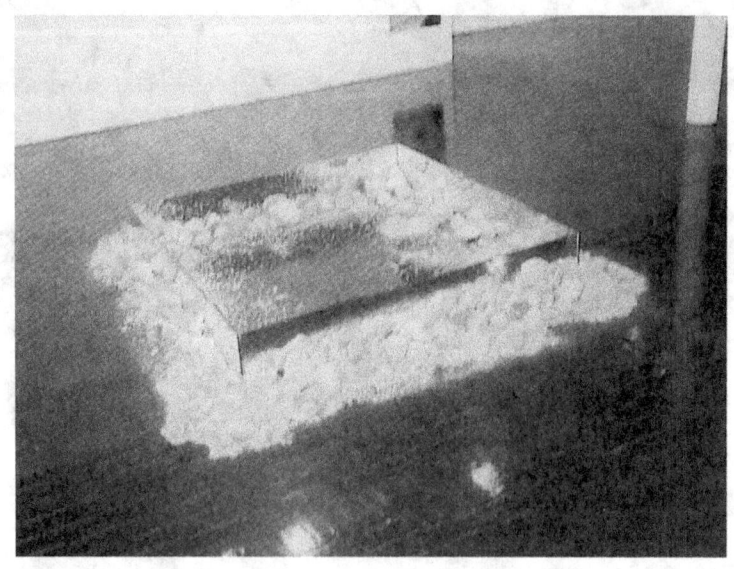

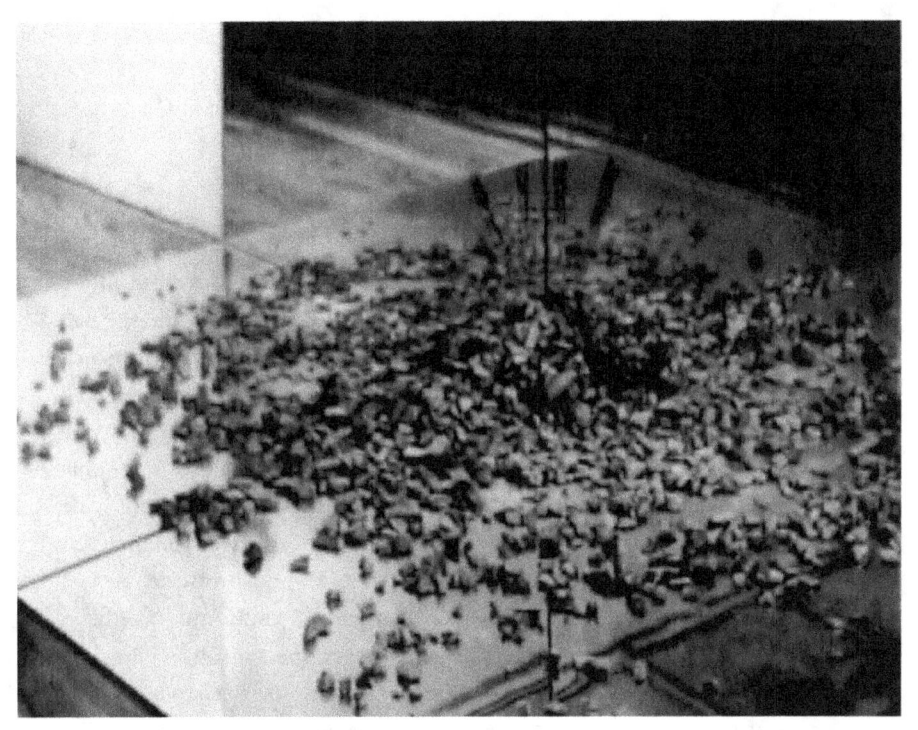

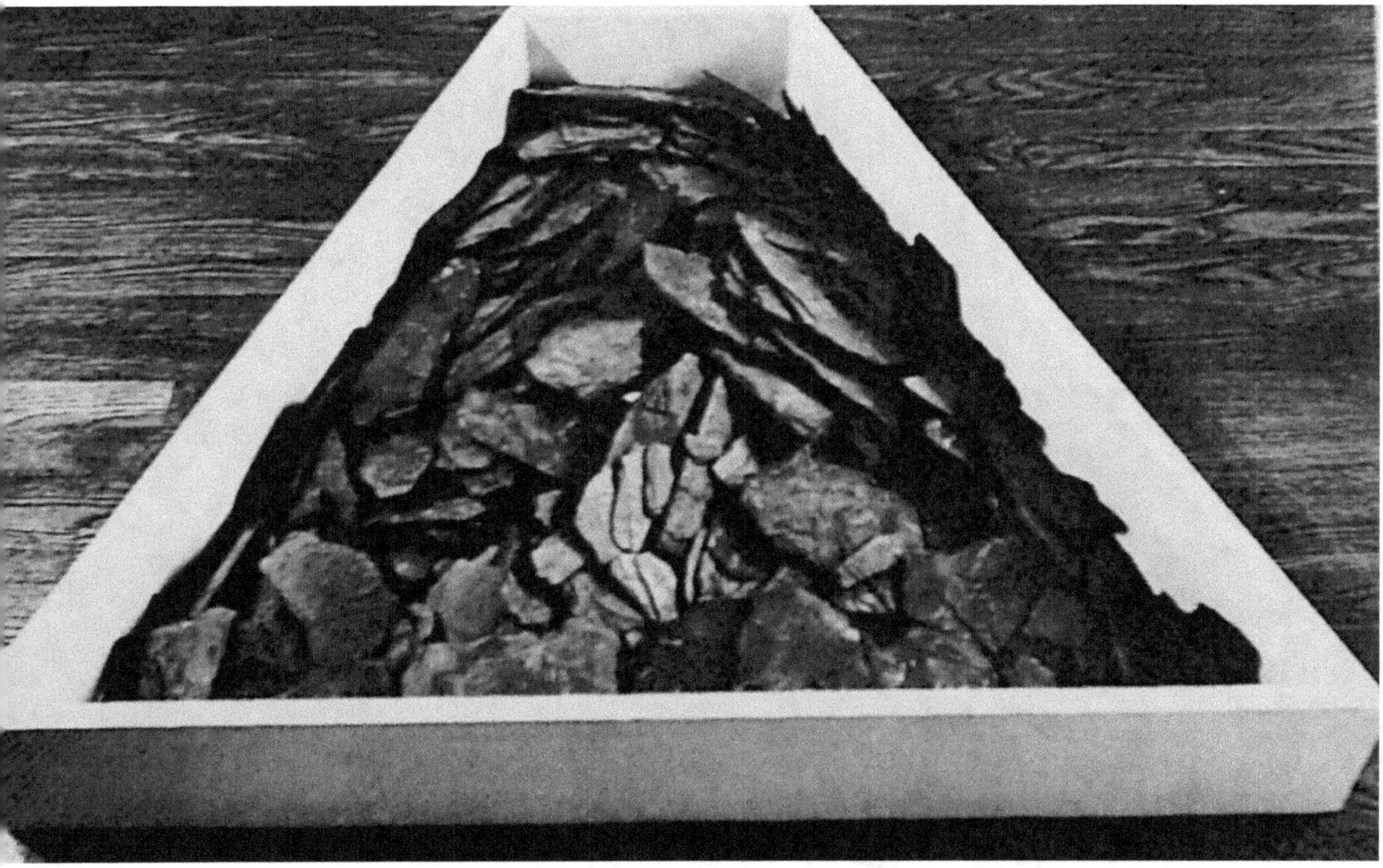

ROBERT SMITHSON: *BROKEN CIRCLE*

Robert Smithson's 1971 *Broken Circle* was another large earthwork using circular motifs that was set adjacent to the land and extended out into a lake. Smithson chose a quarry site near Emmen, Holland. Again, the site had an interesting geological aspect, which was in keeping with Smithson's love of rocks and minerals. Glacial action had formed unusual layers of soil. Unlike *Spiral Jetty*, which was subsequently submerged, *Broken Circle* remains on display, and is maintained by local funds. It is a 140 foot circle comprising one half of soil and one half of water, with a twelve foot wide canal cutting round the earth section of the circle, forming a semicircle. At the centre of *Broken Circle* is a very large glacial boulder. It was supposedly one of the largest in the Netherlands. Significantly, Smithson allowed nothing at the centre of *Spiral Jetty*: the spectator walked round the inward-turning spiral to find nothing. Smithson was exasperated by the prehistoric stone at the centre of his *Broken Circle*, but he let this 'accidental center' stay there, commenting 'it became a dark spot of exasperation, a geological gangrene on the sandy expanse'.[1]

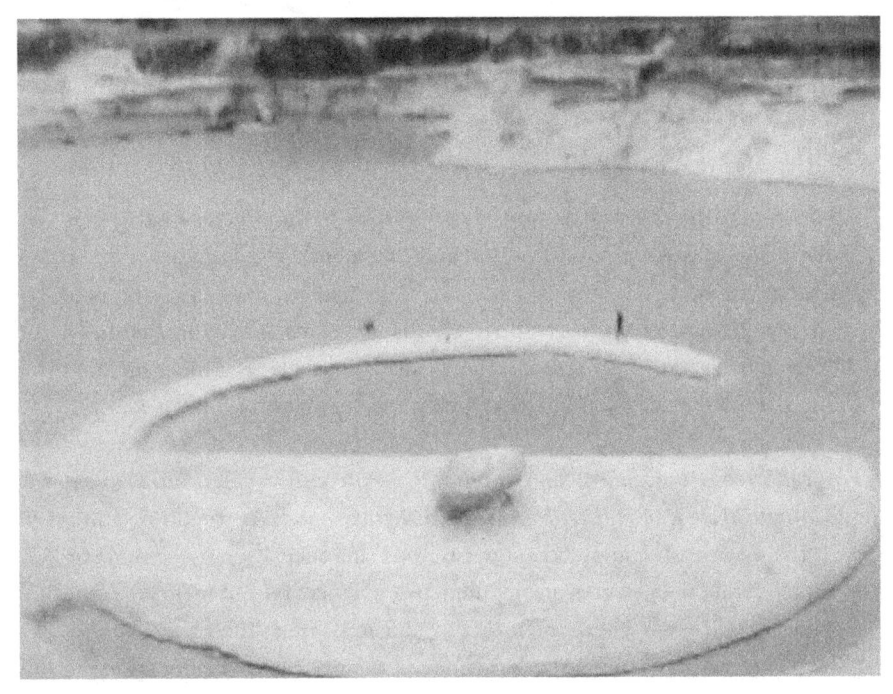

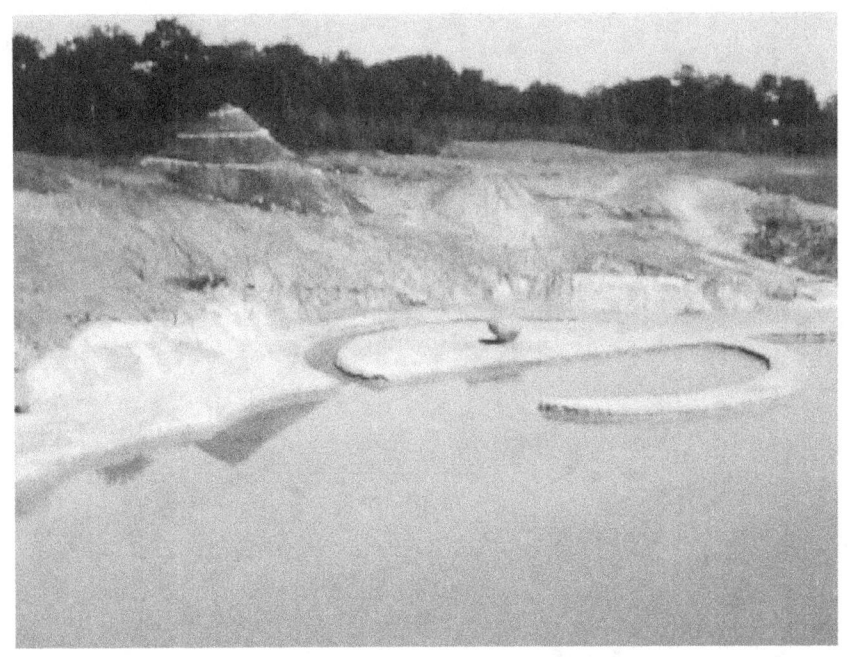

ROBERT SMITHSON: *AMARILLO RAMP*

Robert Smithson's last major work, before his untimely death, was *Armarillo Ramp*, one of many land artworks conceived as an observation structure. Nancy Holt worked with one of the major American sculptors of the era, Richard Serra, to complete Smithson's plans. *Amarillo Ramp,* 15 miles north-west of Amarillo in the Texas Panhandle, is a huge inclined ramp or road, made from quarried rocks. The summit of *Amarillo Ramp* is a viewing point.[1]

Taken together, Smithson's three large-scale earthworks, *Spiral Jetty, Broken Circle* and *Amarillo Ramp* all revolve around circular or spiral motifs, a sense of temporality, of decay and transience, each uses primitive, mythic forms and gestures in a monumental manner. Two of them are set in wilderness spaces, where the marks of humanity are at their weakest. Yet each earthwork of course speaks acutely of the mark of humanity upon the Earth, and a very particular kind of mark: that of late 20th century American (New York) art-making.

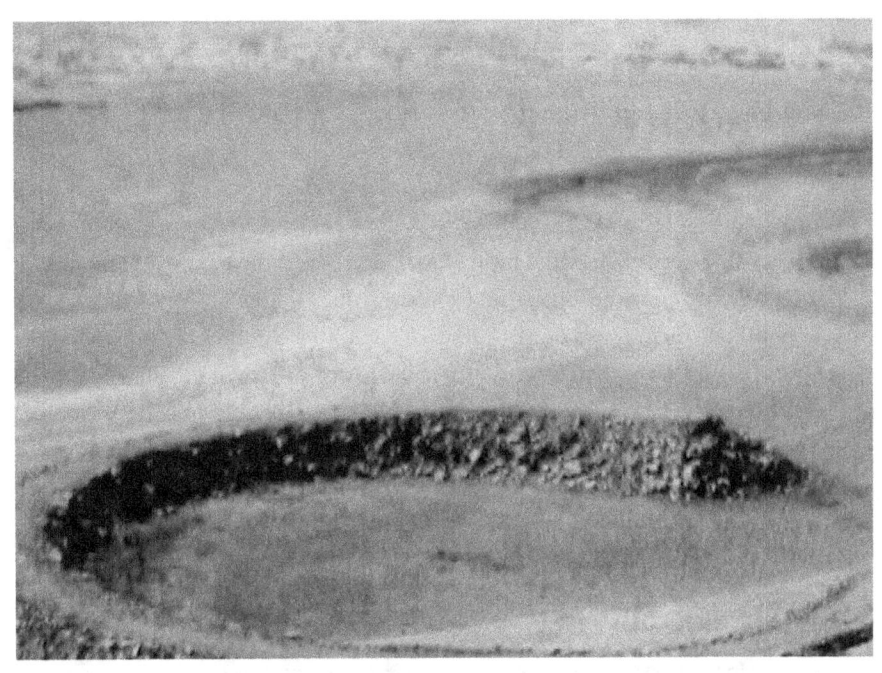

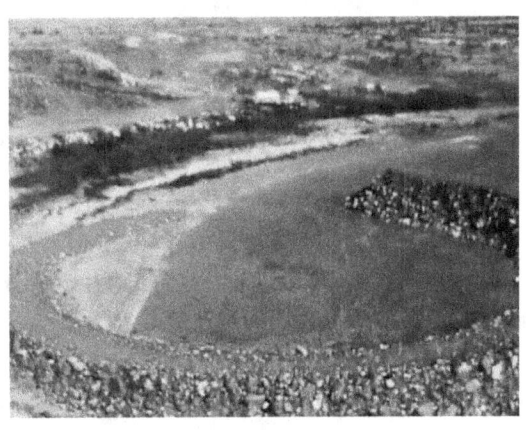

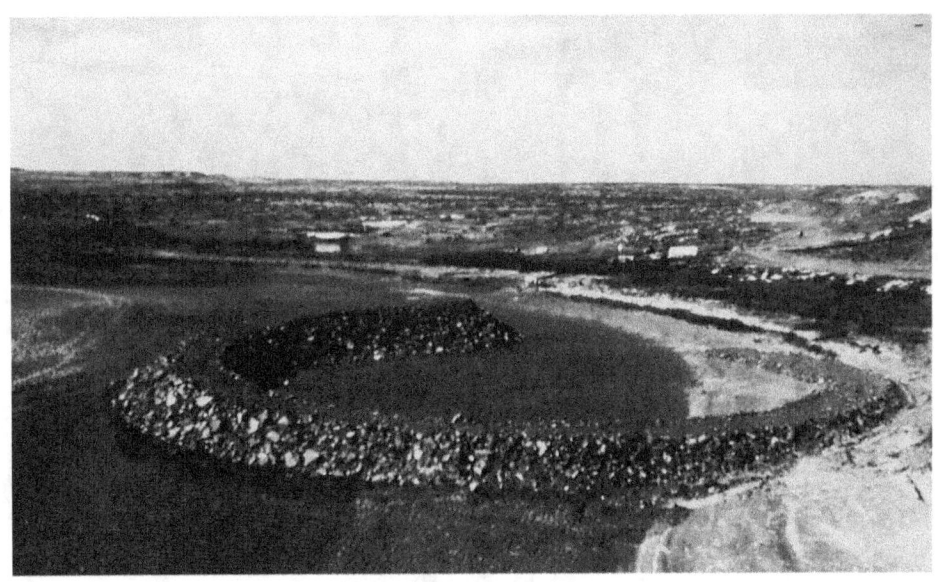

ROBERT MORRIS: *OBSERVATORY*

Robert Morris was one of the most eloquent theorists of Sixties and Minimal sculpture (along with Donald Judd and Carl Andre). Robert Morris had, like Donald Judd, begun in painting, but moved on to sculpture. Morris studied at Kansas City Art Institute, California School of Fine Arts and Hunter College, New York. In San Francisco in 1961 he worked with the dancer Anna Halprin. He was part of the Fluxus school, alongside Yoko Ono, Simone Forte, Walter de Maria and Henry Flynt. Morris wrote many artistic statements, the most famous probably being the articles published in *Artforum* entitled "Notes on Sculpture". For Robert Morris, one of the things that was new about 1960s sculpture was the object's relationship with the viewer. Before, Morris argued, the viewer related to the object as something separate; the new æsthetic put the viewer into the same space as the object. 'One is more aware than before that he himself is establishing relationships as he apprehends the object from various positions and under varying conditions of light and spatial context.'[1] This is a crucial concept in Minimal art, which is nearly always viewed in an object-viewer continuous space. Robert Morris's concept of 'objecthood' was central to his notion of sculpture.

Robert Morris has produced gigantic circular works, such as his *Observatory*, which is a huge earthwork recalling the megalithic structures of ancient times, such as Avebury stone circle. His *Labyrinth* is a maze-size sculpture, the kind of maze one finds in theme parks and country houses, except that Morris' *Labyrinth* uses the ancient pattern of the Cretan labyrinth, itself a motif some see as distinctly feminine, speaking of Goddess mysteries.

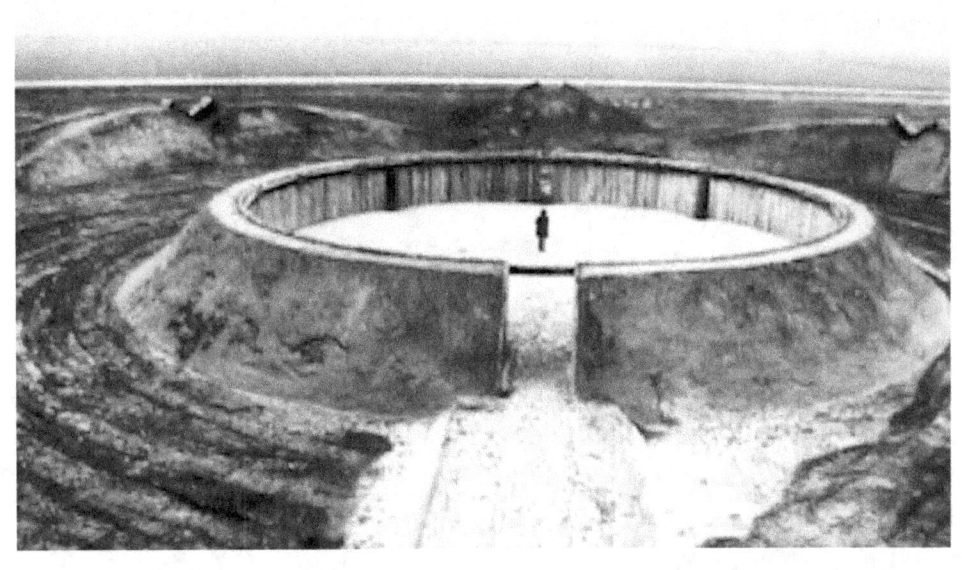

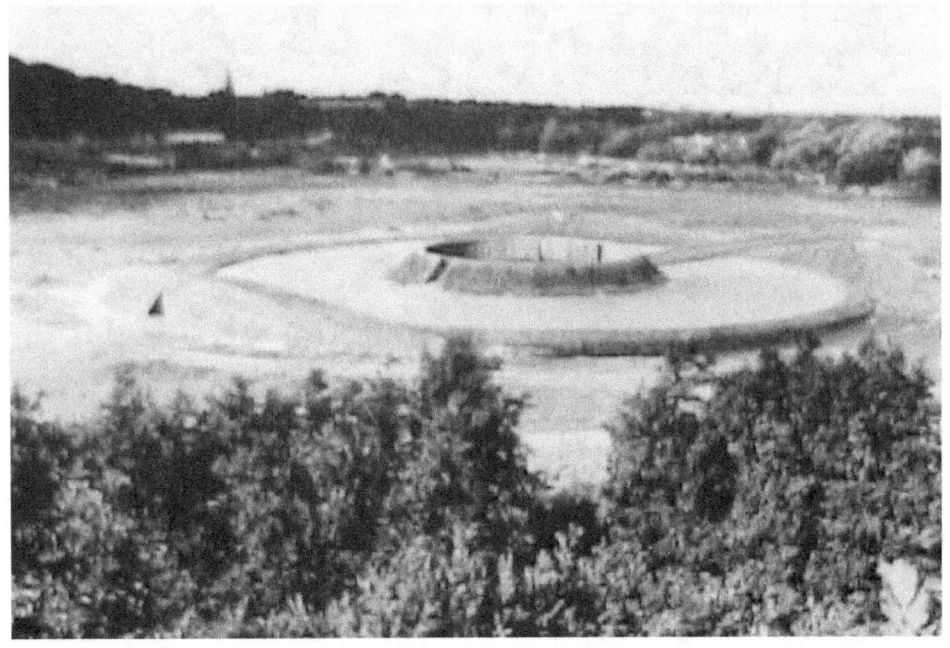

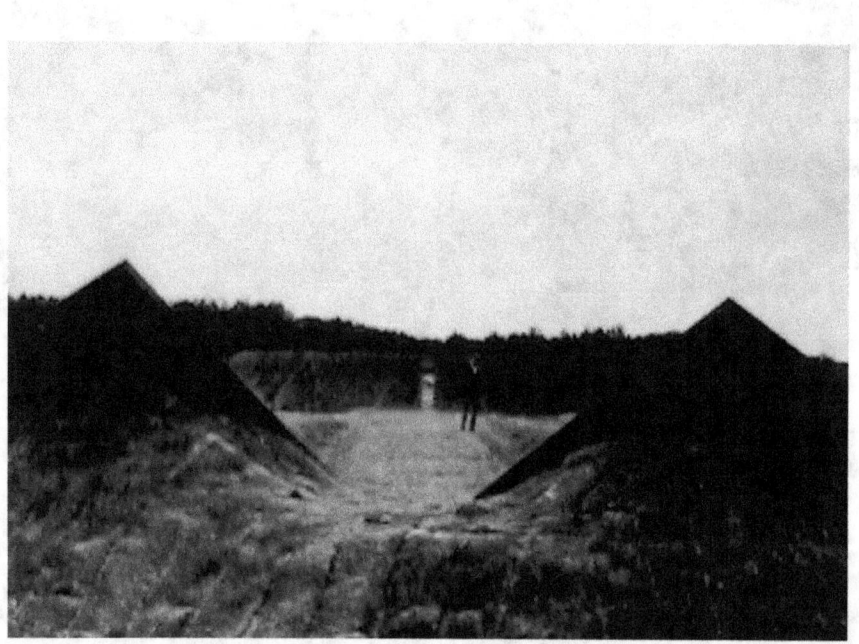

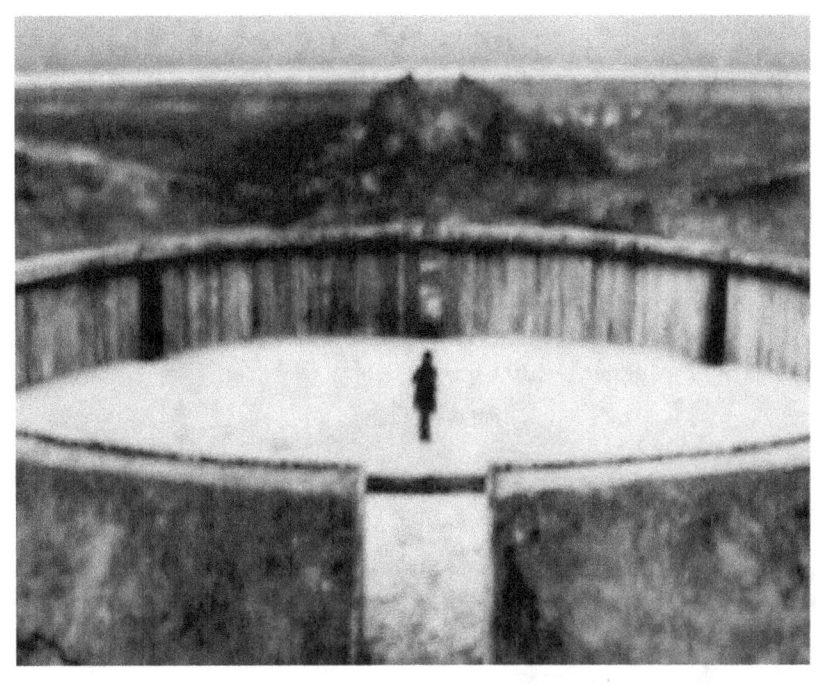

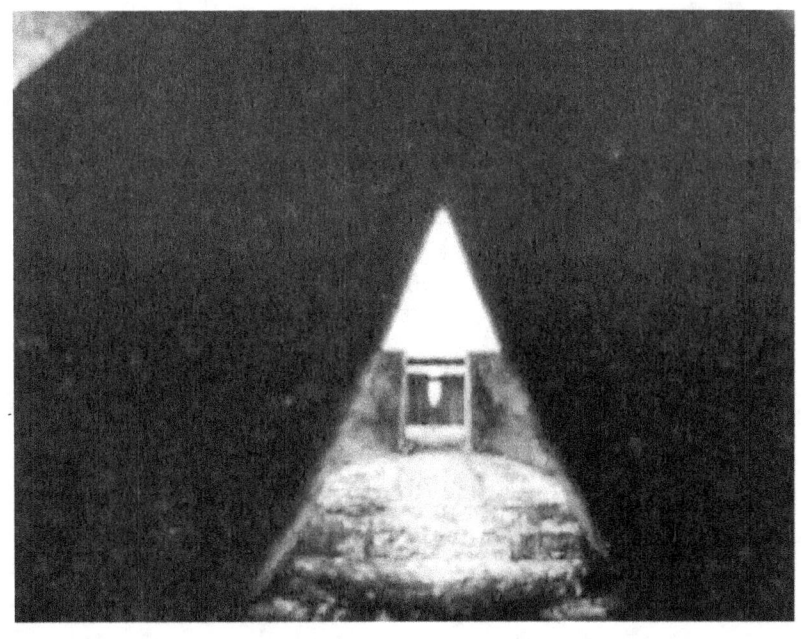

ROBERT MORRIS:
UNTITLED (STEAM PIECE)

Robert Morris produced some works of a highly 'ephemeral' nature, such as his 'steam piece' (*Untitled*, 1968-69), which was made out of doors on a patch of grass. How the work turned out was dependent upon physicalities such as humidity, air pressure, wind speed and direction, and temperature. Clouds of steam drifted over the grass.

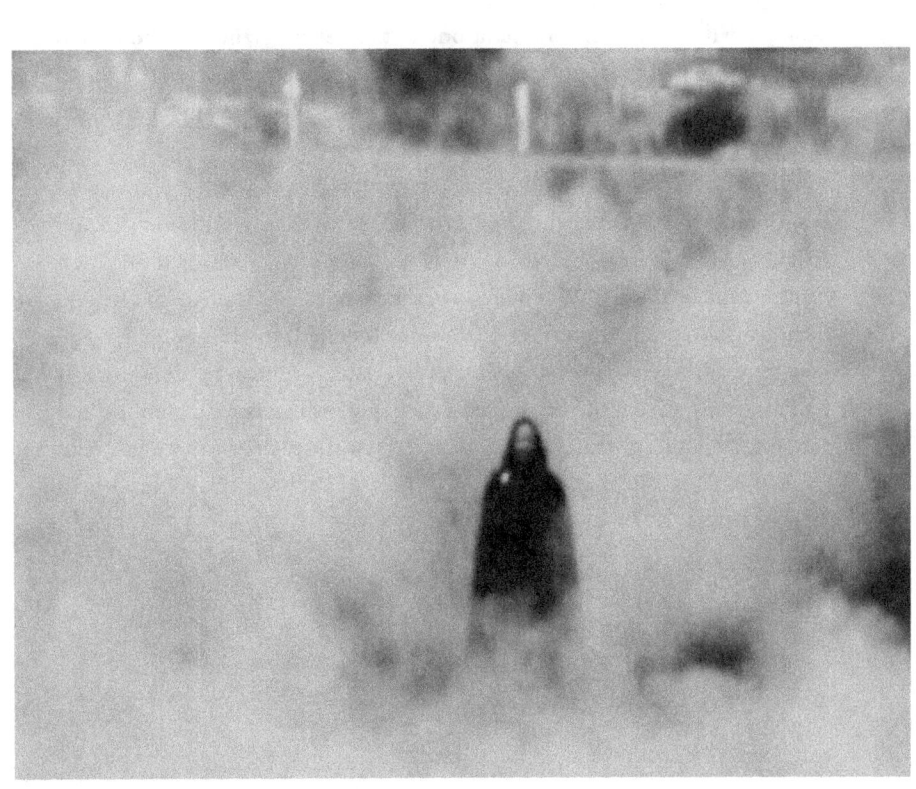

ROBERT MORRIS: *UNTITLED*

In *Pace and Progress*, Robert Morris made a work by walking a horse back and forth over a piece of grass until a path had been worn. The action of walking the horse rubbed down the grass. In 1975 Robert Morris wrote "Aligned with Nazca", an article in one of the key magazines of the period (*Artforum*) which related earthwork art with ancient art such as the Nazca lines. However, such connections with ancient art had already been made by artists and critics of land art.

Morris's later works included the felt sculptures, where an element of randomness and chance dictated how the felt strips would hang. Each installation would be different. Some of the later felt pieces used thick felt (such as in *Untitled 1996* [collection: the artist]). Another work entitled *Untitled 1996* (collection: the artist) was modelled, the felt being draped symmetrically over a pole. *Untitled 1996* recalled a human figure.[1] Morris's wall drawings were made by the artist covering his hands with graphite and dabbing them on the wall blindfolded. The large areas of smeared graphite (in *Blind Time IV*, 1991, for example) recall Richard Long's mud wall drawings.

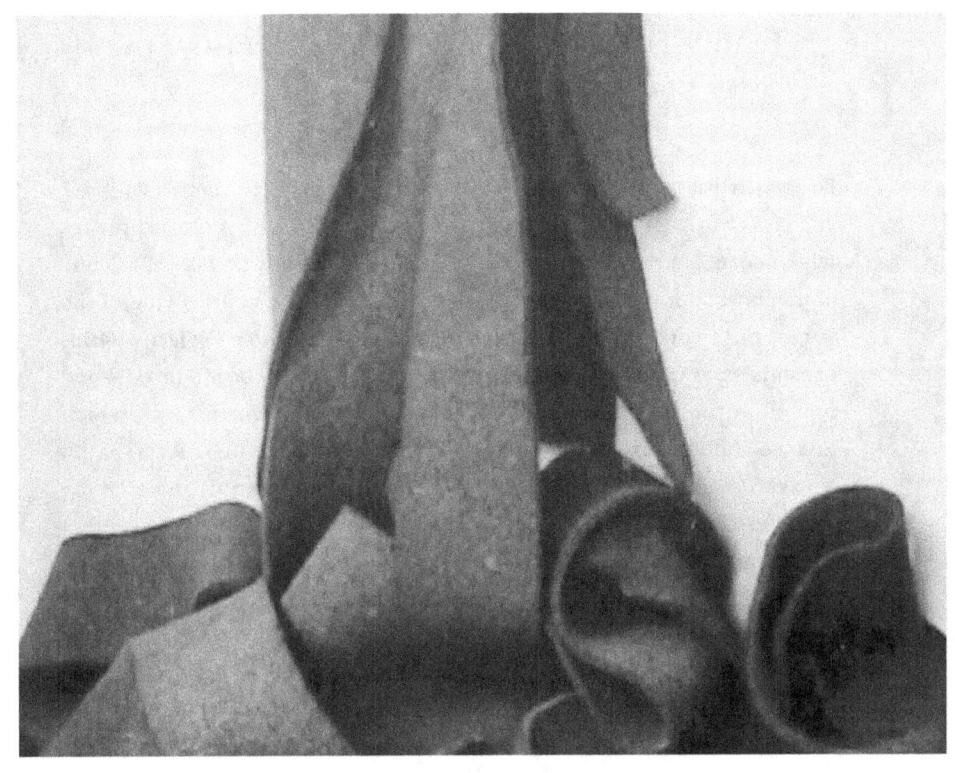

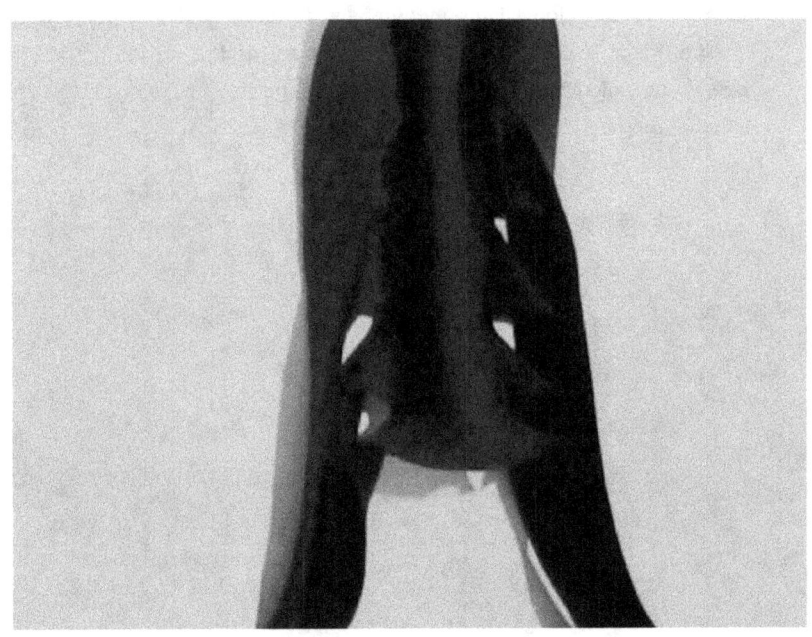

JAMES TURRELL: *RODEN CRATER PROJECT*

Postwar artists, of all kinds, have made massive art. David Smith's *Wagon I* and his *Cubi* sculptures are huge, heavy, chunky, truly colossal pieces which dominate their surroundings. Donald Judd wrote: '[t]his scale is one of the most important developments in twentieth century art'.[1] One of the largest earthwork projects is James Turrell's *Roden Crater Project,* a series of tunnels and chambers in an Arizonan extinct volcano, begun in 1974 and funded by the Dia Foundation. The first stage of Turrell's project, which involved bulldozing 200,000 cubic yards of earth from the volcano's rim, 'so as to shape the sky'. Turrell also planned tunnels, pools and viewing chambers. Turrell said '[m]y art is made for one person. I like the solitary experience. Standing alone at night, perceiving the Roden Crater and the moon and stars, you really feel the vastness of the universe and yourself entering into it'.[2] There were spaces at Roden Crater where clouds were projected onto the floor during the day, which at night were related to the procession of equinoxes. Richard Long's art is not monolithic in scale, usually: but his works can stretch over many miles, far longer than even Christo's fences. The Abstract Expressionists, such as Helen Frankenthaler, Mark Rothko, Franz Kline and Barnett Newman, produced huge paintings, which swallow up the spectator when s/he moves close to them. One can get up close to a Morris Louis and be enveloped by it. Similarly, postwar sculptors have made massive works. Artists such as Christo made pieces that were 24 miles long. Even medium-sized pieces, such as Donald Judd's wooden boxes, are sometimes seen as monumental. A critic on *The New York Times* called Judd's 1977 installation at the Heiner Friedrich Gallery a 'majestic and finely measured presence'.[3]

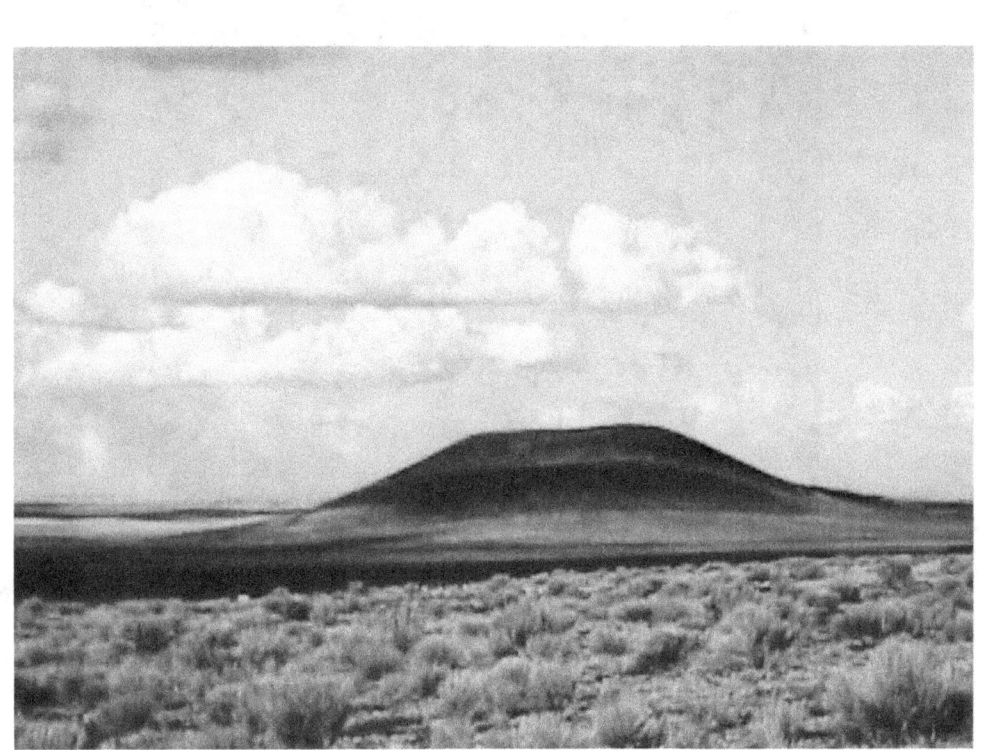

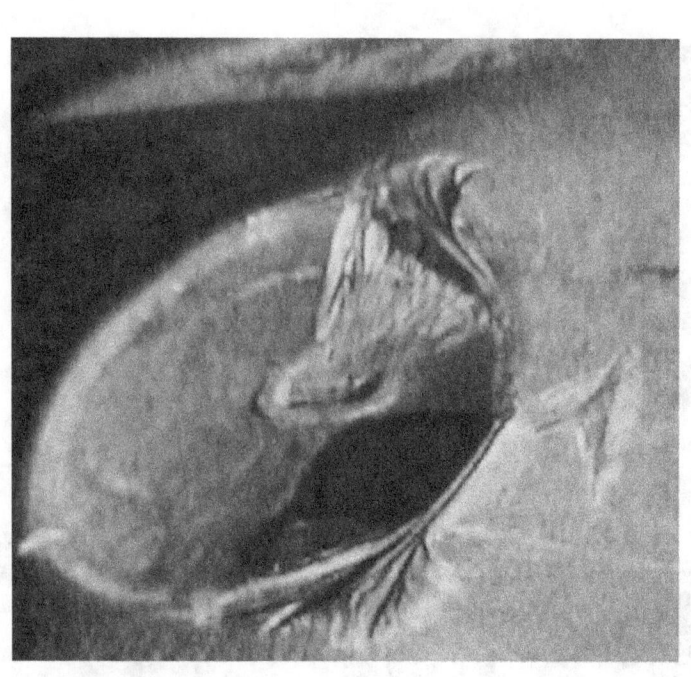

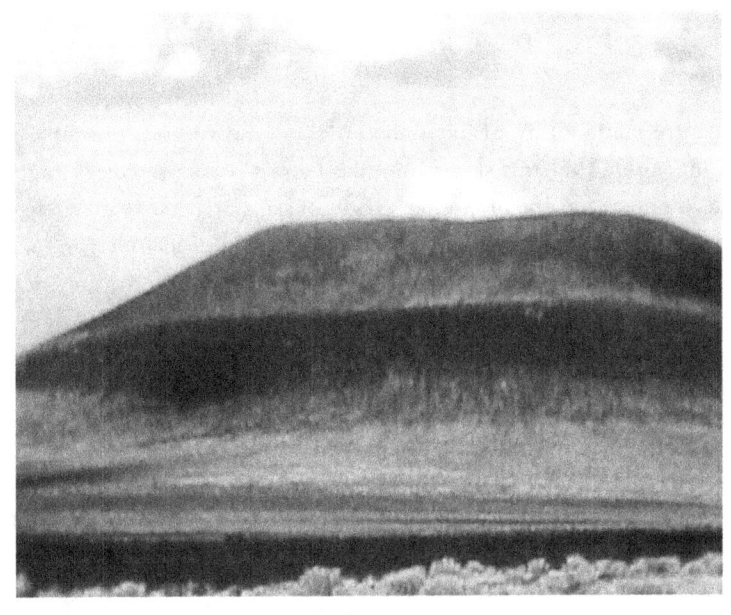

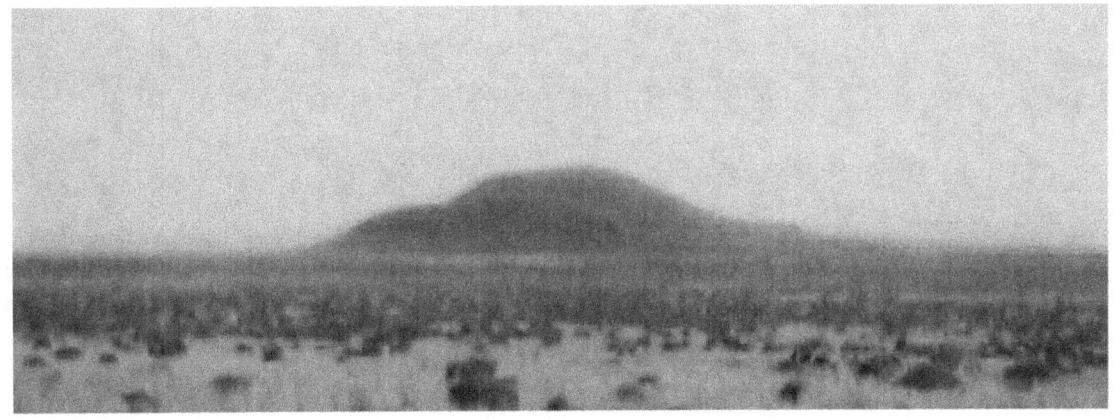

CARL ANDRE: *JOINT*

Carl Andre made a line of hay bales, placed end to end, in a field in Vermont (*Joint*, 1968). It was a line like Long's rows, or Tony Cragg's spreads. Andre made one of his floor pieces of slabs of metal deliberately so it would be altered by being outside. It was called *Small Weathering Piece* (1971), and contained a large number of metals (large for an Andre sculpture): lead, zinc, aluminium, copper, steel and magnesium.

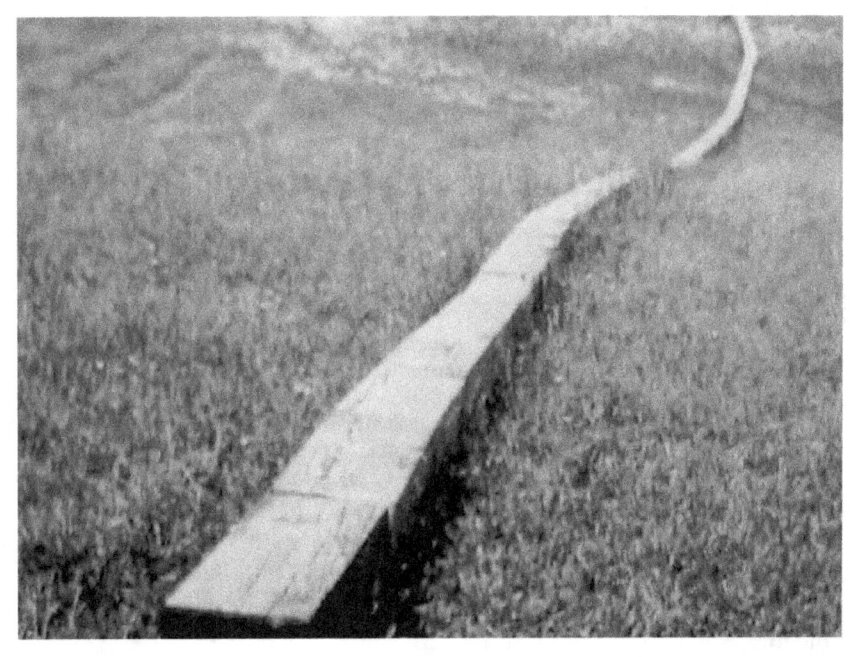

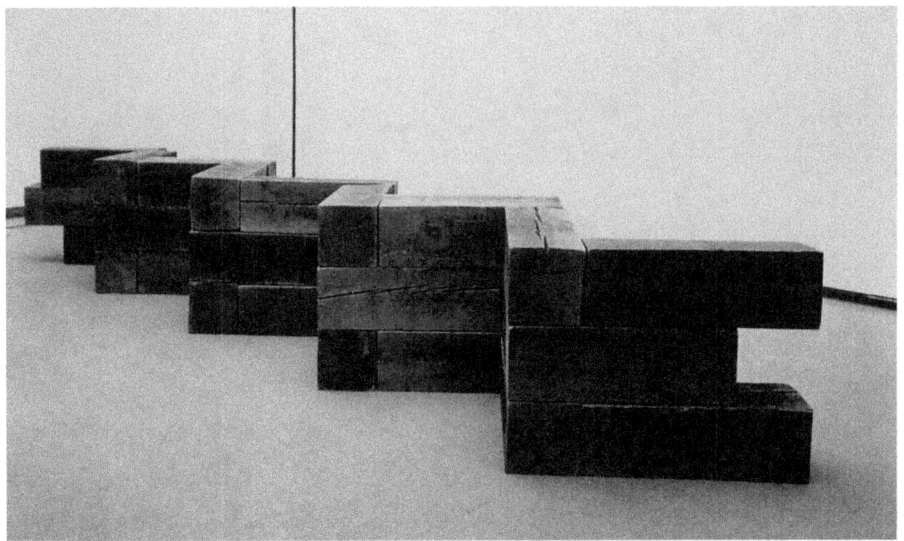

CARL ANDRE: *37 PIECES OF WORK*

Carl Andre's *37 Pieces of Work* is a good example of Minimal æsthetic permutations taken to extremes. It is a sculpture that is typical of Andre's art:

> Taken as a whole *37 Pieces of Work* consists of 1,296 plates, 216 each of aluminium, copper, steel, magnesium, lead and zinc. Each metal appears alone in individual six-foot square plains. Then alternates with another, checkerboard fashion, in every possible permutation. Since each of the six metals in the large piece was laid out in the alphabetical order of its chemical symbol, alternating successively with the others, there are two versions of each combination.[1]

37 Pieces of Work is a 432 inch wide 'floor-hugging' square, in which the colours of the copper, aluminium, lead, steel, zinc and magnesium is to the fore.

Many of Carl Andre's floor-pieces are similar (*Twelfth Copper Corner*, 1975, *Brooklyn Field*, 1966, Belgium, *8 Cuts*, 1967, Switzerland): the spectator is aware of the material first and foremost: the colour, mass, weight, size and texture of the metals.

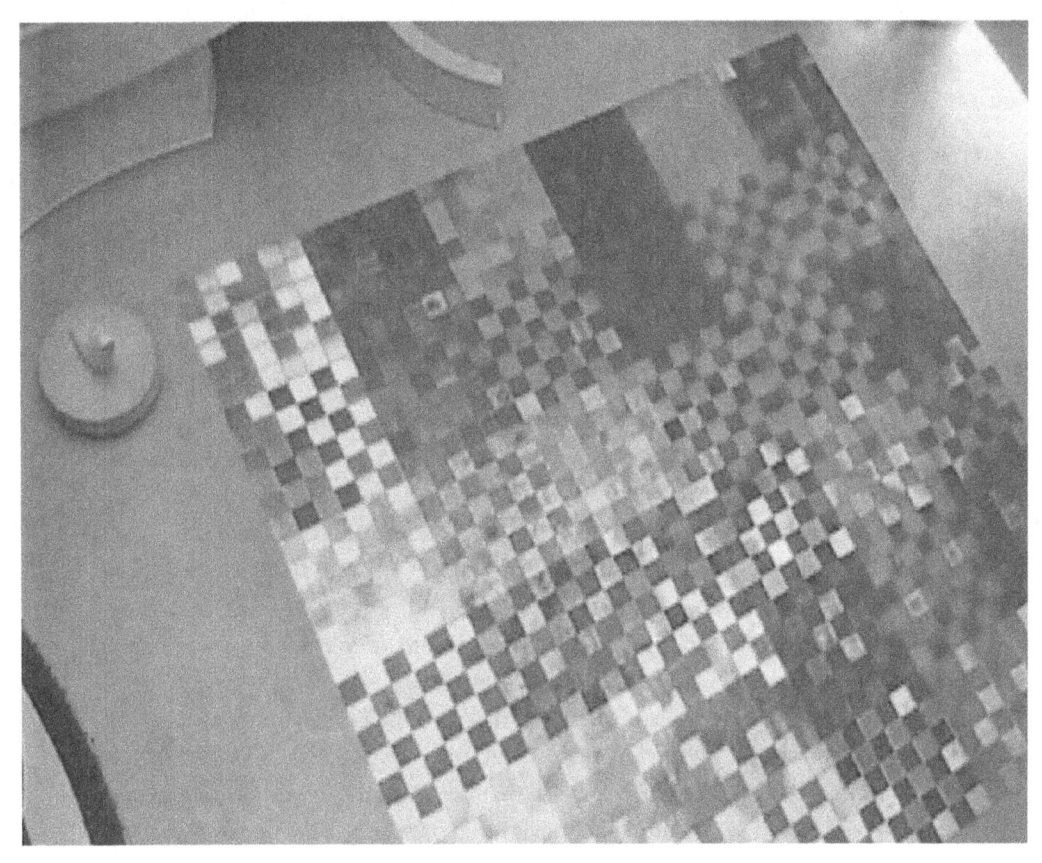

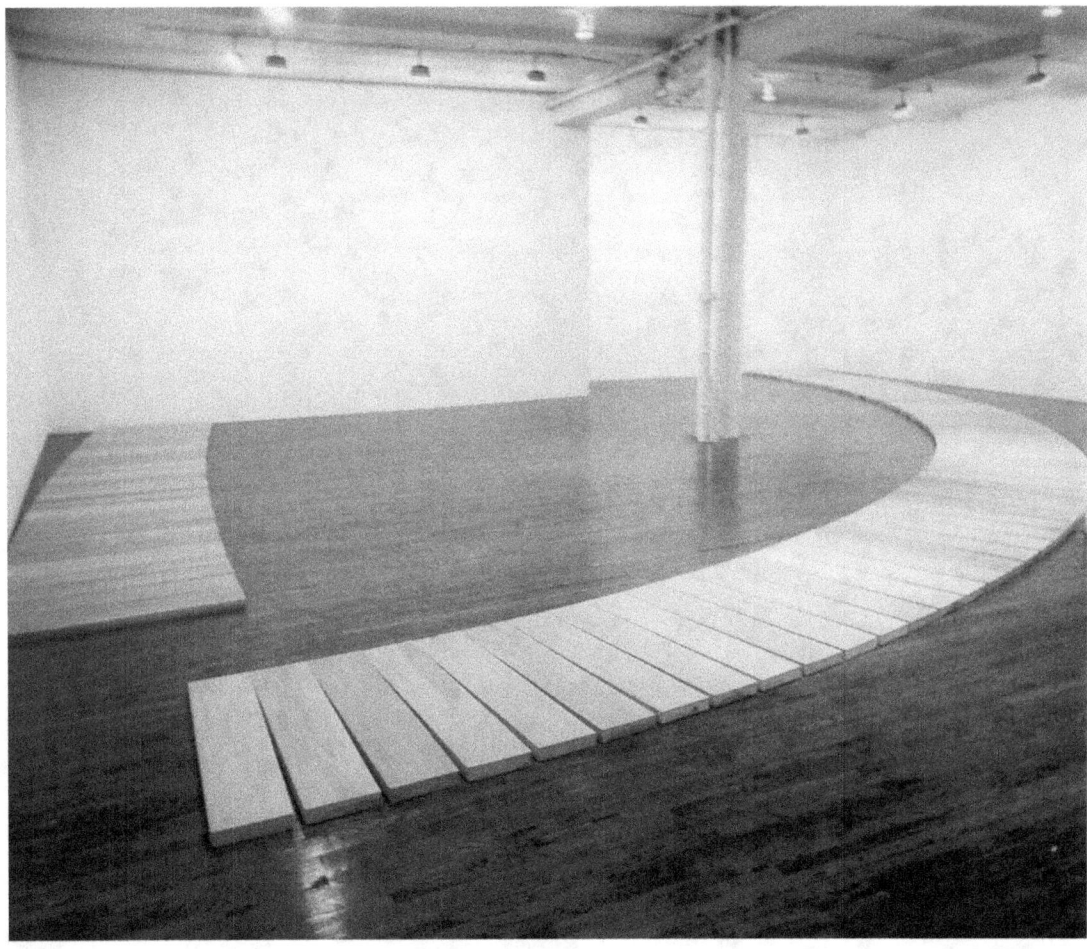

CARL ANDRE: *EQUIVALENT VIII*

Carl Andre's *Element* series consisted of wood-carved beams that recalled Brancusi; Andre's *Equivalents* were 'floor-hugging' sculptures shown in 1966. The magnet pieces, which preceded the metal squares, also hugged the floor, so much so that the third dimension was nearly expunged. The floor-pieces neatly rid the sculptor of dealing with pedestals. They became 'place-markers'.[1] They have no space, according to one critic, they have 'no appearance of inside or center. Rather they seem to be co-extensive with the very floor on which the viewer stands' (R. Krauss, 271f). Place, not space or sky, became what matters for Andre. Andre's floor-pieces are viewer-friendly, too: the viewer is invited to (or allowed to) walk over them. Like Judd, Andre wanted his sculptures to be seen from a variety of viewpoints. Instead of a single viewpoint, one could have a number of angles; he compared viewing his sculptures to walking on roads: '[t]hey cause you to make your way along them or around them or to move...over them' (1970, 57). Andre's works seem to be slight, almost insubstantial, but, simultaneously, 'their matter-of-factness that makes them in a multiple sense *present*'.[2] Stella influenced Andre's way of making sculpture: Andre often stayed with Stella in the early years, and worked in Stella's studio: when Andre was working on a large log, Stella told him that unworked the wood could be sculpture too. Andre considered what Stella had said, and thereafter used materials in an untouched state, 'using them as 'cuts' in the space that surrounds them, shaping the space itself'.[3]

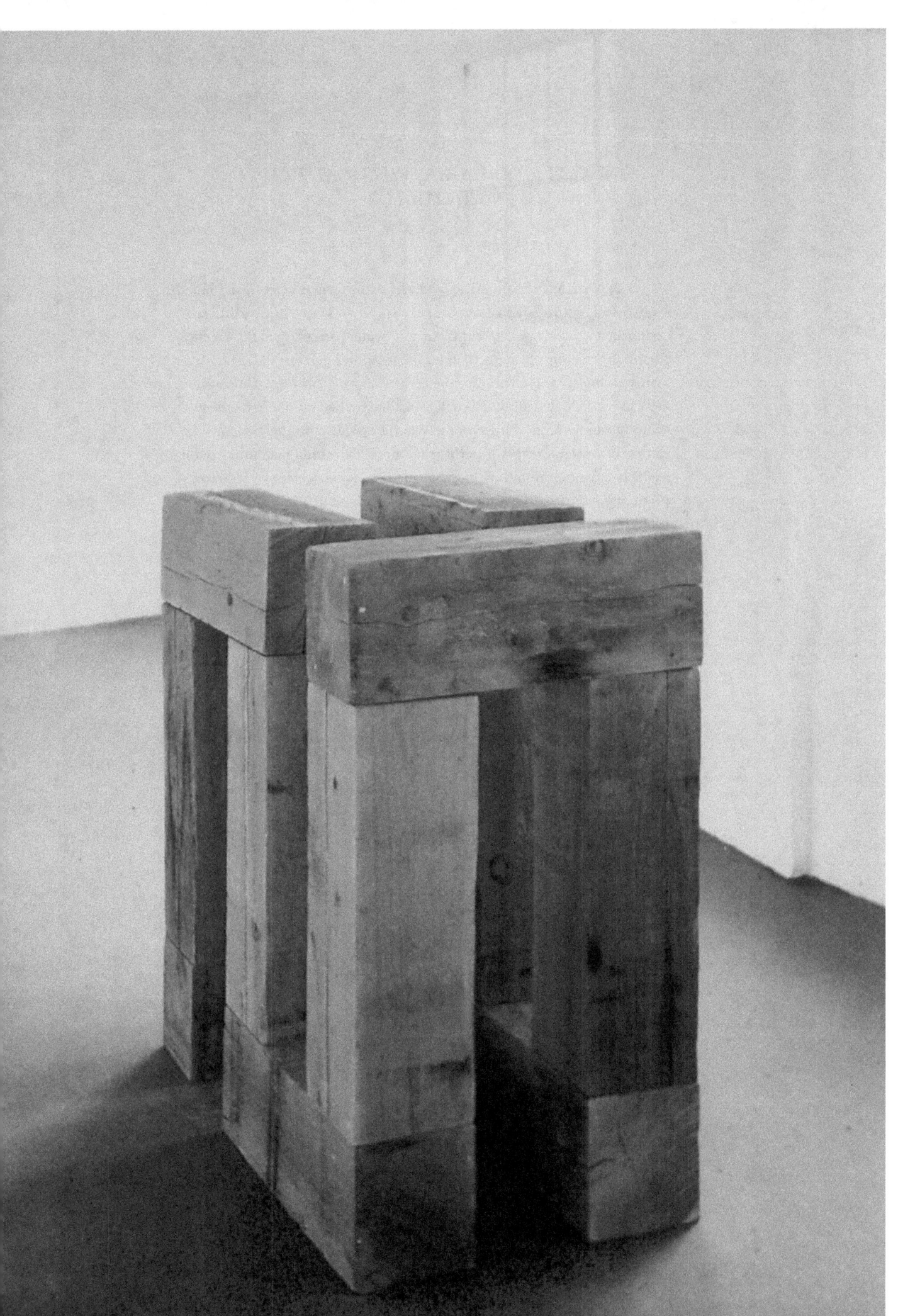

WALTER DE MARIA: *VERTICAL EARTH KILOMETER*

Walter de Maria made a dramatic land art gesture when he cut a 4.5 mile-long 6 foot-wide scar in the desert in Nevada with a bulldozer. Commentators have spoken of this cut as a 'wound' or 'scar' on the Earth (a wound in the body of the Earth in its Great Mother persona). The ultimate in ithyphallic, male land art must be de Maria's *Vertical Earth Kilometer*. At a cost of $500,000, de Maria sunk a 1-kilometre brass rod into the planet. Nothing can be seen of it except a 2 inch brass disc on the ground. The making of de Maria's work is perhaps far more interesting than the artwork itself. It must be the ultimate art statement/ non-statement. De Maria's *Vertical Earth Kilometer* remains practically invisible. It neatly melds two 1960s æsthetic movements: Conceptualism (wow, what an idea, sticking a kilometer of brass into the Earth!) and Minimalism (there's nothing to see of it except... a two-inch brass disc!). Yeah, that's *real art*, a kilometer-long piece of metal stuck into the ground with nothing of it showing except a tiny disc. Shown at Kassel Dokumenta 6 in 1977, de Maria's *Vertical Earth Kilometer* annoyed British artist Stuart Brisley so much he made *Survival in Alien Circumstances*. This was a hole in the earth dug with his bare hands, which Brisley lived in for 2 weeks, intending to mock de Maria's overblown American earthwork. In 1979 de Maria exhibited *The Broken Kilometer*: 500 brass roads each two metres in a New York gallery.

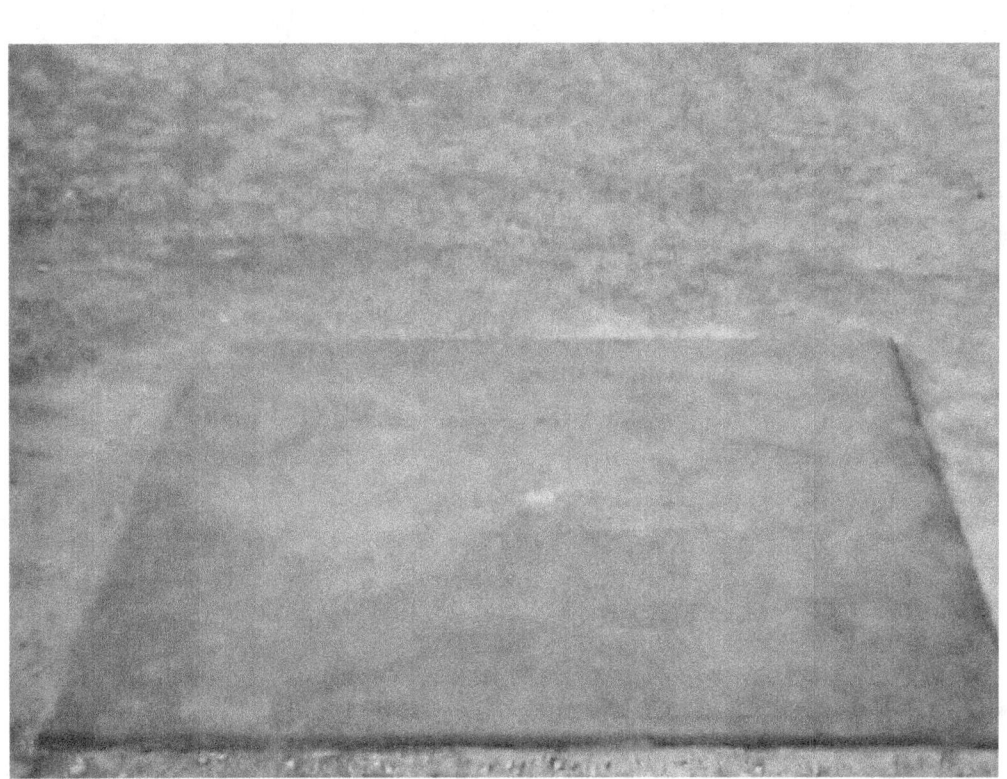

WALTER DE MARIA: *EARTH ROOM*

Walter de Maria's *Earth Room* was a gallery full of dark earth made in 1968 in Munich and later in New York (*The New York Earth Room*, SoHo Gallery, 1977). It consisted of 125 tons of soil, taking up 3,600 square feet, 22 inches deep. This was a vivid (and aromatic) example of bringing the Outside inside, one of land art's key projects. The contrasts were immediate, between the flat, clean, white, controlled gallery space and the 1,600 ft3 of uneven, 'dirty', dark, organic soil. Roberta Smith said it was a 'shock' to see the soil taking up the interior space usually reserved for things such as furniture and people. 'The dirt carried its own absence, was somehow a living substance' (1978, 104).

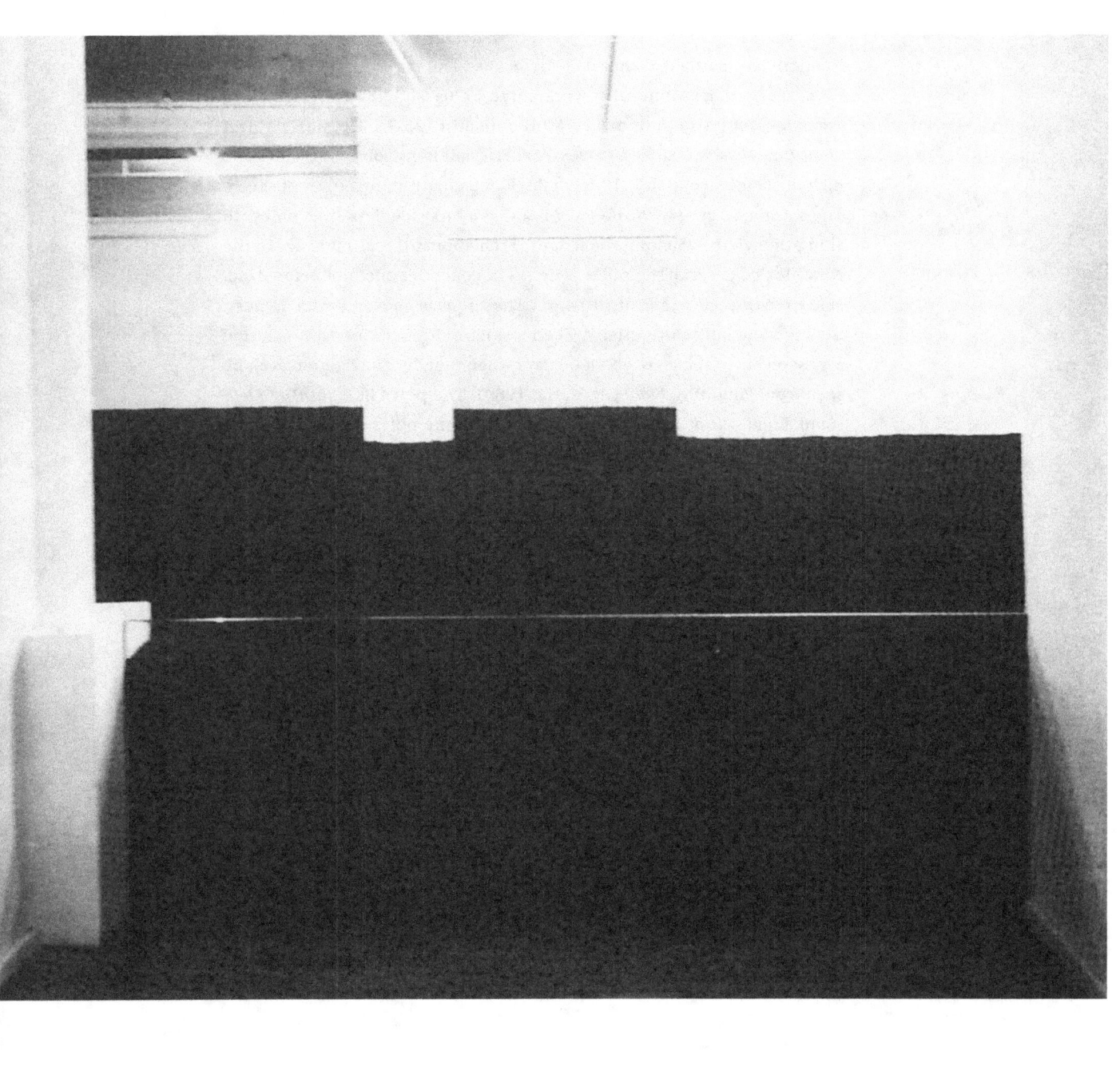

WALTER DE MARIA: *LIGHTNING FIELD*

Kenneth Baker called Walter de Maria's most famous work, the *Lightning Field,* the 'grandest Minimalist work of the 1970s' and 'the closest thing to a masterpiece to come out of Minimalism' (125-7). De Maria's firat *Lightning Field* was sited 40 miles from Flagstaff in Arizona, consisting of 2 inch diameter steel poles, 18 feet tall, 30 feet apart, in five rows of seven. The second, larger *Lightning Field* is a grid of 400 stainless steel poles, 16 along the width, 25 along the length, each about 20 feet high, set in the New Mexico desert.[1] The poles were set in concrete, one foot below land, able to withstand winds of 110 mph. The site was chosen for its flatness, isolation and lightning activity. The most lightning activity occurs during May-September; there are about 60 days when thunder and lightning can be seen from *Lightning Field* (de Maria, 1980). The poles in *Lightning Field* stand alone, about 220 feet apart. The tips of the poles define a plane in space parallel to sea level: the length of each pole varies according to the contours of the landscape. The *Lightning Field* is an exact, mathematically precise human site laid onto nature, where the poles are tiny mirrors which mark out and calibrate the landscape. The site looks like a scientific or industrial project – like a radio telescope site, say, or a military communications centre. *Lightning Field* is spectacular, with masculine and phallic connotations (lightning is related in symbolism to male creativity, sperm, fire, power and shamanism).

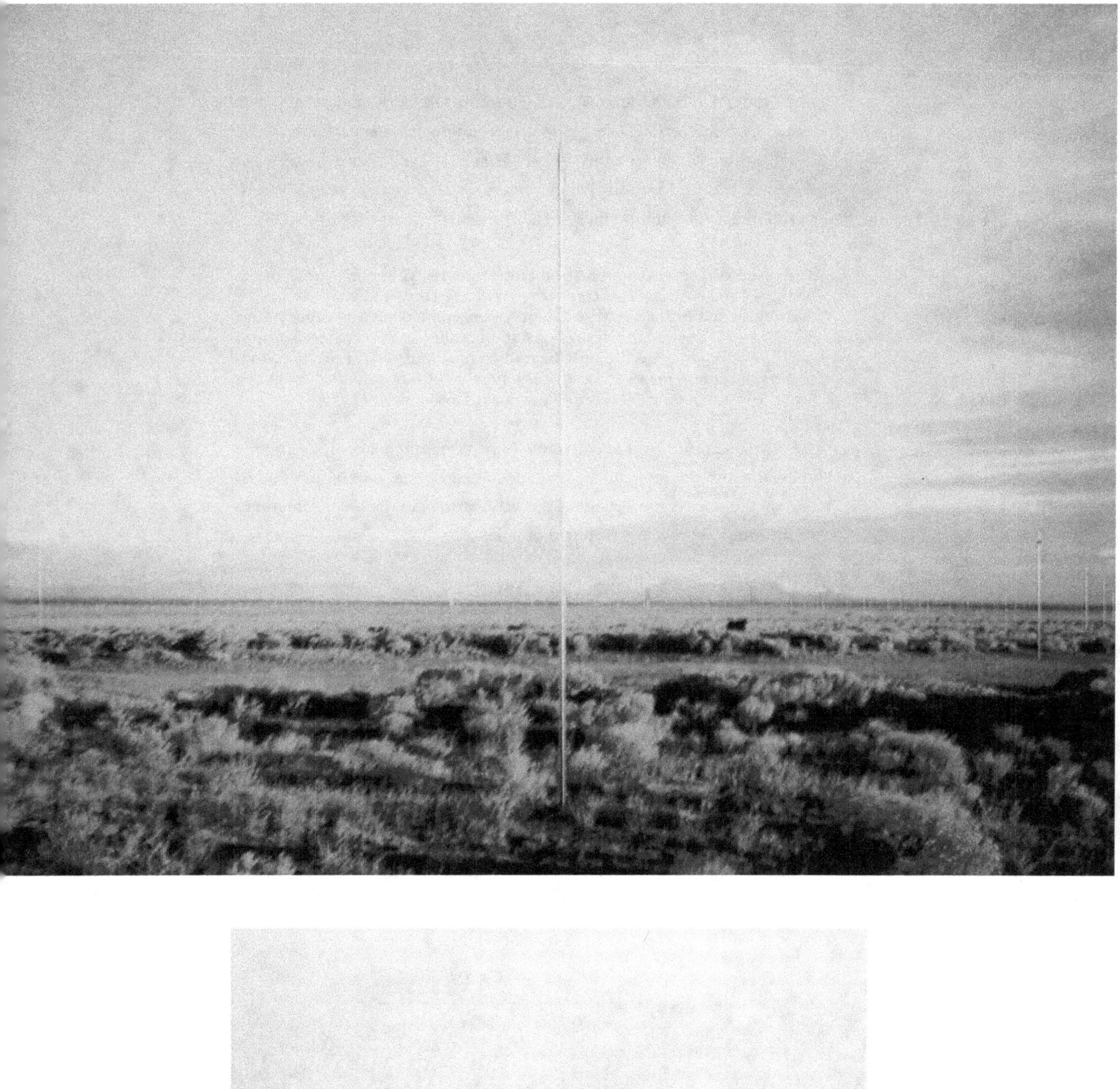

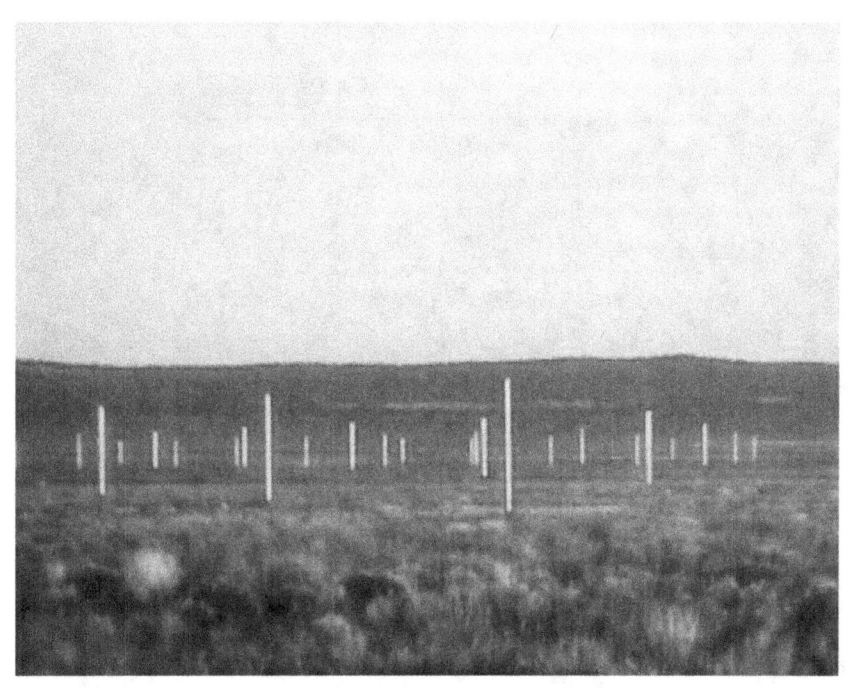

Lightning Field is ambiguously related to the Dia Art Foundation, which financed its construction. The site recalls technological experiments, while the poles themselves recall Brancusi's *Birds in Space*, and his *Endless Column*. Art critic Kenneth Baker relates de Maria's *Lightning Field* to issues of philosophy and politics:

> The piece also serves as an instrument for intensifying one's grasp of the beauty of the earth... The *Lightning Field* acquaints the visitor with the possibility that beauty may be the only conscionable and feasible refuge from history. That is, the apprehension of reality as everywhere *radiant with its being* may be the only bearable consciousness of life that does not entail repressing awareness of the horrors of our time. Beauty in this sense is just what the *Lightning Field* makes available... (127)

De Maria's *Lightning Field* attracts lightning, and a storm, as anyone knows, is about the most erotic and spectacular phenomenon in nature.[2] May to September is the season of the great storms in the area, sometimes 'two or three a week cross this field of poles'.[3]

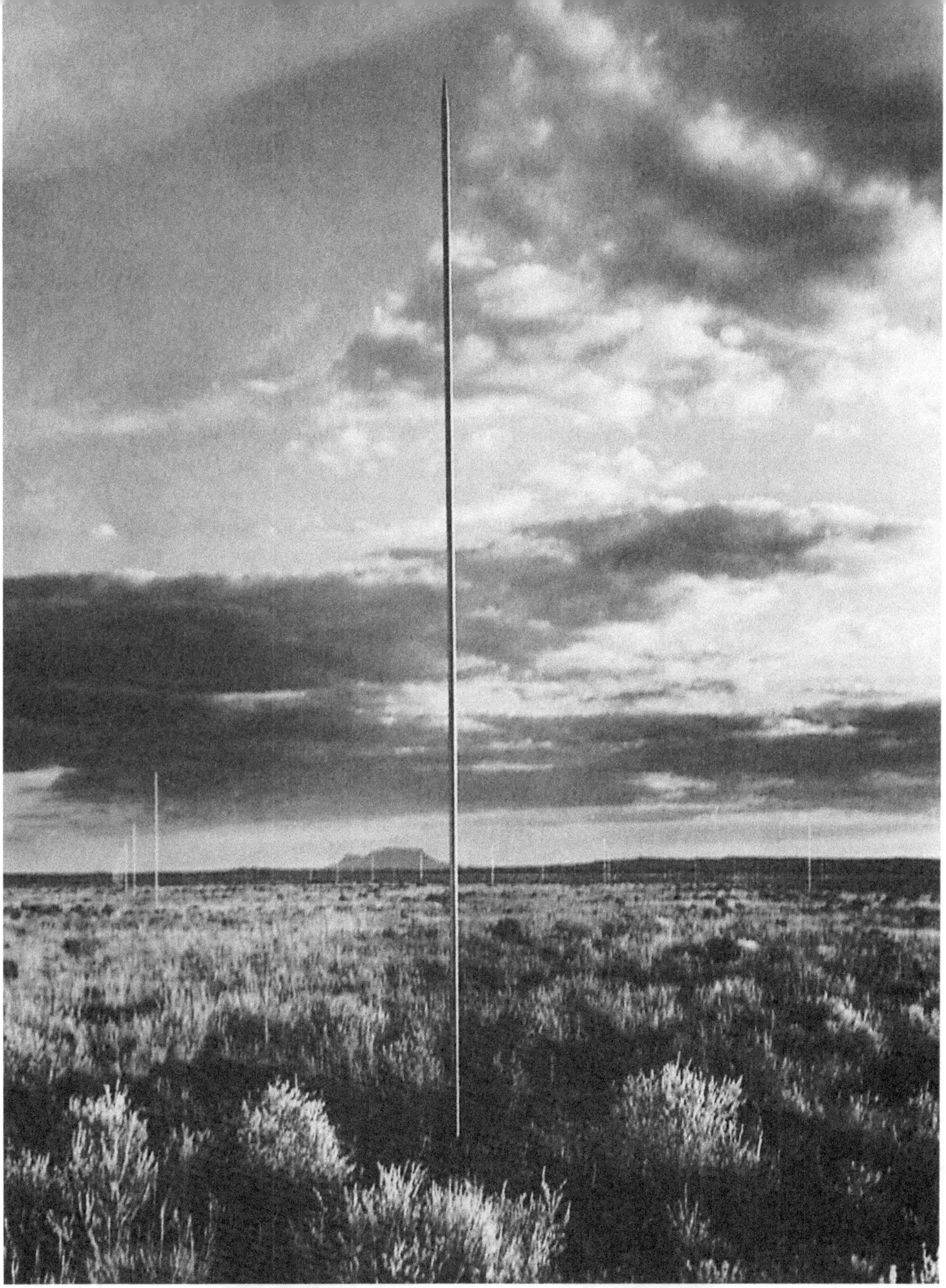

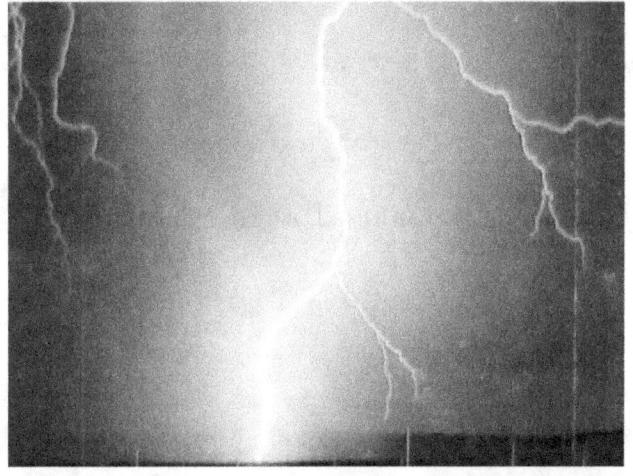

CHRIS DRURY: *MEDICINE WHEEL*

Chris Drury, one of the key British land artists, was born in 1948 (in Sri Lanka), and educated at Camberwell School of Art in London in the late Sixties. Drury belongs to the generation of Alan Sonfist, Charles Simonds, Michael Heizer, William Furlong, Alice Aycock, Mary Miss, David Nash and Richard Long (all born between 1944 and 1946). Drury had started out in the field of figurative sculpture. Among the artists that Drury admired were Roger Ackling and Constantin Brancusi (Drury said he found Joseph Beuys 'immensely irritating' and 'too self-obsessed').[1] Drury has exhibited in many solo shows, including the Henry Moore Centre in Leeds, Royal Botanic Gardens in Edinburgh, and London's Serpentine Gallery).

A key sculpture in Chris Drury's *œuvre* was his *Medicine Wheel* (made in 1983), a calendar work which collected 365 found objects strung on bamboo stalks mounted around the edge of plant papers and a mushroom spore at the centre. Drury wrote his diary in lines spreading outwards from the centre (a recurring motif in his work). Among the objects were hen feathers, wheat, runner beans, snail shells, pebbles, twigs, bark, berries, acorns, flowers, seeds, fish bones, grass, grapefruit, cherry blossom, hawthorn, crab, mussels, sheep bone, mistletoe, seaweed, cork, walnuts, quinces, rabbit skin, figs, and a cat's skull. The *Medicine Wheel* inspired many new forms in Drury's art:

> out of that came different categories of work. It started me off on making shelters and baskets, and then the shelters led to cloud chambers, and the baskets and the large, woven works I've made outside led me to the dewpond works. I've made woven maps, weaving ideas of landscape. And then there are the found objects.[2]

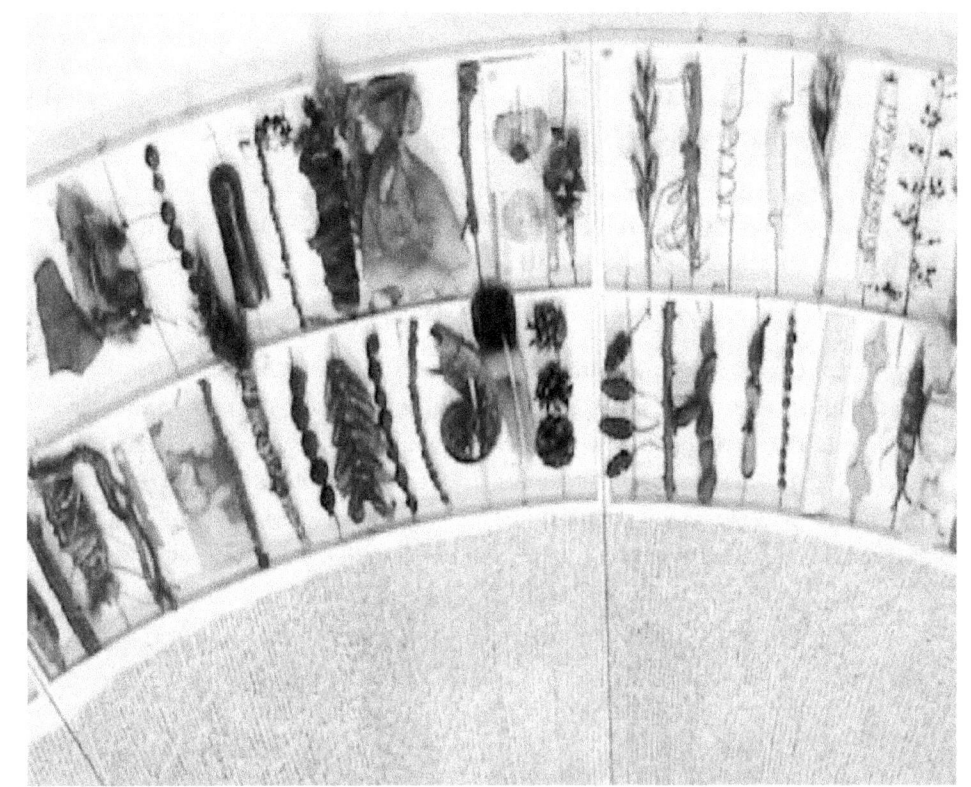

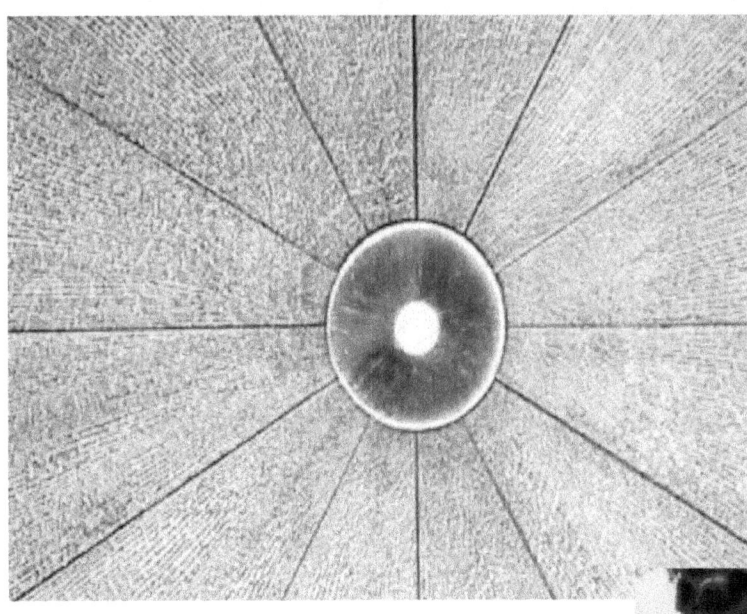

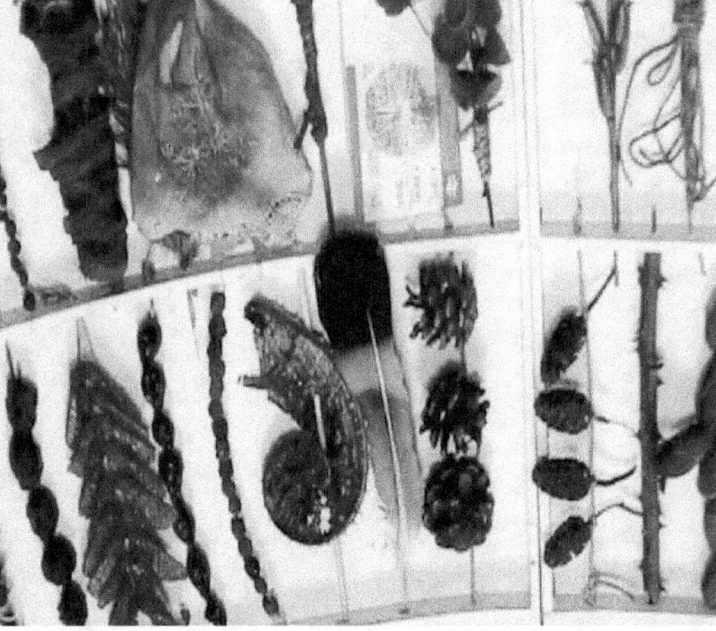

CHRIS DRURY: *STONE WHIRLPOOL*

One of Chris Drury's most striking sculptures was *Stone Whirlpool* (1996), built from river stones arranged into a spiral in a Japanese river (in Okawa-mura), near a waterfall. It was one of a number of Drury's works which explored vortexes and spirals. An associated work which took on currents of energy was *Edge of Chaos* (2000), a large paper work covered with handwritten texts describing the world's ocean currents and winds. One of Drury's largest vortex works was *Heart of Reeds* (2000).

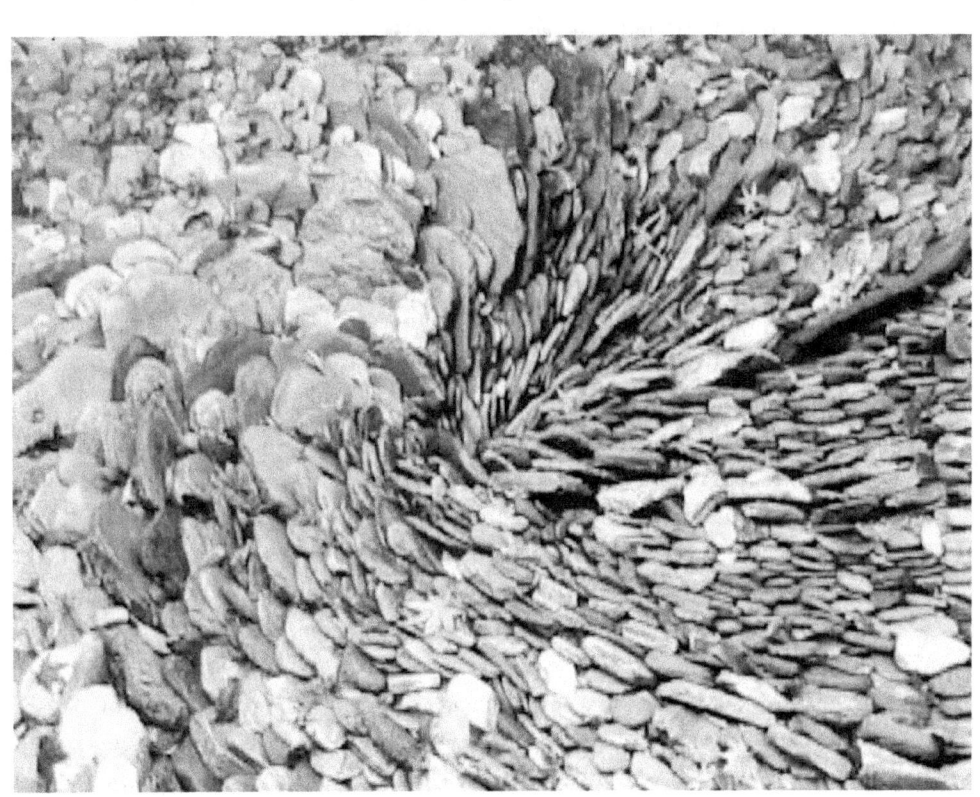

CHRIS DRURY: *CAIRNS*

Chris Drury has treated his cairns in different ways: many of the stone cairns have had fires lit inside them, such as *Midsummer Fire Cairn* (1989), *Falling Water Fire Cairn* (1997, Norway), *Fire Cairn* (1993, Ireland), *Fire Mountain Cairn* (1996, Japan), and *Fire Cairn* (1989, Colorado). Some cairns have been enclosed with basket weaving (such as *Basket Cairn*, 1991) and *Covered Cairn* (1993, Denmark).

Like Long's stone rows or Goldsworthy's cairns, Drury's stone cairns are usually erected in wilderness or spectacular scenery: Norway (1988), New Mexico (1993), De Lank River, Cornwall (1990), Lappland (1988), Webster Ross, Scotland (1992), Kintail, Scotland (1994), Ladakh (1997) and Colorado (1989). For Drury, the cairns are about commemorating a particular moment in a special place: 'they're just saying, 'this is an extraordinary place. Grab a few rocks, put them up before the moment's gone and photograph it'' (2002, 79). If the shelters were the stopping-places on a journey, the cairns were the 'markers of highpoints/ moments of exhilaration along the way' (1998, 58).

Another favourite Drury motif is the shelter: low, squat structures, sometimes like teepees or witches' hats, some like prehistoric beehive huts. The shelters were often made from stone (but also in chalk, turf, ice, wood, plants and coal. Some of these materials, such as turf, coal and chalk, are unexpected, and give Drury's shelters a very particular quality). The shelters are usually (but not always) constructed at human scale. That is, in the correct scale for someone to enter them bodily. *Beara Shelter* (1995), in West Cork, Ireland, was a squat, square, stone structure, with views of the sea and Bulls Rock. 'The intention was to provide a space for being and contemplation' (1998, 20). Some of the shelters, such as *Shelter For the Winds That Blow From Siberia*, made near Drury's home in Lewes in 1986, have a distinctly Goldsworthyan flavour: blocks of ice mounted on a hazel frame, looking like an igloo. *Shelter For the Northern Glaciers* (1988) was constructed in the spectacular coastal setting of Seiland island, in Norway, surrounded by snow-capped mountains. Geoffrey Harris has also constructed wooden shelters in forests (*Hollow Spruce*, 1988).

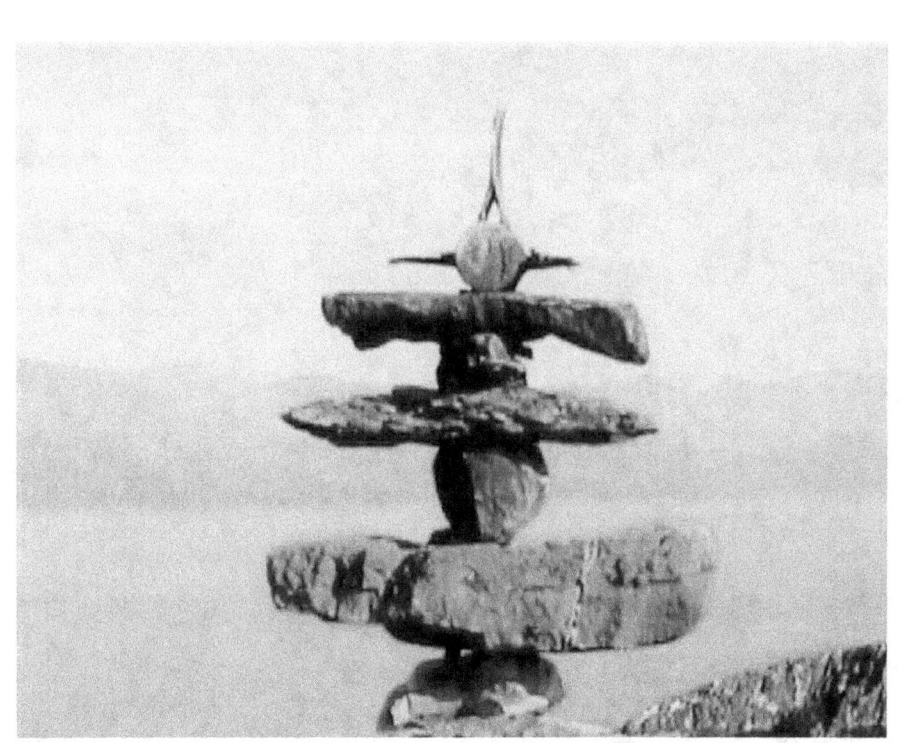

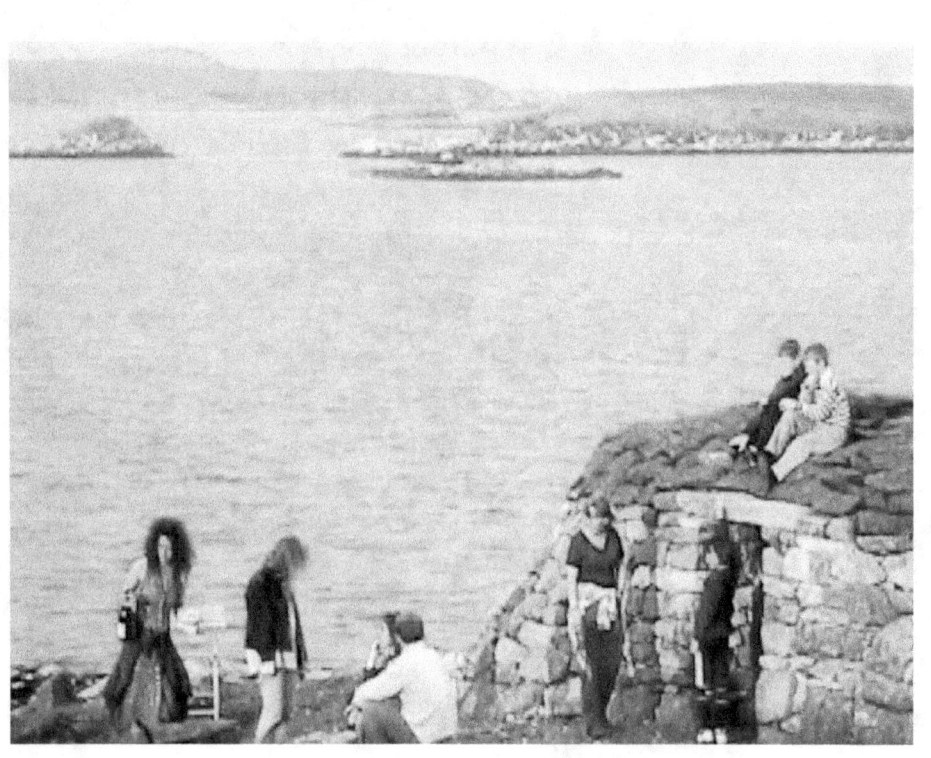

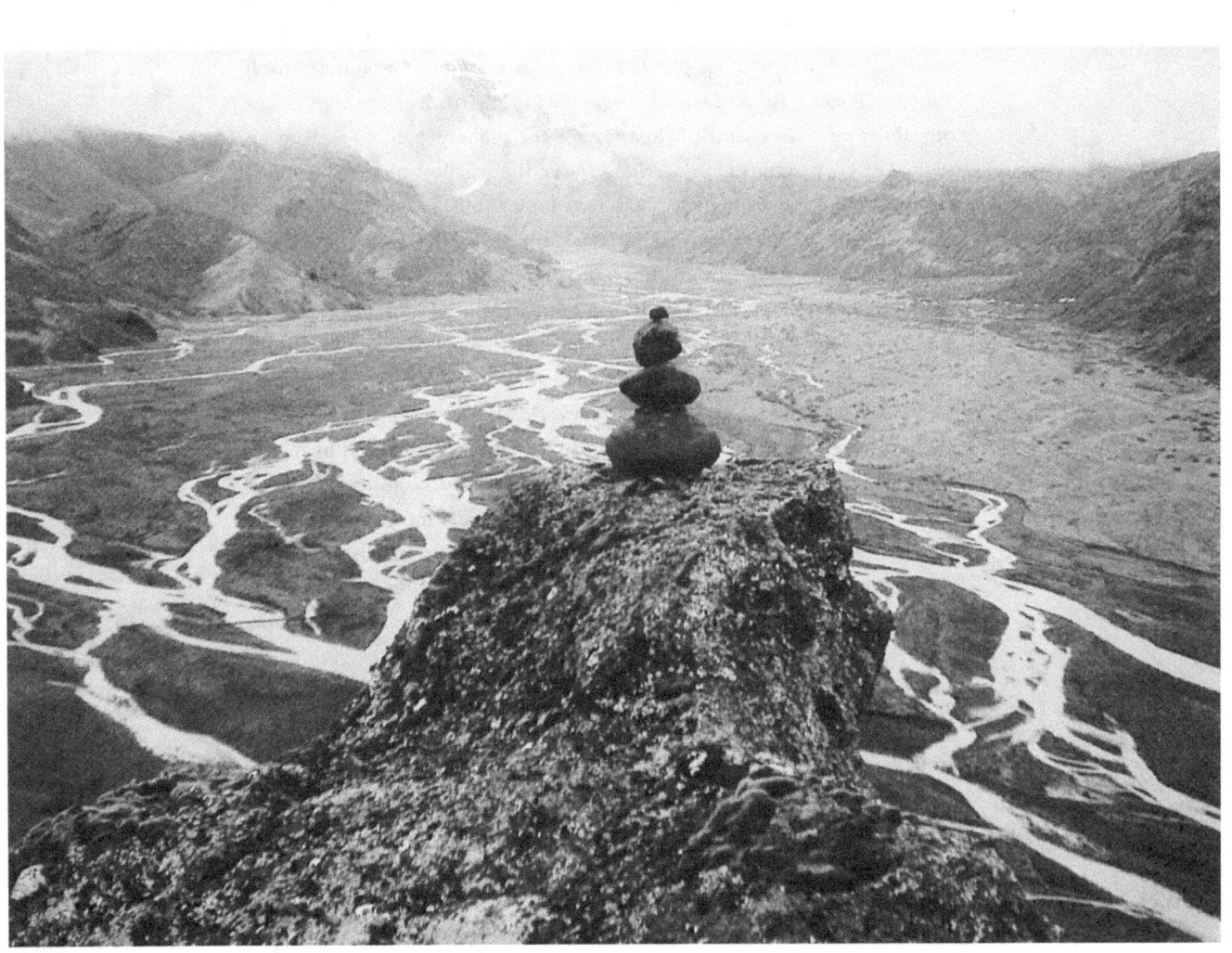

MICHAEL HEIZER: *DOUBLE NEGATIVE*

Land art or earthworks have proved to be the most arrogant, phallic and patriarchal of postwar productions.[1] Christo works on a gigantic scale, wrapping buildings or stretching curtains across valleys or surrounding islands. Some of the most phallic, domineering works of land art are by Michael Heizer.[2] In his *Double Negative* (1969-70), he took two chunks out of the earth, a gigantic 'violation' of the planet, in ecological/ green terms.[3] (Heizer claims *Double Negative* is 'the smallest piece I've done in relation to the size of the site').[4] Heizer gouged out 240,000 tons of earth from the site at Mormon Mesa in Nevada with bulldozers. The cuts are ramps, going down 50 feet through the cliff of the canyon. The spectator can walk down them. The overall dimensions of *Double Negative* are 1,500 x 42 feet. Heizer is very much concerned with *scale*, as well as other formal characteristics of a work. He has said that '[m]an will never really create anything large in relation to the world.'[5] Heizer's *Double Negative* is a widely celebrated example of land art. The photographs of it have been reproduced in many art history books. *Double Negative* appeals to trendy 1960s notions of Zen, existentialism, negativity and emptiness. The point about *Double Negative* was its sense of symmetry and relationship, the one cut reflecting the other across the Nevada canyon. Some viewers saw Heizer's enterprise as combining the subliminity and grandeur of Abstract Expressionism with the emblematic forms of Minimalism. American earthworks art rejuvenated the myth of the sublime West.[6] Mary Miss was not convinced. When she looks at the work of Heizer or Smithson 'there's always been an aspect which impedes my relating to it... It's like a mark on the earth' (1981, 6-7).

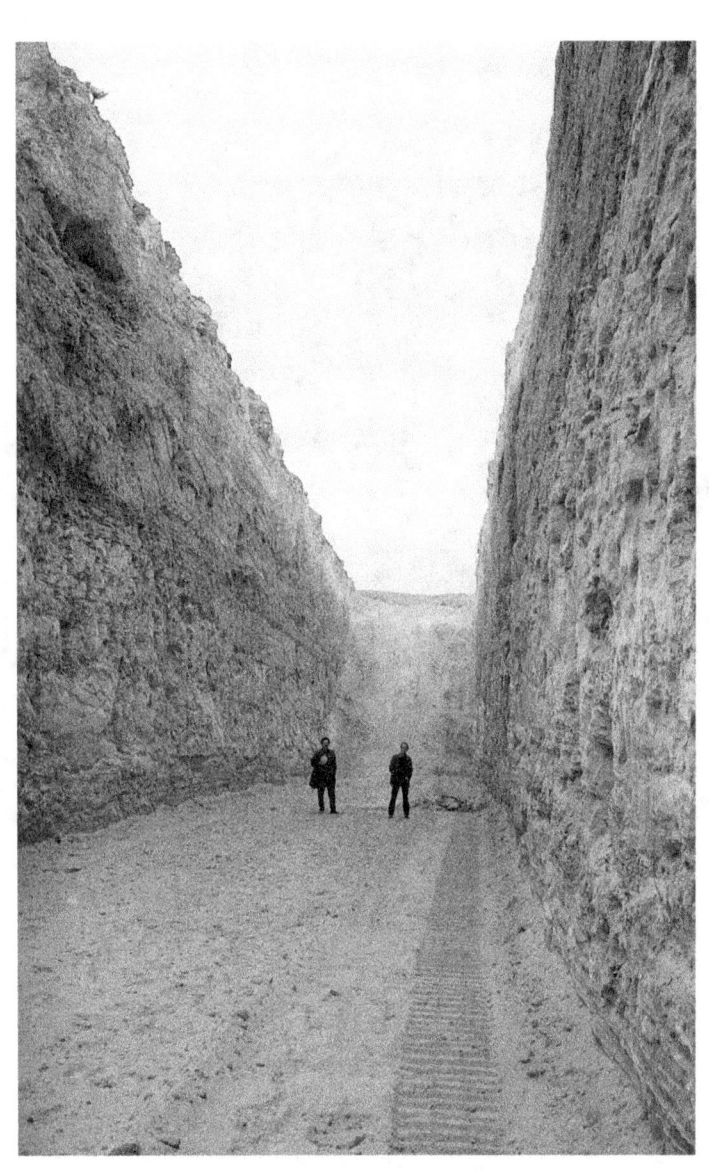

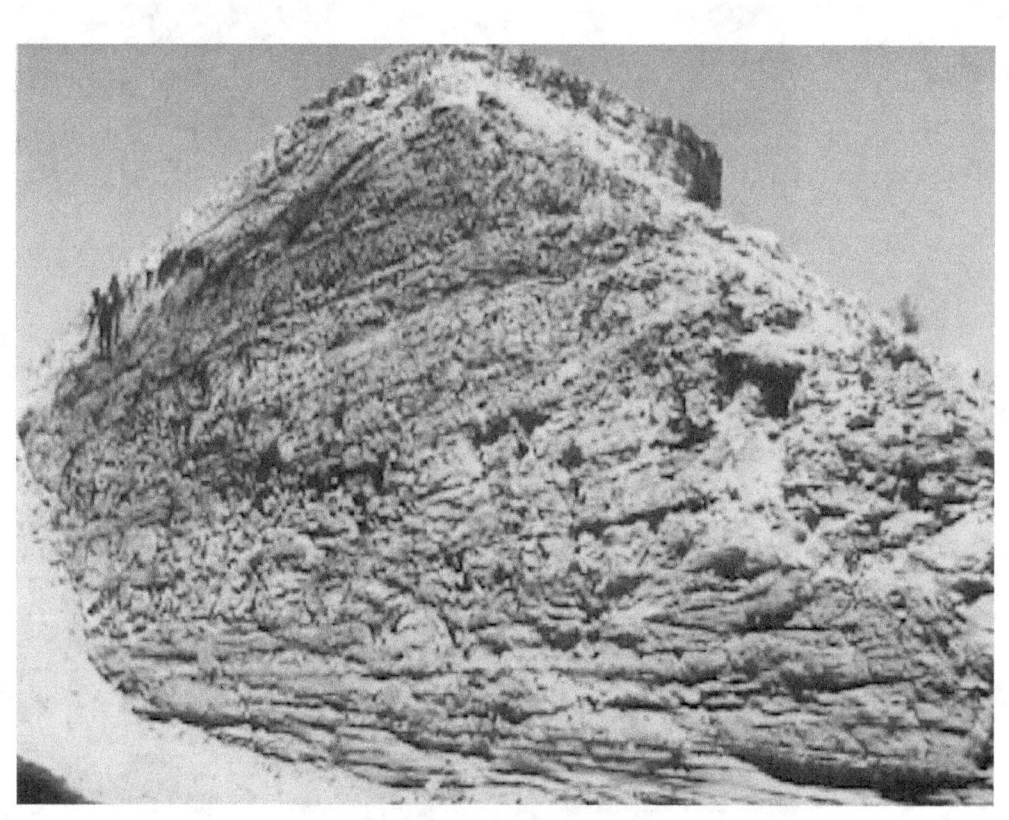

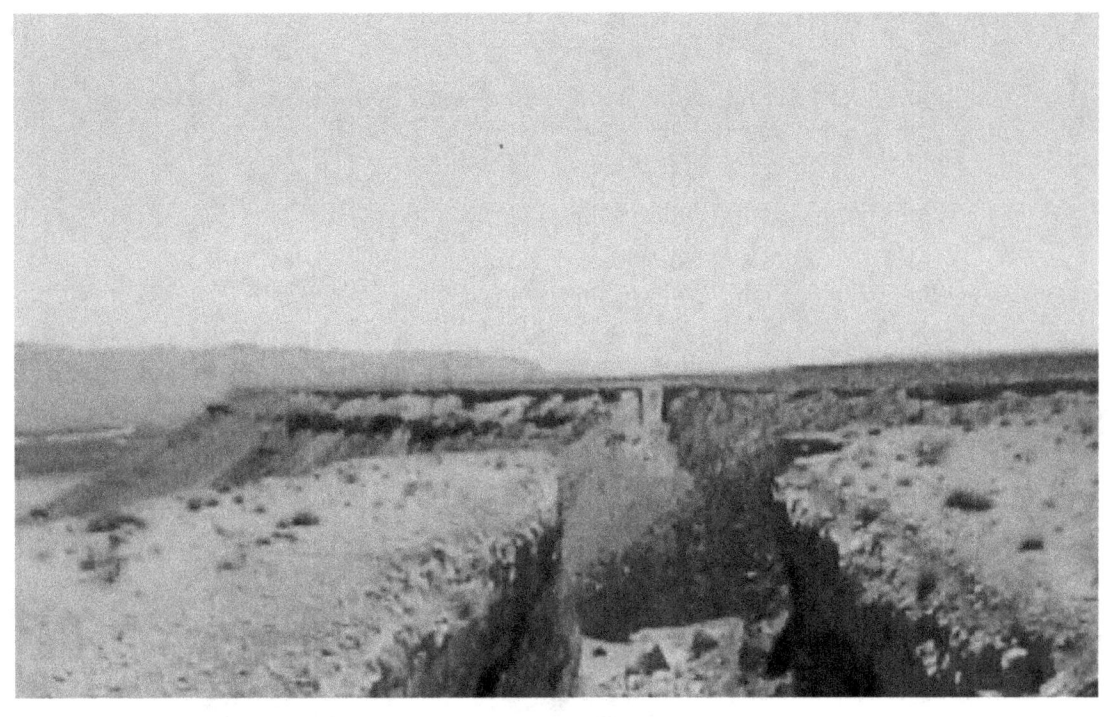

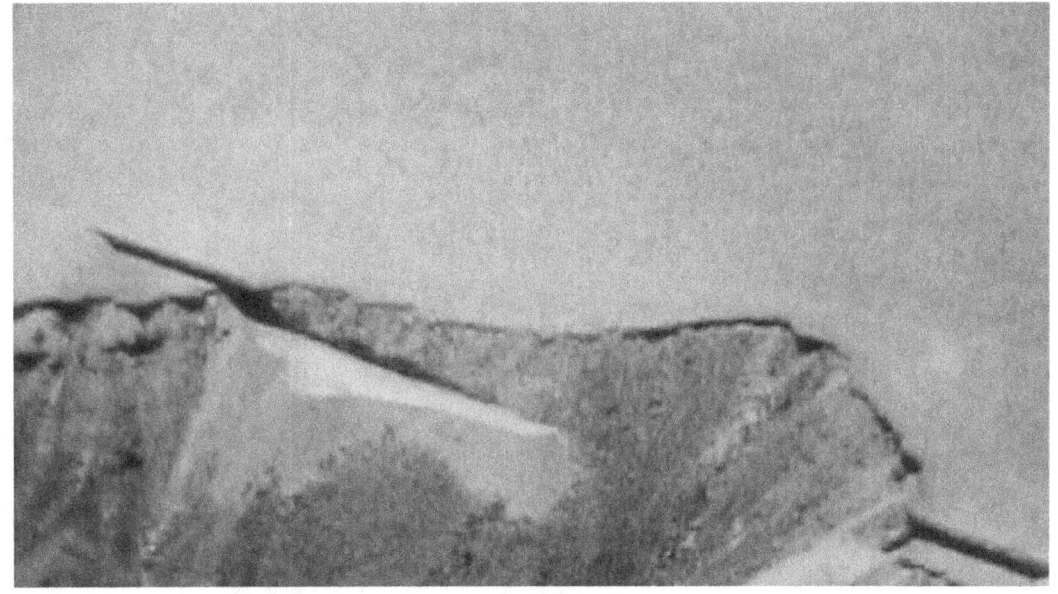

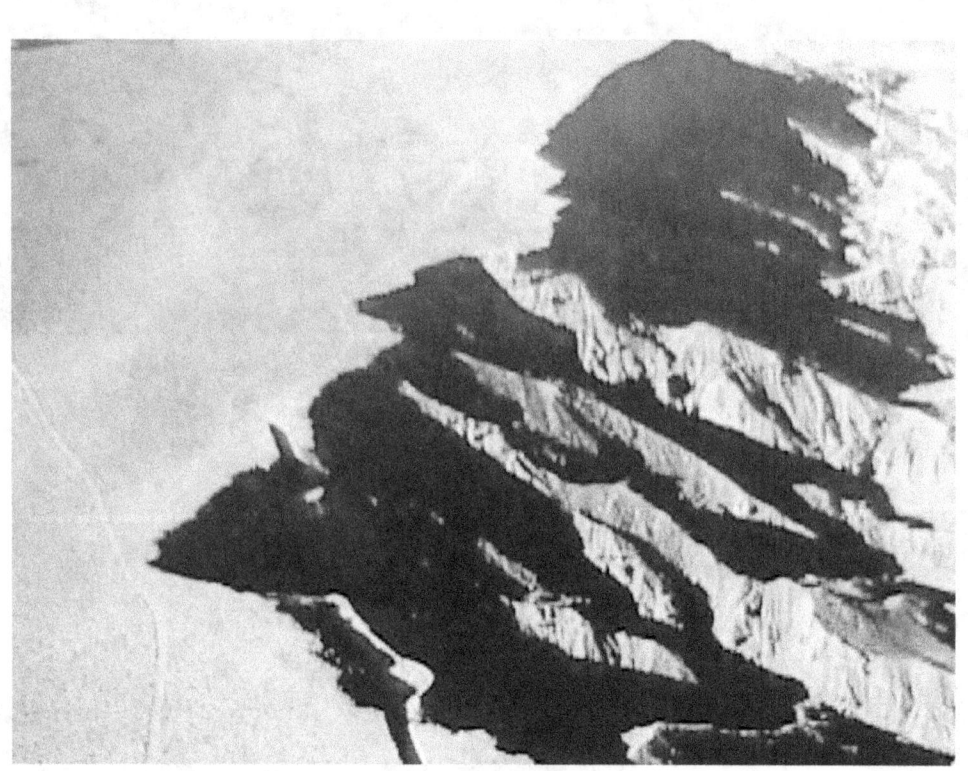

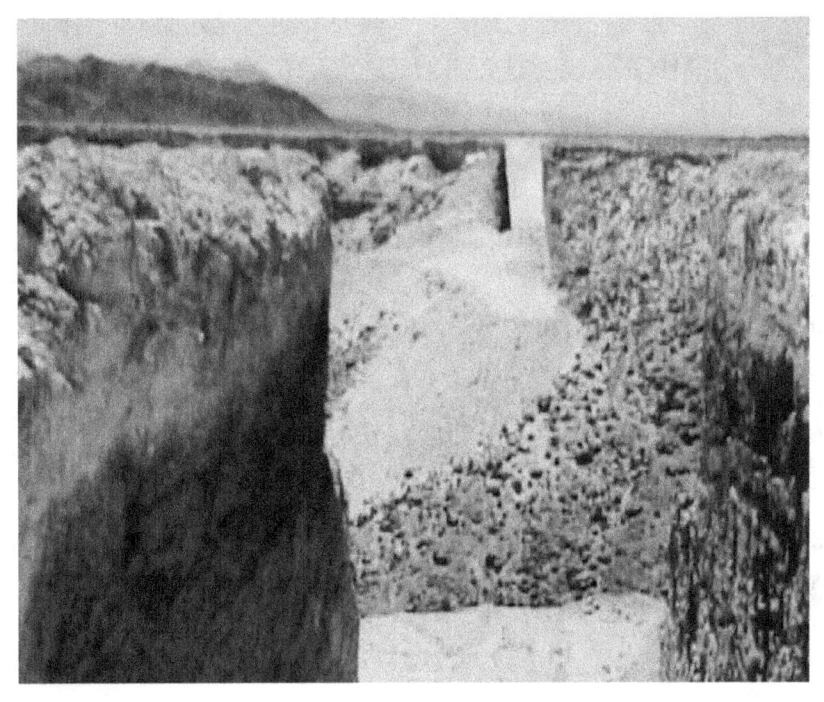

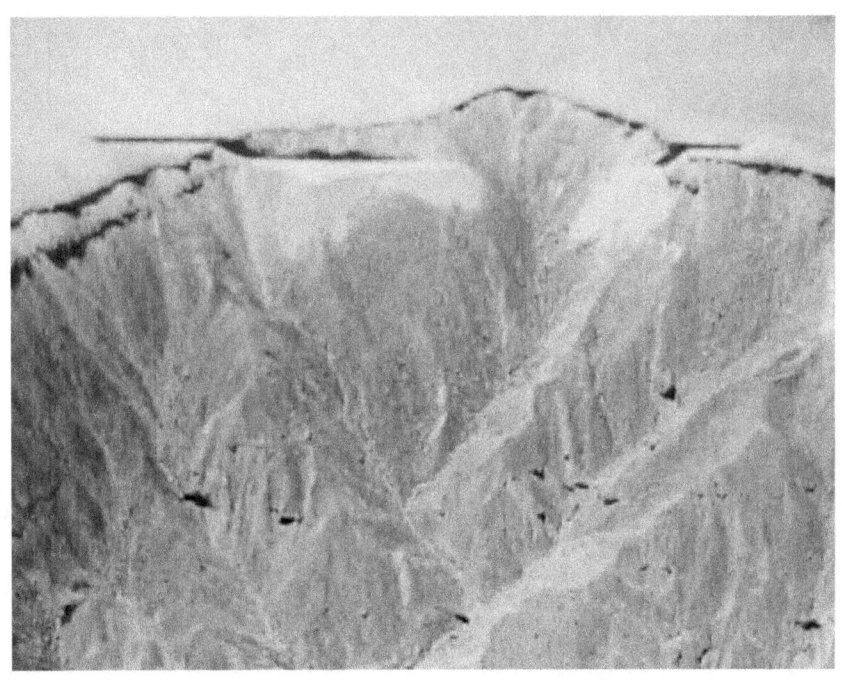

MICHAEL HEIZER: *DESERT CUTS*

Michael Heizer went on archælogical digs as a child with his father. He started out with the ambition to be a painter, which he studied at San Francisco. He made his first earthwork in 1967, and accompanied Smithson on geological expeditions. In 1968, Heizer collaborated with Smithson and Nancy Holt on a Super-8 film, *Mono-Lake*. (Heizer had invited Holt and Smithson to his parents' house at Lake Tahoe). Heizer's motorbike earthwork was entitled *Circular Surface Displacement*; it was made at Mono Lake.

Michael Heizer's other works include gouging huge holes in the ground and putting great chunks of rock in them. *Nine Nevada Depressions* (1968) was 5 cuts in the Blackrock desert, each one twelve feet long in an area 50 by 50 feet. *Munich Depression* (1969) was another cut, a line 15 feet deep.

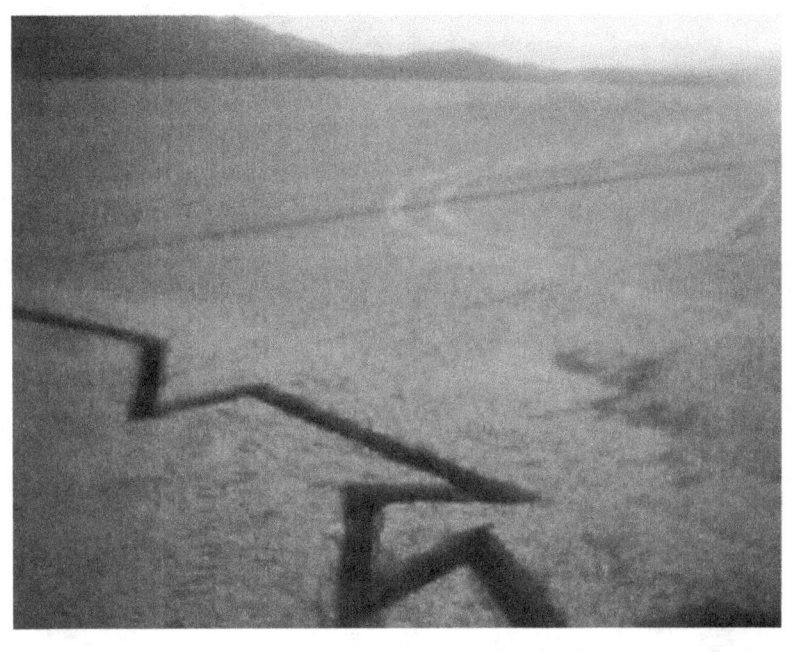

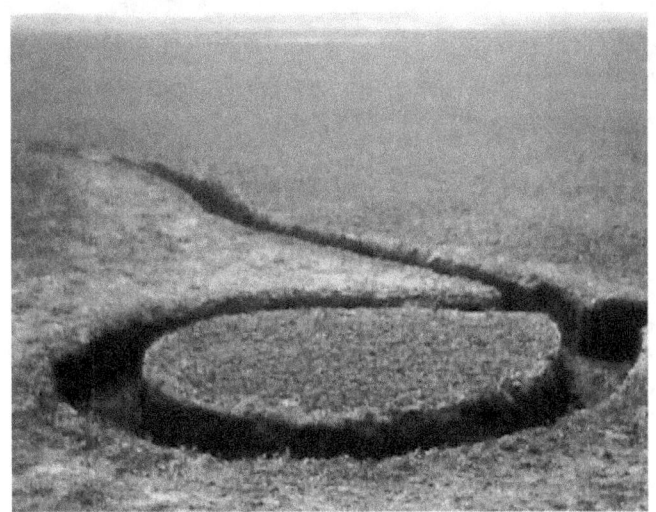

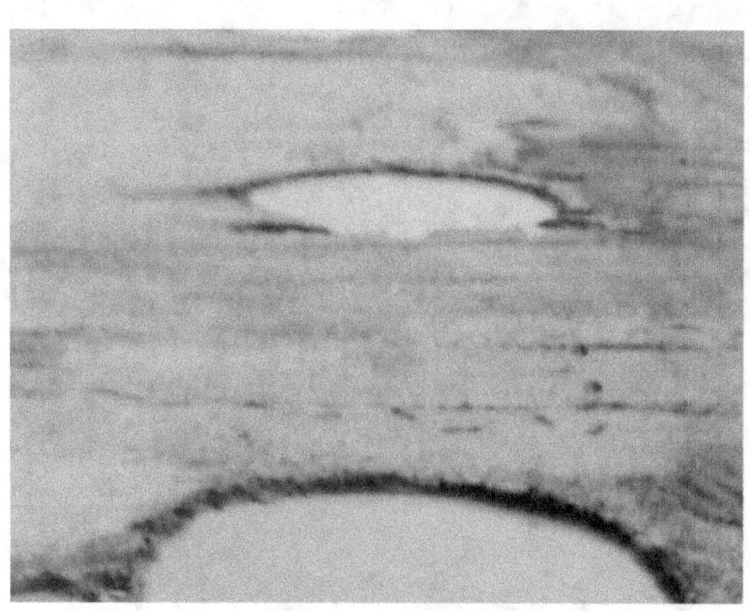

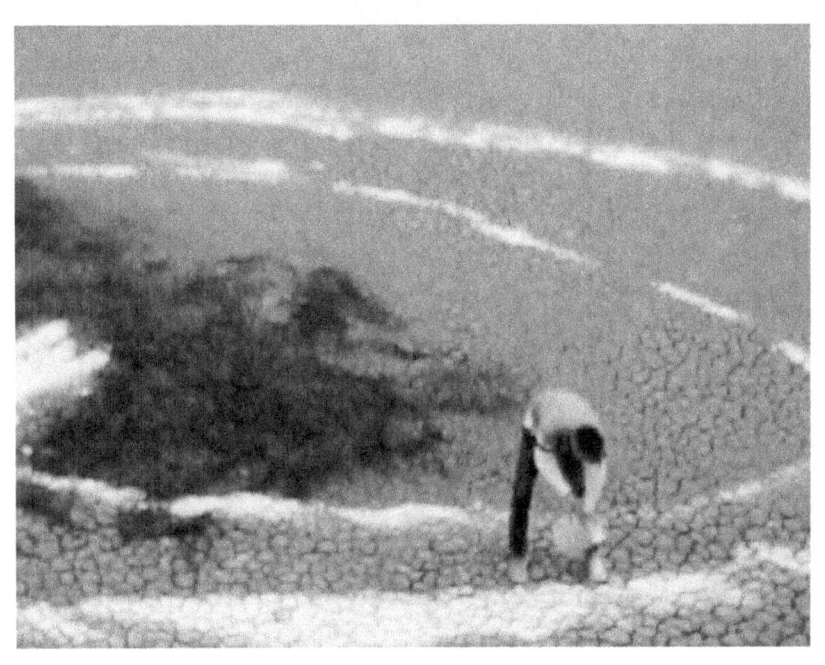

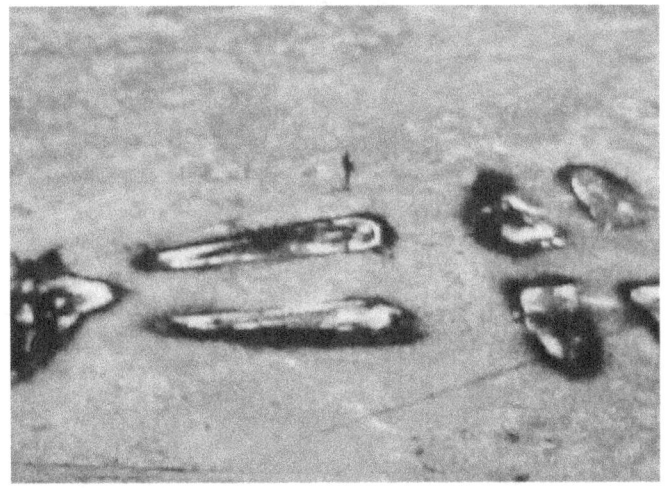

MICHAEL HEIZER: *COMPLEX ONE*

Michael Heizer's *Complex One* (1972) was a huge bunker-like mass of earth built with the aid of two assistants in Nevada. It was 23.5 feet high and 140 feet long. Each end of the hill had a cut-off triangle of reinforced concrete like giant bookends. Over the work were cantilevered concrete beams. '*Complex One* is a magnificent spectacle. Even its minatory look, suggesting a bunker, seems proper to the site – the edge of the Nevada nuclear proving-ground'.[1]

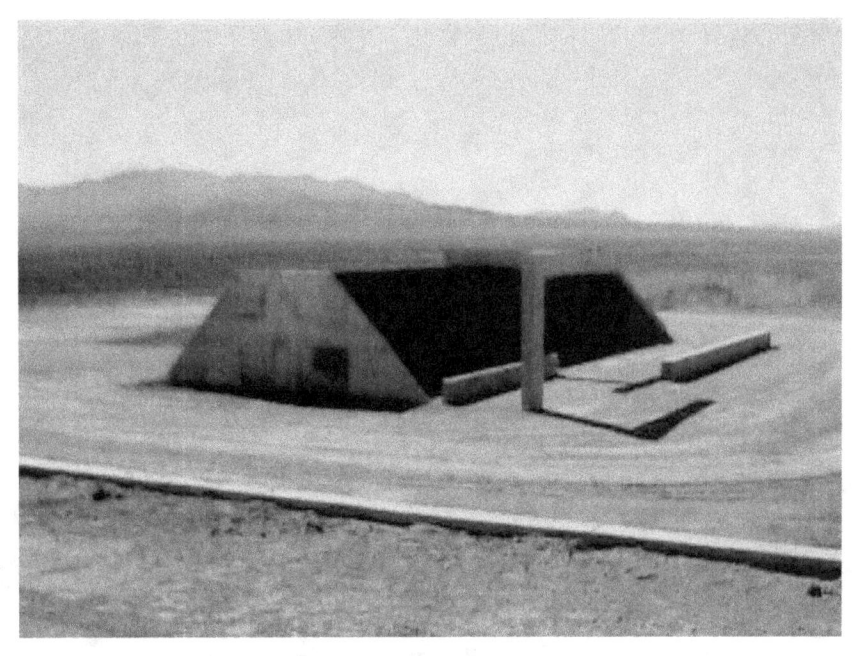

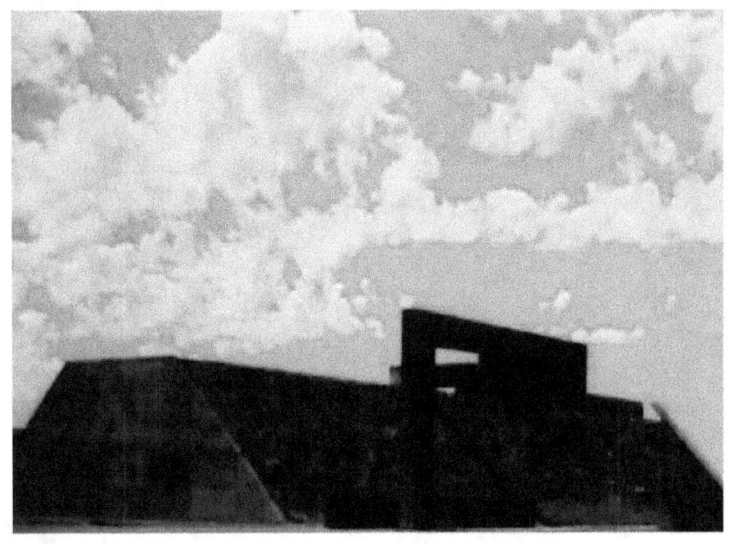

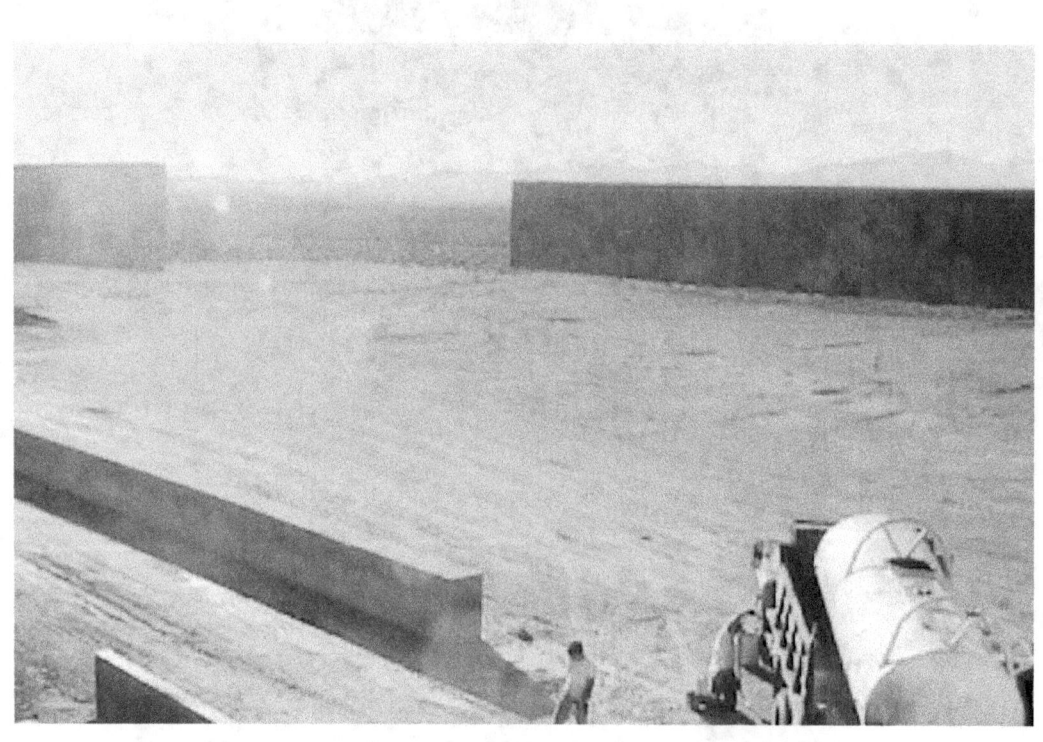

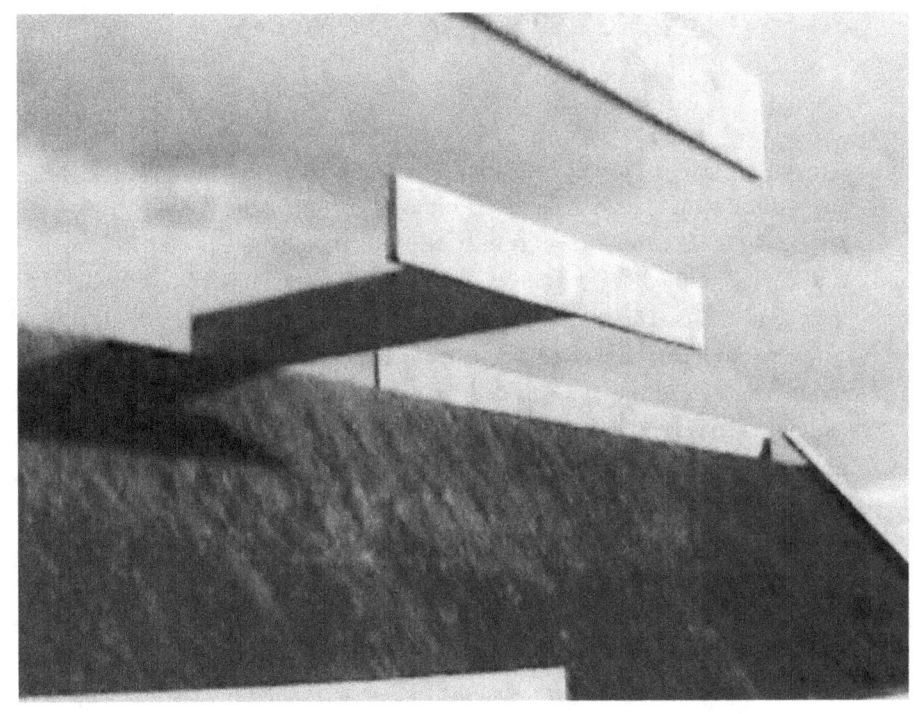

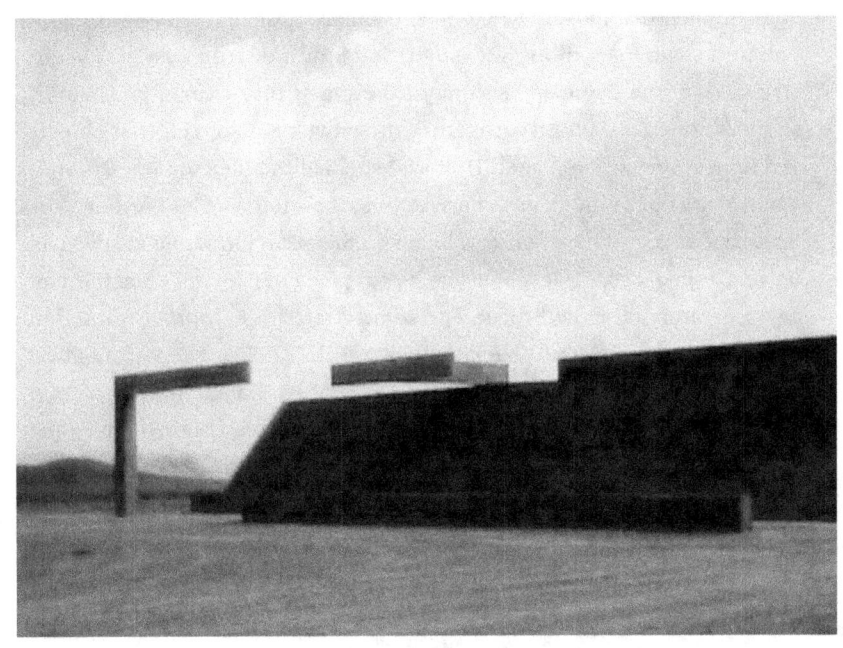

NANCY HOLT: *SUN TUNNELS*

Nancy Holt married the key earthwork artist, Robert Smithson, in 1963. She worked with him on his non-site projects, including the famous *Spiral Jetty* and *Amarillo Ramp*. Nancy Holt's art, with its large, heavy landscaping gestures (such as her *Dark Star Park*), is comparable with the male land artists. The globes and pools of water, though, are traditional 'feminine' volumes, here given a new, monumental turn. Holt's art concerns the movements of the heavens. Her sculptures focus the viewer on the motions of the earth, moon, sun and stars. Holt's art is concerned with the notion of time, in particular with geological time, the relation between time and the Earth. Holt was impressed by the desert when she visited it in the late 1960s with Smithson and Michael Heizer.

While working on Smithson's enormous *Amarillo Ramp* after his death in a plane crash, Holt developed the idea for the gigantic *Sun Tunnels*, 18ft long pipes that were 9 feet high with many holes punched in the side, to let light in.[1] She searched for a suitable site – a desert floor surrounded by low hills. The site she chose (and bought) was in the Great Basin Desert of Utah. *Sun Tunnels* was finished in 1976, with holes in the side of each concrete tube 7, 8, 9 and 10 inches diameter. The holes corresponded with star constellations (Capricorn, Draco, Columba and Perseus), as with *Hydra's Head*. During the day the sun creates points of light on the bottom of the tunnels that move. The moon also shines through the holes by night. The pipes were set about 32° North and South of true East and West, aligned with the rising and setting of the sun at the Summer and Winter solstices. *Sun Tunnels* links together the movements of celestial objects and the viewer on the planet. Holt said she had the idea for *Sun Tunnels* while being out in the desert and watching the sun rising and setting. The flat desert area evoked 'a sense of being on this planet, rotating in space, in universal time' (1977). It is a cosmological piece of land art, something of an observatory, like the Bronze Age stone circles of Europe. 'I wanted to bring the vast space desert back to human scale' (1977). The astronomical observatory has been an enduring theme in land art. Robert Morris, Michael Dan Archer, Julia Barton and Andy Goldsworthy have also made viewing sites.

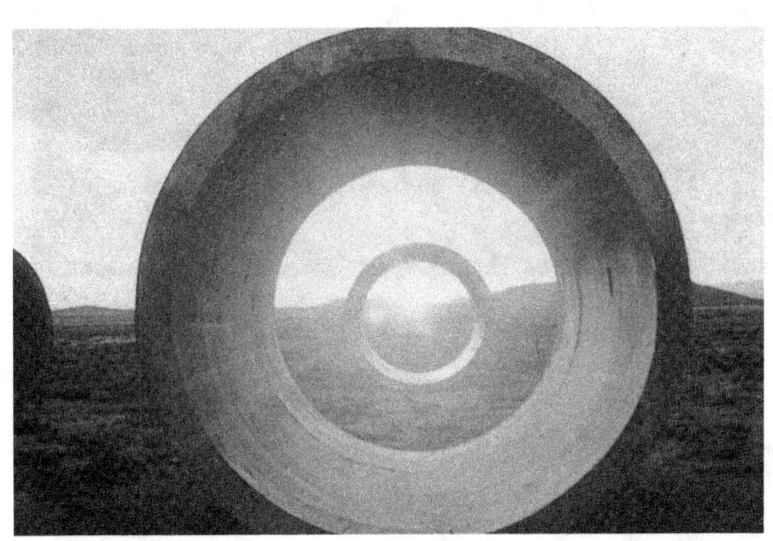

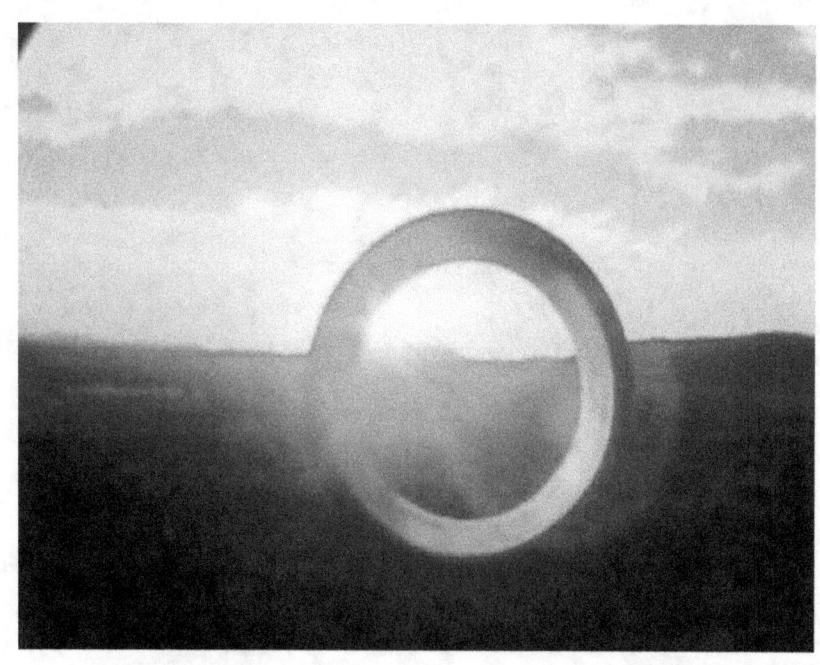

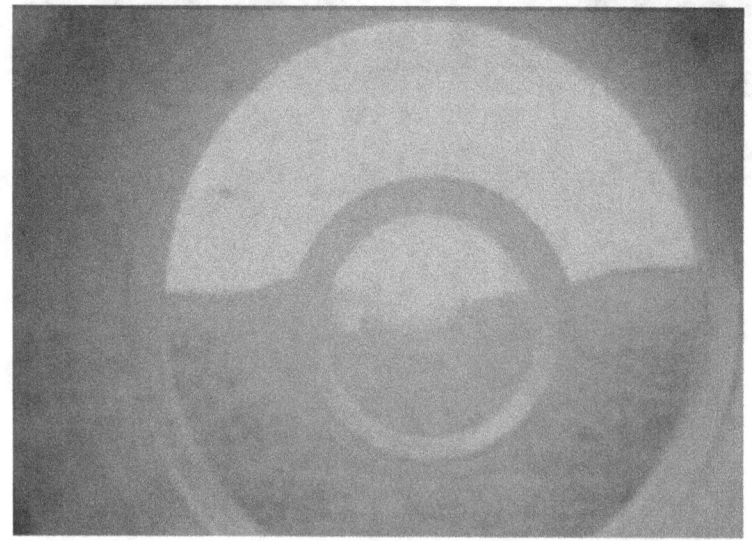

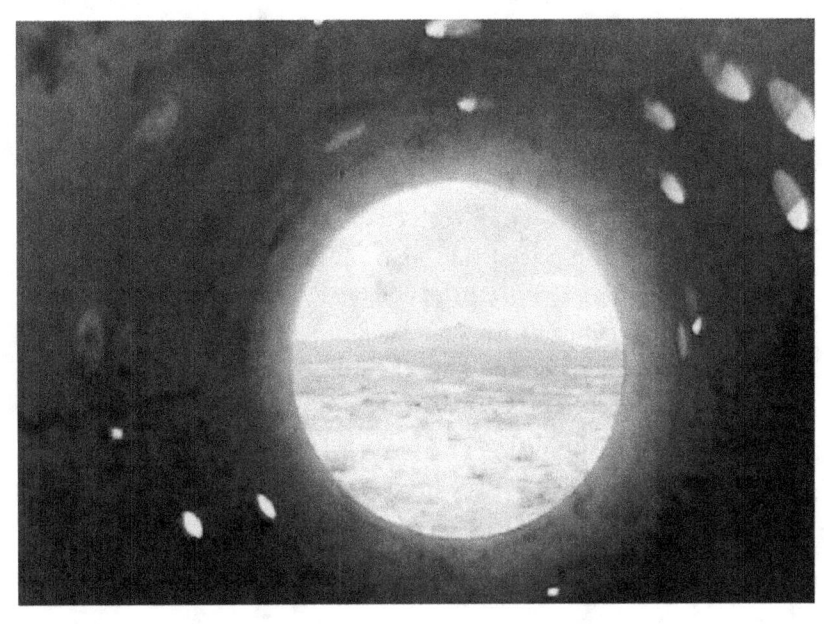

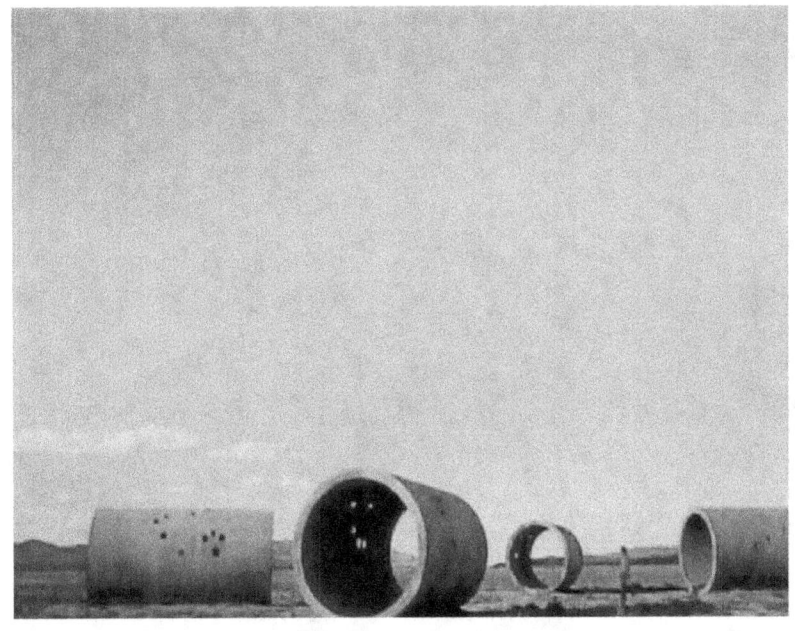

NANCY HOLT: *HYDRA'S HEAD*

Nancy Holt's *Hydra's Head* (1975) also concerned the relation between the heavens and earth. Next to the Niagara River at Art Park, Lewiston, New York, Holt sank 6 concrete tubes into the soil. Each three foot pipe was filled with water, so they formed circular mirrors flush with the ground. Again, Holt based the position of the concrete pits on a constellation (Hydra). *Hydra's Head* combined the presence and noise of the rushing Niagara River with the reflections of the sky, stars and moon. Holt's concrete pipe sculptures use the prime symbol of change and all things cosmic, the circle. The *Sun Tunnels* are like enormous telescopes or astrolabes, while *Hydra's Head* evokes six fallen stars, the circles of water reflecting the sky and stars.

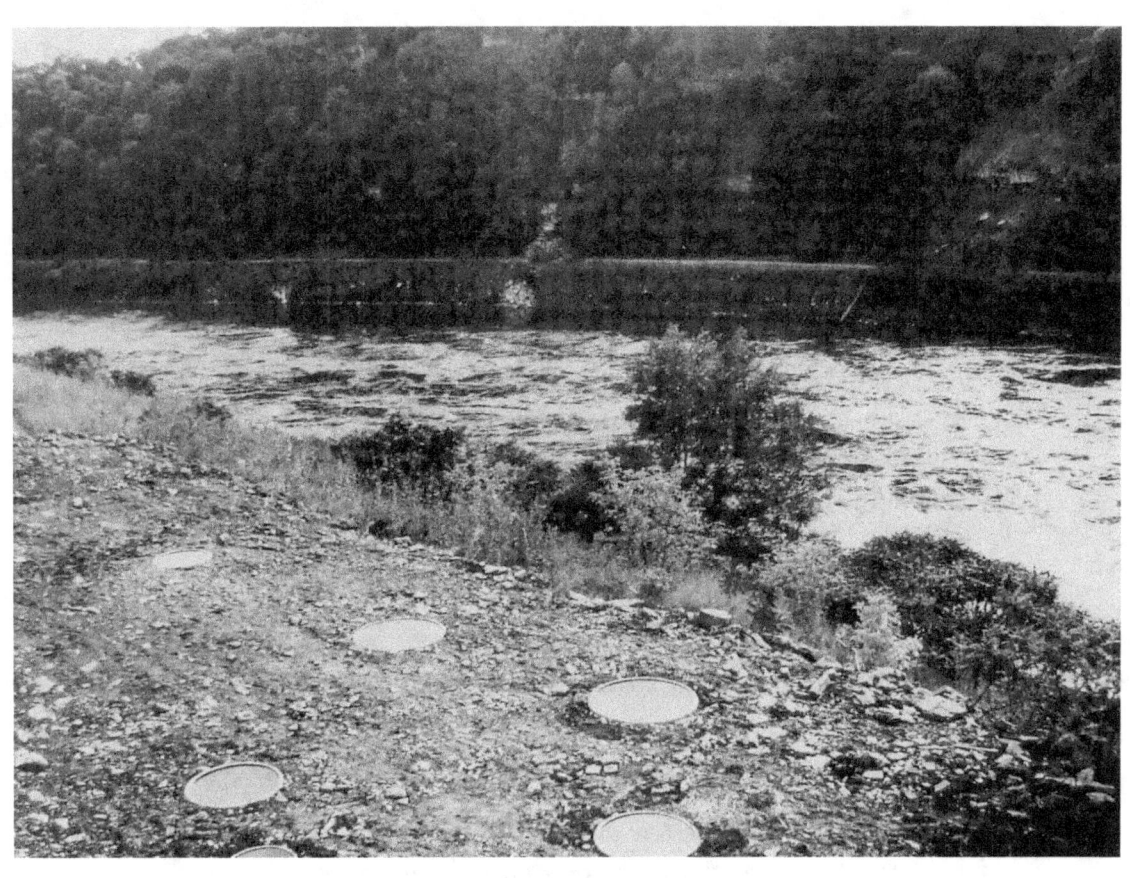

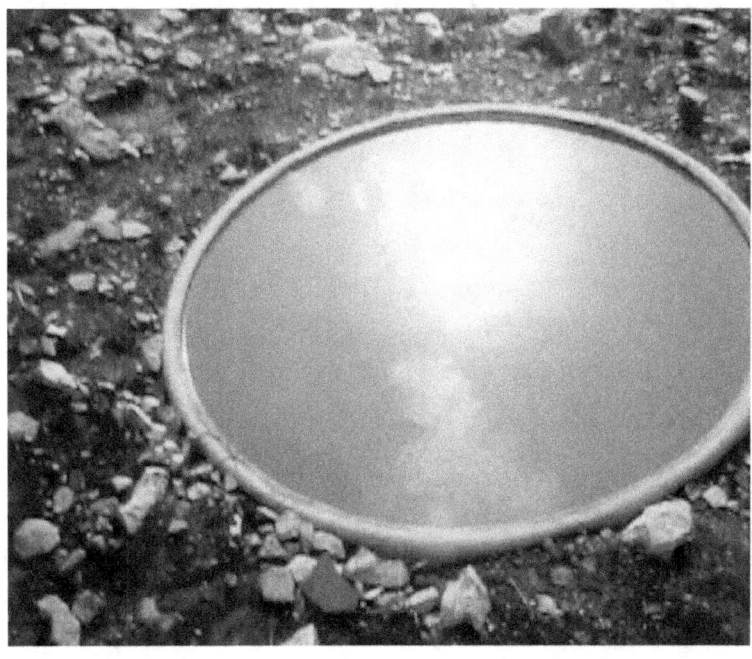

NANCY HOLT: *STONE ENCLOSURE: ROCK RINGS*

Nancy Holt's romantic evocations of stellar, cosmological themes in concrete and soil flourished again with *Stone Enclosure: Rock Rings* (1977-78) constructed at Western Washington University Bellingham. Holt's *Stone Enclosure* directly recalled, even emulated, prehistoric stone circles, in particular Stonehenge. Holt used ancient schist rocks, between 200 and 230 million years old (known as brown mountain stone) to construct two concentric rings 10 feet high. In each wall of stone Holt made 4 arches, each 8 feet high, and 12 'portholes'. It was not a large stone ring, in terms of diameter (outer diameter was 40 feet), but being ten feet high it was much taller than most Bronze Age stone circles. The arches and holes provided views to the cardinal points, and to NE, SW, EW, NW-SE. Holt's *Stone Enclosure* makes the connections with ancient astronomy and stone circle building explicit, not slyly implied, as in much of land art. Holt is clear that she is dealing with the ancient astronomical realities of weather, seasons, cycles, stars and time. Another work, *30 Below* (1980), a tower with arches facing the points of the compass, was positioned around the North Star. The still point in the heavens, the Pole Star, was also one of the keys to *Stone Enclosure*, which, Holt said, related to a true north, a dead centre.[1]

1. C. Robins, 1984, 104.

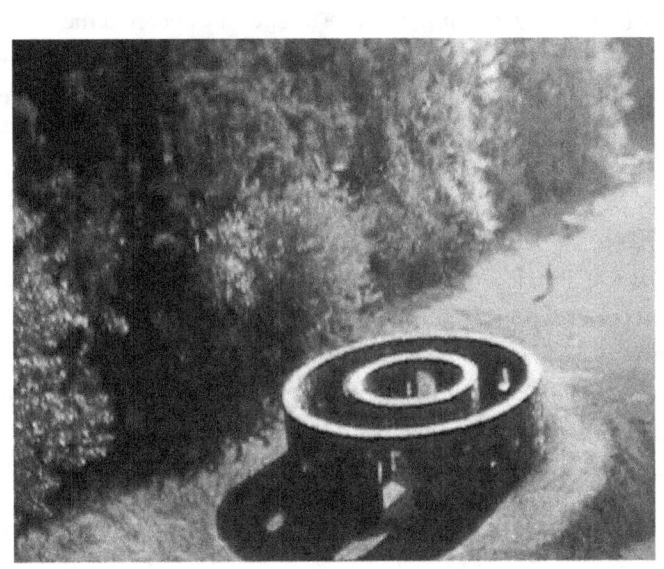

ALICE AYCOCK: *A SIMPLE NETWORK OF UNDERGROUND WALLS AND TUNNELS*

Alice Aycock's land artworks are much more ambiguous and deliberately problematic than Nancy Holt's or Carl Andre's works. Many of Aycock's land sculptures involve underground passages and spaces. In 1972 she constructed a series of underground spaces in *Low Building Made with Dirt Roof (For Mary)* in Pennsylvania. The spectator entered the 20 by 12 feet work through a doorway thirty inches high. The work was experienced by crawling through it. Aycock's intention was to evoke an experience of claustrophia, of being in a cellar. Aycock's works had titles such as *The Machine That Makes the World* (1979), *A Theory of Universal Causality* (1983) and *How to Catch and Manufacture Ghosts* (1979). Aycock's sculpture explored the rationality of machines and technology and irrationality of ghosts and magic (H. Risatti, 37).

Alice Aycock's *A Simple Network of Underground Walls and Tunnels* (1975) was made in a corn field at Far Hills, New Jersey. It consisted of 6 square wells in two rows of three excavated out of a 20 by 50 foot area. Two of the wells had 7 foot ladders that enabled the spectator to climb down and explore the dark connecting tunnels. Some of the wells were capped, others were open. The effect was a series of spaces that recalled 'ominous historical precedents, caves, catacombs, dungeons and beehive tombs' wrote Roberta Smith (1975, 68).

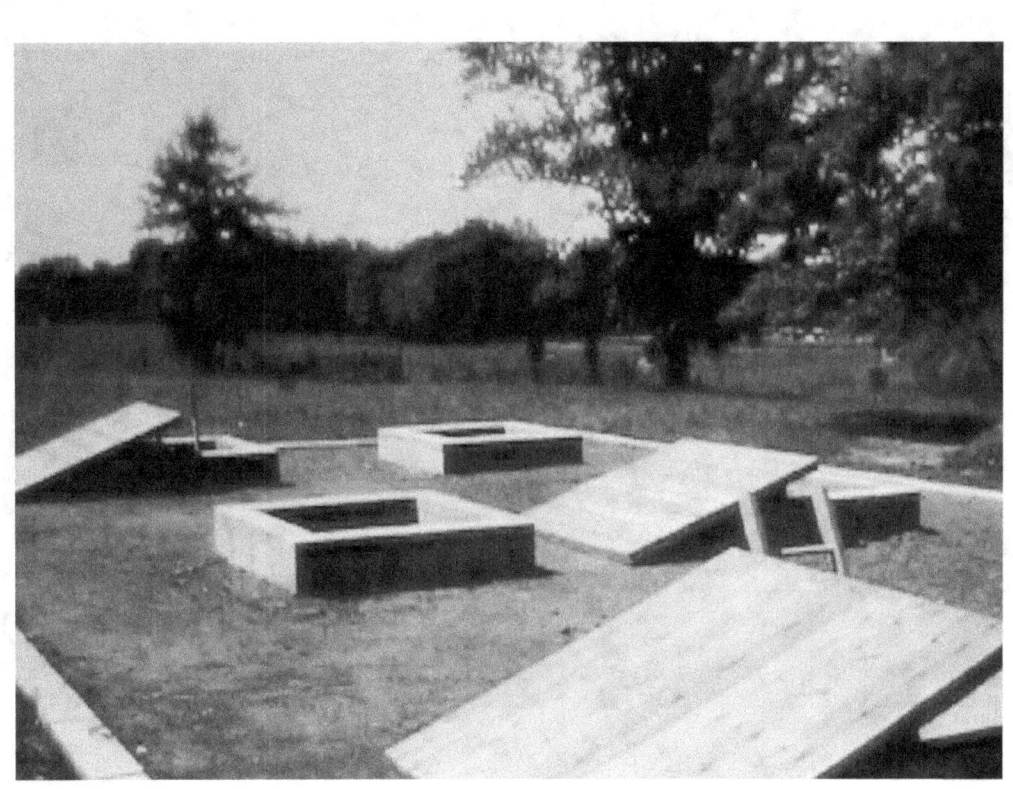

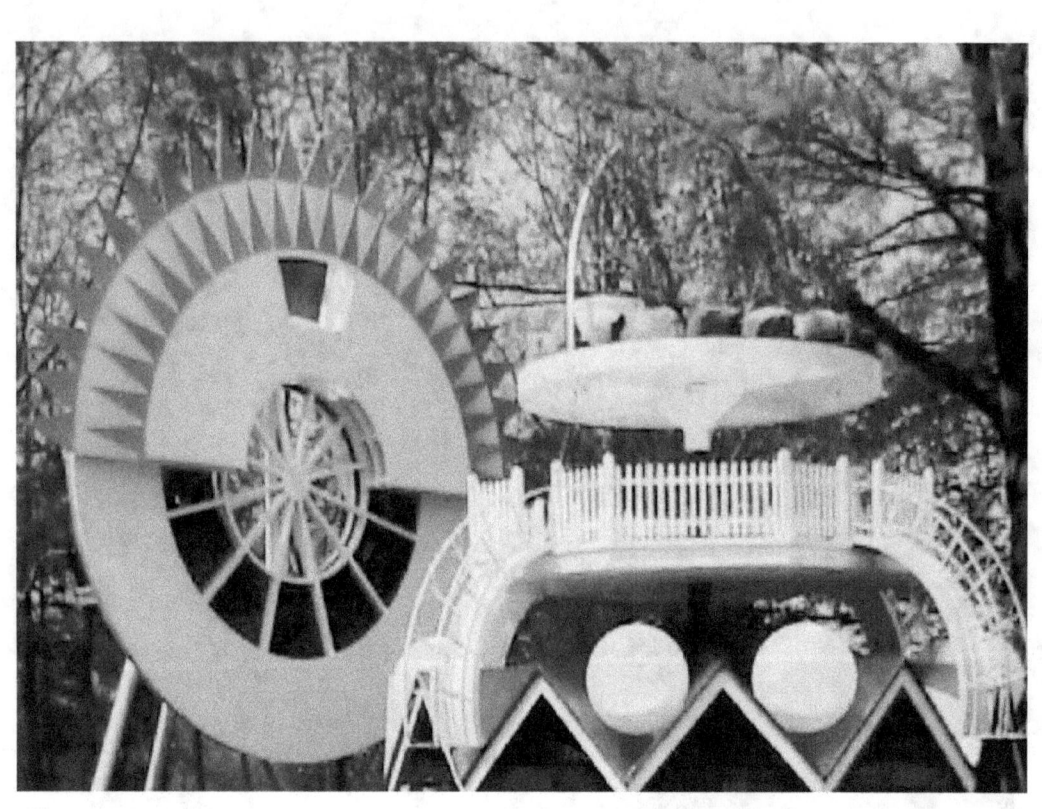

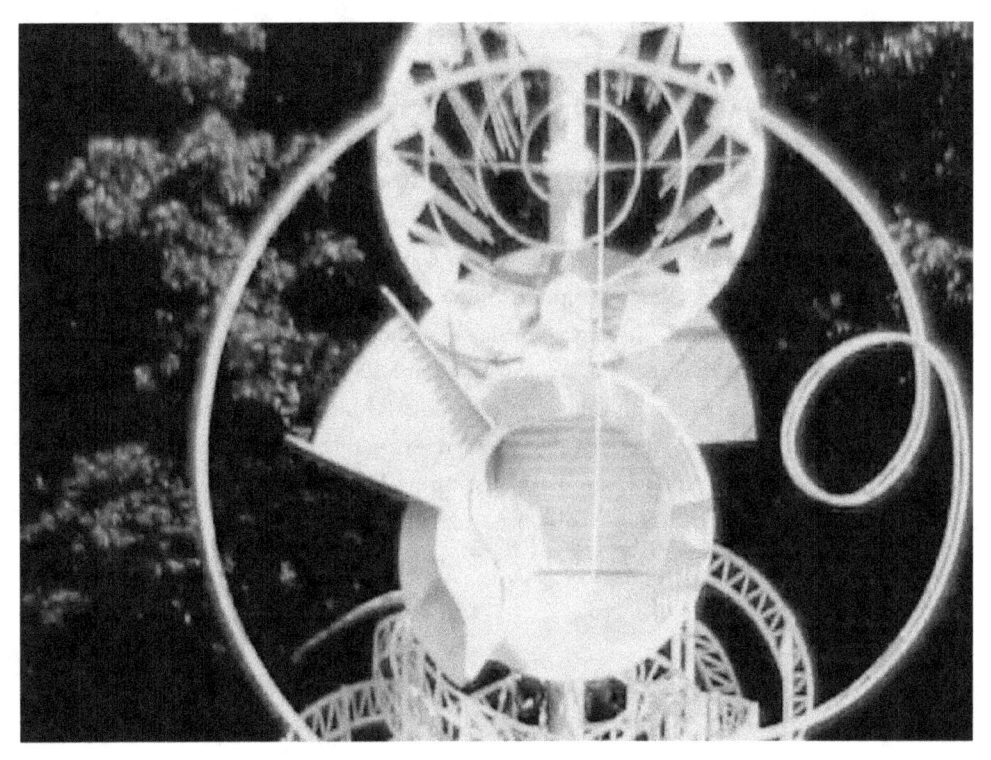

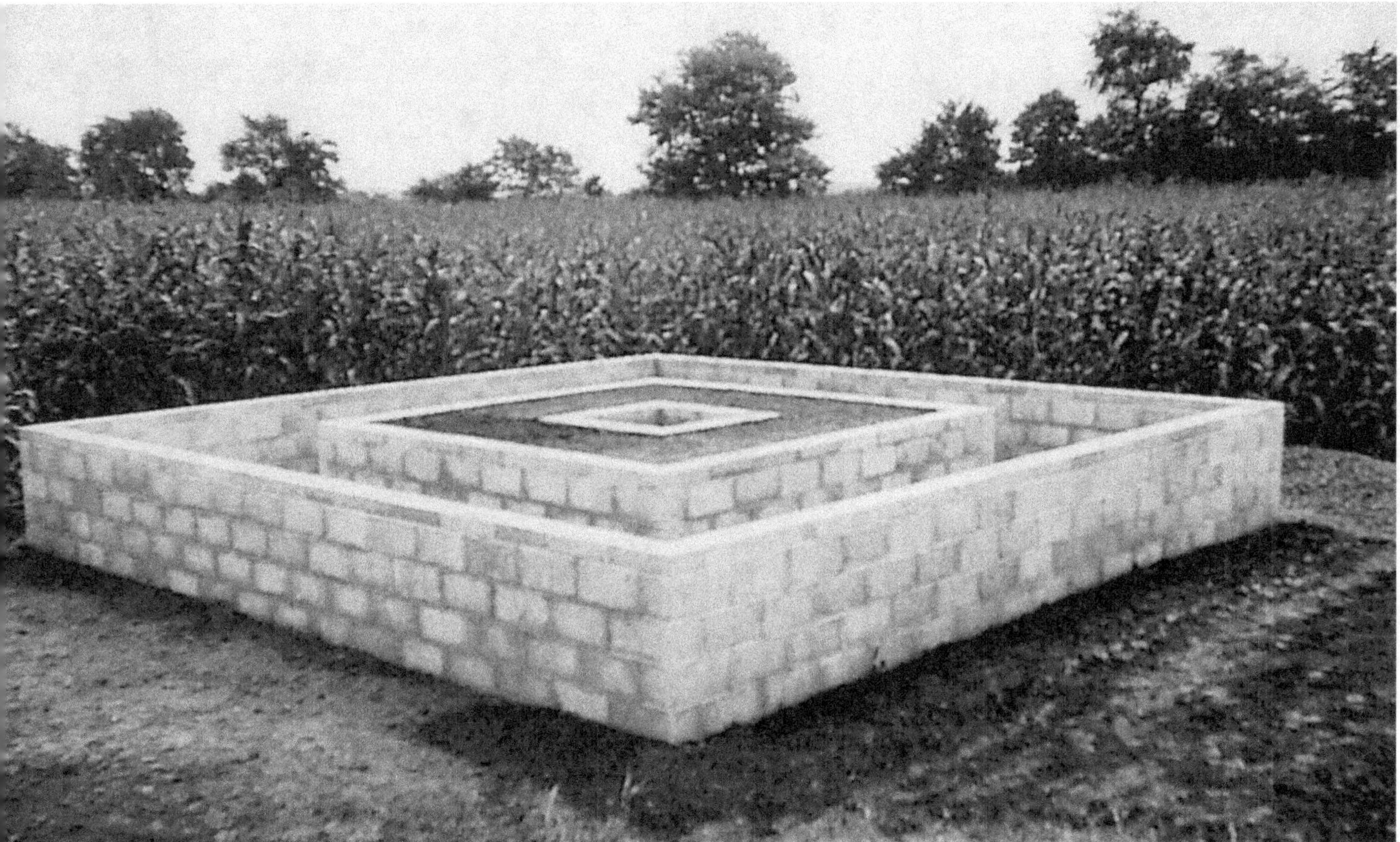

MARY MISS: *BATTERY PARK CITY ESPLANADE*

Mary Miss studied at the University of California at Santa Barbara. In summer 1963 she studied sculpture at Colorado College. After graduating in 1966 from the University of California Miss studied at the Rinehard School of Sculpture at the Maryland Art Institute until 1968. Early works included a 'waterline': at Fountain Creek in Colorado Miss suspended a double knot of hemp rope 100 feet over a dry riverbed; every twenty feet were lines of rope. At War's Island in New York Miss threw 15 foot long wooden stakes into the water which were weighted with rocks. *Battery Park City Esplanade* (1985-87) is a typical Miss work.

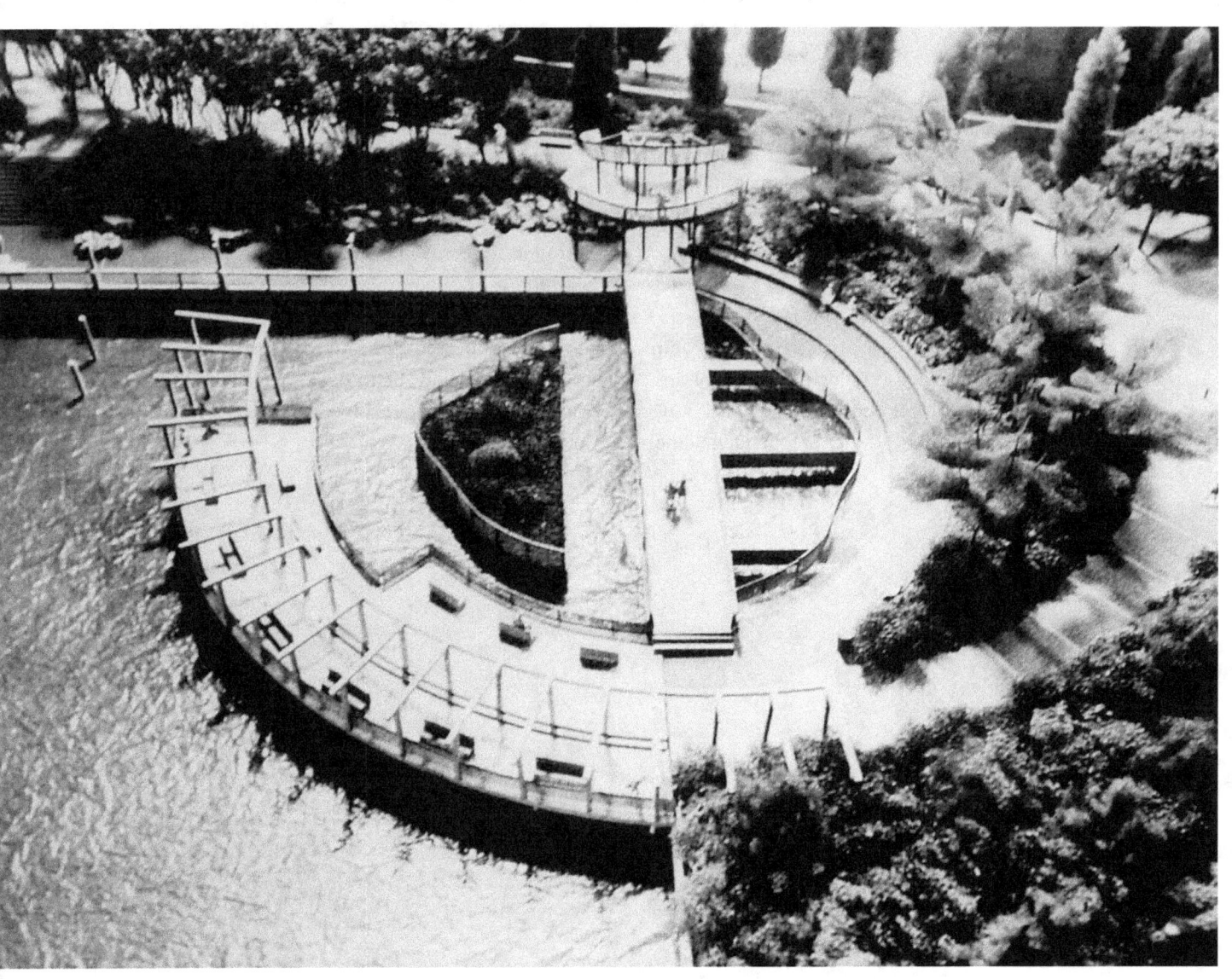

MARY MISS: *PERIMETERS/ PAVILION/ DECOYS*

Mary Miss's 1978 *Perimeters/ Pavilion/ Decoys* was constructed in Roslyn, New York, in a field that was part of the Nassau County Museum's ground. *Perimeters/ Pavillion/ Decoys* consists of three wooden towers, which look like tree houses with four platforms on stilts, two mounds of earth, and an underground space which's accessed by a ladder. The wooden towers are not for climbing on, but for viewing. The tallest is 18 by 10 by 10 feet. The subterranean atrium was for exploring through. It was a 16 ft^2 pit with a seven foot hole acting as an entrance; visitors climbed down a ladder to explore the various underground spaces, some with wooden, others with soil walls. *Perimeters/ Pavillion/ Decoys* was related to Pueblo Indian structres, Pompeiian and Mexican courtyards, and Mesopotamian brick complexes. The site explored the physical and psychological aspects of 'inside/ outside, above/ below, light/ dark, open/ closed, nature/ artifice'.[1] Miss's works are often large, spreading over a wide area of ground. In Illinois she created a 5-acre scale work.[2]

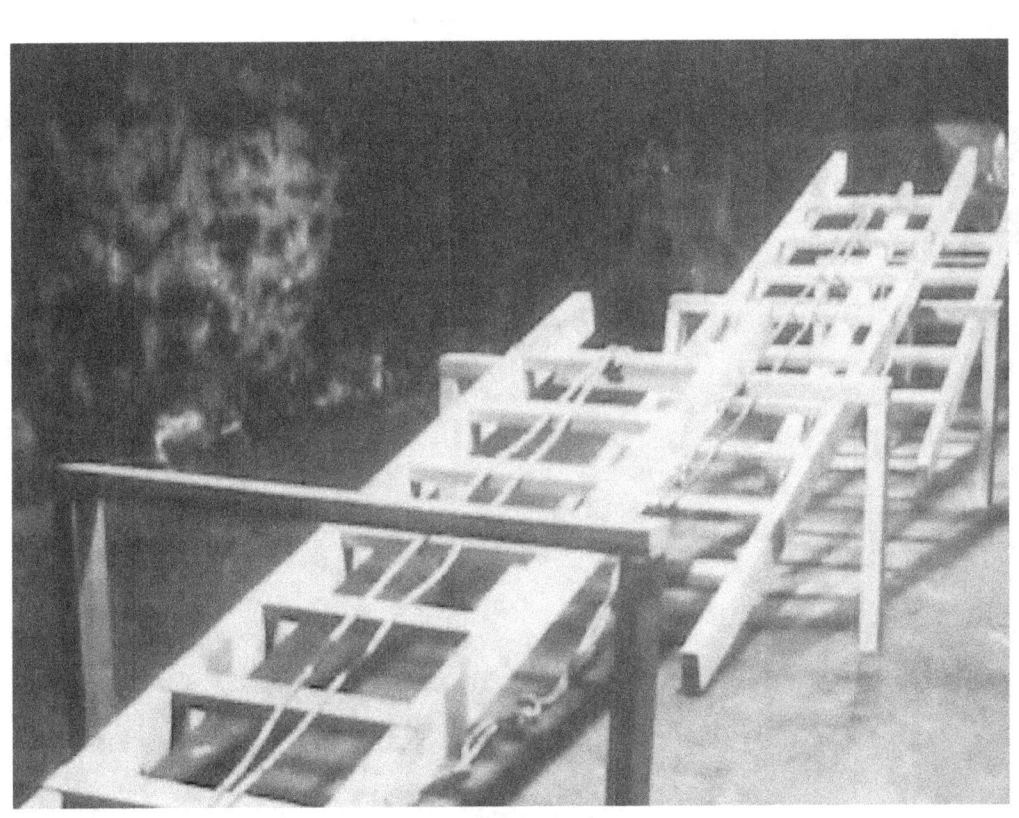

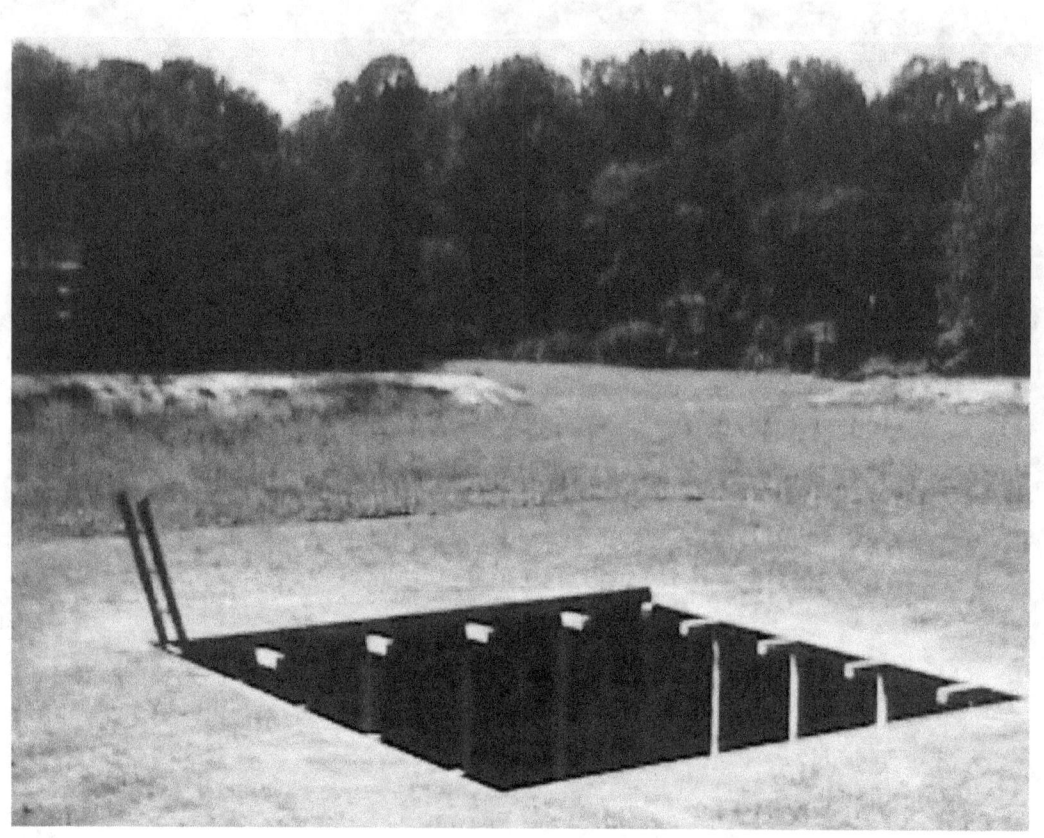

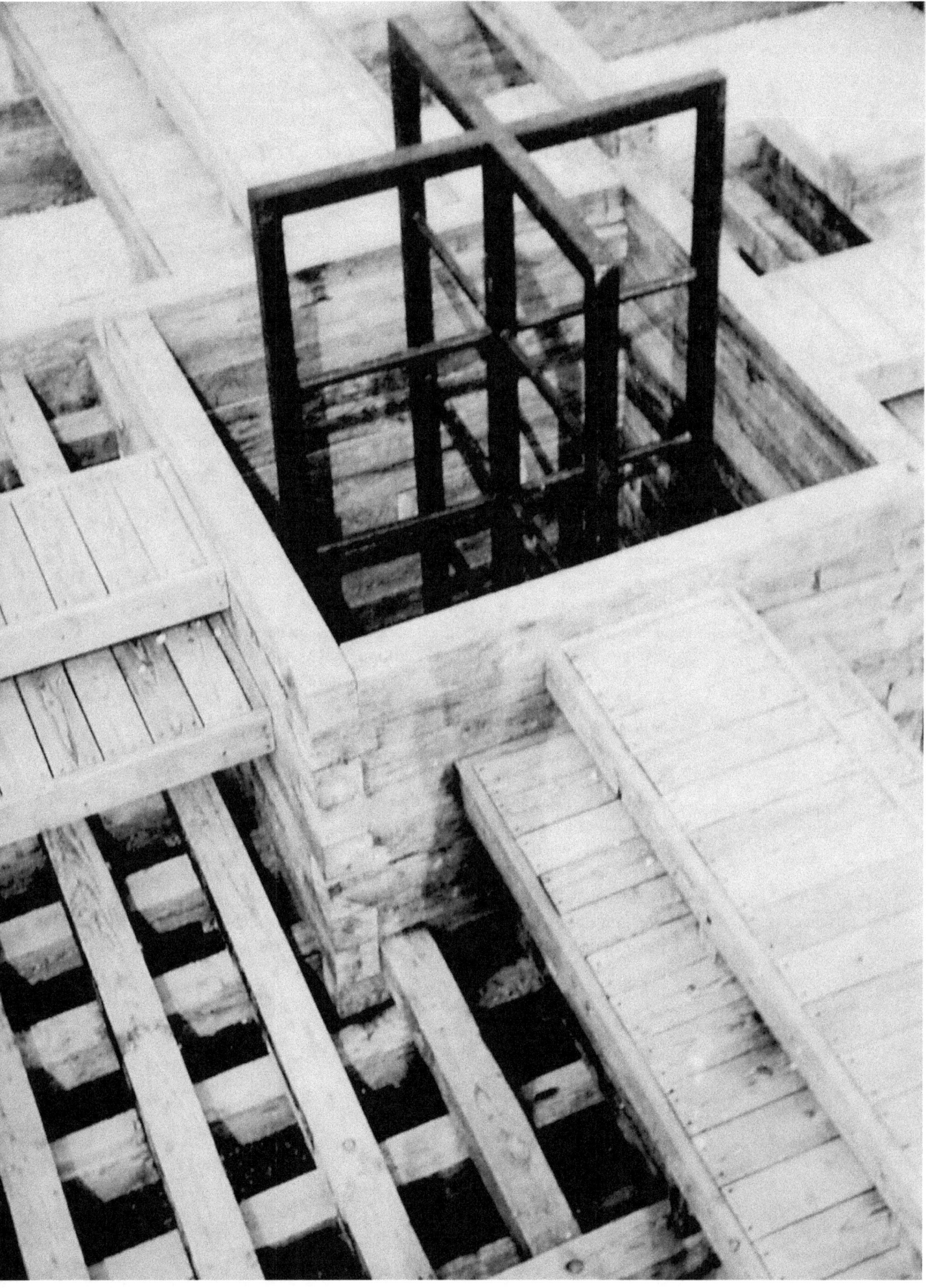

LAWRENCE WEINER: *BILLOWING CLOUDS*

Sixties Conceptual artist Lawrence Weiner produced text works, capital letters on a wall or in a book (Richard Long, Barbara Kruger, the Art & Language group and Michael Craig-Martin have also produced post-Conceptualist wall works). Weiner's solution to making sculpture was that a sculpture on a plinth has to be 'translated' into language, so that people can understand it. Sculpture is language, and words are language, therefore, Weiner reckons, words can be sculpture:

> when you see a piece of wood lying on the ground with a piece of stone on top of it, you must translate that in your own head into language. What I try to do is present language itself as a key to what sculpture is about... It is a presentation of a piece of sculpture in language.[1]

Weiner produces capital letters in short phrases which are about a viewer's relationship with an object. The words are a means or the expression of a relationship with something.

Billowing Clouds is a typical Lawrence Weiner artwork.[2] Richard Long comments that '[t]he discovery [Weiner] made that art does not necessarily have to be made, that was a great breakthrough'.[3] Weiner is right, of course: words alone can be sculpture, for poets have long known that language is an experience, not simply abstractions or concepts. Language really does affect people – otherwise why would they spend so much time consuming language? That is, they consume 40 hours of broadcasting per week – that's over a day and a half spent consuming television and radio per week. So Weiner's and Long's words on a gallery wall don't seem at first to be 'art'. They are not sensual and graspable, like a marble sculpture. Yet those words, whether photocopied on cheap paper or printed by high quality typography on deluxe paper, are 'art', they are communication, language, even sculpture. Conceptual art or Process art is 'possessed' by the viewer, in Weiner's system. Indeed, some Conceptual art requires the existence of the viewer to make the work work at all. The viewer brings the work alive.

BILLOWING CLOUDS OF FERROUS OXIDE
SETTING APART A CORNER ON THE BOTTOM OF THE SEA

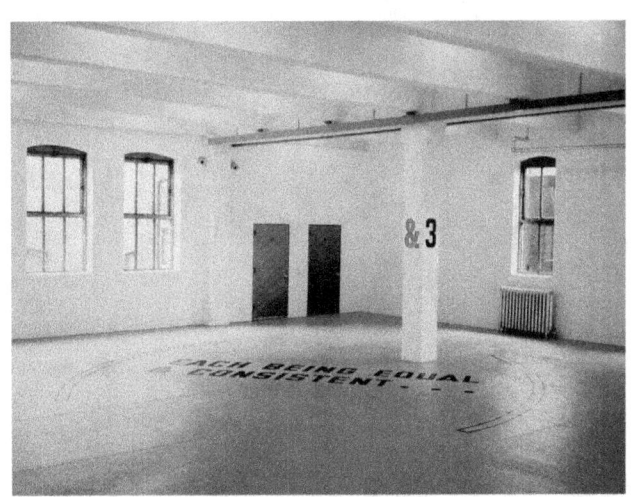

HANS HAACKE: *GRASS GROWS*

The German artist Hans Haacke has produced some of the most intriguing land art works (although Haacke is more usually linked with Arte Povera, Conceptual or process art, than land art). Many of Haacke's early works explored natural or organic systems. Later, Haacke moved on to social, economic and political systems (what Haacke called 'real-time systems'). Haacke's 1965 artistic statements included: 'make something that lives in time and makes the "spectator" experience time… articulate something natural'.[1] One of Haacke's tenets was 'the simpler the better'.

Grass Grows (1966 and 1969) was a mound of soil with grass growing out of it. Haacke later fashioned a row of beans growing along string suspended at an angle, in soil mounted on glass on the gallery floor (*Directed Growth*, 1972), and in tropical plants growing on a circular area of soil, *Rye in the Tropics* (1972). *Condensation Cube* (1963-65) was a Plexiglas cube (a metre on each side) with water inside which condensed on the clear sides of the box, an exploration of process. 'It is changing freely, bound only by statistical limits' remarked Haacke of his 'Weather Box'. In *Sky Line* (1967) Haacke released white helium balloons over Central Park. Hans Haacke commented that 'in spite of my environmental and monumental thinking I am still fascinated by the nearly magic, self-contained quality of objects. My water levels, waves and condensation boxes are unthinkable without this physical separation from their surroundings'.[2]

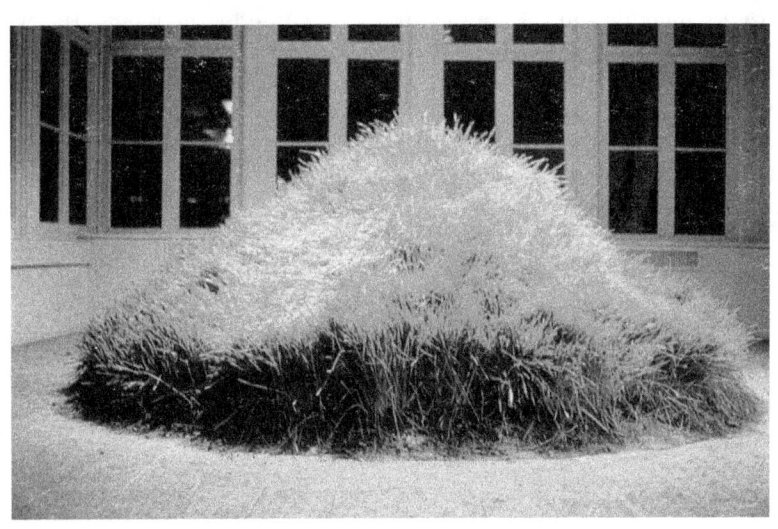

HANS HAACKE: *FOG, FLOODING, EROSION*

Many of Hans Haacke's most compelling artworks were made to explore the ephemeral qualities of ice, snow, fog, steam, smoke and water. *Fog, Flooding, Erosion* (1969) employed a sprinkler system to turn a lawn in Seattle (WA) into mud. *Fog Dripping From or Freezing On Exposed Surfaces* (Boston, 1971) and *Spray of Ithaca: Falls Freezing and Melting On Rope* (1969) explored water and fog freezing on waterfalls and trees. One of Haacke's air and wind constructions comprised a fan blowing a seven by seven foot chiffon sail hung parallel to the gallery floor. Another air sculpture was a balloon balanced above an air jet (a favourite with science and natural history museums). He had proposals for monumental-sized windmills and sails, all naturally powered by the winds. Haacke preferred to use unmechanical sources of energy.

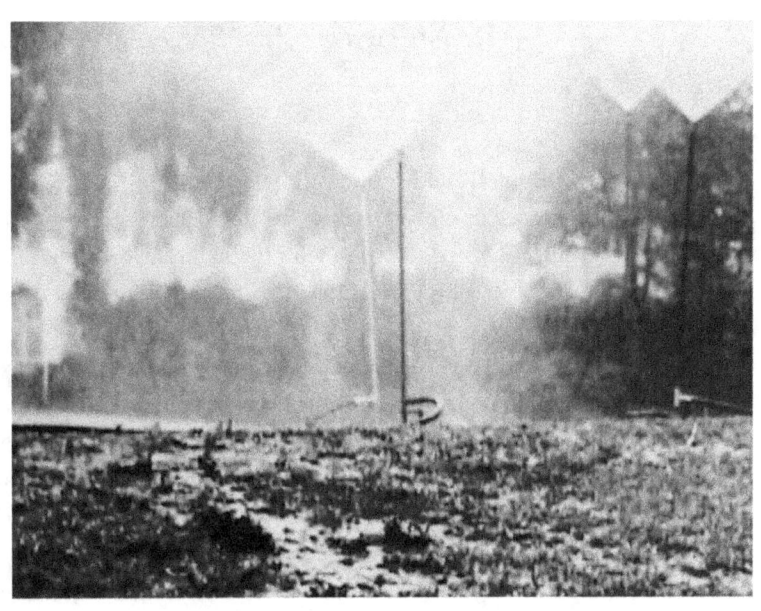

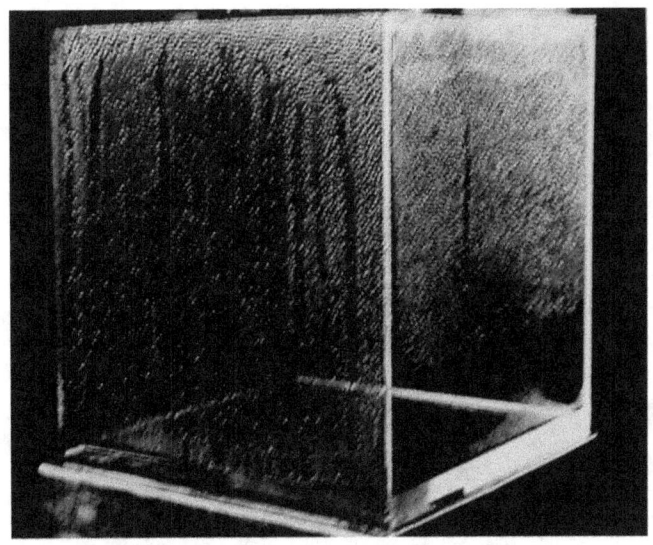

HANS HAACKE: *TEN TURTLES SET FREE*

In Hans Haacke's piece *Ten Turtles Set Free* (1970), the animals were released in a forest near St Paul-de-Vence (France), a symbolic gesture about humanity's relationship with the natural world and its inhabitants. Haacke photographed seagulls feeding on bread scattered on a lake in *Live Airborne System* (1965/68).

Hans Haacke later considered economic systems in works such as *Shapolsky et al, Manhattan Real Estate Holdings, a Real-Time Social System* (1971). For the *Information* show at Gotham's MOMA (in 1971), Haacke exhibited a poll about Governor Rockerfeller running for election, inviting visitors to vote. Haacke took on cultural institutions such as museums, landlords, and politicians such as President Reagan and British PM, Margaret Thatcher. On a few occasions Haacke's proposals were negated by the authorities of the Guggenheim, Wallraf-Richartz and Metropolitan museums, with works and shows being cancelled as a result. Other artists (such as Daniel Buren) protested in support of Haacke.

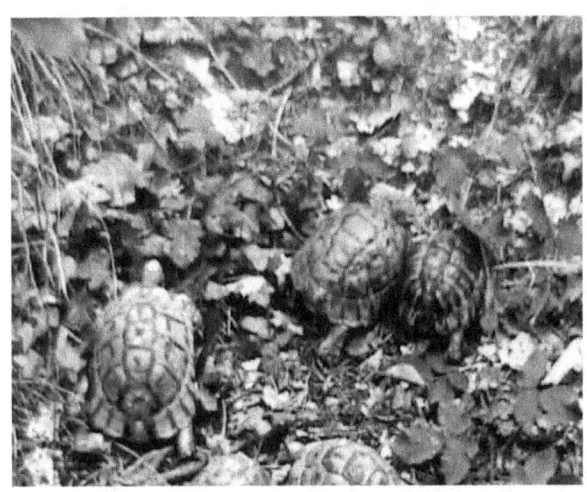

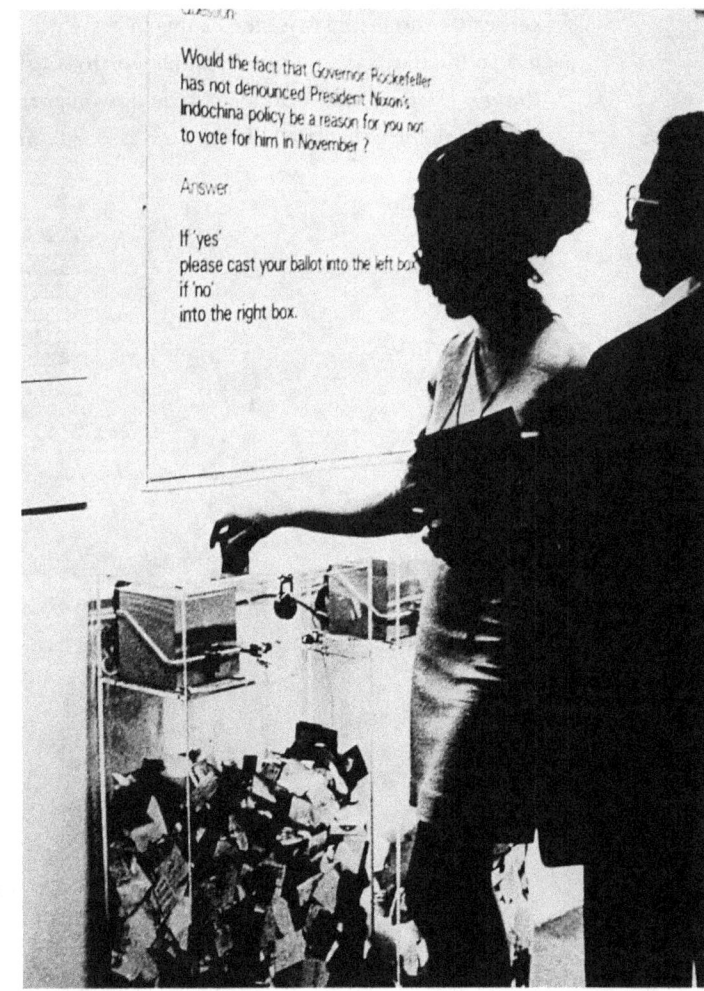

Question

Would the fact that Governor Rockefeller
has not denounced President Nixon's
Indochina policy be a reason for you not
to vote for him in November?

Answer

If 'yes'
please cast your ballot into the left box,
if 'no'
into the right box.

CONSTANTIN BRANCUSI: *BIRDS IN SPACE*

One of the most ancient religious functions of the tree was the World Tree of shamanism, the oldest of all religions. The World Tree was the mythic centre of the world of the community, it was the *axis mundi*, the pivot of time and space. The archaic shaman had many tasks: one of them was to travel to the Other World, to bring back news of what happened there, and to guide the souls of the departed to the Land of the Dead. The shaman did this by climbing up the Cosmic Tree: the shaman's magical flight to the Other World was linked with climbing the World Tree. What has all this to do with 21st century land art? A lot. Constantin Brancusi, more influential on land art than Picasso, Arp, Giacometti, Rodin, Matisse or Maillol, worked notions of shamanic flight into his *Birds in Space* sculptures, and most especially in his *Endless Column*, which is cited by many key sculptors (Judd, Andre, Morris) as an important inspiration. Brancusi's *Birds in Space* aimed to express the essence of flight, the moment when a quivering verticality is released from the chains of gravity and flies upward. One only has to look at Nash's *Tripods*, Goldsworthy's tower of rocks, Newman's *Broken Obelisk*, Judd's ladders, to see how important Brancusi's sculptures were, with their shamanic, World Tree associations.

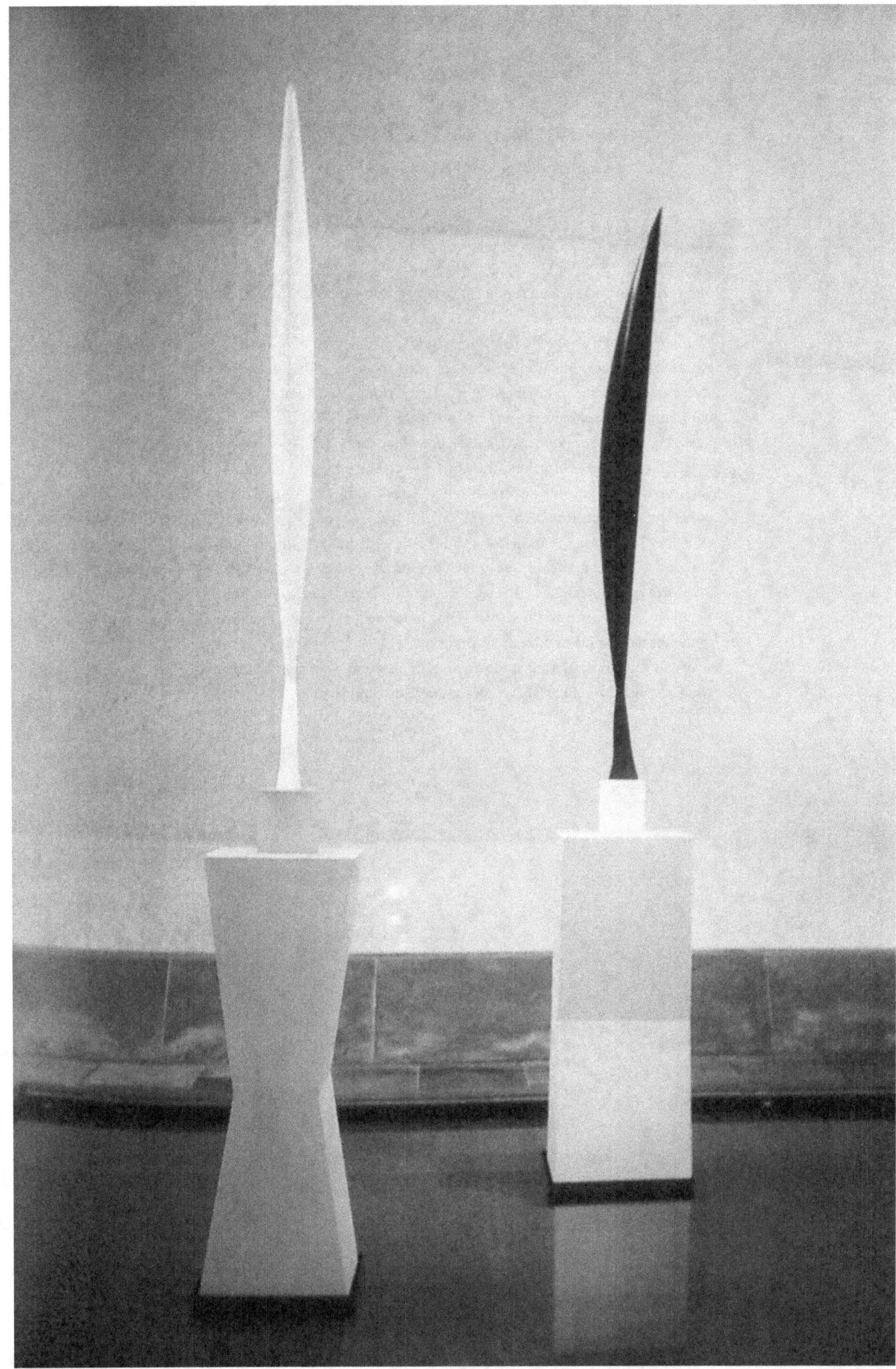

CONSTANTIN BRANCUSI:
THE GATE OF THE KISS

The variations on *The Kiss* (Brancusi regarded them all as one work) reveal interesting departures from that first, Craiova *The Kiss*. The 1908 Diamond *The Kiss* is much rougher, in its grey limestone, with the strokes of the chisel still visible, but the eyes bulge, with those heavily-lined eyelids. These eyes became so enlarged in the later works they filled up the face until, in the late columns, all you can see is the great orbs of the eyes, fused together, in *The Gate of the Kiss* and *Column of the Kiss*.

The late *Kisses* sculptures, the column and the gate, are monumental versions of the Platonic *syzygy*, the Platonic soul union, but erotic and cosmological versions. The 'eyes' are biological 'cells', as Brancusi explained. They are the basic form of life, the organic cell, from which all life grows. These 'eyes' are also circles, and in *The Column of the Kiss* and *The Gate of the Kiss*, Brancusi uses the circle as the prime symbol of life. He cuts it in two, and so those two semi-circles become the perfect symbol of the Platonic souls finding their 'other half'. Circles split in two also have sexual associations, hinting at the genitals of men and women. The bisected circle can be, if you like, labia, or testes, or glans, and so on.

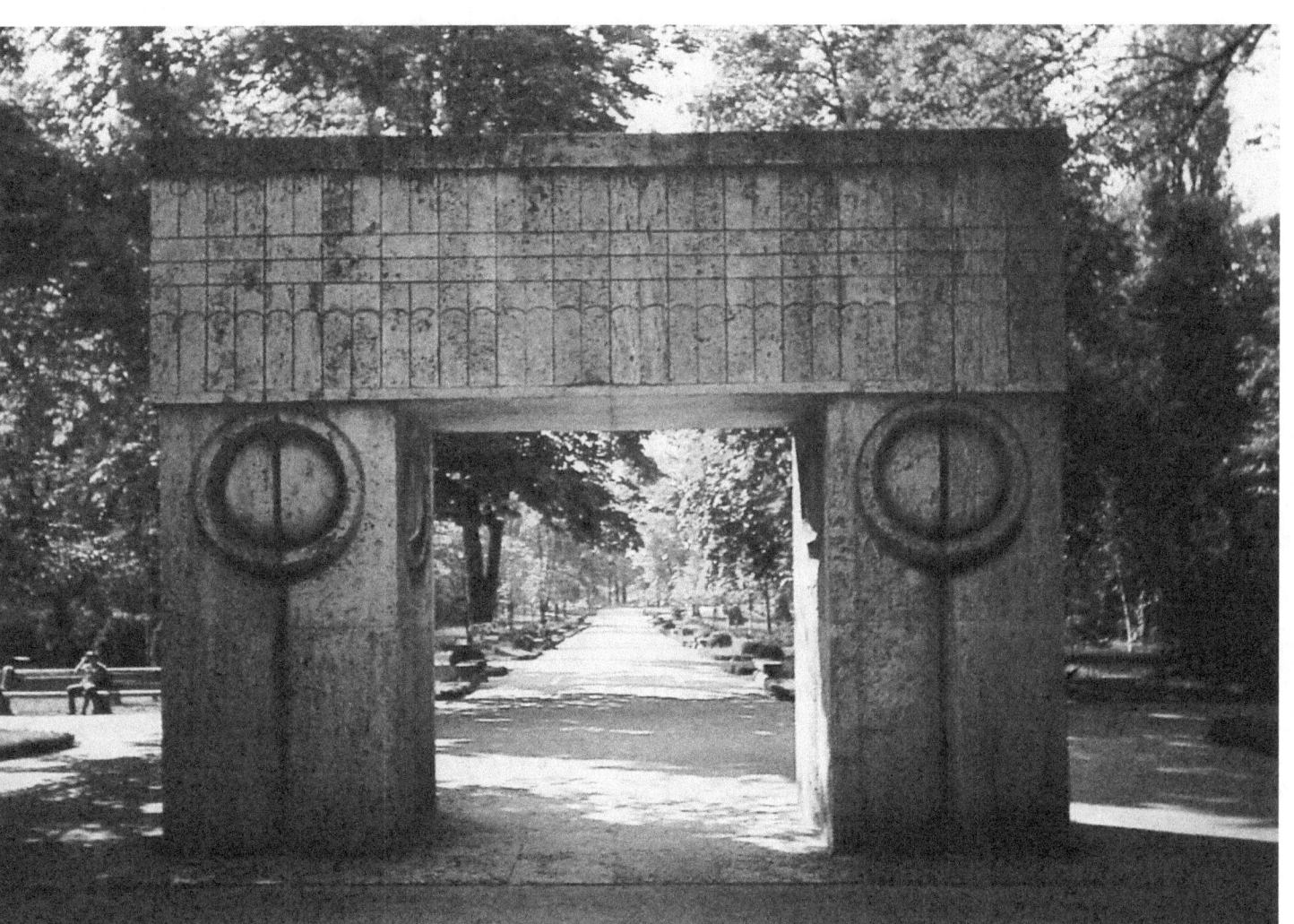

CONSTANTIN BRANCUSI: *ENDLESS COLUMN*

The giganticism of the American 'earth artists' is not something of which Brancusi would approve, one imagines. The enormous cuts into the Earth's surface by Michael Heizer, or the long fences of Christo, seem at odds with Brancusi's philosophy. However, Brancusi did make a large piece of sculpture that can be seen as 'land art', the *Endless Column*. When it suited him, Brancusi liked to make a powerful impact in a space. The site in Romania can be seen as an early work of land art, very much in the subjective, visionary vein of Sixties land art.

The influence of Brancusi is apparent in Minimal and Arte Povera sculpture. Morris, Judd, Andre and Flavin acknowledged Brancusi's art, in particular his *Endless Column*. Andre's early work *Last Ladder* is something like Brancusi's *Endless Column*. Andre said: '[a]ll I am doing is putting Brancusi's *Endless Column* on the ground instead of in the air... The engaged position is to run along the earth'.[1]

The Brancusi ethics, of simplicity, purity, smoothness, interiority and organic form are found in the Minimal sculptors, as well as the Constructivist notion of working with materials in a 'natural' way, so that the material dictates the form you create with it. Barry Flanagan has commented that sculpture works directly with materials: '[t]he convention of painting has always bothered me. There always seemed to be a *way* of painting. With sculpture, you seemed to be working directly, with materials and with the physical world inventing your own organisations'.[2]

For a long time the shadow of Brancusi lay over Carl Andre's art. When he came to explain his floor-standing works, such as *Lever*, a line of firebricks, he said he was 'putting Brancusi's *Endless Column* on the ground instead of in the sky... Most sculpture is priapic with the male organ in the air. In my work, Priapus is down on the floor. The engaged position is to run along the earth' (in ib., 104).

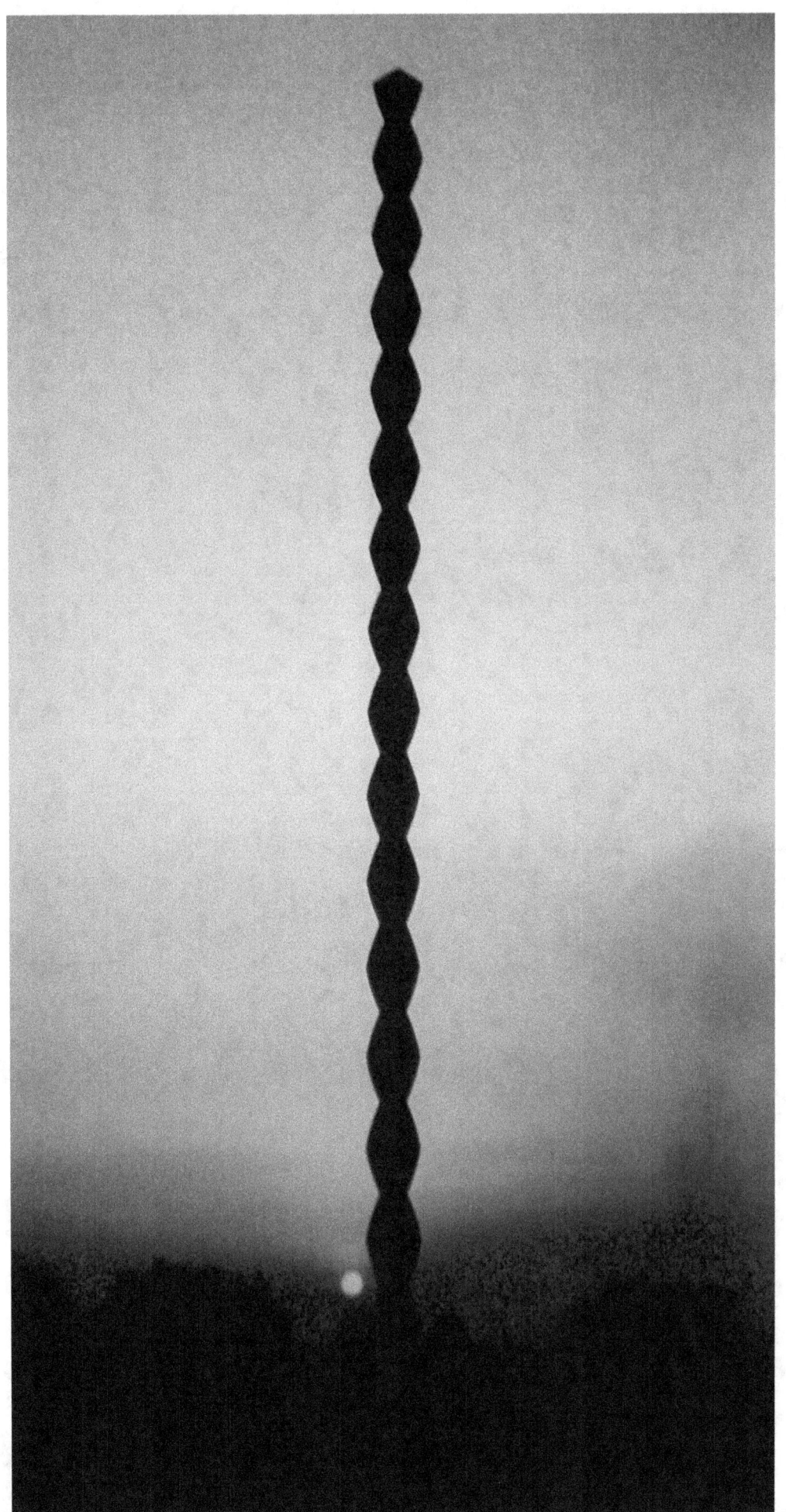

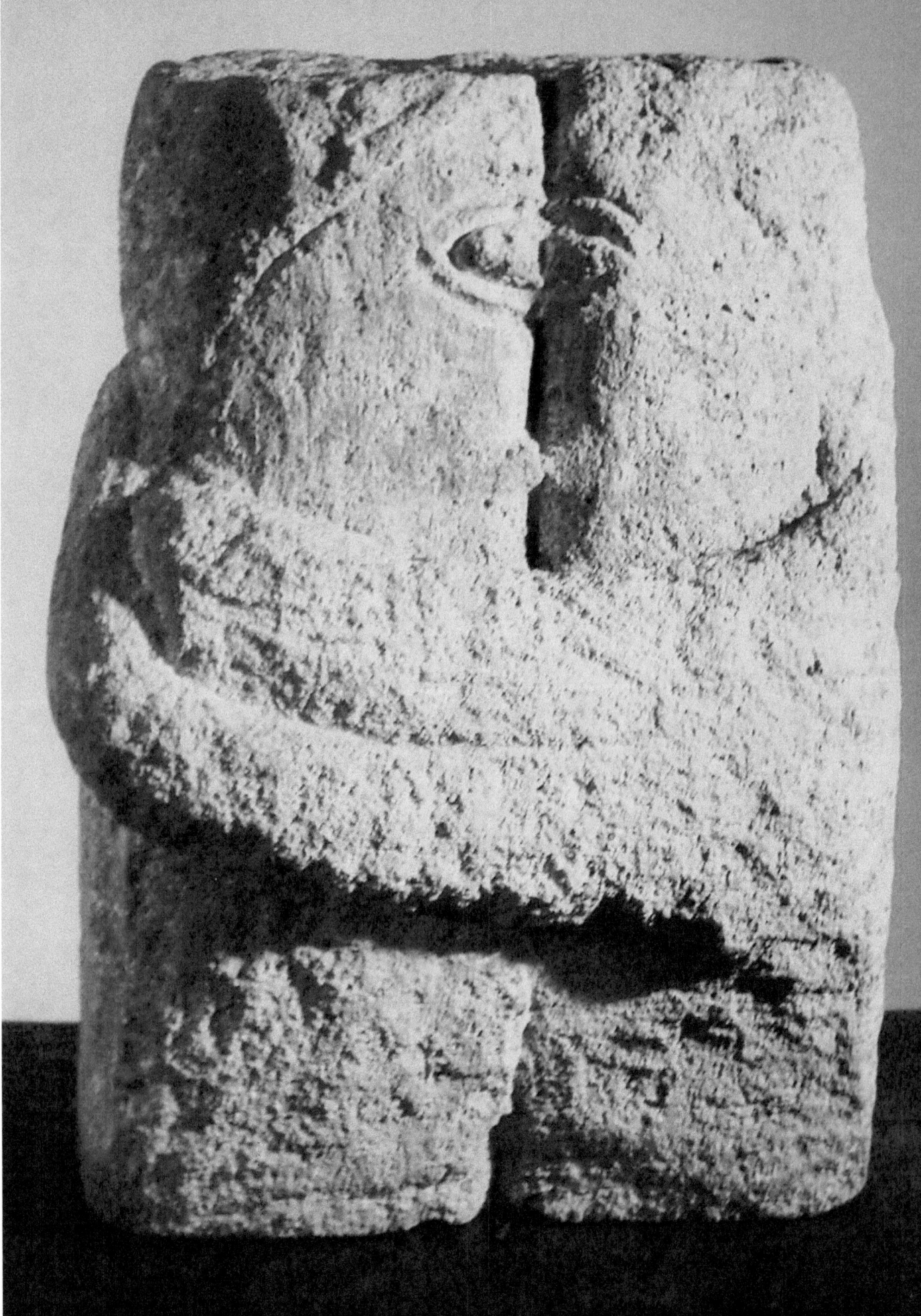

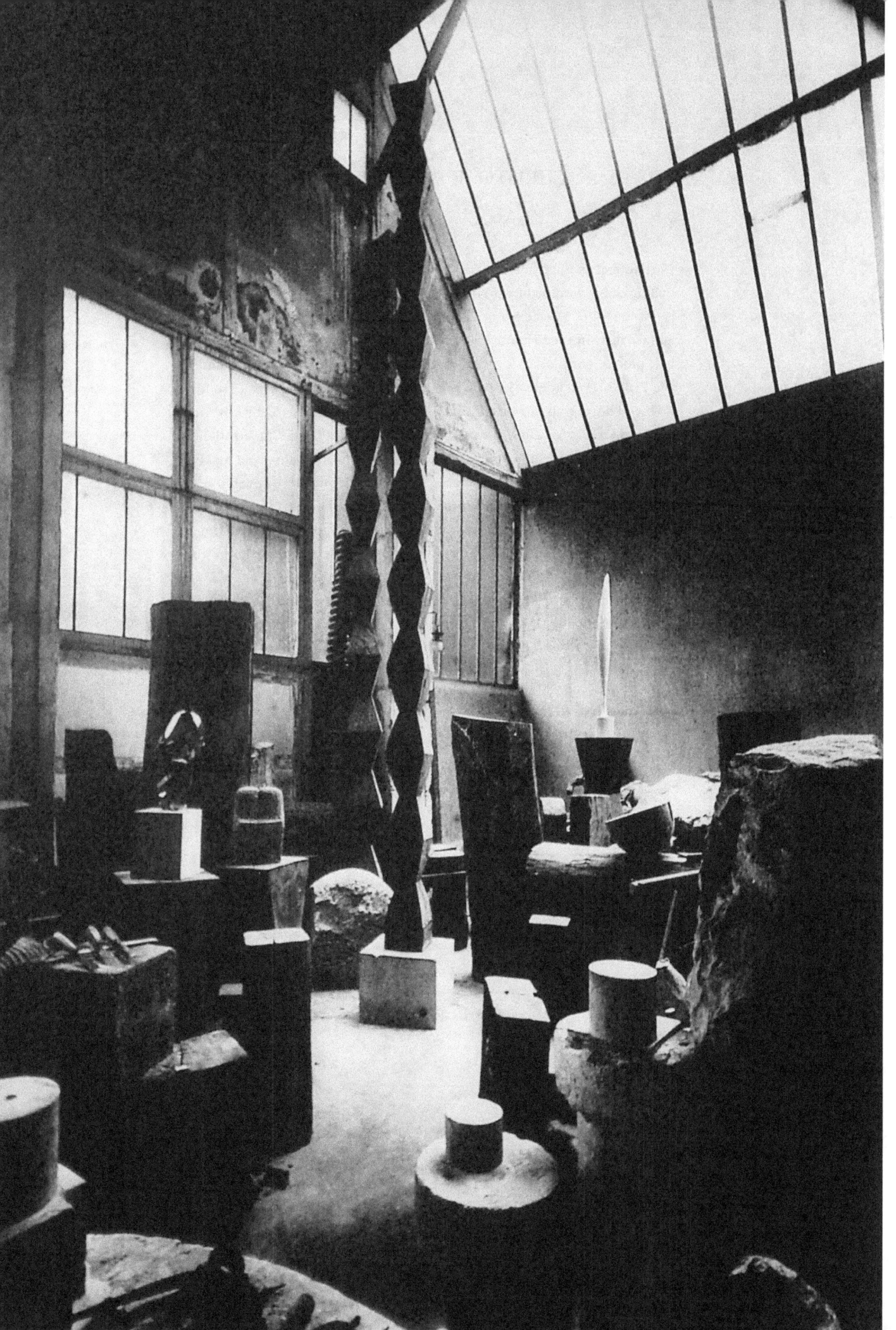

CHRISTO: *WRAPPED COAST*

Christo makes huge gestures everyone can see, with his plastic-covered buildings, his wrapped Pont Neuf or curtains hanging across valleys. His art is not 'invisible' like de Maria's kilometre-long brass rod which only reveals a brass disc on the ground, or Long's walks, which are only memories or text pieces. Born in 1935, in Bulgaria, Christo (Christo Javacheff) attended the Fine Arts Academy in Sofia. One of his early activities as a student involved tidying up the Orient Express route through Bulgaria by covering old farm machinery and haystacks with tarpaulin. At Prague Christo studied set design, and one of his mid-1960s works in New York involved making replicas of shopfronts, like a stage set, but the windows were covered with cloth or paper. In his early works, Christo wrapped up items such as books, bottles, tins and boxes. Other Assemblages or *empaquetages* (Assemblages as packages) included nude models, cars, chairs and motorbikes.

In 1969 Christo wrapped a mile-long section of the Australian coastline. The use of open weave cloth (1 million ft²) meant that wildlife would not be affected. *Wrapped Coast*, at Little Bay near Sydney, stayed for 4 weeks. It was a dramatic land art gesture, difficult to ignore.

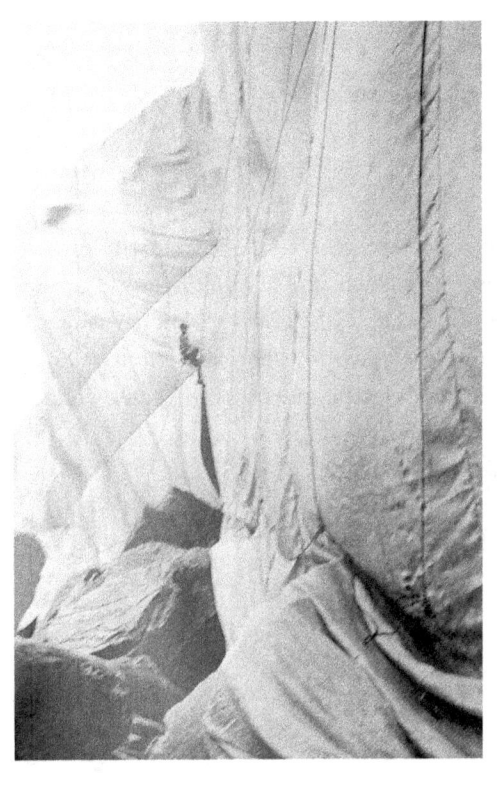

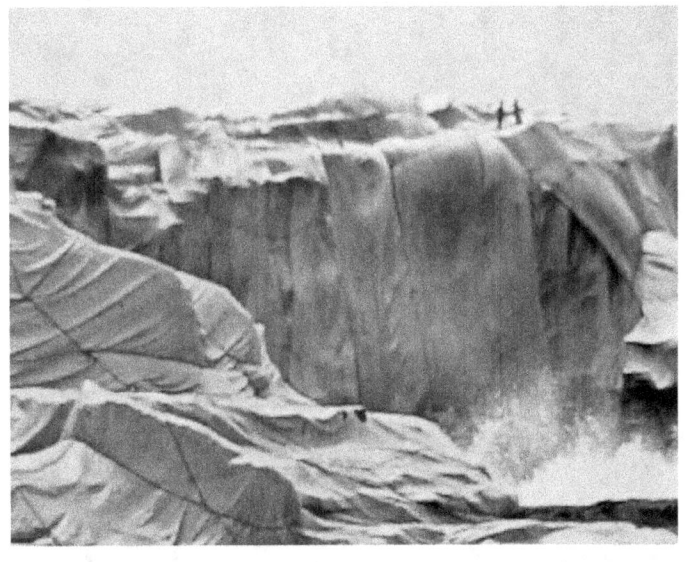

CHRISTO: *THE UMBRELLAS*

Christo's large-scale works are expensive: *Running Fence* cost over $3 million, *Surrounded Islands* cost $3.5 million, and *The Umbrellas* in Japan and California cost $26,000,000. Denigrators of Christo's work have noted the expense of the projects, but Christo pays for them himself, by selling photos, drawings, collages, models, lithographs and plans and other works, and by collaborating with industry.

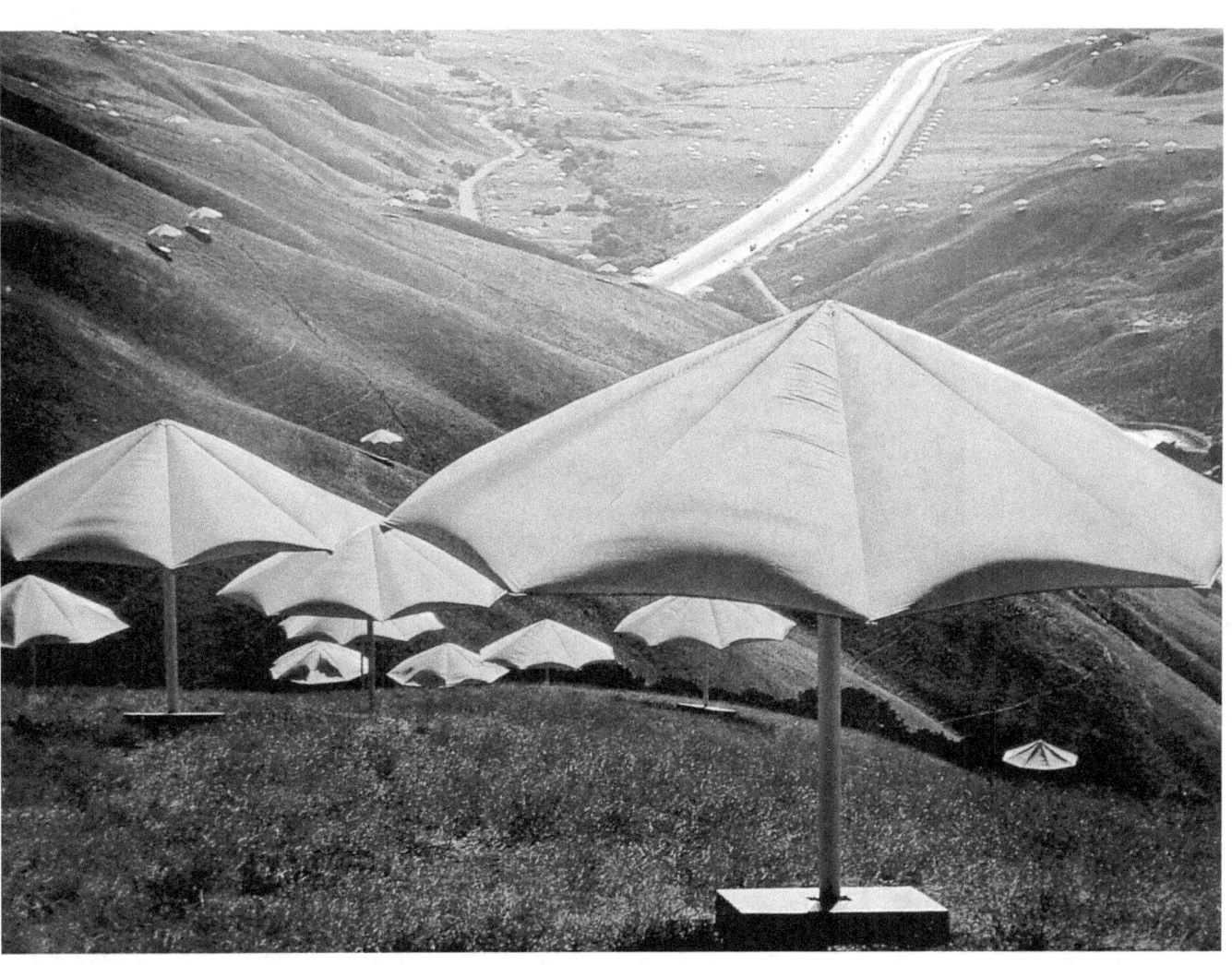

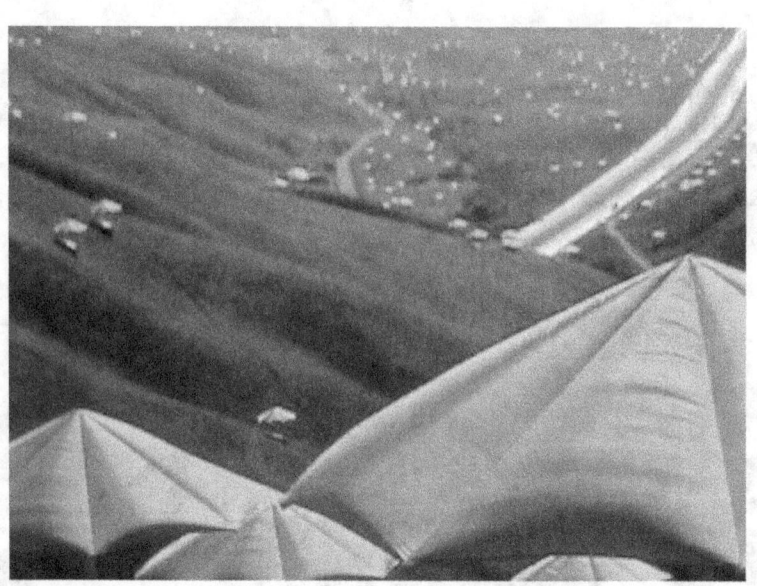

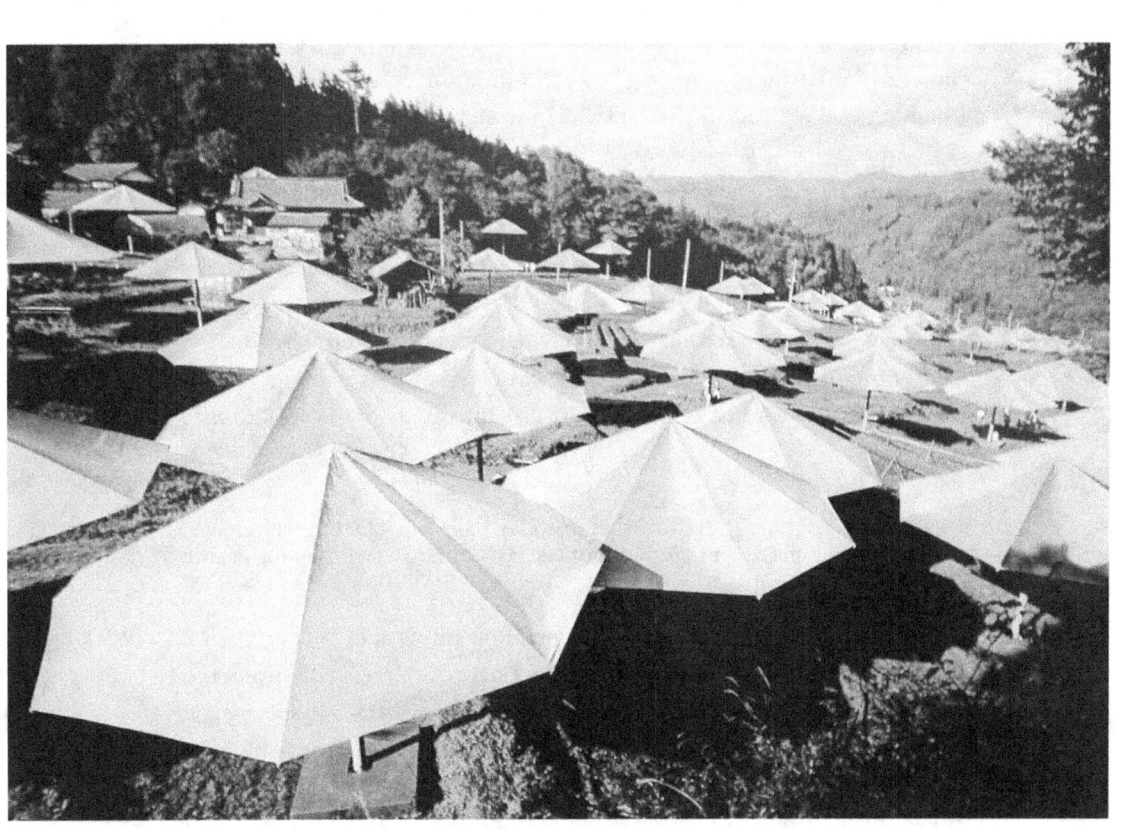

CHRISTO: *RUNNING FENCE*

Running Fence (1972-76) consisted 2,050 18 foot panels of white nylon attached to steel poles, running across Marin and Sonoma counties and 12 roads in California. As with Christo's other mammoth project, there was much opposition to *Running Fence*. A committee designed to 'stop Running Fence' brought the subject to the Superior Court of the State of California 3 times. The subsequent report on the environmental impact of the *Running Fence* project found that there were no endangered species in the region, except for the Brown Pelican, and virtually no wildlife would be affected by it. *Running Fence* went ahead, and stayed up for two weeks in September 1976.[1] When it was taken down, nothing remained of it in the area: the holes were filled in, and bare parts of soil were reseeded. As with other Christo projects, when it was taken away some locals were dismayed, the work had helped them realize the beauty of the area. Christo says his art is

> about displacement. Basically even today I am a displaced person. And this is why I make art that does not last. Of course, it will stay for ever in the minds of people.[2]

Christo here espouses the fundamental Romanticism in land art: that it will live on in the memories of people. Christo's large-scale projects – *Running Fence, Surrounded Islands, Wrapped Coast* – are spectacular works, part of the land art tradition which moves towards the sublime in landscape art (which resurfaced in the Abstract Expressionism of Rothko, Newman and Motherwell). The ocean end of *Running Fence* is particularly impressive: at Bodega Bay the *Fence* extended gracefully into the Pacific, 558 feet, descending from a height of 18 feet on land to 2 feet at the section which was anchored to the bottom of the sea.

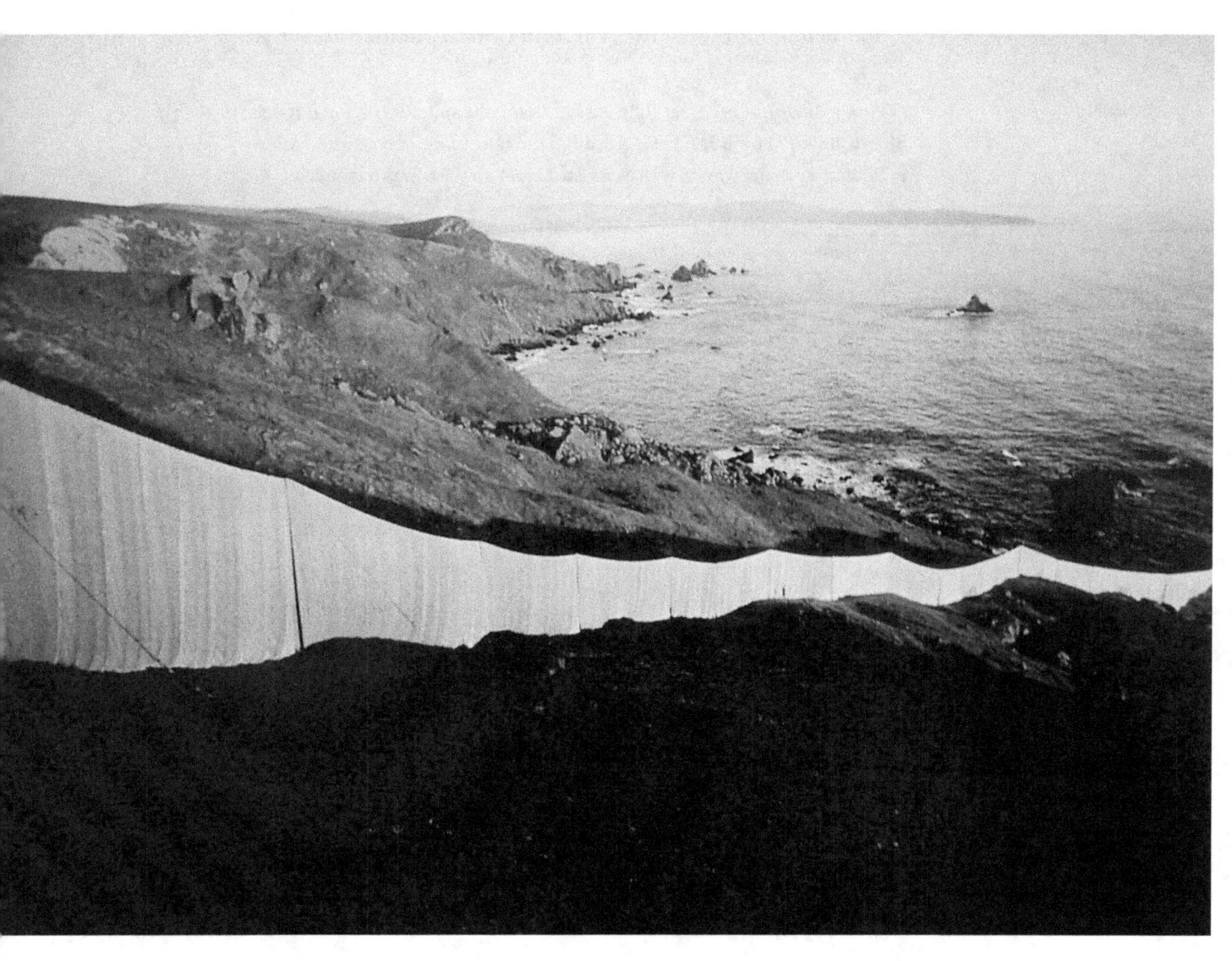

CHRISTO: *VALLEY CURTAIN*

When I was doing *Valley Curtain* [Christo wrote] everybody knew that this is a huge curtain crossing a valley. Now everybody knew what it is that is behind the valley. The thing that is behind is not so important...only that motion, the passing through.[1]

Valley Curtain (1972), at Rifle Pass in Colorado, did not last long. It was blown down. The huge bright orange curtain hung across the valley, providing a passageway as well as a visual block to what was beyond.

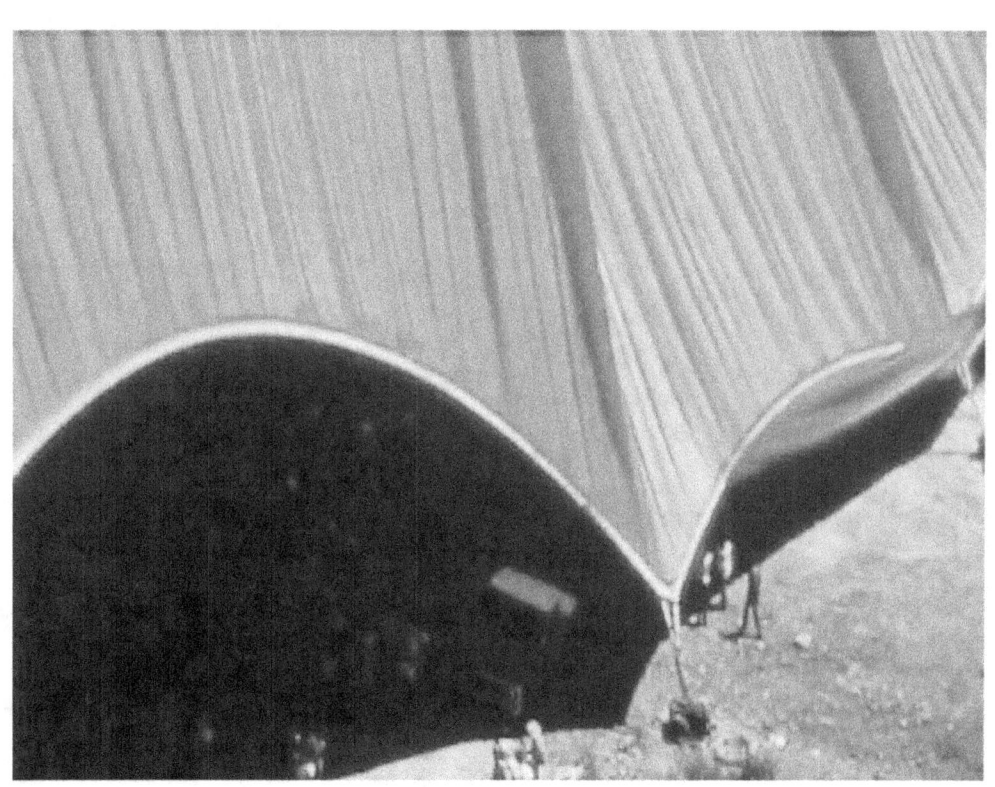

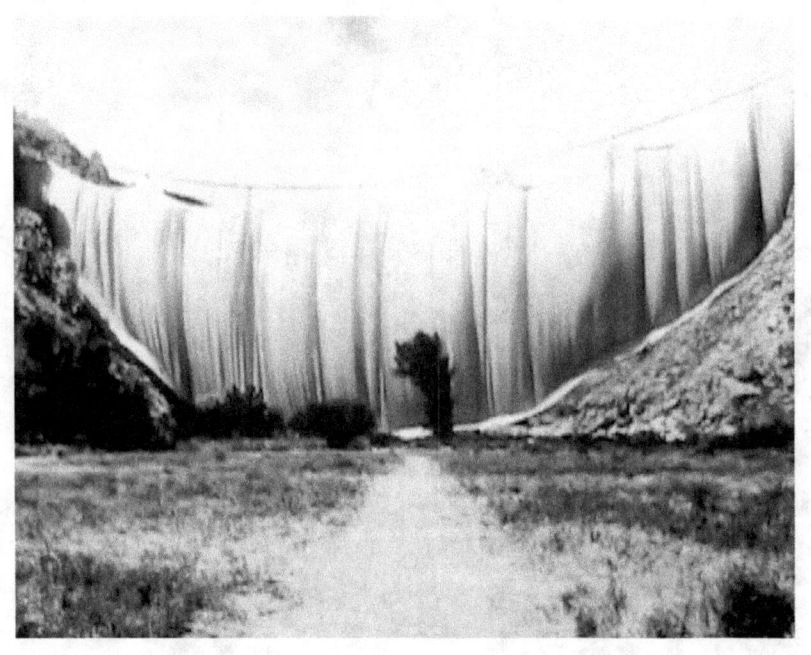

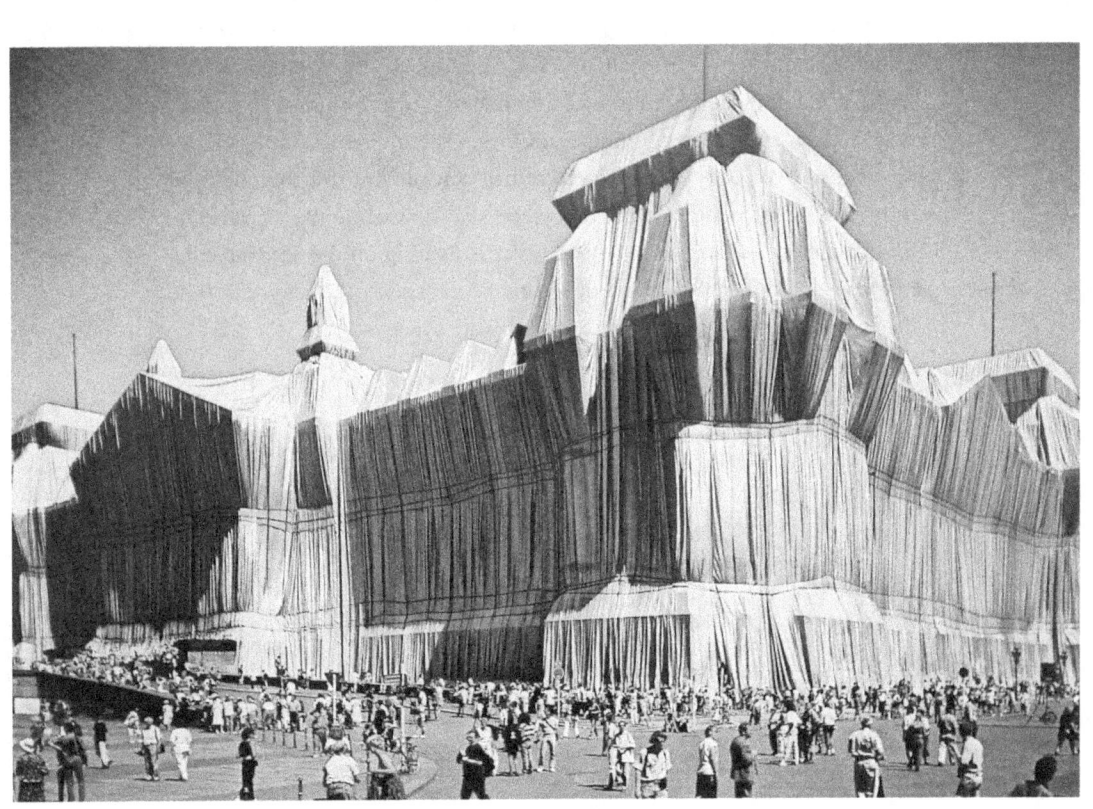

CHRISTO: *SURROUNDED ISLANDS*

Many of Christo's large-scale wrappings take place next to water: *Running Fence* plunges into the sea; *Wrapped Coast* is submerged by the tides; *Surrounded Islands* floats on the ocean; *Pont-Neuf* stretches over the Seine. *Surrounded Islands* (1980-83) was one of Christo's largest works. Not a wrapping this time, but still involving masses of fabric (6 million ft^2 of it). With a budget of $3.5 million, 4 engineers, 2 ornithologists, a marine biologist, 2 attorneys and 430 helpers, Christo surrounded 11 little islands for 2 weeks in May 1983. The choice of brilliant pink meant the enclosed islands stood out vividly against the green sea at Biscayne Bay in Florida. The pink-enclosed islands looked like flowers floating on the sea, recalling the Japanese Buddhist ceremony of setting flowers afloat. Or, more in tune with Western art history, recalling Monet's waterlilies.

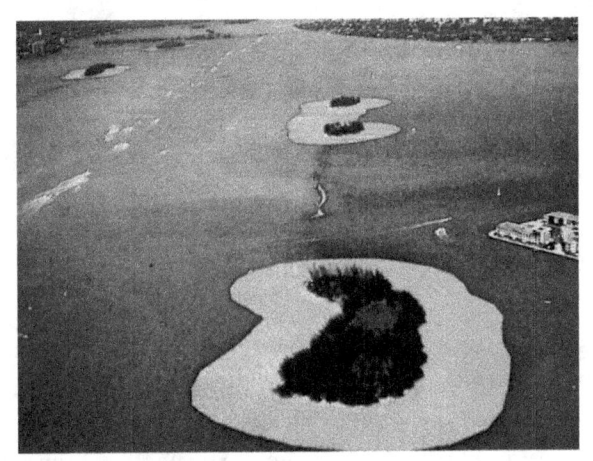

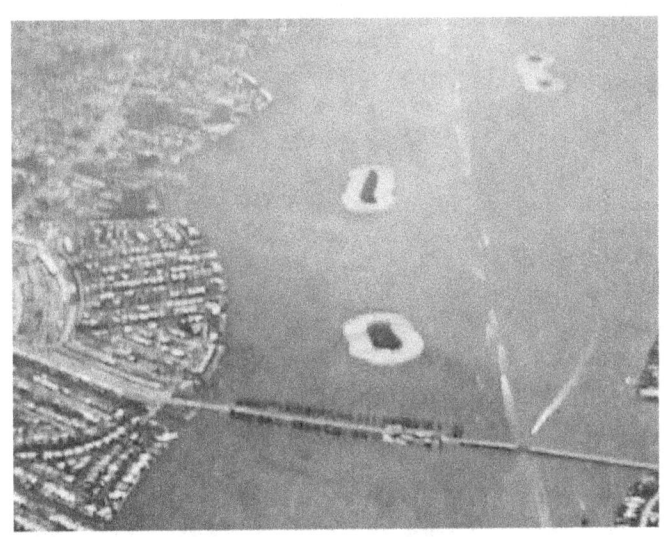

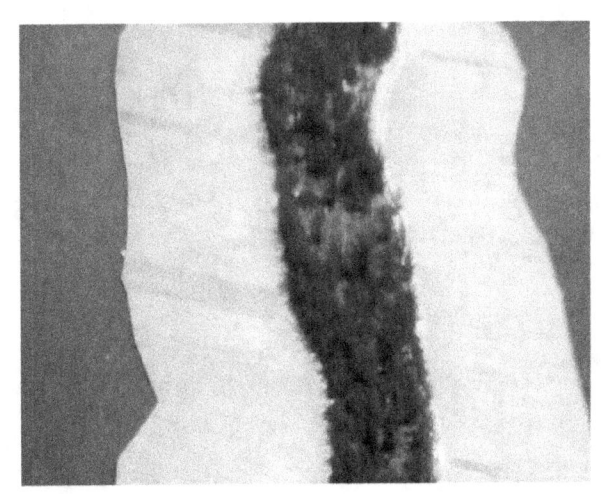

CHRISTO: *WALL OF OIL BARRELS*
- IRON CURTAIN

Christo's most famous Assemblage was on a larger scale, the *Wall of Oil Barrels - Iron Curtain* (1962). This was a pile of barrels stacked across and blocking one of Paris's oldest streets, Rue Visconti. *Wall of Oil Barrels - Iron Curtain* parodied the Berlin Wall, which had recently been constructed. The sculpture annoyed the locals, and Christo's large-scale works have been upsetting neighbours ever since.

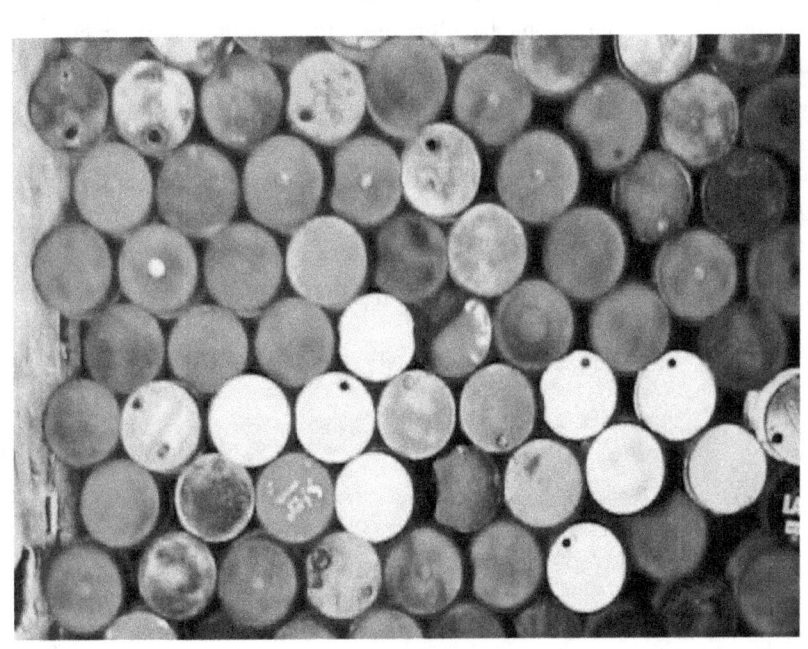

CHRISTO: *WRAPPED MUSEUM OF CONTEMPORARY ART, CHICAGO*

Christo's first large-scale wrapping was to cover the Museum of Contemporary Art in Chicago with 10,000 ft² of brown tarpaulin. Christo's wrapping of the museum made it the focus of attention in the neighbourhood – some people hadn't realized the museum was there until it had been wrapped. The museum's director reckoned Christo had parodied 'all the associations a museum evokes: a mausoleum, a repository for precious contents, an intent to wrap up all of art history'.[1] Inside the museum was the *Wrapped Floor*, consisting of 2,000 ft² of rented drop cloths.

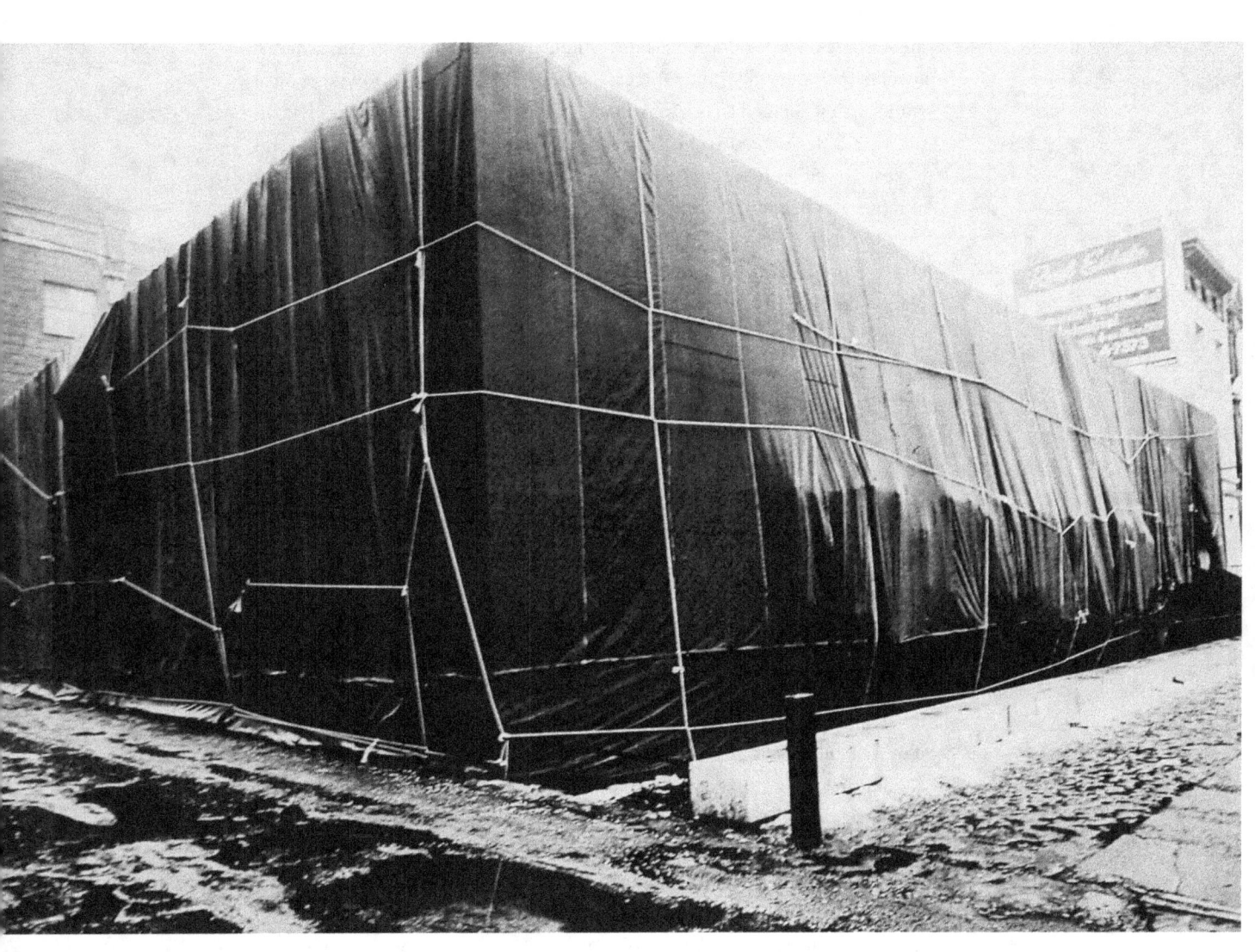

DONALD JUDD: *UNTITLED*

Donald Judd was one of the most learned of Minimal artists: he had a BA in philosophy and an MA in art history (at Columbia University). Judd's theorizing on art and Minimalism was influential in the Sixties (his famous articles included "Specific Objects" and "Local History"). Donald Judd's works at first seemed to be firmly fixed in a monotonous rectilinear view of the world. It seemed to be an arid, vacuous world of boxes and more boxes. Looking closer, one saw that there was a great sense of play and humour at work in the choice of materials (sometimes wood, sometimes steel, or glass, or copper, or lacquer, or Plexiglas). Sometimes Judd's serial boxes were open, and one could see inside them; at other times, Judd placed coloured Plexiglas over the end, and the interior was hidden or vaguely discernible; sometimes the boxes were sprayed with Harley Davidson motorbike lacquer and enamel, so they'd be bright green, or red. Using Plexiglas meant the colours would deepen across the row of boxes. The emphasis on hollowness meant there was nothing to hide; there was mystery, but no deliberate mystification on the part of the artist. Seemingly hollow and fragile, with their thin walls, Donald Judd's 'specific objects' were also constructed from strong materials, and were fixed, immobile, to the wall. The wall-mounted objects did not require a base; they seemed to float in space. They were unitary, modular: there was no single unit that stood out from the others. The gaps between each object was also regular. Hierarchy was avoided. There was in fact a lot going in Judd's works. Robert Hughes, in *American Visions*, defined Judd's work as the product of 'esthetic fanaticism' and uncompromising reductionism: 'Judd was the doyen of "high" Minimalism: inorganic materials (steel, tin, colored plastic, aluminium), blatantly artificial colors (Harley-Davidson red lacquer was a particular favourite), geometric rigidity (but without the Utopian overtones of earlier geometric abstraction), industrial process, and, in its refusal of touch, an address to the eye alone' (1997, 563-4).

Many of Donald Judd's best Minimal works are housed in his permanent installation in Marfa, Texas. One of the main works at Marfa is the epic *Untitled* (1980-86), one hundred large (41 x 51 x 72 inch) mill-aluminium boxes, each one apparently the same, yet each one different. The field of boxes was funded by the Dia Art Foundation, and made by the Lippincott Foundry, New Haven.

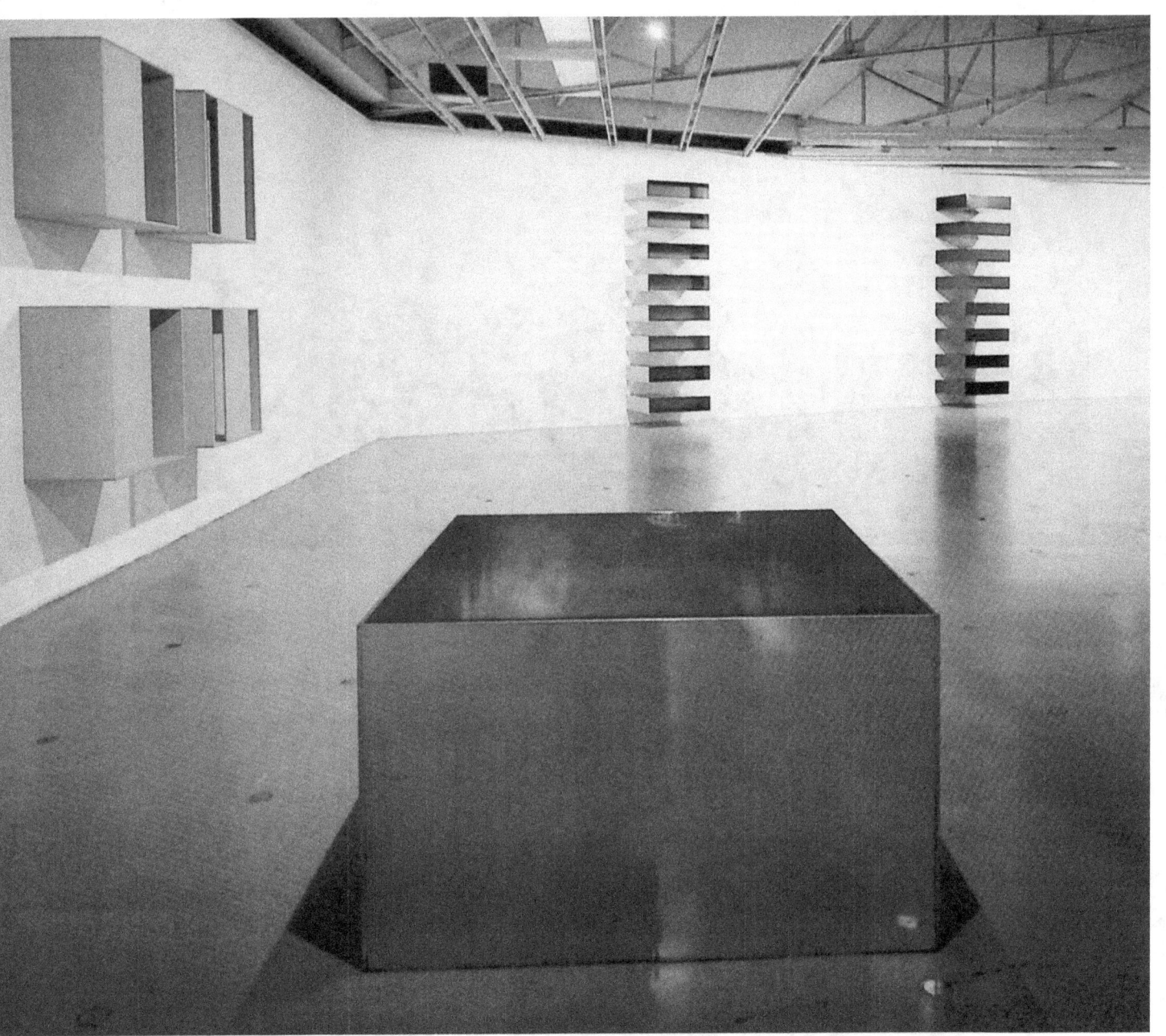

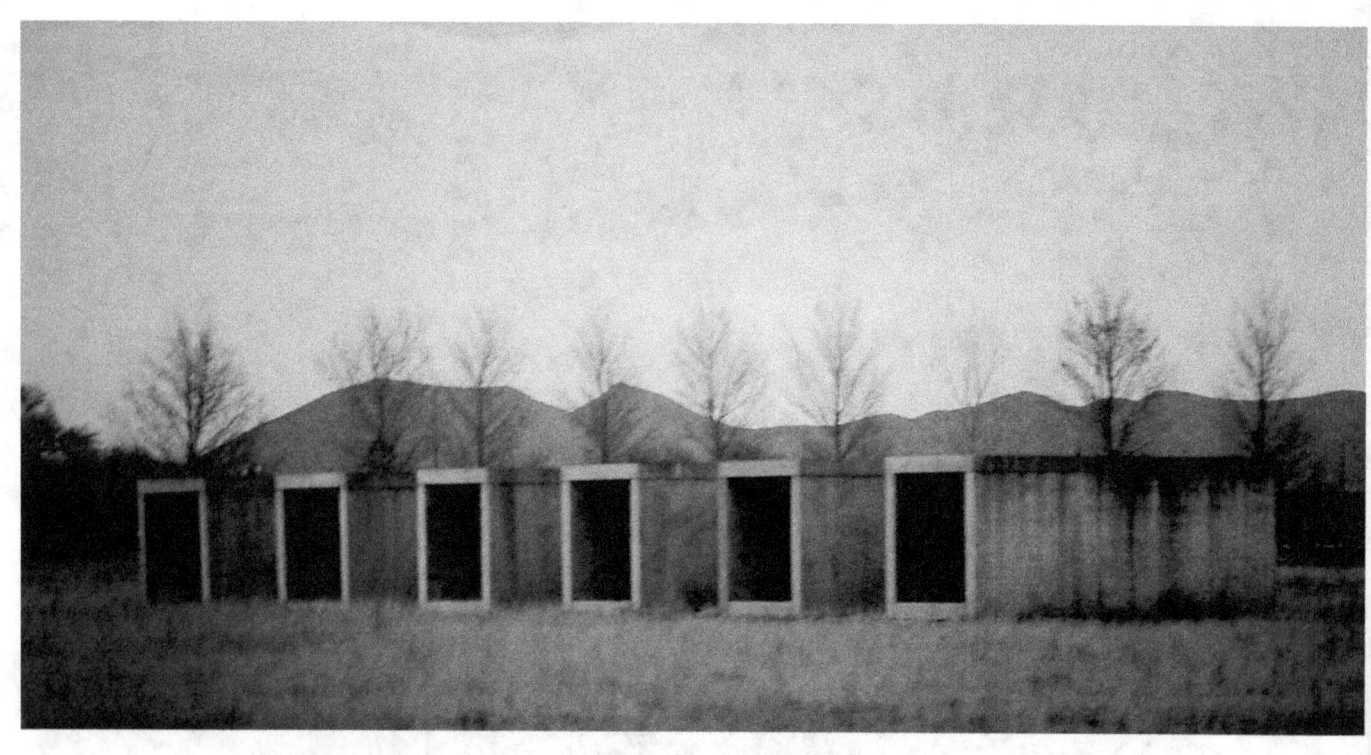

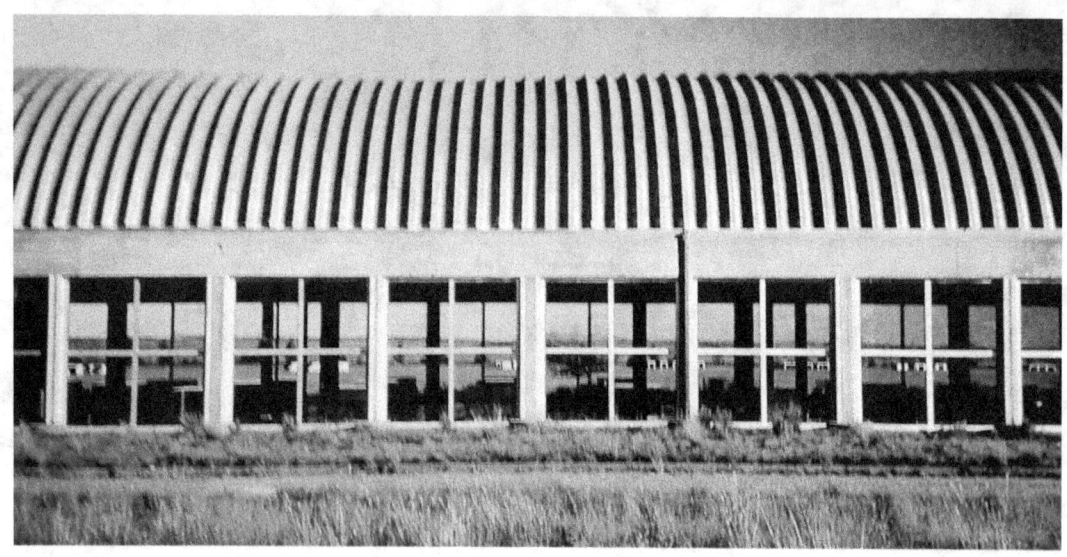

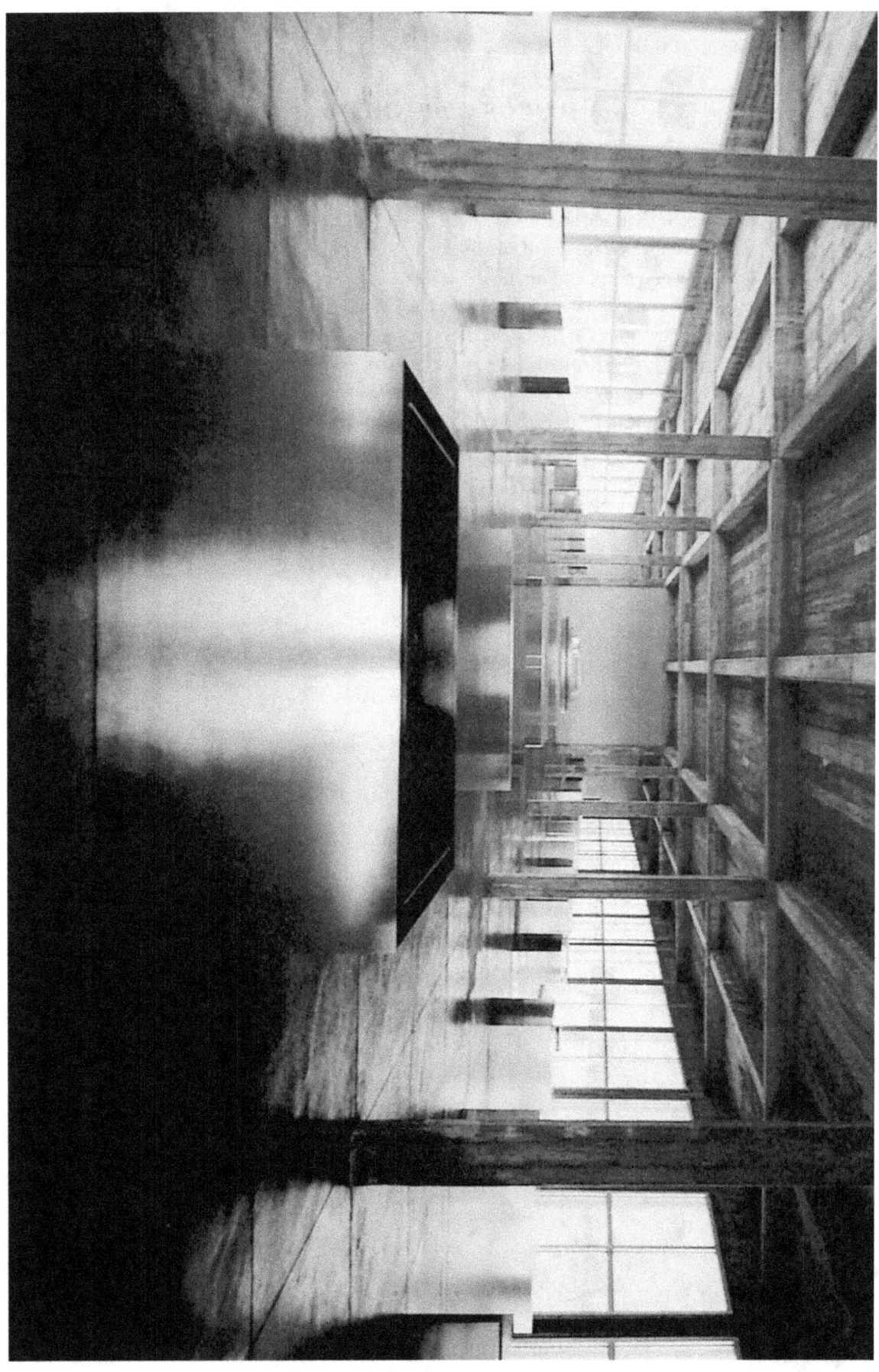

DENNIS OPPENHEIM

Like Robert Smithson and James Turrell, Dennis Oppenheim was one of the most interesting of US earth artists, an artist who produced an amazing body of work. It's significant, for instance, that Dennis Oppenheim was the first US land artist to work with snow on a grand scale. Oppenheim began making snow works in the late Sixties. The only other important environmental artist who regularly used snow and ice, really, was Hans Haacke. But, more than any of the other first generation land artists, Oppenheim made snow one of his primary media.

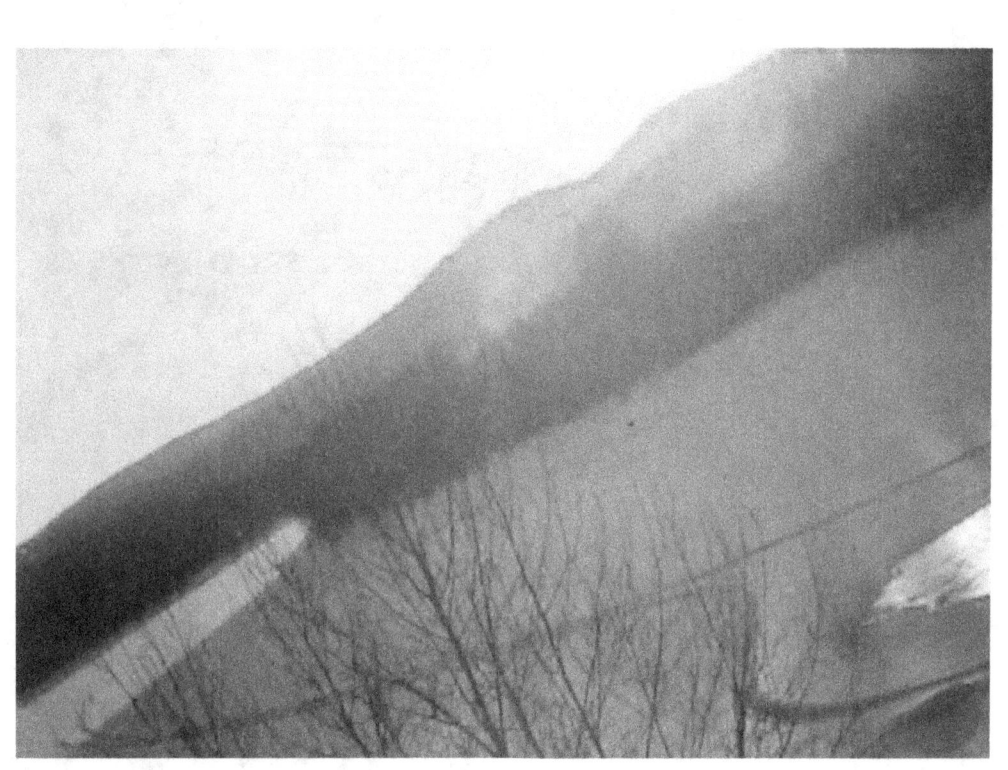

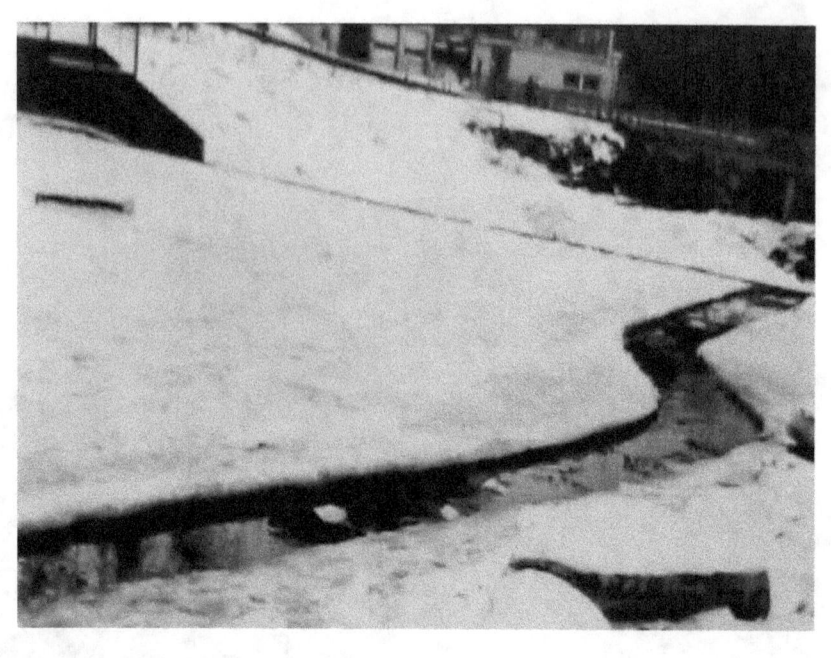

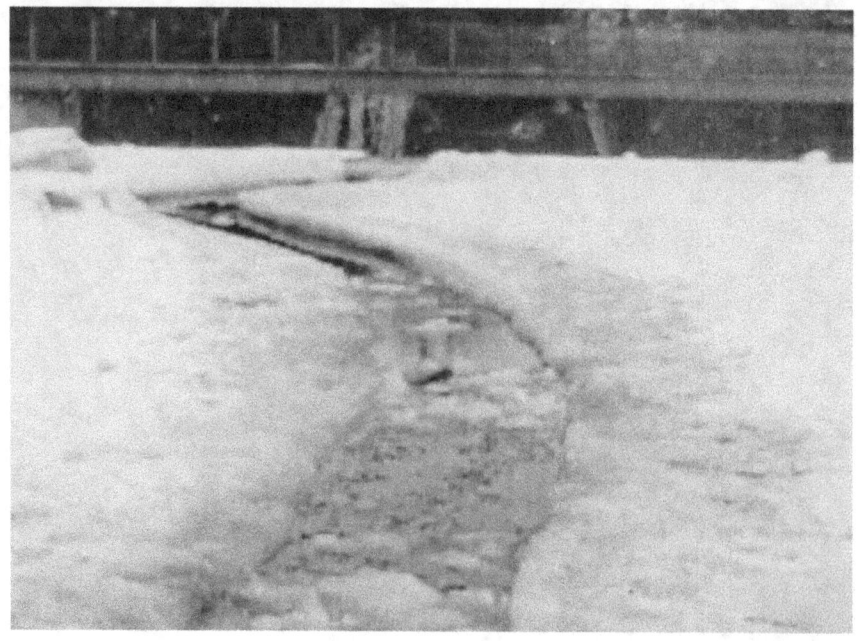

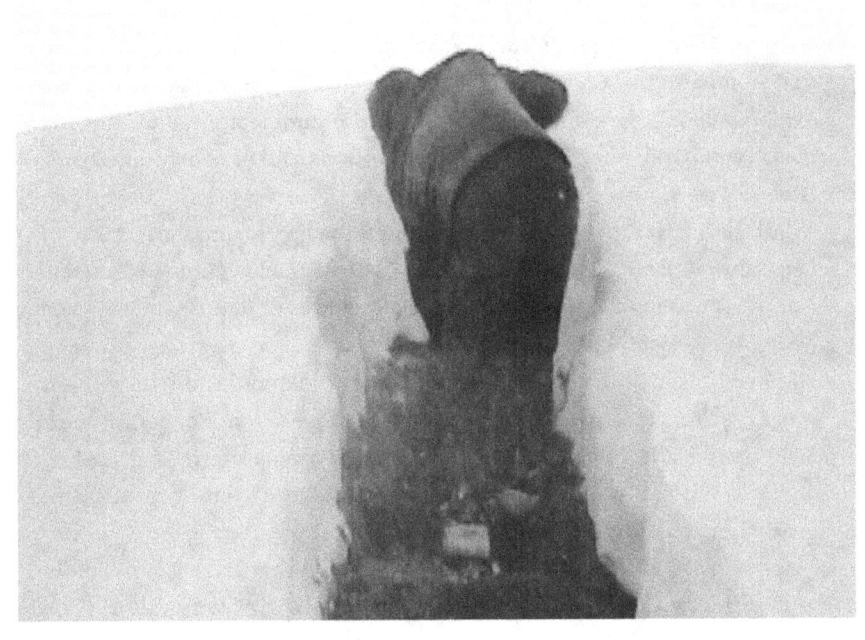

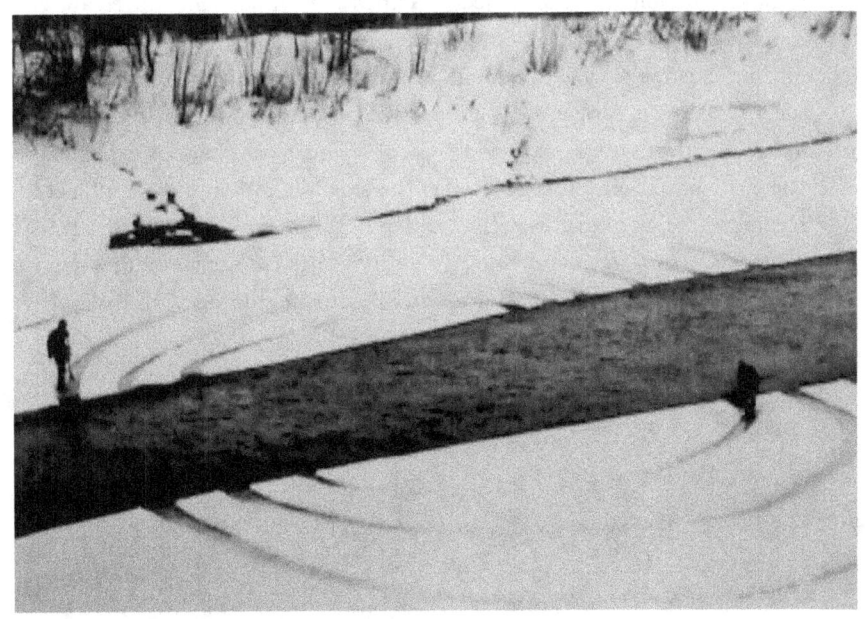

DENNIS OPPENHEIM: *ANNUAL RINGS*

Many of Dennis Oppenheim's artworks are conceptual pieces in the tradition of Sixties Conceptualism. That is, many are works made to be exhibited in galleries, on walls. They comprise photographs, drawings and maps, with Oppenheim's typewritten captions and explanations: *Three Downward Blows* (1977), *Salt Flat* (1969), *Boundary Split* (1968), and *Negative Board* (1968) (maps were central to Oppenheim's art). Many of Oppenheim's land artworks also existed as these framed photo-text-sketch-map works. One of Oppenheim's specialities was to impose humanmade geometries, symbols and ideas onto the landscape: to transpose map contours, for instance, or the rings of a tree trunk onto snow (in *Annual Rings*), or the International Date Line in snow (*Time Pocket*). Robert Smithson remarked that Oppenheim was 'transforming a terrestrial site into a map'.[1] Generally, Oppenheim tended to enlarge symbols or ideas or images, and recreate them on a colossal scale in the landscape.

Speaking in 1970, Dennis Oppenheim opined that art was now 'more concerned with the location of material and with speculation' (i.e., locations or ideas). Now, art was meant to be visited (location) or 'abstracted from a photograph' (conceptualized).[2] Oppenheim moved towards a kind of art that would be discovered or visited by the spectator, rather than 'made' in the old, traditional manner (this was part of the 'dematerialization' of the art object in Sixties art). Oppenheim moved away from the idea of the special, unique art object, towards found objects, and utilizing existing sites. Oppenheim was replacing objects with locations. The *Site Markers* series (1967) comprised posts in locations which were documented with texts, maps and photos. The maps and photos explained where the posts were situated, so that the location, rather than the object, became the centre of the piece. As Oppenheim pointed out, the *Site Markers* works were intended to be about the sites themselves, rather than the manipulation of replication of an object: 'beginning with the site-markers started in a sense a journey: art is travel'.[3]

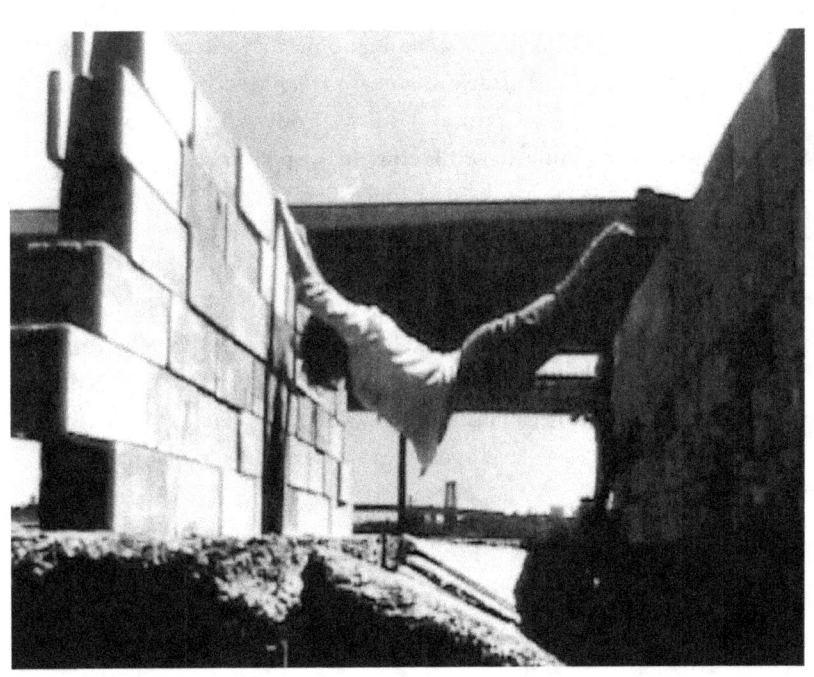

ANA MENDIETA

Ana Mendieta covered herself in mud (while nude, of course) and stood against a tree (for *The Tree of Life* series, 1977, made in Old Man's Creek, Iowa), a combination of Goddess art, performance art and environmental art. In *The Tree of Life* series, Mendieta left the outline of her body in leaves on a tree trunk. In the *Silueta* series (1979), Mendieta imprinted her body in the snow in Amana, Iowa, and in mud on a river-bank, or set the form on fire in the earth, or made a silhouette from flowers. These pieces echo Andy Goldsworthy's rain and snow 'body prints' (however, Mendieta's art has an undisguised ideological, spiritual and ecological agenda; some of Mendieta's works are explicit performance explorations of rapes, and Mendieta was also exploring her Cuban and Latin American heritage).

In some pieces Mendieta remodelled the entrance of a cave and a ravine into her Goddess shape. She also buried herself under turf – a literal Earth-Goddess mound, and had herself photographed in an ancient Mexican stone grave. Mendieta also lit fires in sculptures (such as *Volcano*, 1979), like Chris Drury and David Nash, and lit candles and fireworks in the shape of a woman.

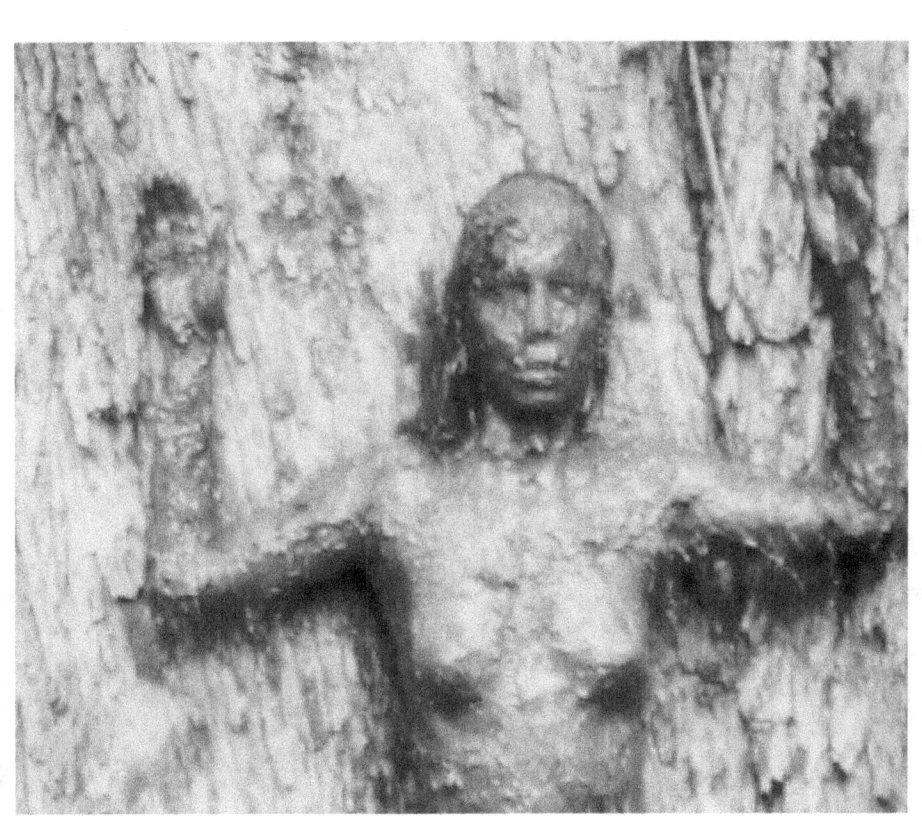

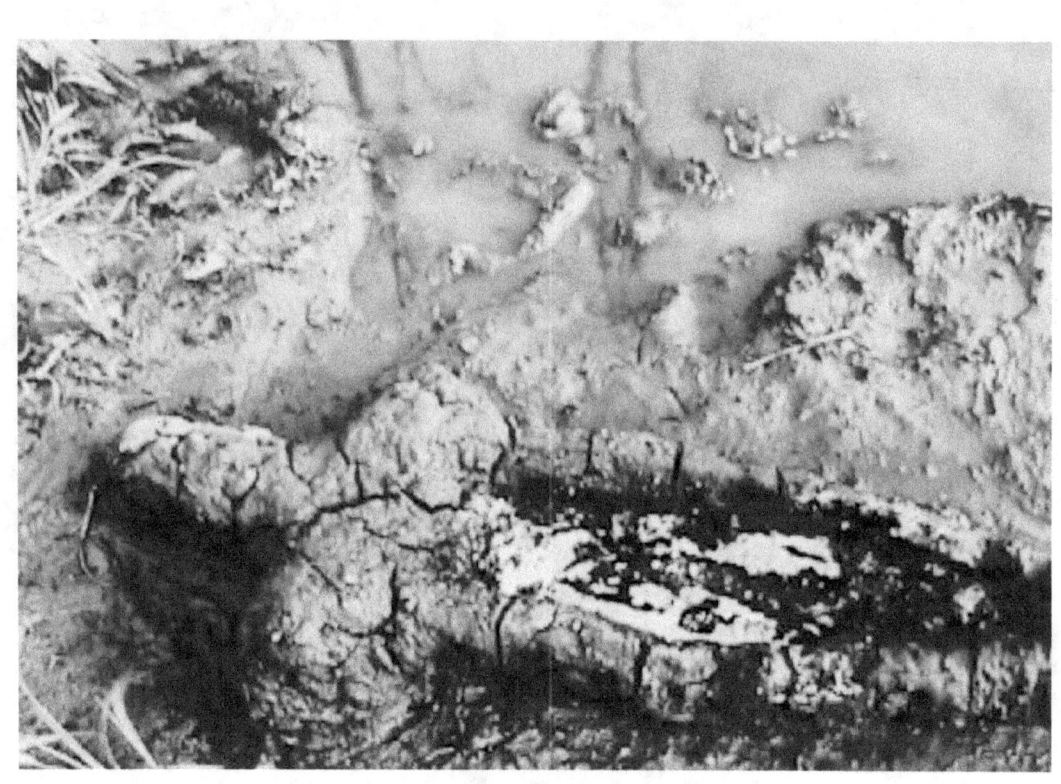

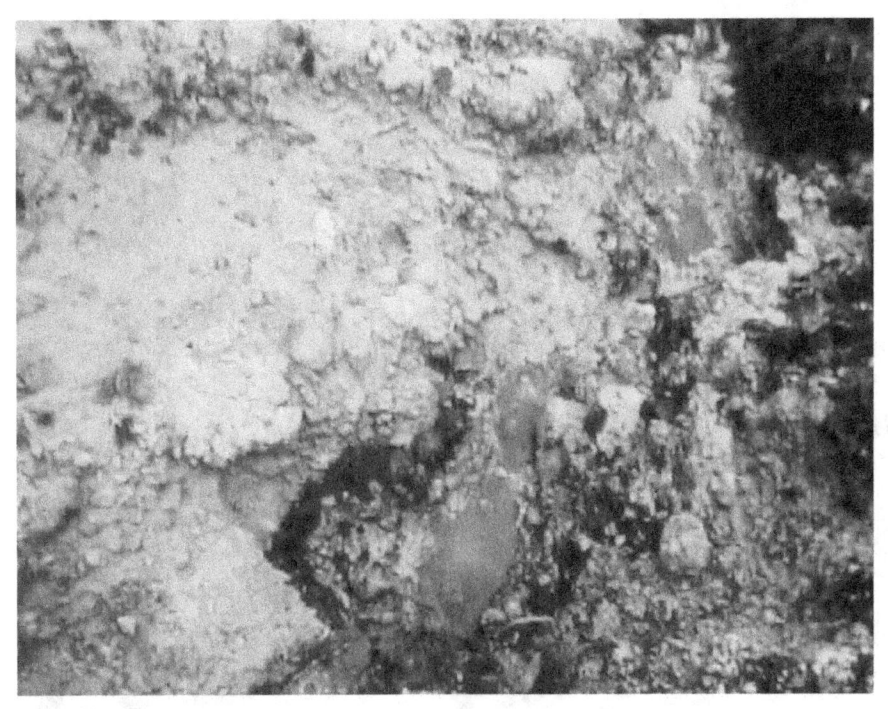

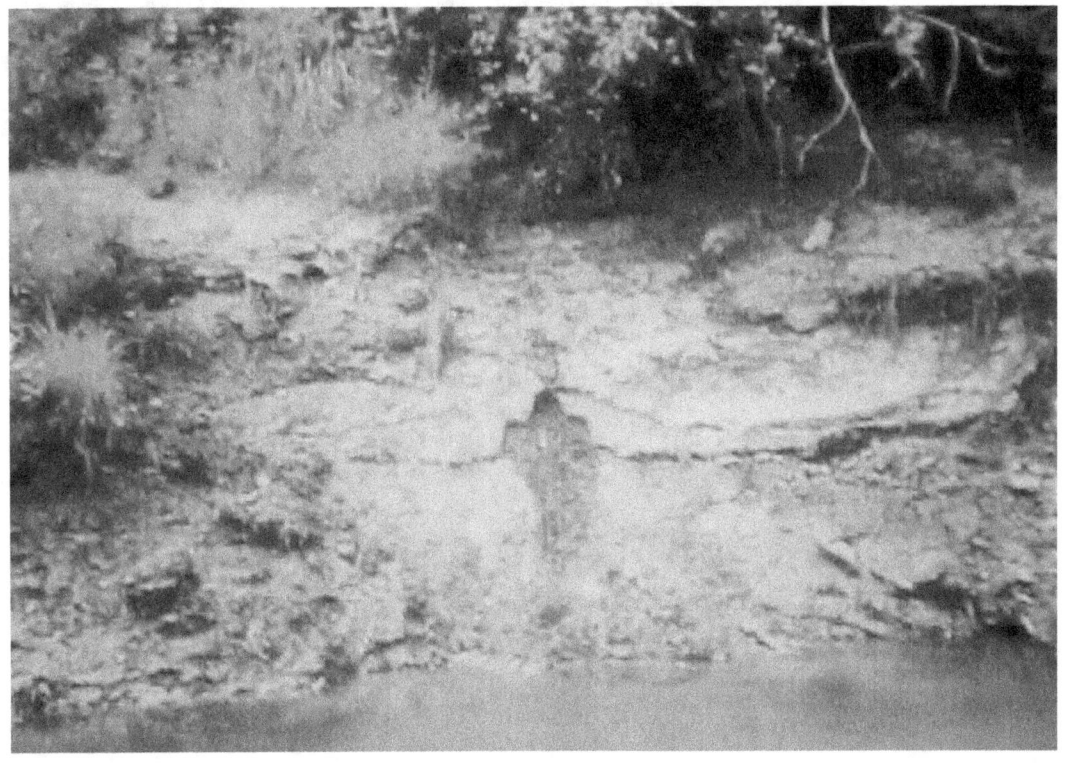

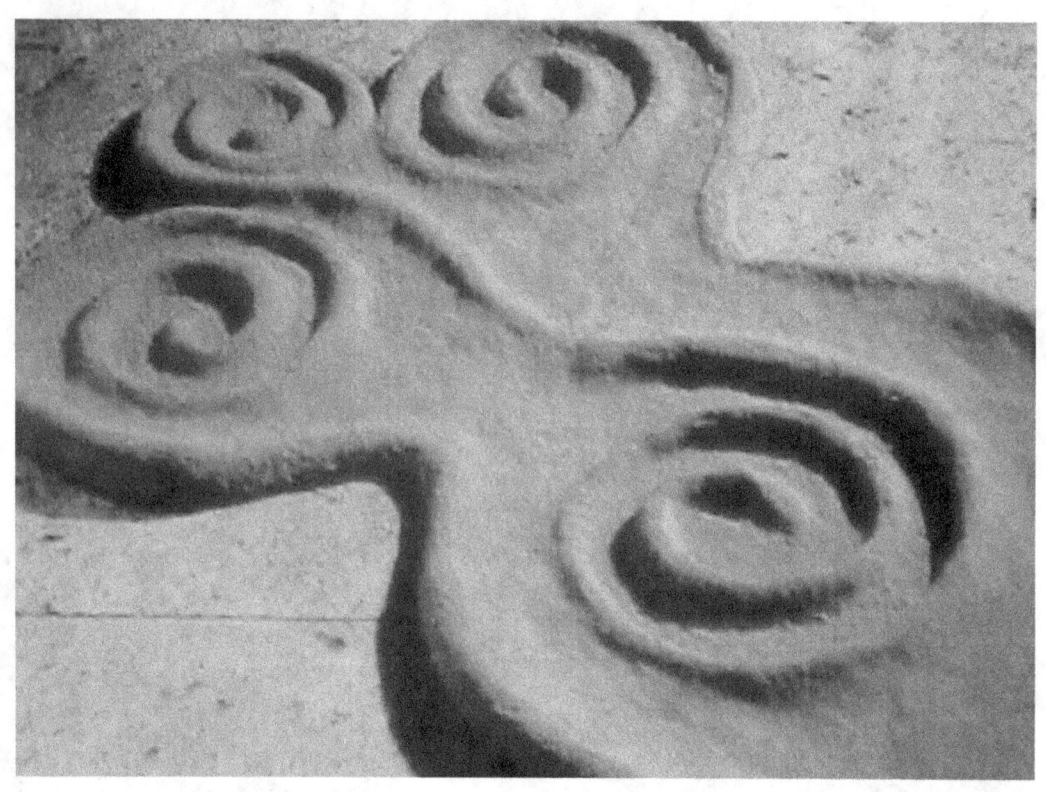

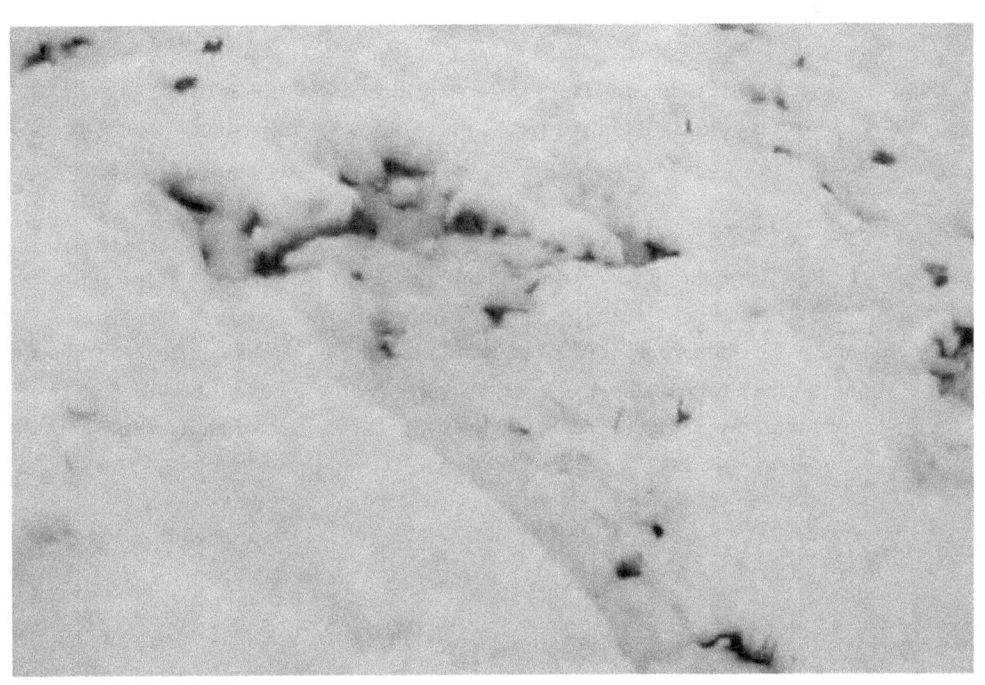

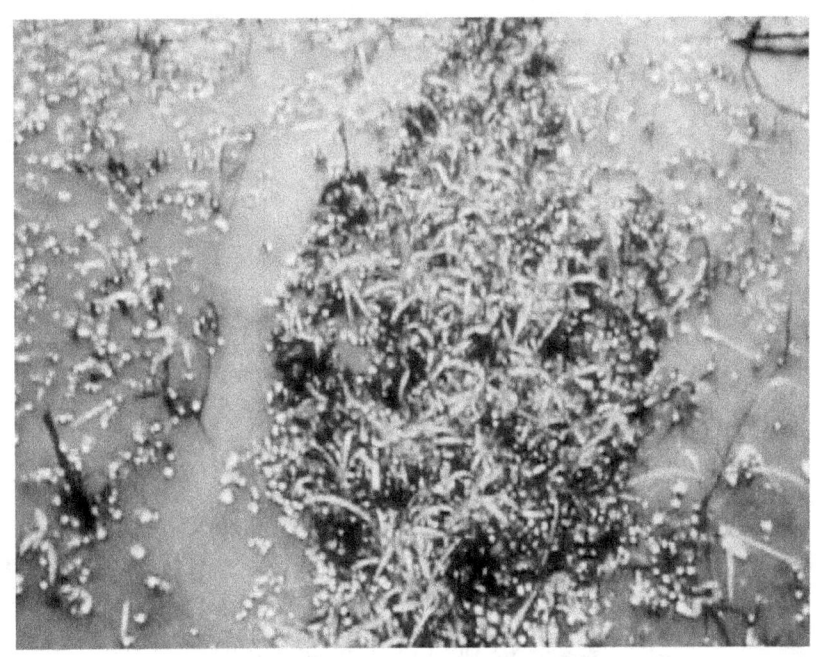

GORDON MATTA-CLARK

Gordon Matta-Clark was famous for transforming buildings by knocking enormous holes in them (*Conical Intersect,* 1975), or cutting a house in New Jersey in half (*Splitting,* 1974). But these were not sculpted spaces or physical gestures so much as Conceptual reorganizations of a structure. It's easy to discern the influence of Matta-Clark's interventions in houses and buildings (which he called 'unbuilding') on Andy Goldsworthy's holes and Rachel Whiteread's works (such as her impressions of rooms and houses). Matta-Clark bought up pieces of land in the borough of Queens (in 1973), in another Conceptual piece; none of them were big enough for housing of for much else (some were only 2 by 3 feet, tiny strips of land). *Reality Positions, Fake Estates* explored the notion of land ownership.

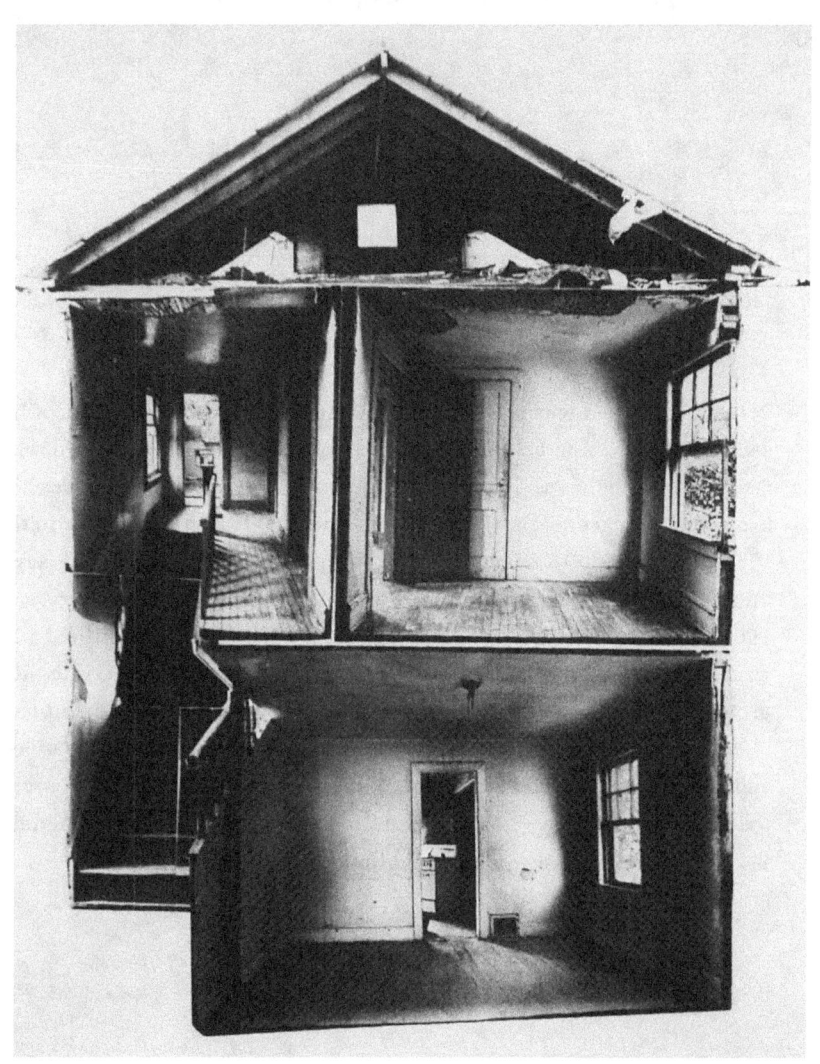

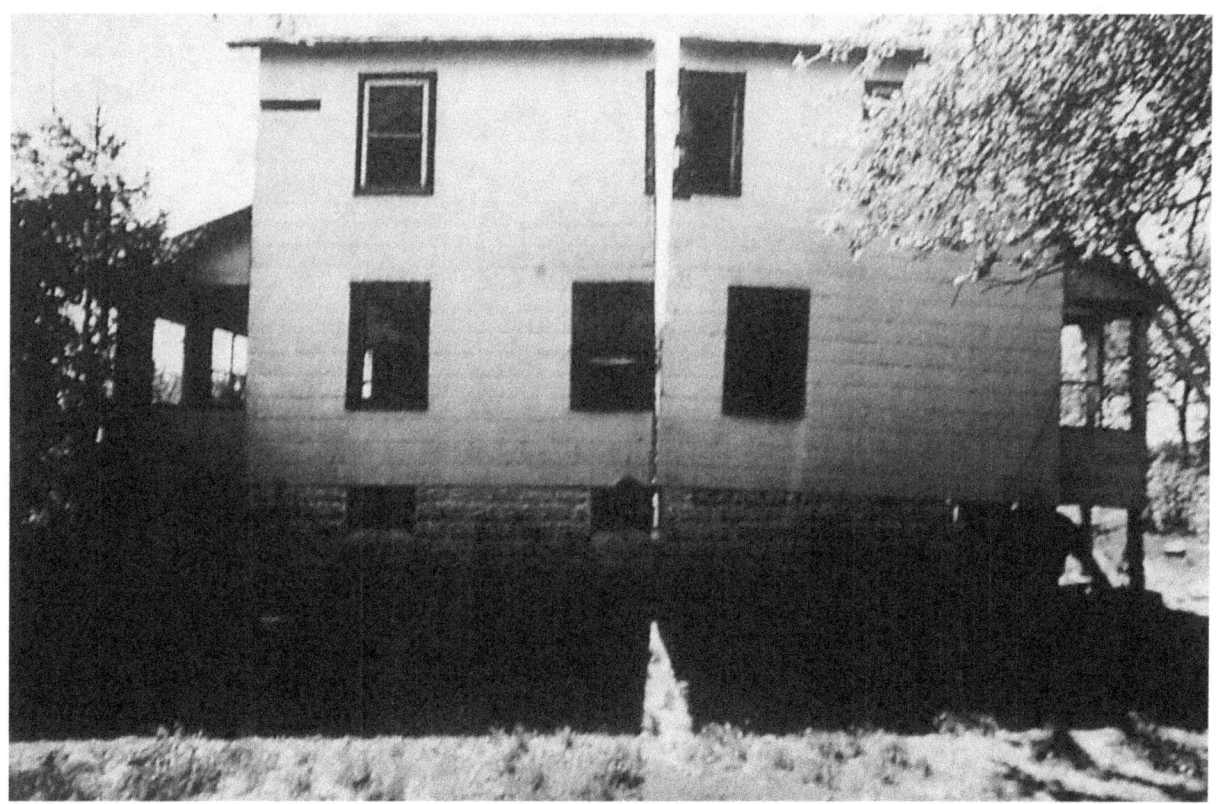

PETER HUTCHINSON

Peter Hutchinson was born in England (in 1930), but spent most of his artistic career in the US (based in Massachusetts). He collaborated with Dennis Oppenheim on a series of underwater works: fruit, vegetables and bread were packed in plastic bags and suspended from a fishing line in the West Indes (1969). Hutchinson also planted flowers in the sand underwater, and made a dam from sand bags in Tobago (*Underwater Dam,* 1969). Along the rim of a volcano (Paricutin, 1970), Hutchinson sited a 76 metre line of white bread wrapped in plastic. Hutchinson recorded the growth of mould and decomposition. Later works include *Ice Sandwich* (1994), a Brancusi-like tower of slabs of wood interlaced with blocks of ice, and 'thrown ropes' of flowers planted in the ground in the shape of a rope that Hutchinson threw (1996). Hutchinson preferred works that combined his love horticulture, science, art and botany.[1]

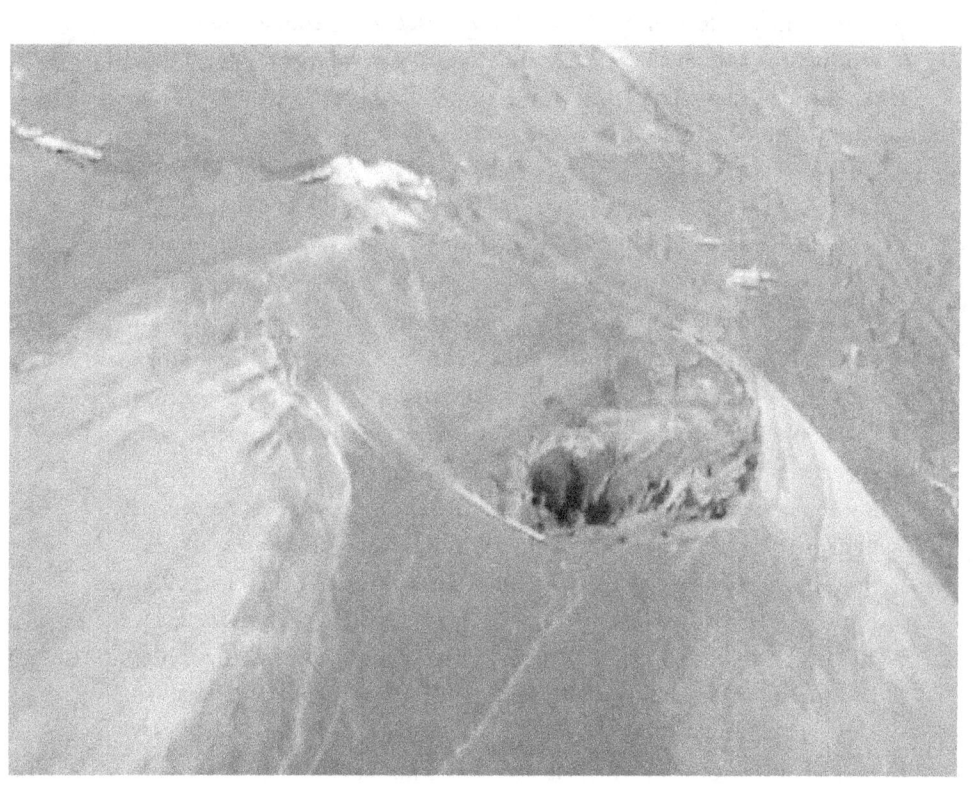

ANDY GOLDSWORTHY: *LEAFWORKS*

It is the leafworks that are the most colourful of Andy Goldsworthy's sculptures. What the leaf sculptures show is how beautiful the colours of nature are: Goldsworthy shows the viewer these subtle colours by contrasting one leaf with another. *Maple patch* grouped the red/ orange/ yellow of Japanese maple leaves together; *Poppy leaves* contrasted the red poppy leaves against the mid-green of an elderberry bush; a Stone Wood sculpture of 1992 consisted of poppy leaves wrapped around a hazel branch, the red constrasting vividly with the wet green leaves; *Dock Leaves* interwove red leaves in green grass stalks. Two sycamore leafworks of 1980 and 1981 are very simple: a leaf black from cow shit is placed against pale Autumn leaves; another leaf, bleached white, is set down on a bed of dark leaves. He pins together two colours of sycamore leaves (sycamore is a favourite Goldsworthy medium) in *Sycamore leaf sections* (1988), and hangs the line of leaves from a tree. Shot with the sun behind them, the photograph of the leaves shows them glowing green and gold, the two classic colours of poetry and alchemy. The Autumnal colours of course connote nostalgia, decadence, sensuality, Romanticism, time passing, the decay of the year, and so on, all those things John Keats wrote about in his 'Ode: To Autumn', and in a billion other poets. Goldsworthy's aim in the leaf pieces, though, draws attention to the fragility and delicacy of leaves, as well as their strength and function. A leaf, after all, is a complex biological factory, so the natural scientists say. 'There is a whole world in a single leaf' says Goldsworthy.[1] Goldsworthy's leafworks do not have a scientific agenda. Rather, they celebrate the presence of leaves, the being-in-the-world of leaves, so to speak.

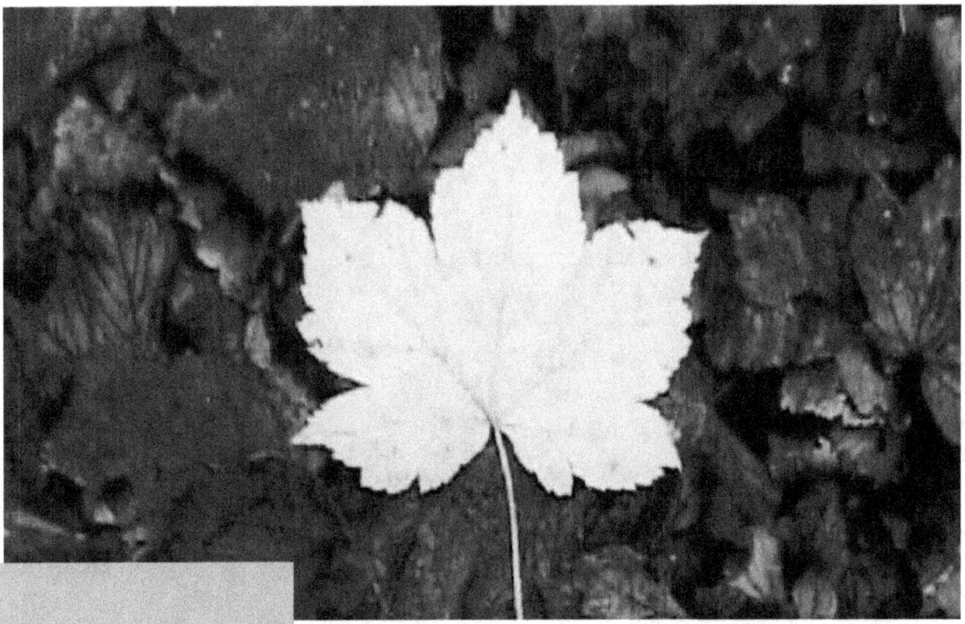

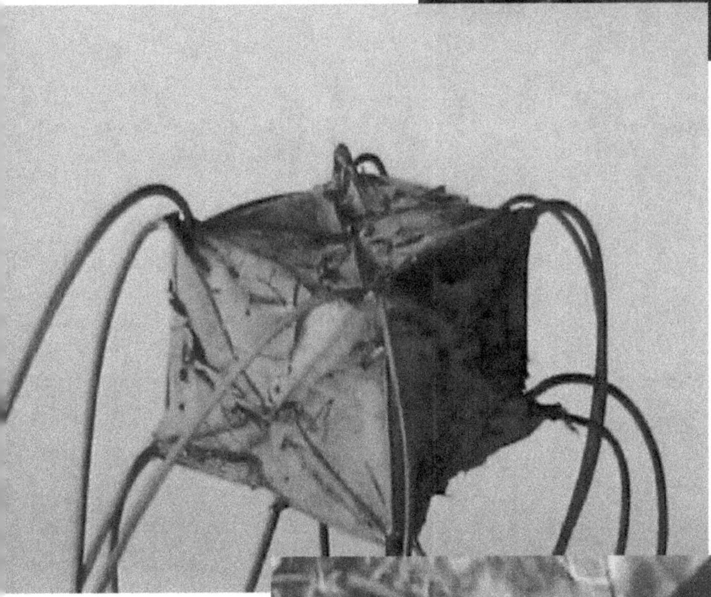

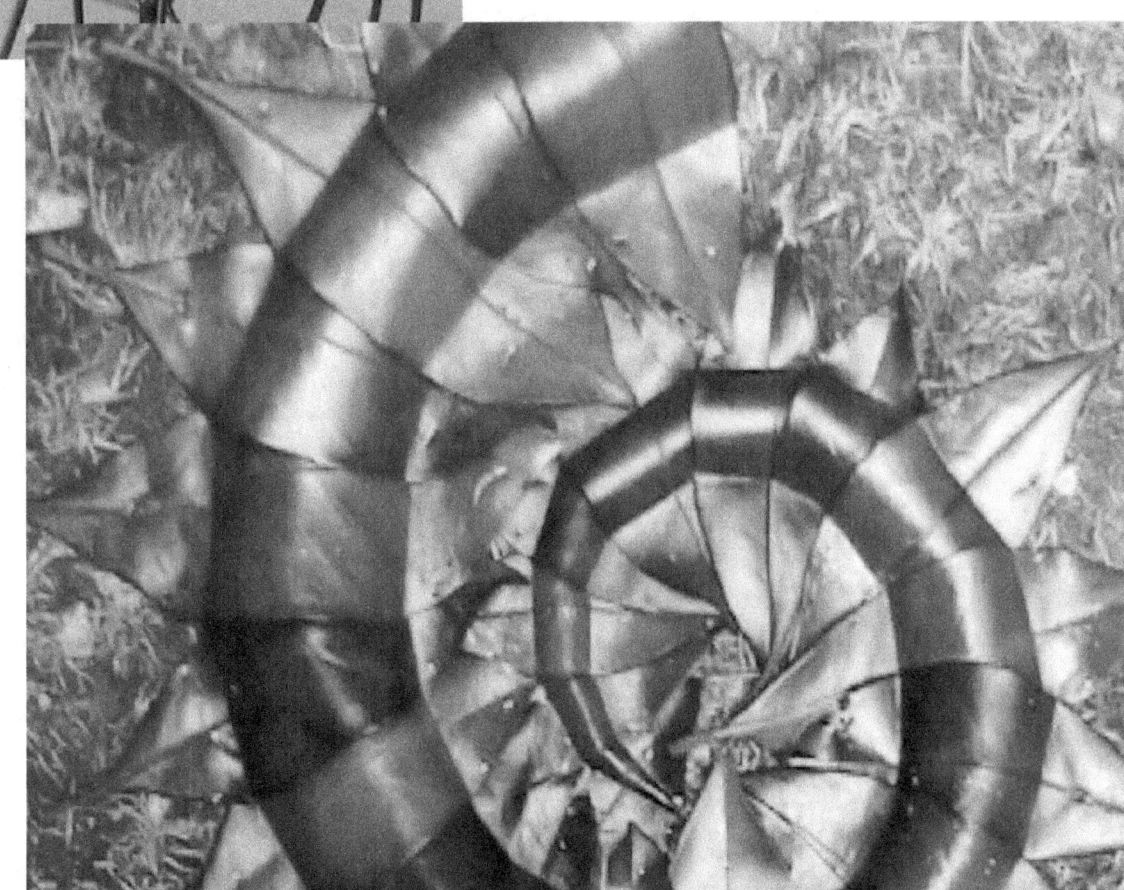

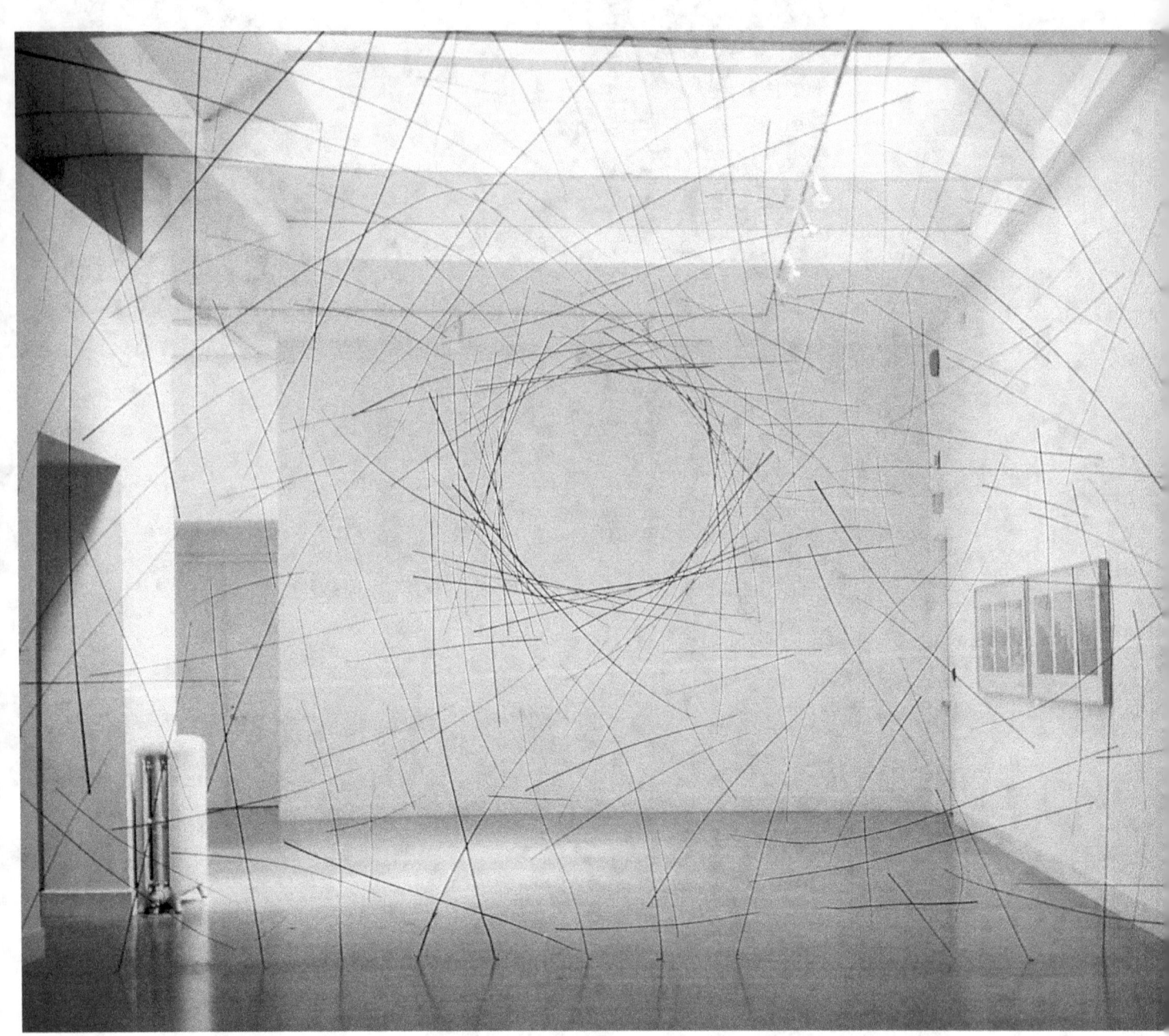

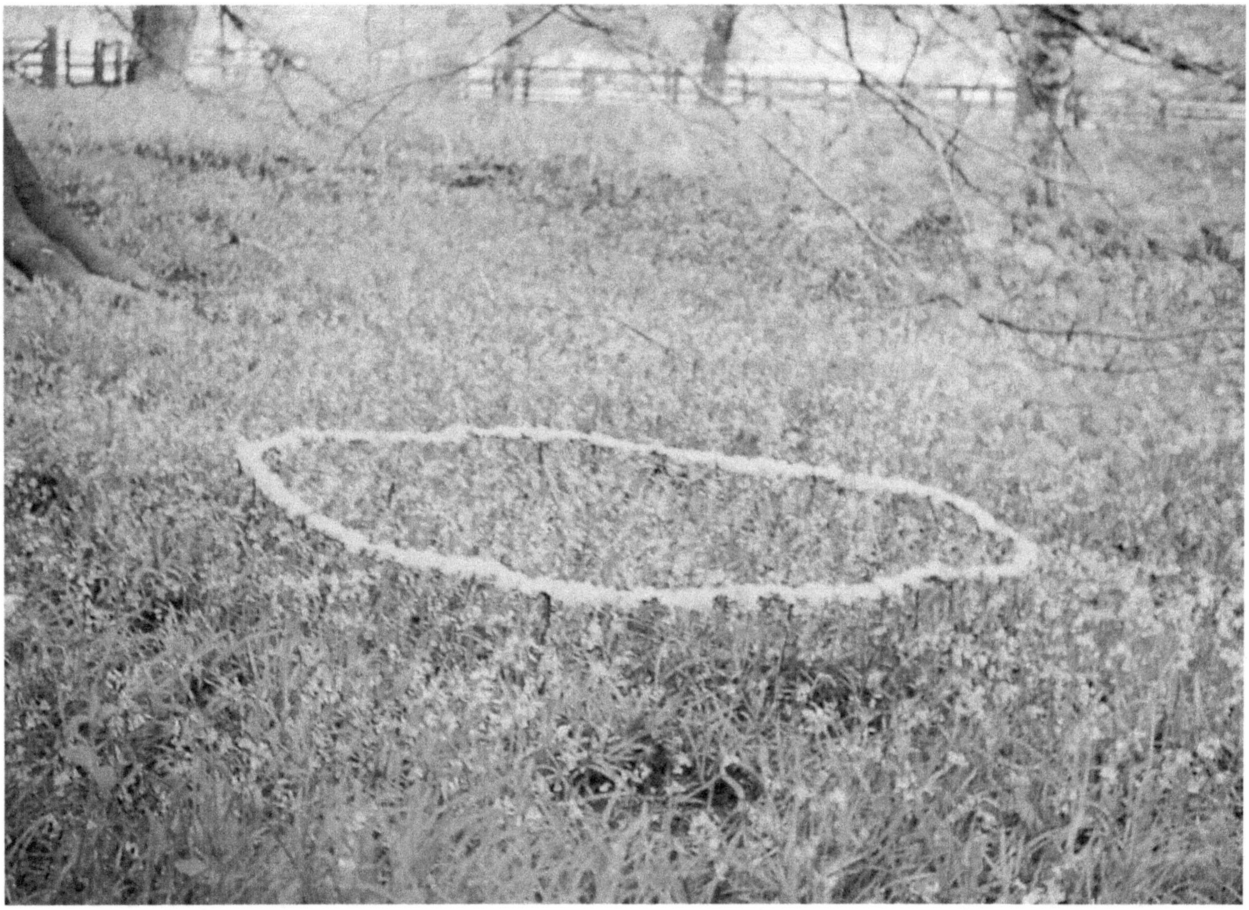

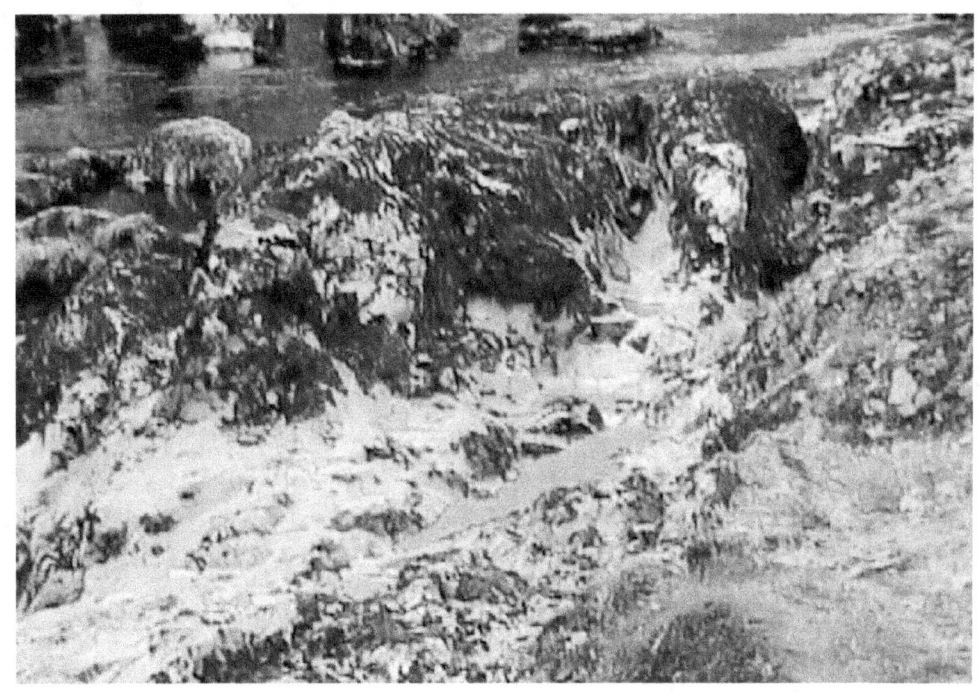

ANDY GOLDSWORTHY: *STONE CAIRNS*

Many of Andy Goldsworthy's cairns are made from slate (such as *Slate cone*, 1987, 1988); others from branches (*Oak branches*, 1990); or sandstone (*Sandstone*, 1990). Others are put into groups (such as the proposals for stone cone groups at Vassivière, Newcastle and Penpont). The cairn form is about the process of growth and energy. It is a form that celebrates 'the fullness, vigour, heavy ripeness and power generated from a centre, deep inside' Goldsworthy claimed (*Stone,* 37). Like D.H. Lawrence and Friedrich Nietzsche, Goldsworthy here makes the age-old links between 'ripeness' in nature and femininity and pregnancy. The Goldsworthy cone, then, can be seen as another expression of female fecundity, in the Lawrencean manner, an equivalent for a pregnant woman (like the prehistoric "Stone Venuses", the squat, callipygous figurines): in short, stone Mother-Goddesses.

'Cone' is perhaps not quite the right term for an image or expression of fullness and ripeness: Goldsworthy's 'cones' look more like fruit. The imagery of fruit would accord with Goldsworthy's ripeness discourse. 'Cairn' is also not quite the right word, though some of the 'cones' on rocky mountainsides (*Cone to mark day becoming night at Glenleith Fell*, and *Cone to mark night becoming day*, Scaur Glen, both 1991) have affinities with natural cairns and outcrops of rock. Some of the cairns were made at night, to be seen at night, as hymns to the night, or the dawn, or the sunset. Working on the Yorkshire *Ice hole,* Goldsworthy spoke of 'working with the moonlight' which was a 'very strange intense light' (1987, *Hand to Earth*, 147). Working at night, Goldsworthy spoke of approaching 'the most beautiful point, the point of greatest tension, as one moves towards daybreak'.[1]

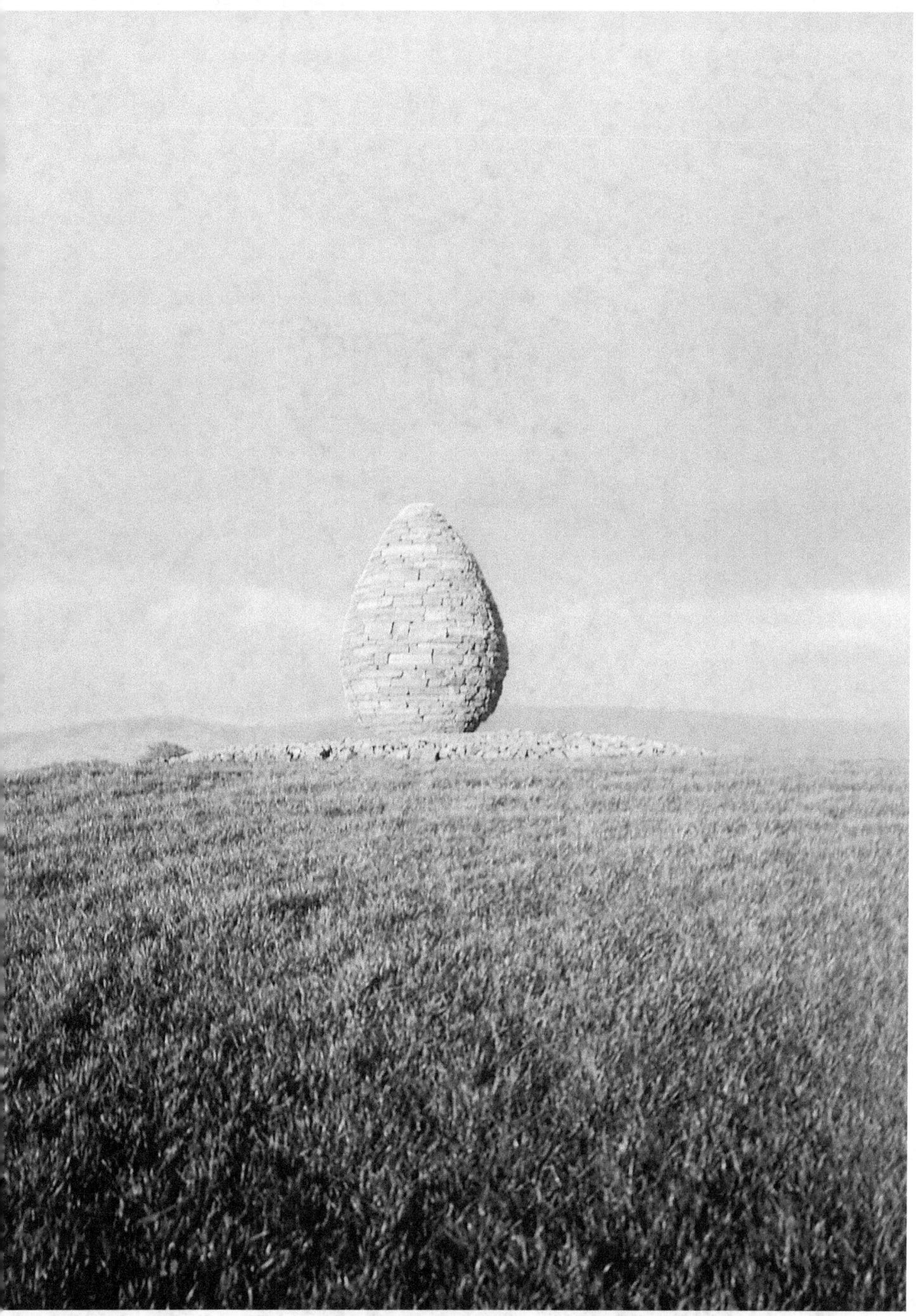

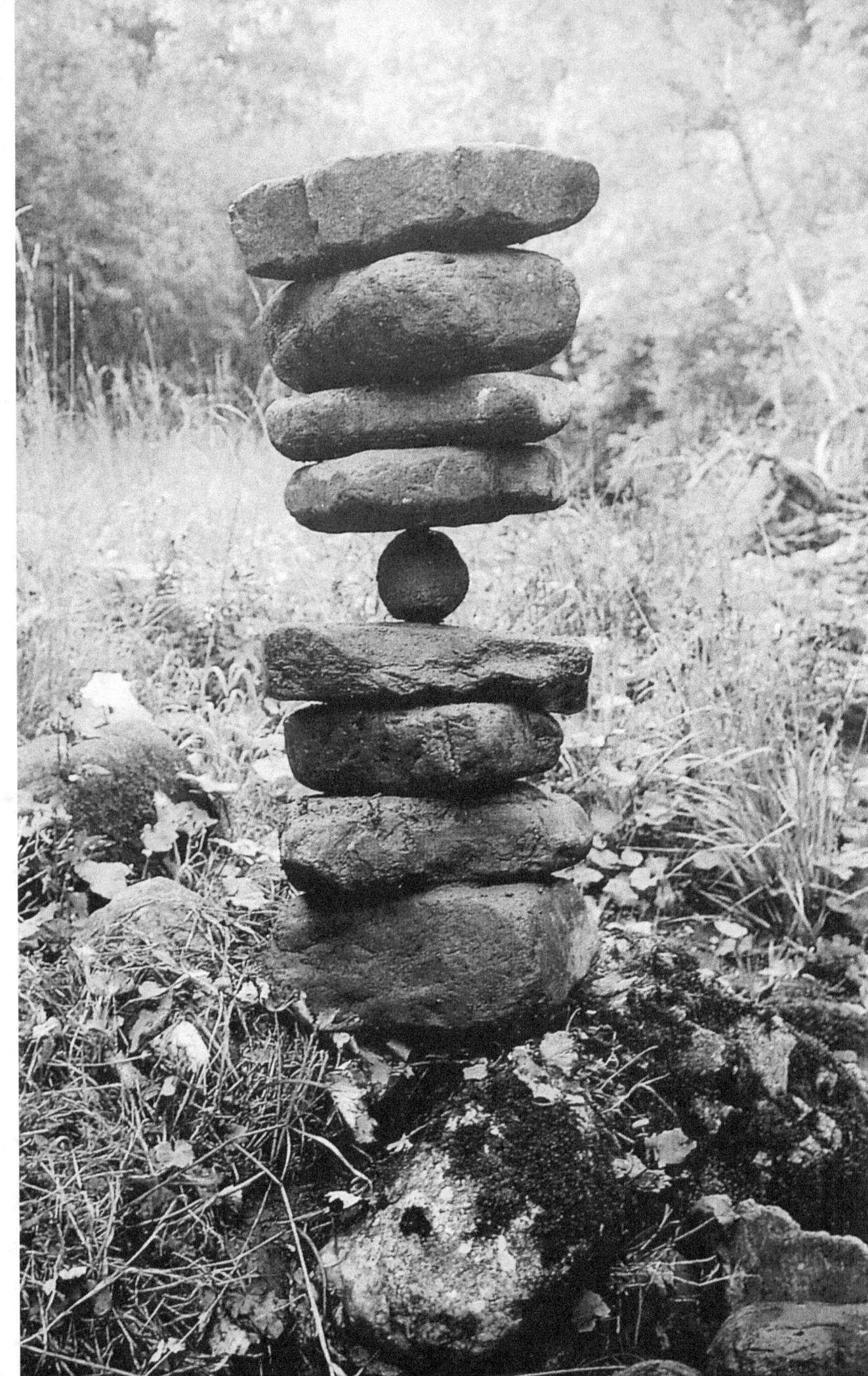

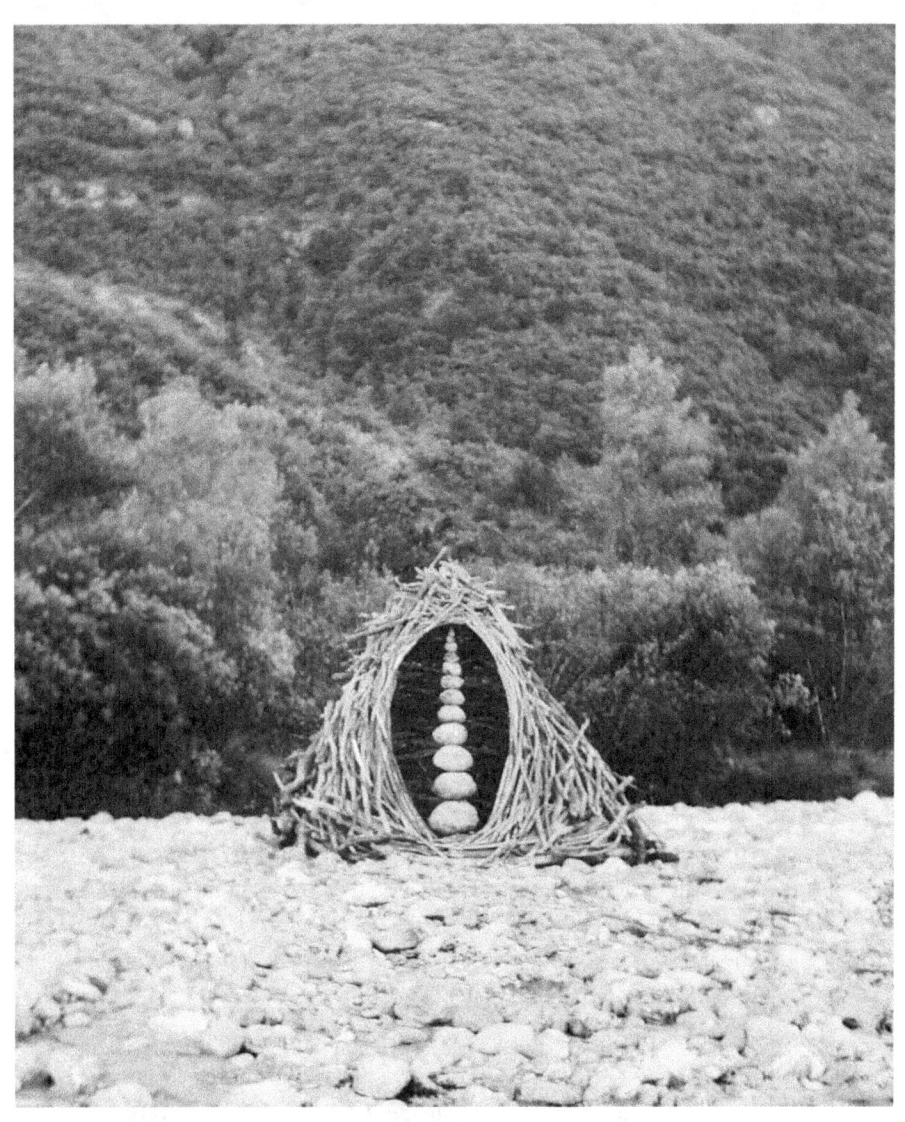

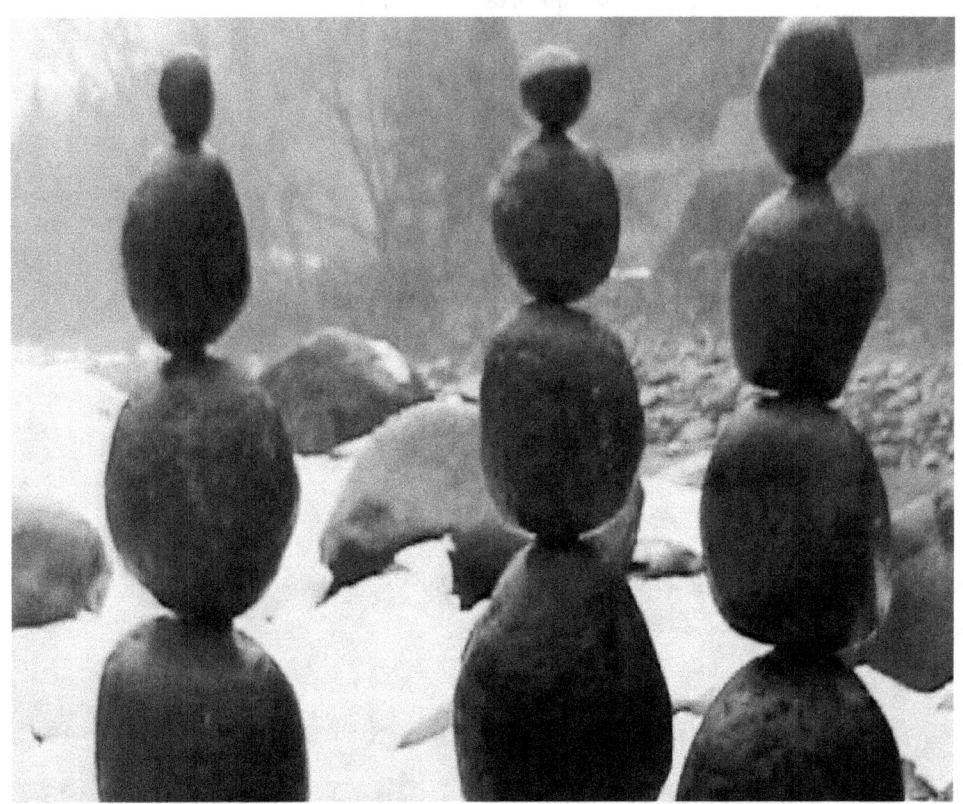

ANDY GOLDSWORTHY:
THROWS AND SPLASHES

Andy Goldsworthy says that he is really working with time. 'If I had to describe in one word what I do, I'd say I work with *time*'.[1] Although it seems, at first glance, to be all about space, about particular spaces and how materials react with certain locations, time is an important element in Goldsworthy's art. He speaks of adding another layer to preceding layers of 'human understanding and character' when he makes work in the landscape.[2] He is conscious of the past and its layers of time on/in the landscape. 'The land is an expression of its past' he says (*Hand to Earth*, 189). He investigates moments, the instant of a splash; then there are works that last a few minutes or hours: the soil drying after Goldsworthy's laid on it after rain; or days - the rocks covered in clay; then works that study seasons (Autumnal leaves, snow and ice works); and works that explore the slow, cosmic time of enduring media - stones, the sun, the sea. What counts, Goldsworthy says, is not the duration of the work, but 'the experience of making.'[3] 'I've always been interested in the moment a work is made' (*Sheepfolds,* 15).

Many of the photographs in his exhibitions document very brief occurrences: the red earth in the river, or mud being thrown in the shallows on a beach, or on a misty hillside: *Rainbow splashes* were made with a stick in Yorkshire (1980), *Slate throws* (Cumbria, 1988) consisted of throwing slate into the air, like *Hazel stick throws* (1980) and *Leaf throws* (Tayside, 1989). *Maple leaf throw* was made in Japan in 1990. In 1995, Goldsworthy had the Ballet Atlantique dance troupe throw sticks and soil into the air at once. In California (1994), Goldsworthy threw dust into the air against the sun, which he called *Breath of Earth* works. It is the shapes the mud and earth and sticks make in the air that fascinates Goldsworthy. He is seen in various photos, throwing the mud and earth, his legs and arms raised high, caught in a moment of release. These photos are about time, about letting something go, and capturing the trajectory. Mud and earth is not 'alive', as a bird is, but Goldsworthy seems to throw the mud and earth as if he's releasing a bird. He wants the earth to fly. It doesn't: it arcs back to the ground, but these arcs are elegant, and become the subject of many photographs.

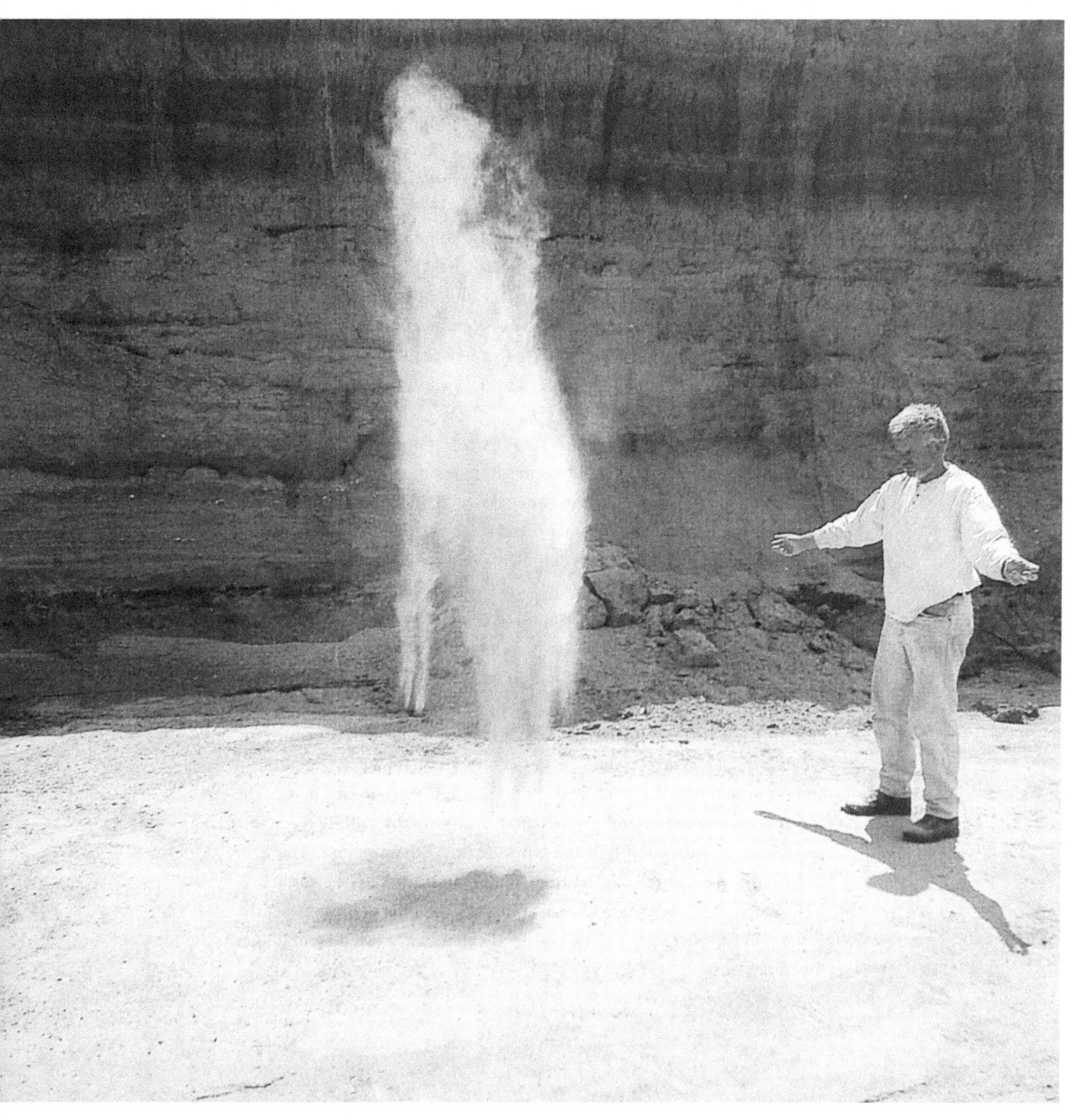

ANDY GOLDSWORTHY: *ICICLES*

The biting cold maybe gives Andy Goldsworthy a sense of heroism, for suffering invariably enhances a work (as in, 'this work was difficult, made under adverse conditions'). After all, Goldsworthy is not an artist who prefers to make work in the 'comfort' of a home or a studio (working indoors doesn't feel 'real' to him). No: he ventures out into the wilderness, where it can be uncomfortable and challenging. He claims to know the landscape around his studio in Penpont, Scotland, very well (he would do - after creating sculptures in the area regularly since the 1986), so that the snow does not hide the world: 'I know what lies under the snow - I know the earth beneath' (HE).

Always Andy Goldsworthy stresses the intimate relationship he has with nature. Part of this intimacy comes from returning to the same patch of land again and again. Through successive visits, layers of touch and meaning in the landscape are uncovered by the artist. An artist returning to the same space always works in time as well as space, for s/he creates a personal history of that place. S/he works with her former selves, as well as in the present - with the artist and ideas s/he had two years ago, ten years ago, twenty years ago. 'Some places I return to over and over again, going deeper - a relationship, made in layers over a long time' commented Goldsworthy (AG). For an artist like Andy Goldsworthy, the land around Penpont, Thornhill, Burnhead, Keir Mill, Cleuchhead, Carronbridge, Closeburn and Tynron would be very, very familiar. Weeks or perhaps months would be spent each year fashioning sculpture in this part of the South-West Scotland. One can bet that Goldsworthy will be out there making art in the area, if he's not working on a commission in Digne or California or wherever, or dealing with admin, or on vacation. Goldsworthy's sculptures will be situated all over this part of the world. Some will be extremely ephemeral, and some might last a little longer than a day or so.

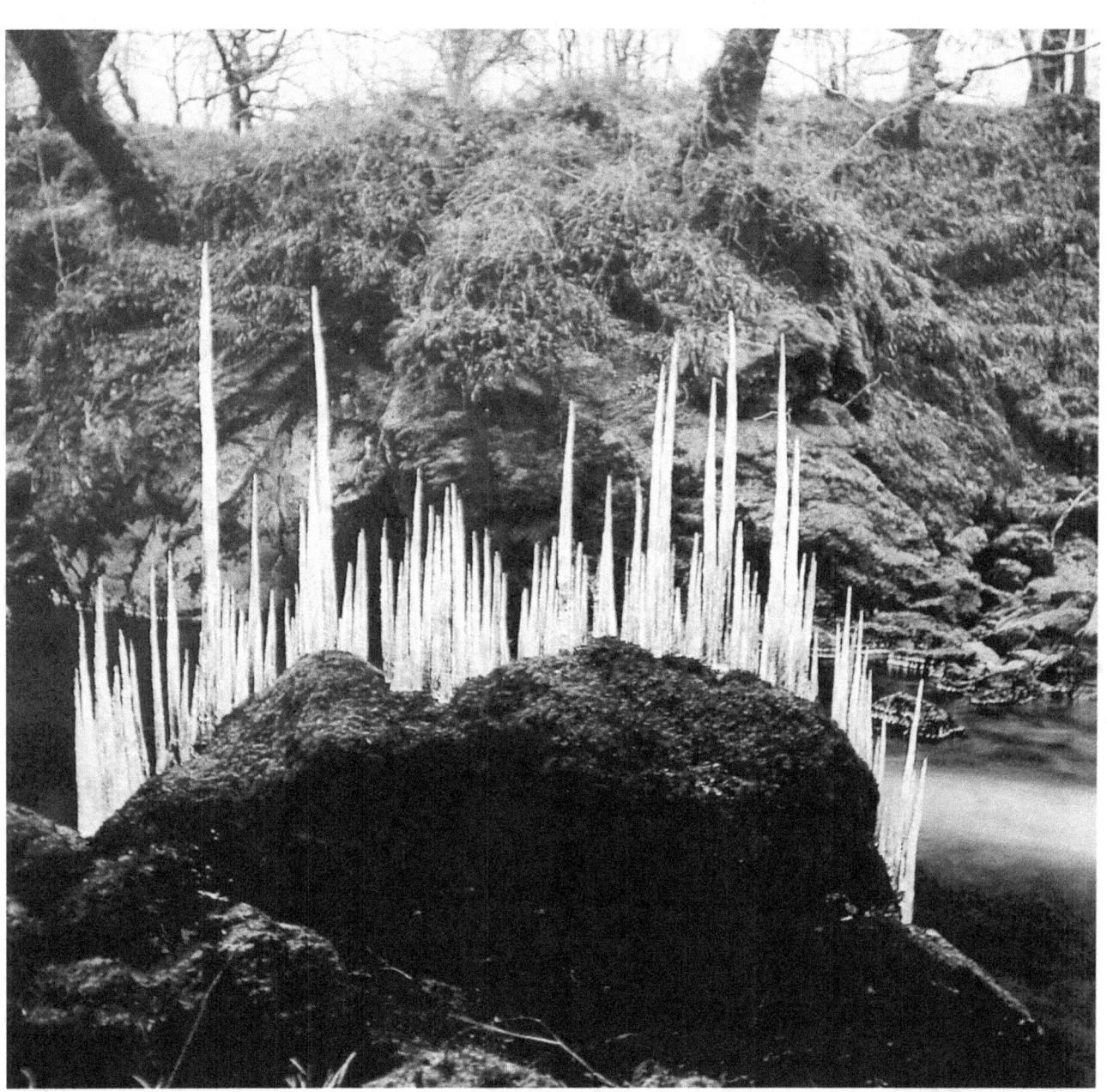

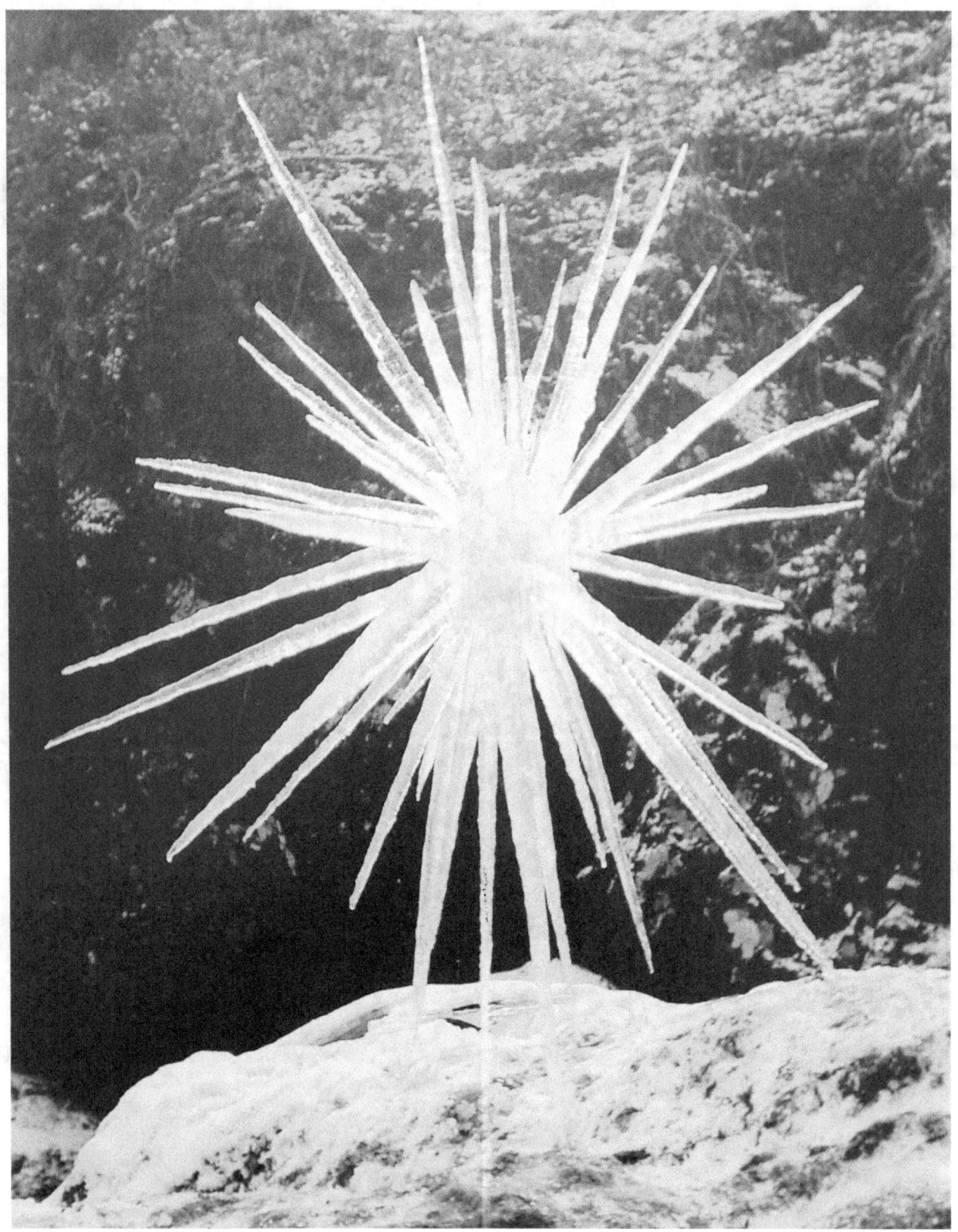

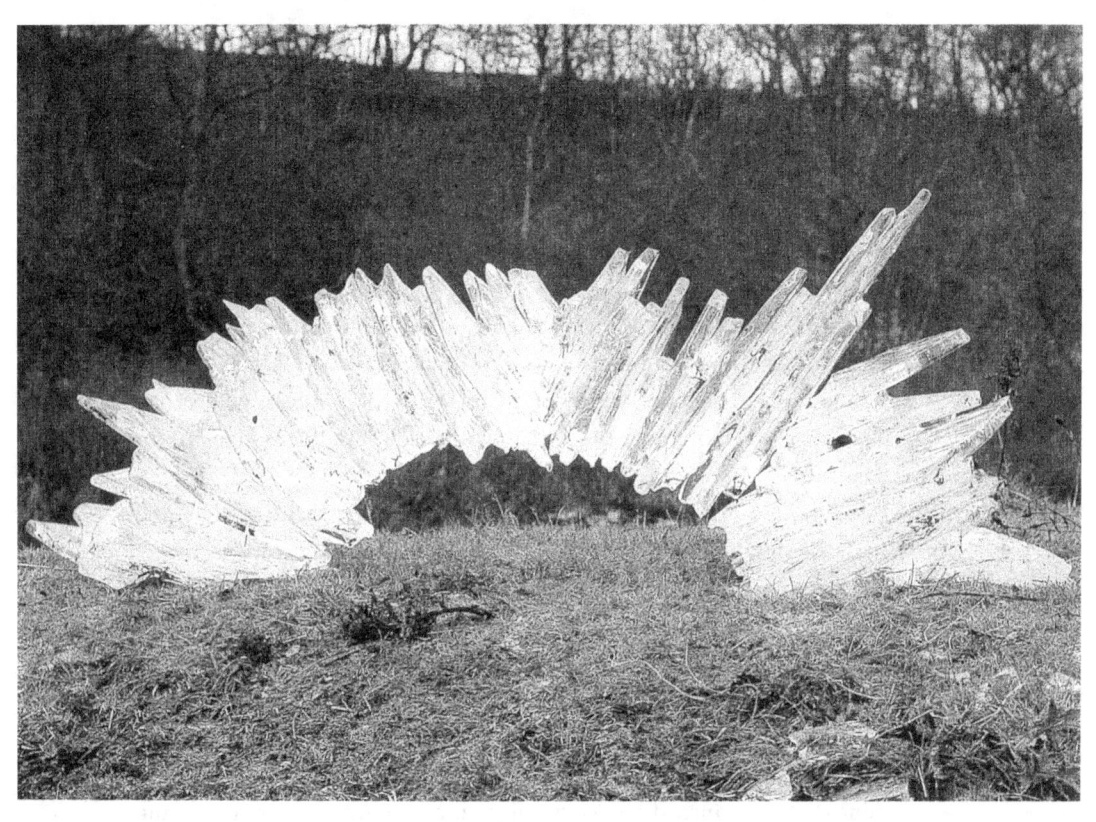

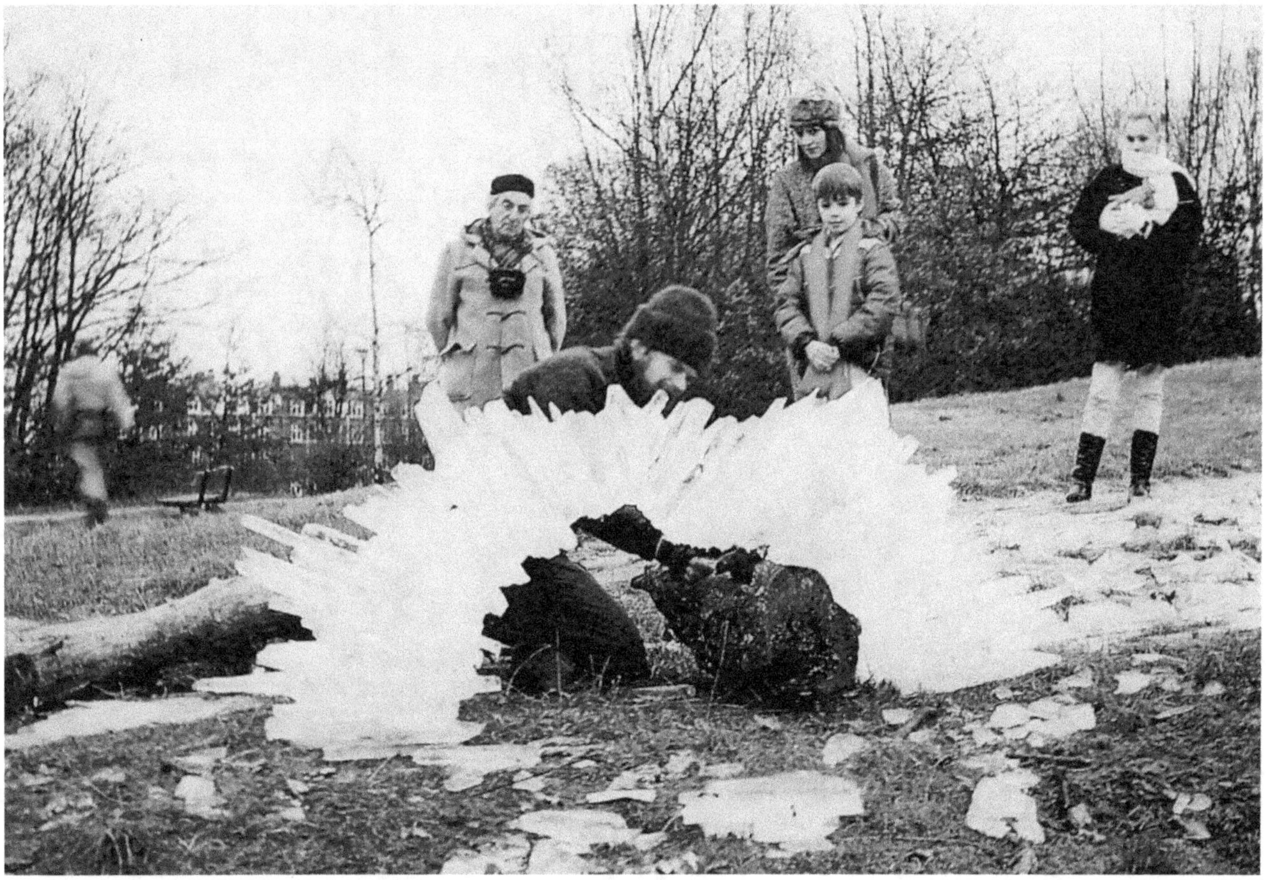

DAVID NASH: *SLATE STOVE*

One of the most intriguing and sensual of land artists is David Nash (born in the same year as Richard Long, 1945), with whom Goldsworthy worked. Nash's æsthetics chime with those of Richard Long and Andy Goldsworthy among British artists.[1] Hugh Adams sees David Nash as a kind of 'fixed abode Richard Long', working from one place (North Wales), while Long travels the globe, regarding the whole world as his studio, as material for making art.

David Nash has built a number of 'stoves' and 'hearths', out of natural materials - snow, slate, wood. These structures burn away - fire as 'living' sculpture. *Snow Stove,* made in Japan in 1982, burns beautifully - a snow pyramid, fusing those two eternal mysteries - fire and snow, fire and ice. Nash has also made a *Wood Stove* (1979), a *Slate Stove* (1981) and also a *Sea Hearth*. Anyone who's lit a fire right next to the ocean will know what a magical experience it can be, and Nash's *Sea Hearth* is certainly rich in magic. Nash set his fire built of large stones inches from the waves, to accentuate the contrast between the two elements. Nash's stoves and hearths are rich in alchemical and elemental allusions: they are a poetry of elements, the basic elements out of which everything is made.

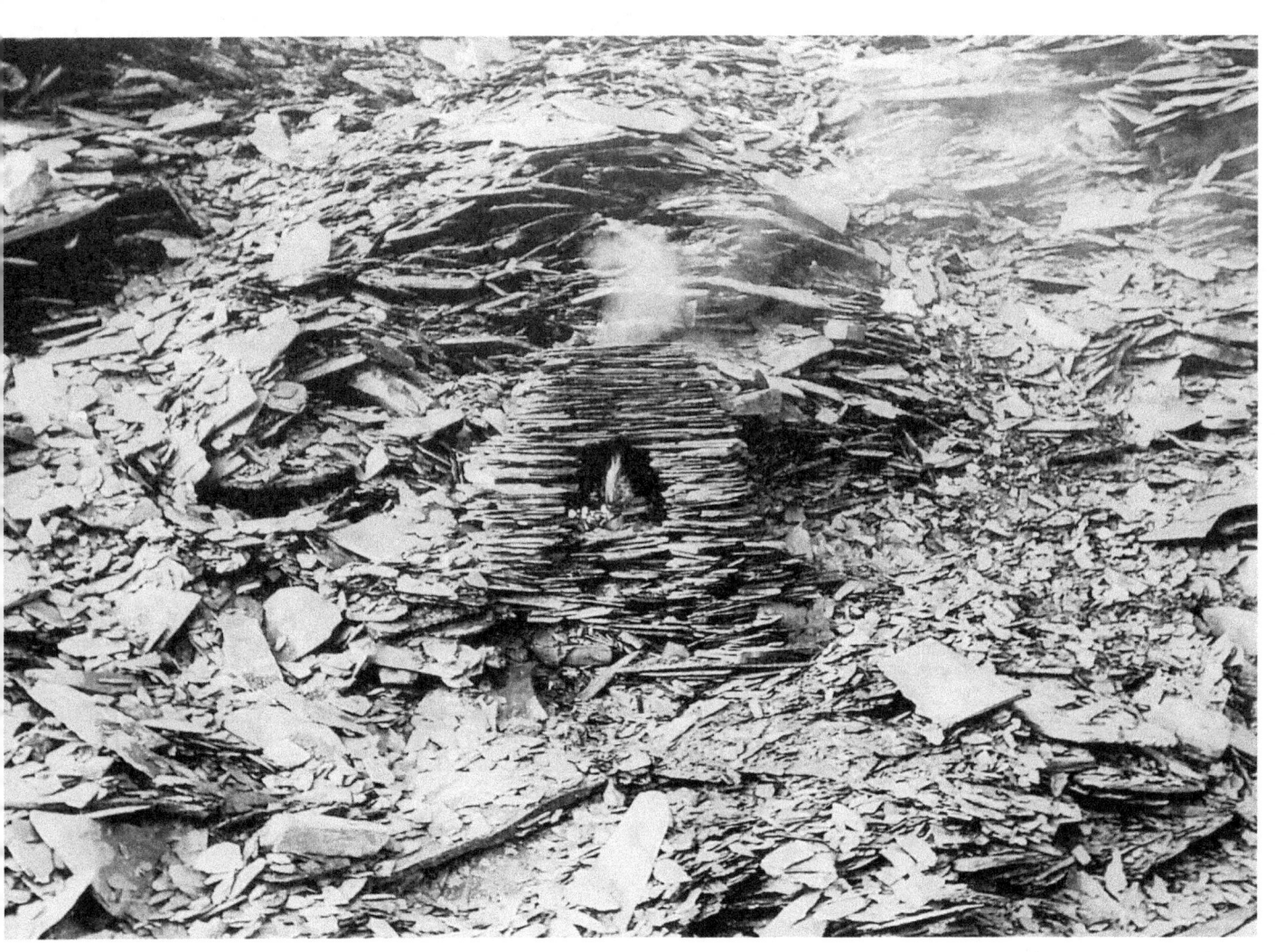

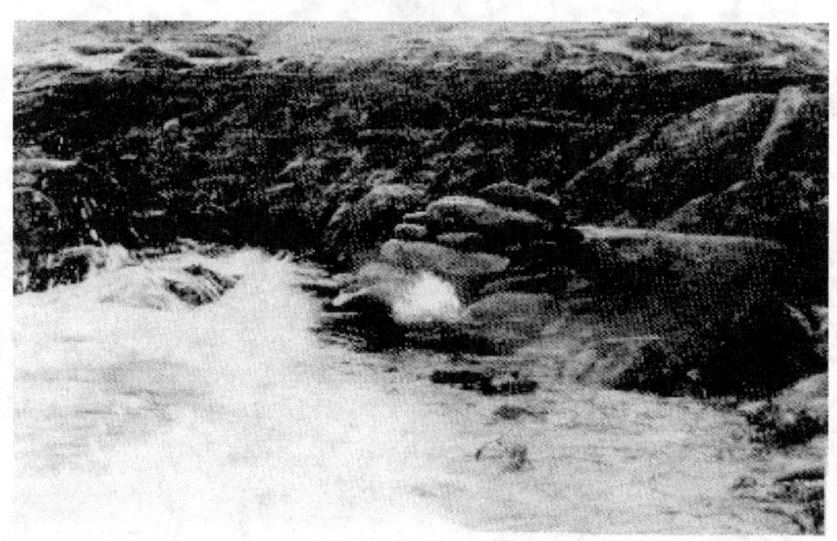

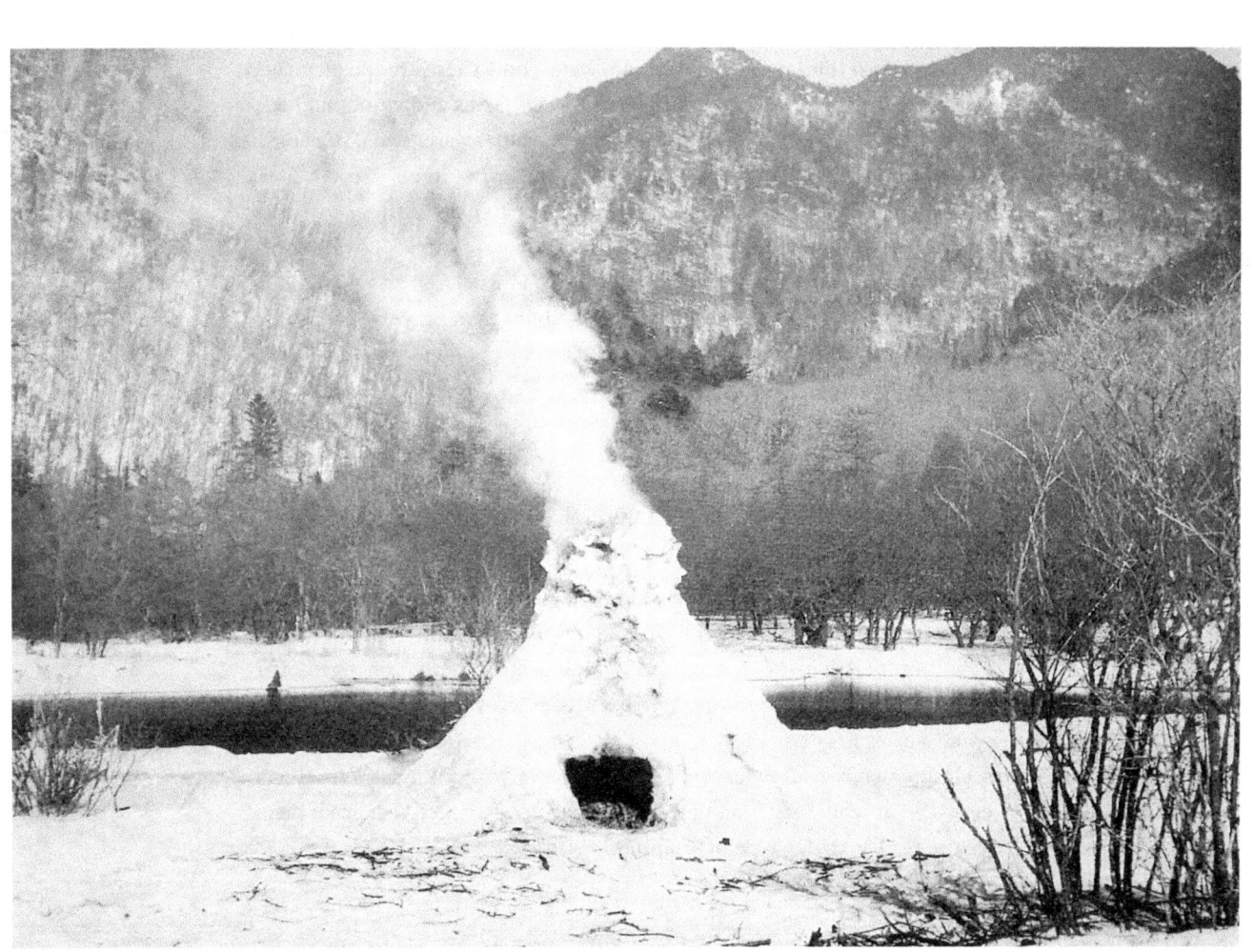

DAVID NASH: *FLETCHED OVER ASH DOME*

David Nash makes fascinating pieces, works which are instantly appealing, partly because of the materials, the natural materials which urban-based cultures are so thirsty for: wood, stone, water, fire. These are the elements not found in cities. Well, one sees trees, stones, skies and wood in cities, but it's not the same: land artists make the spectator aware, again, of nature, of natural materials. How refreshing it is, after being encased in grey concrete and a maze of straight lines in the city to imbibe these works of Long, Nash, Goldsworthy and Pope. What a wonder, really, is David Nash's marvellous *Fletched Over Ash Dome*. This is a circular group of trees in Wales which Nash planted in 1977: it is a 'living' sculpture, which, over thirty years, will be trained into a dome. It will be not only a circle of trees, but a dome of trees. Nash explains:

> A circle of young ash trees fletched and woven into a thirty foot dome fletched three times at ten year intervals then left alone. A silver sculpture in winter, a green canopy space in summer, a volcano of growing energy. (1978)

While Robert Morris uses steam, and Nancy Holt uses stone, Nash's use of living trees (such as in his *Fire Engine Sweep*, planted in 1980) creates a new form of sculpture, a sculpture which is alive, which changes over decades, rather than seconds. Morris's steam works last mere moments, while Nash's fires last a few hours. *Fletched Over Ash Trees*, though, is a sculpture that lasts decades, and changes year in year out. Nash's trees will grow and develop for a long time before they decay, which will make them a particularly exciting type of sculpture.

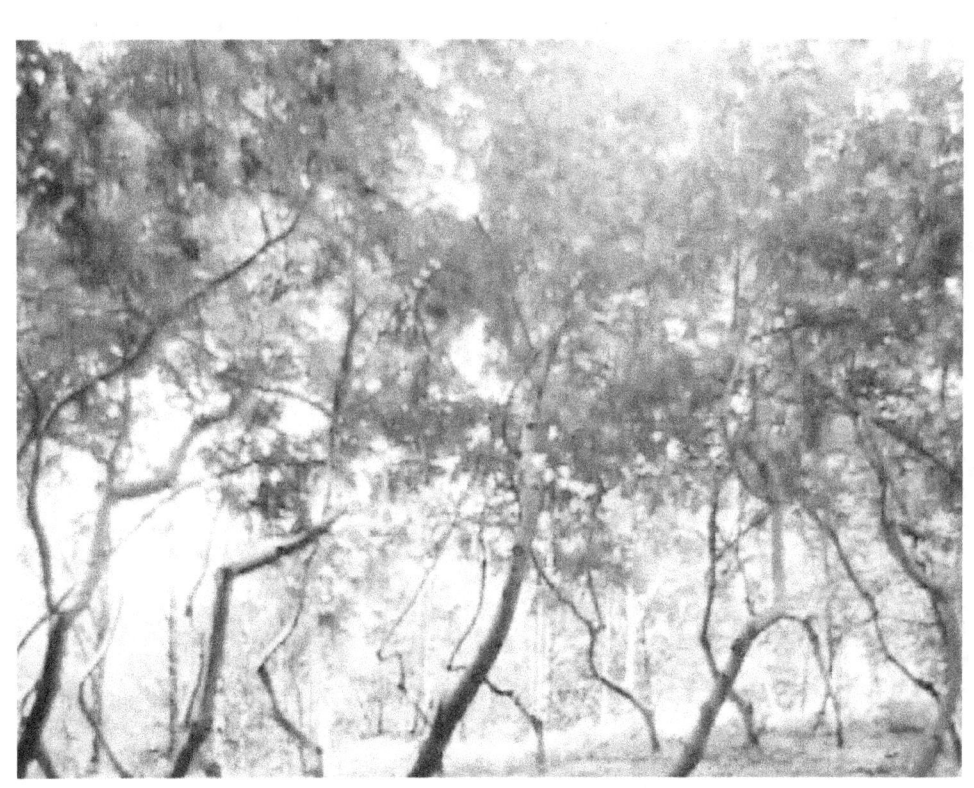

DAVID NASH: *WOOD SCULPTURE*

David Nash discusses the indoor/ outdoor problem in a 1978 interview:

> An object made indoors diminishes in scale and stature when placed
> outside. The reverse happens when an object made outside is brought
> inside, it seems to grow in stature and presence. It brings the outside in
> with it. The object outside has to contend with unlimited space, uneven
> ground and the weather. The sculpture I show inside is meant to be seen
> inside, it relates to the limited space, the peculiar scale, and the still air.[1]

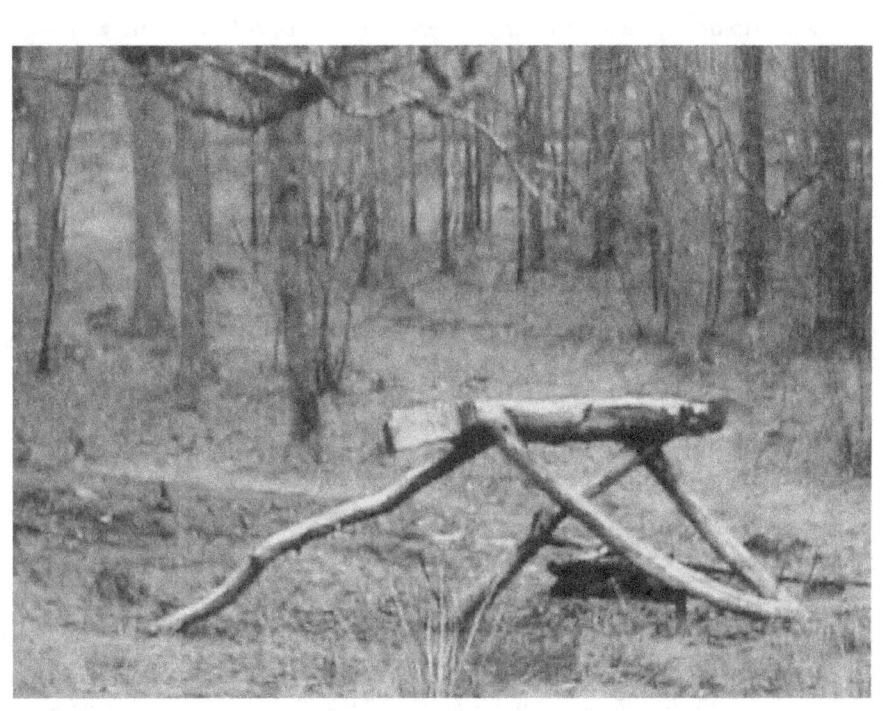

RICHARD LONG: *A LINE MADE BY WALKING*

Richard Long walks. This is the central fact of his art. His work is founded on the art of walking, and on walking as art. His walks become 'artwalks', artwalks which become artworks. For Richard Long, (art)walking is (art)working. As he walks he works. He makes art-walk-works. Art-walking and artworking become interchangeable. Born in 1945, the same year as David Nash, Long studied at the West of England College of Art (Bristol) and St Martin's (1966-68). In 1967 Long made his first important walk-work, *A Line Made By Walking*. Like most land artists, Long makes indoor (gallery) works and outdoor works (not intended for public consumption). He also produces art books, which are not typical exhibition catalogues, but artworks in their own right, usually with text works, photo works, and sometimes map works. Long's has had one-man shows at most of the major Western galleries, including the Whitechapel (1971), MOMA, New York (1972), Venice Biennale (1976), Fogg Art Museum (1980), Stedelijk, Amsterdam (1973), Guggenheim, New York (1986), Hayward Gallery, London (1991), and many one-man shows at Anthony d'Offay Gallery in London, which have produced art books (*Mountains and Waters*, 1992, *Sixteen Works*, 1984, *Five, Six, Pick Up Sticks*, 1980, *Old World New World*, 1988, *Kicking Stones*, 1990, *River Avon Book*, 1979).

Some of Richard Long's early works include: *A Line Made by Walking* (1967), one of his earliest walk-works, which was a short line made on grass and daises by walking repeatedly over the same area. This work had all the hallmarks of the Long walk-work: a definite intention, a clarity of image/ geometry, a countryside setting, a sense of process and formalism, the direct touch of humanity and Nature, the sense of time and impermanence, the relation with Nature, the relation between conception and execution. In the late 1960s Long photographed some concentric plastic stripes in a variety of settings. He made sculptures by cutting into grass (*Turf Circle*, 1966). In 1964 he made a Goldsworthyan sculpture: the track a snowball made as he rolled it along. On a beach in Somerset he made an open square from pebbles (1968). On a beach in Cornwall he made a spiral from seaweed (1970). Cross-shaped sculptures included one submerged in the shallows of Little Pigeon River in Tennessee (1970); a cross on grass and daisies (1968); a cross made by walking on wet sand at half-tide (Ireland, 1971), a very large, wide cross made from pine needles in London (1971).

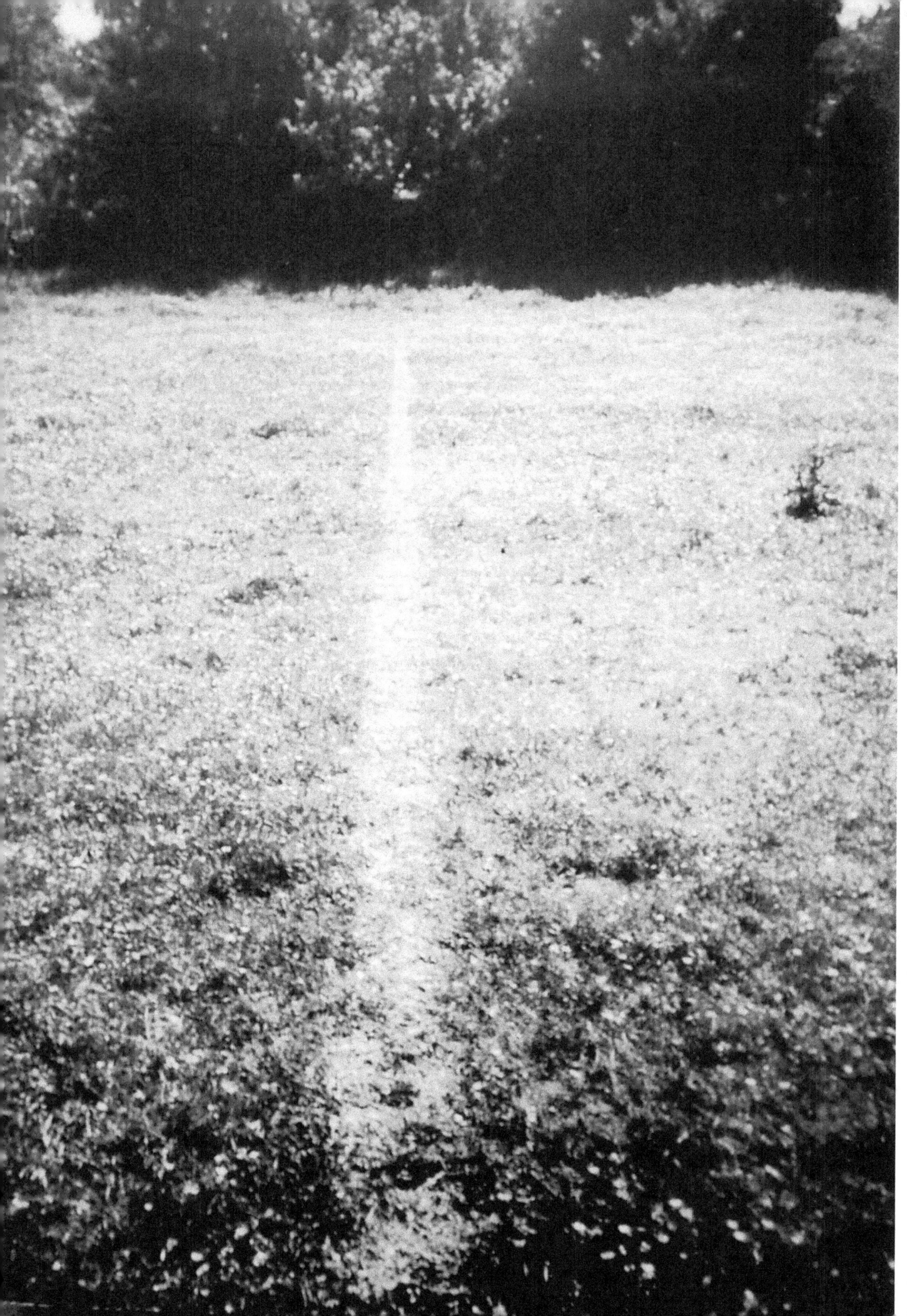

RICHARD LONG: *LINES*

Denying it or hinting at it, Richard Long's sculpture is definitely 'religious'/ 'mystical'/ 'spiritual'. Walking itself is sacred; making art is sacred; the allusions to stone circles are religious; circles themselves are religious; the awe with which viewers regard the sculpture has a religious aspect, and so on. Not all of Long's works are circles - there are always the lines. Long continued to make lines in the shape of a cross from time to time, such as in *Two Places* (Bolivia, 1972), where a small cross is made on marshland in a pile of stalks. Another cross was made in Iceland from some stones (*Stopping Place Stones*, 1974). The crosses are very much like geometric marks 'drawn' onto the landscape, as if to mark a place. Most of the single straight lines are short, like the crosses, such as *Walking Without Travelling* (Sahara, 1988). Occasionally, Long makes a square zigzag line: short right angles are marked upon bare soil, as in *Campfire Ash* (Bolivia, 1972 - all these works are from *Mountains and Waters*). Another zigzag line sculpture, in Antwerp in 1973, extends outwards to take over the gallery: each Long sculpture is made for a particular space, and expands to consume the gallery floor. The zigzag lines recall the Peruvian Nazca animals and symbols drawn on the lava plain (Long had walked along one of the desert lines in 1972: he also made sculptures which employed symbols such as the puma, condor, falcon, moon, sun and rain.)

The rows are really lines - Long calls them lines. *A Line in Ireland* (1974) is a short pile of flat rocks in a line, while *A Line in Australia* (1977) is a wider line, more like a row of red rocks (RL, 54-55). *A Line in Scotland* (1981) is a row of small flattish rocks that were stood on end at Cul Mór, like a row of prehistoric standing stones. In *Ash Line* and *Bushfire Line* (both 1994, Australia), Long dropped wood ash in a short line in a forest. In Yorkshire in 1977, as in Bolivia in 1981, Long cleared a space each side of the line as he picked up rocks (RL, 124, 126). The opposite of this line is the 'negative' line, made by leaving a path through a tangle of rocks, as in *A Line in California* (1982).

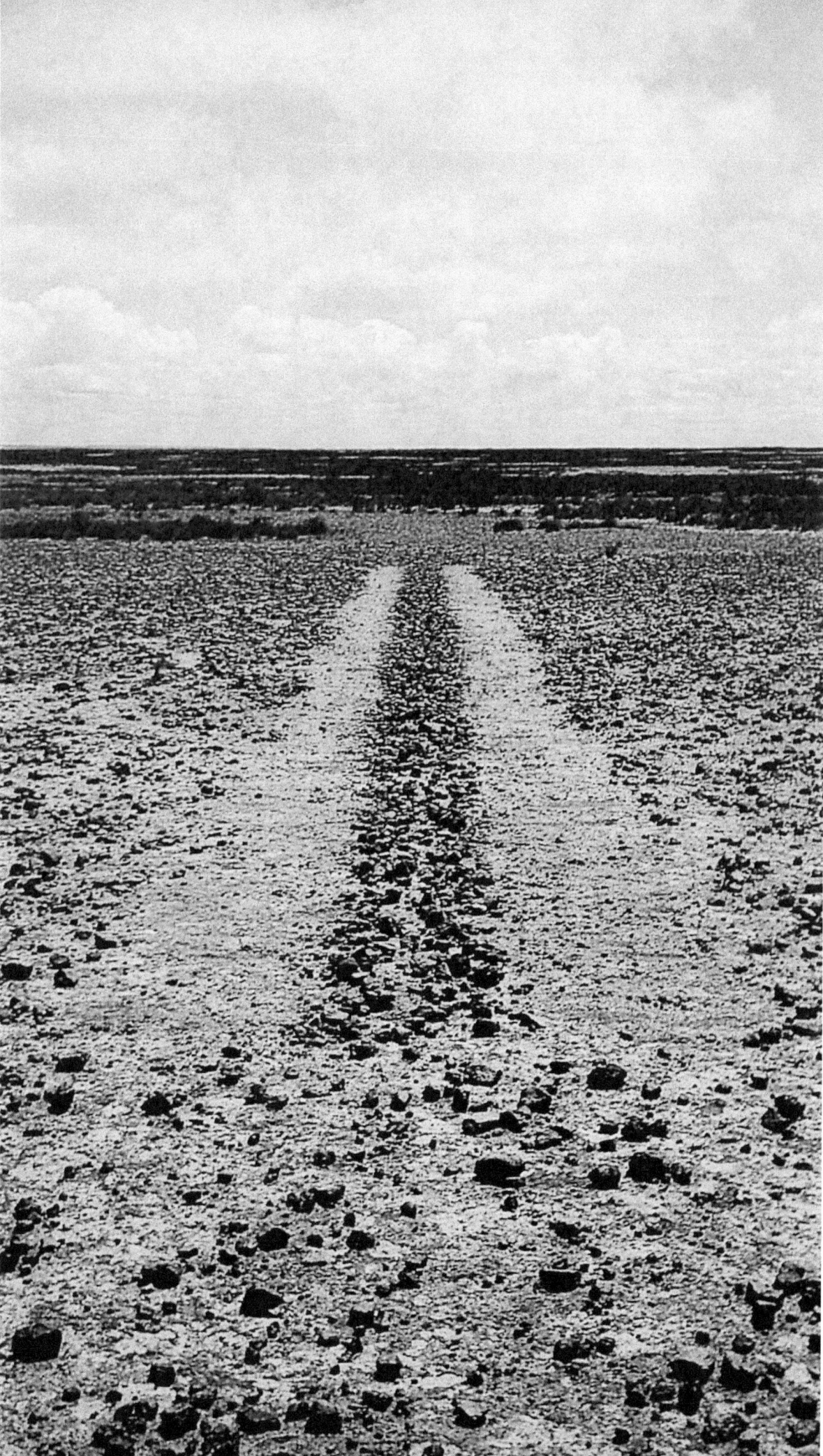

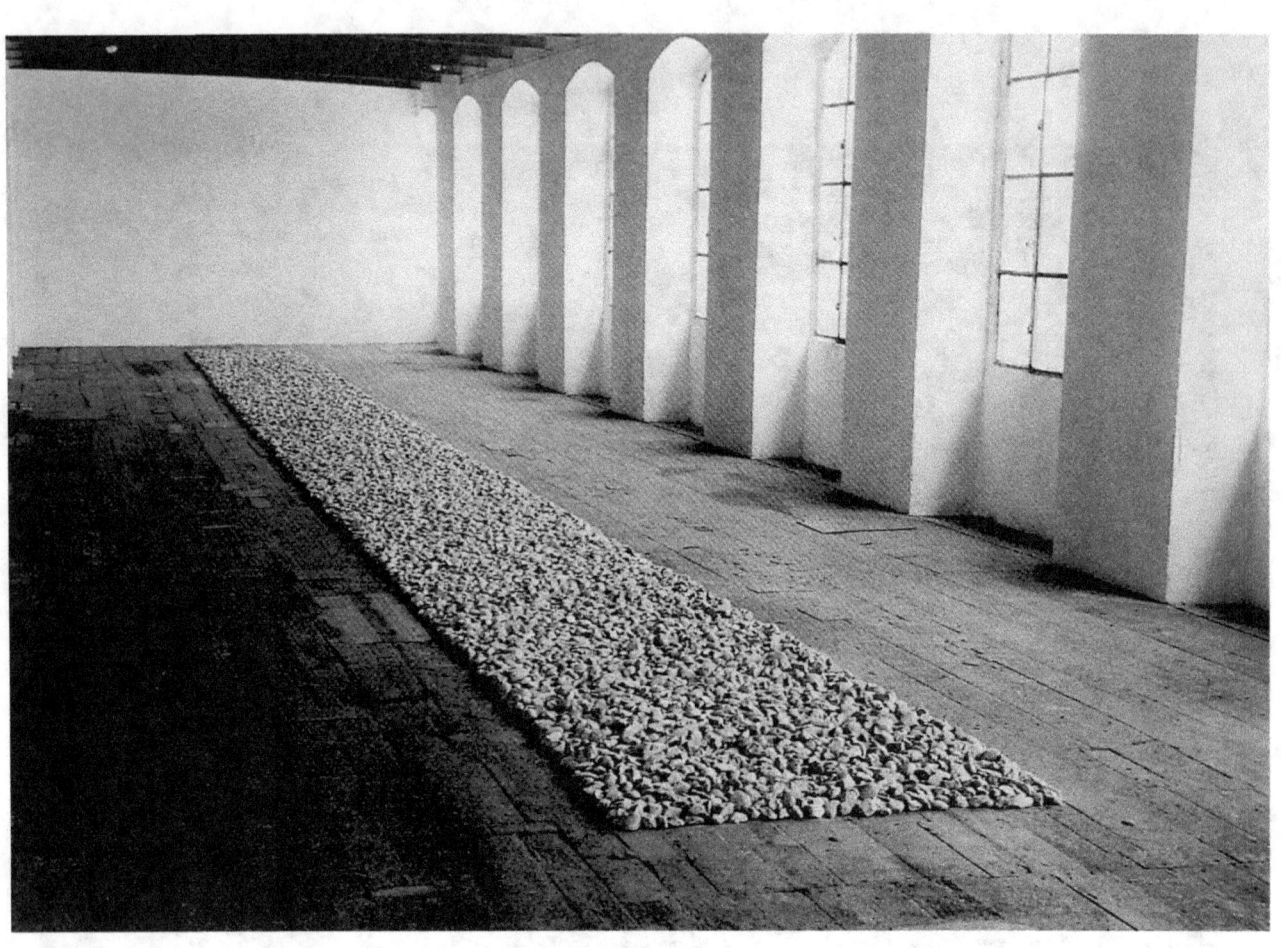

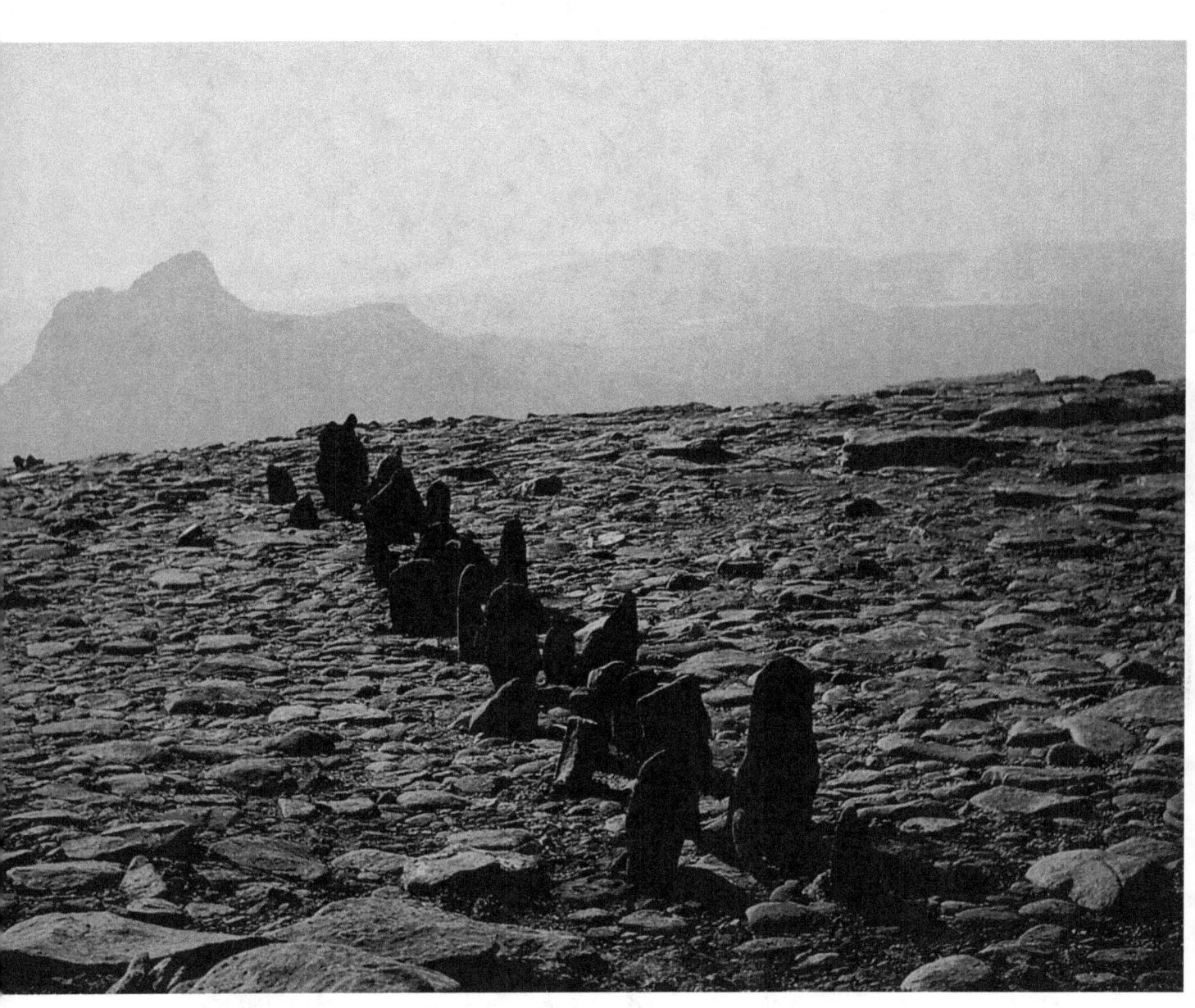

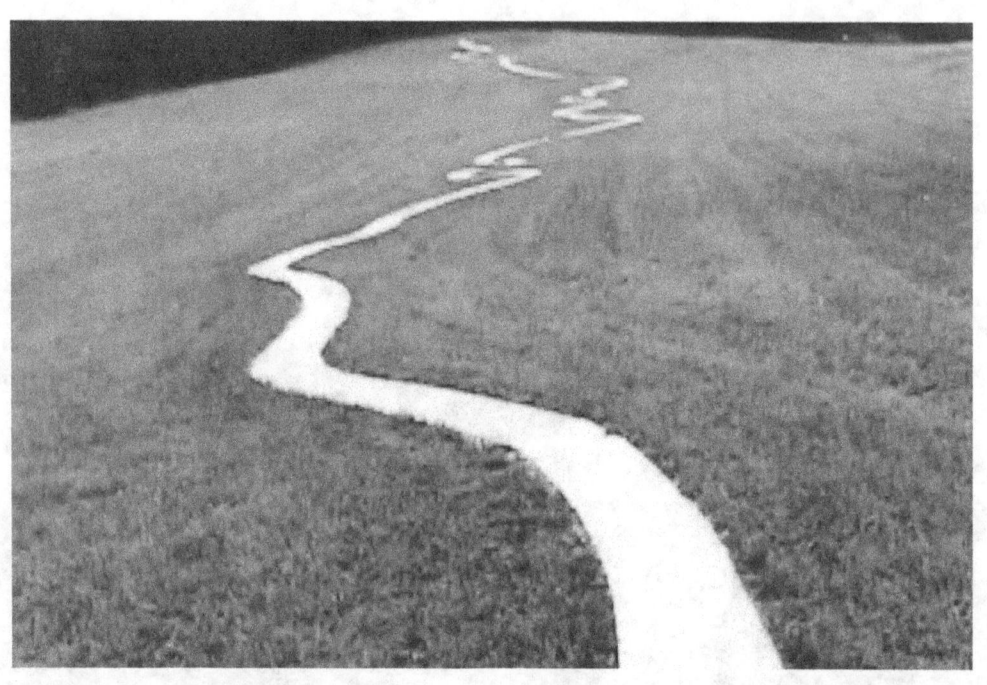

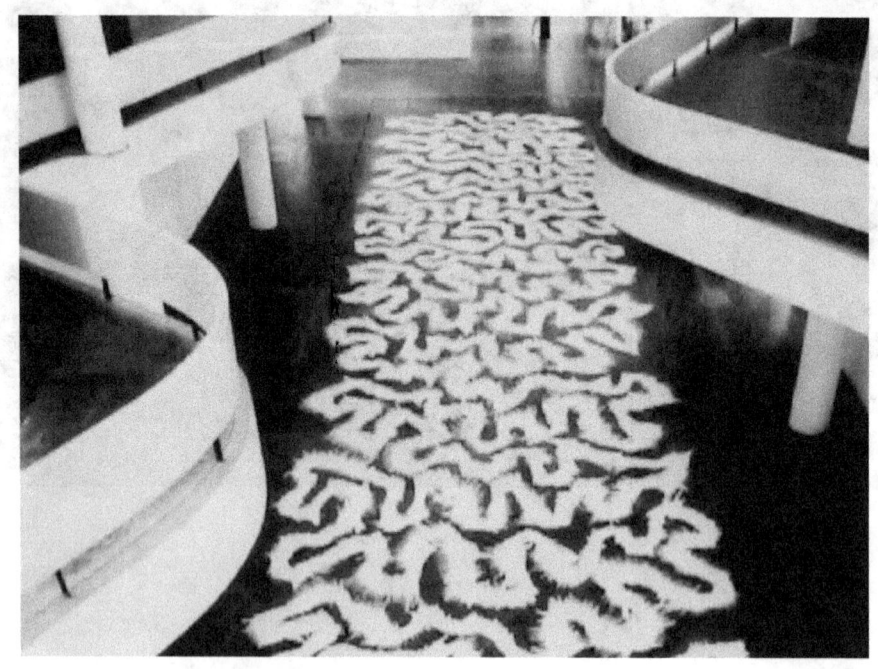

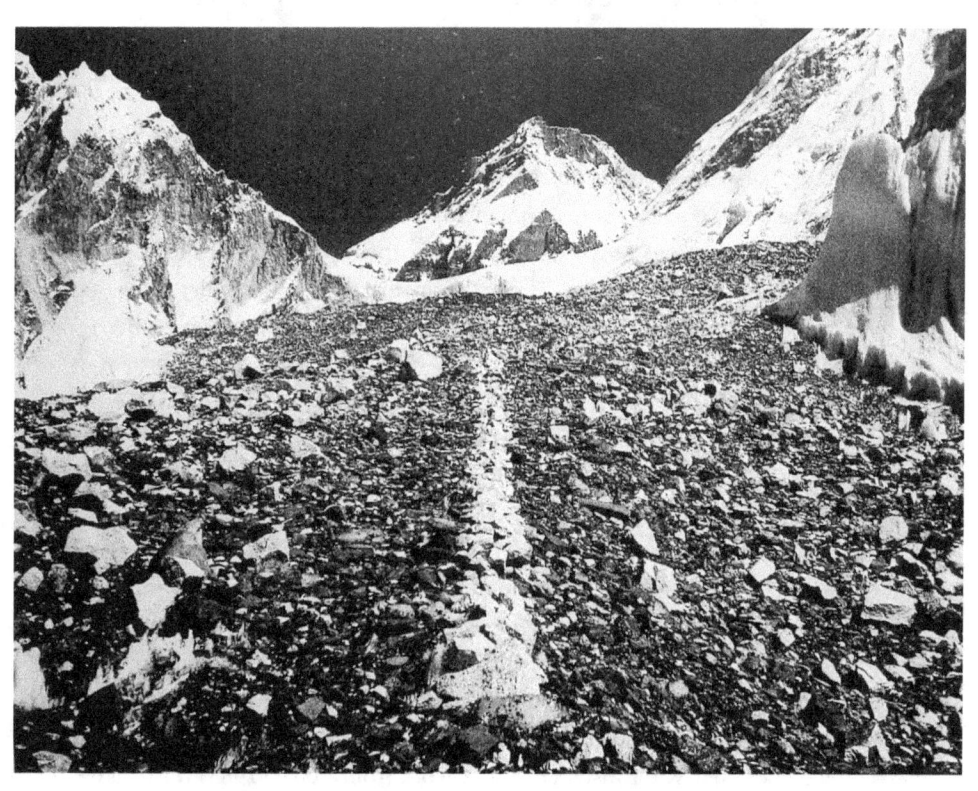

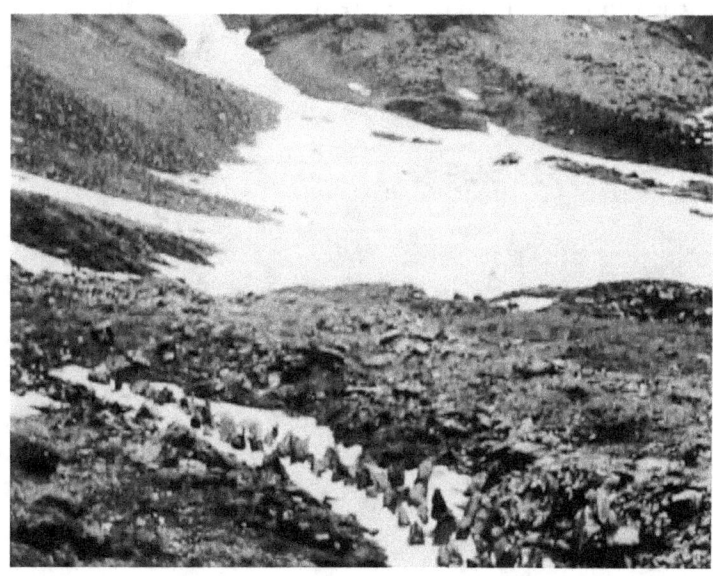

RICHARD LONG: *A FOUR DAY WALK*

Land art is meta-art, art about art, art that relies on other art to 'exist'. It's Conceptual, 'art as language'. Land art exists for a brief moment, then becomes myth, gossip, photography, words. Many of Richard Long's works are simply collections of words, printed in capitals, in Eric Gill's font, Gill Sans, on large pieces of paper. The text printed opposite is be very close to being a Richard Long artwork in itself (although he likes them printed larger).

There's no picture, no map, no reference to anything other than itself. This work is simply these words. At the same time, Long's works have all sorts of readings. He chooses particular words, often plain words, or words used in simple phrases and clauses. The vocabulary Long employs – *road, grass, fields, mud* – is simple and direct, with few embellishments. Nevertheless, Long's text works echo concrete and visual poetry at many points. In the book *Mountains and Waters* there are works with distinctly 'poetic' titles: 'November Sunshine', 'A Spring Walk', 'In the Cloud', 'Dorset Song Lines', 'Walking Up Cedar Creek', 'Dartmoor Stones' and 'Mind Rock'. Long also uses descriptive words which are usually the province of poetry: for instance, a text work from Nepal (1983) reads like cut-up poetry, a poem with verbs and pronouns excised:

GREAT HIMALAYAN TIME A LINE OF MOMENTS
MY FATHER STARLIT SNOW
HUMAN TIME FROZEN BOOTS

A FOUR DAY WALK

A LINE OF GROUND 94 MILES LONG

ROAD STONY TRACK ROAD GRASS FIELD
ROAD BARE ROCK LANE ROAD STONY PATH
HEATHER BURNT MOOR STONY PATH ROAD
ROUGH GRASSLAND RIVERBED SHEEPTRACKS EARTH WALL
ROUGH GRASSLAND GRASS FIELDS BRAMBLES GRASS FIELD
PATH ROAD DUSTY LANE
ROAD GRASS FIELDS EARTH PATH ROAD
SAND BEACH CLIFF PATH ROAD ROCKS
CLIFF PATH SAND DUNES SAND PATH EARTH PATH
ROAD OLD RAILWAY TRACK MUD FLATS SEA WALL
MUD FLATS ROAD RIVERBANK ROAD

ENGLAND 1980

A FOUR DAY WALK

A LINE OF GROUND 94 MILES LONG

ROAD STONY TRACK ROAD GRASS FIELD
ROAD BARE ROCK LANE ROAD STONY PATH
HEATHER BURNT MOOR STONY PATH ROAD
ROUGH GRASSLAND RIVERBED SHEEPTRACKS EARTH WALL
ROUGH GRASSLAND GRASS FIELDS BRAMBLES GRASS FIELD PATH
ROAD DUSTY LANE
ROAD GRASS FIELDS EARTH PATH ROAD
SAND BEACH CLIFF PATH ROAD ROCKS
CLIFF PATH SAND DUNES SAND PATH EARTH PATH
ROAD OLD RAILWAY TRACK MUD FLATS SEA WALL
MUD FLATS ROAD RIVERBANK ROAD

ENGLAND 1980

STONE WALK

FROM ONE STONE TO ANOTHER, PICKING UP AND
CARRYING
EACH STONE TO THE PLACE OF THE NEXT STONE

STONE TO STONE ALLT TO BLANYOY
STONE TO STONE BLANYOY TO HAY BLUFF
STONE TO STONE HAY BLUFF TO TYMPA
STONE TO STONE TYMPA TO Y DÂS
STONE TO STONE Y DÂS TO GIST WEN
STONE TO STONE GIST WEN TO CORN DÛ
STONE TO STONE CORN DÛ TO PEN Y FAN
STONE TO STONE PEN Y FAN TO CRIBIN
STONE TO STONE CRIBIN TO WAUN FÂCH
STONE TO STONE WAUN FÂCH TO PENTWYNGLAS
STONE TO STONE PENTWYNGLAS TO TAL TRWNAU
STONE TO STONE TAL TRWNAU TO Y FAN
STONE TO STONE Y FAN TO TWYN TAL-Y-CEFN
STONE TO STONE TWYN TAL-Y-CEFN TO BLWCH-BACH
STONE TO STONE BWLCH-BACH TO BÂL-MAWR
STONE TO STONE BÂL-MAWR TO GARN-WEN
STONE TO STONE GARN-WEN TO SUGAR LOAF
STONE TO STONE SUGAR LOAF TO ALLT

A 101 MILE WALK IN THE BLACK MOUNTAINS AND BRECON
BEACONS

WALES 1984

RICHARD LONG: *STONE CIRCLES*

Some land artists, such as Richard Long, maintain that their stone circles are subjective, private, individual works, quite different from the public, social art of the prehistoric stones circles. The ancient stone rings were made by a group of people, a society, constructed, perhaps, according to the plans of a priestly elite. Land art circles are the work of one person, but a major postwar artist is no less a member of the cultural, æsthetic elite. Prehistoric stone circles may have been made for religious rituals, perhaps connected with the position of certain astronomical bodies. Land art stone circles are for private consumption, for an onlooker who wanders into a gallery or a space then out again, back into the hurly burly and stench of the city. Yet the ancient sacred sites and land art/ Postminimal/ Arte Povera earthworks have much in common, because art and religion join at so many points.

One or two of Long's stone circles are small - *Circle of Standing Stones* (1983), which is 26 stones arranged in a circle of a half metre in diameter, *Cornwall Slate Circle* (1982), 34 stones in a 2 metre circle, and *Standing Stone Circle* (1982), 36 stones in a similar size circle. The small stone circles are often made of standing stones, and many of the outdoor circles are of this type (*Stones in Bolivia*, 1981, for instance). Long's use of standing stones, rather than ones laid flat, echoes prehistoric stone circles – for instance, the Scottish stone circle (*Stones and Stac Pollaidh*, 1981), or the Icelandic *Touchstone, Shelter From the Storm* (1982). Long's small stone circles are intimate works compared to the broad, large pieces. In Britain there are a number of small stone circles which produce similar atmospheres of human-scale and intimacy (such as the small circles on the ridges of hills in Dorset). 'I like simple, emotional, quiet, vigorous art' says Long.[1] While the large circles in the galleries of Western cities speak of polished, upmarket art, the small, 1.5 metre stone circles speak of small wayside shrines. The large gallery circles are planned and organized months in advance, but still look spontaneous. Long's small outdoor stone circles, though, are direct and spontaneous responses to a landscape.

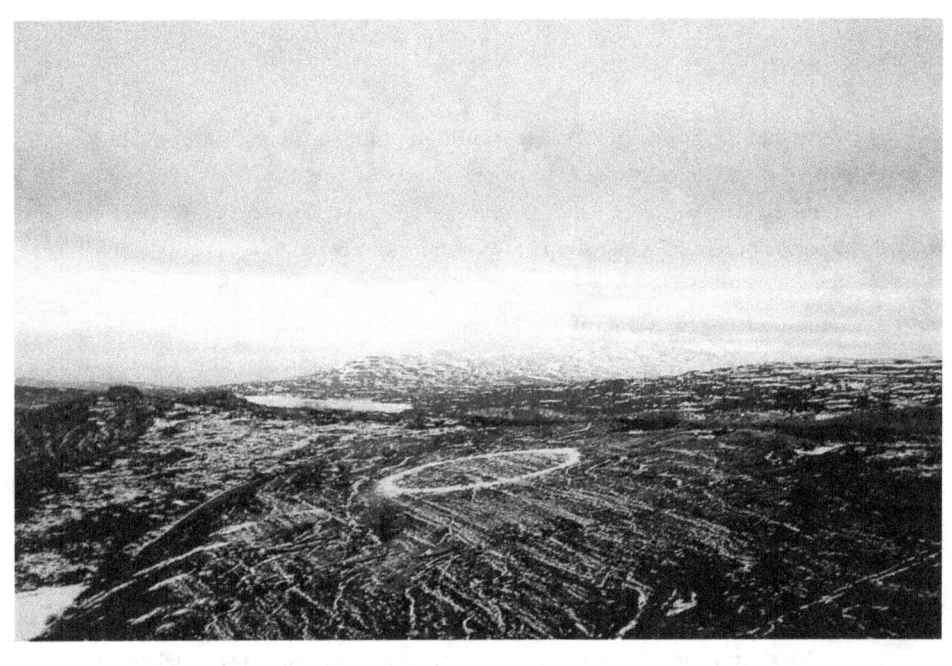

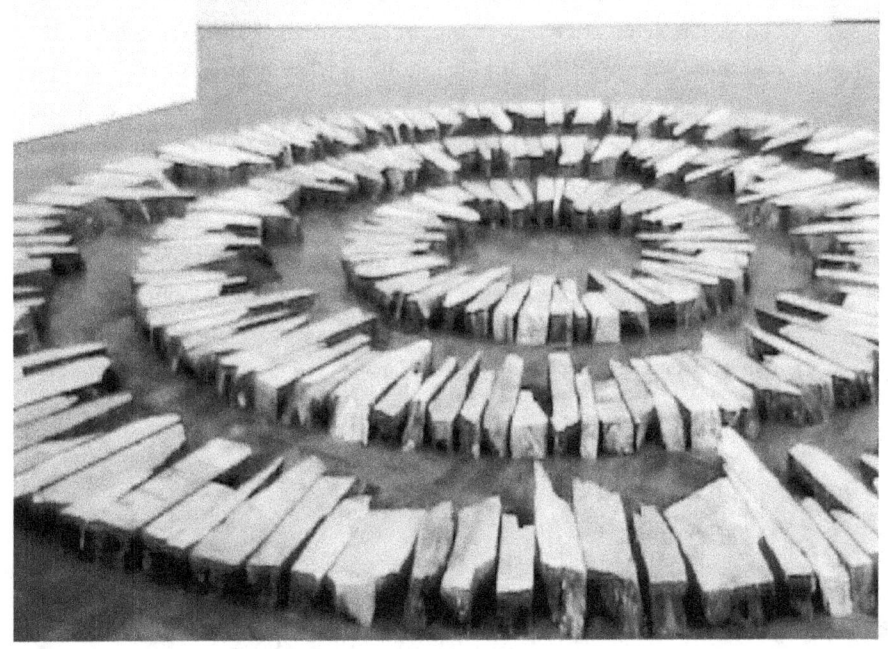

RICHARD LONG: *CIRCLES*

Stressing the Romantic heritage/ tradition of Richard Long's art only makes up part of the picture. Like other artists of the 1960s (whether Pop, Conceptual, Minimal, Process, ABC, 'Cool', Arte Povera, Body, Perform-ance or other art), Long suppresses notions of poetry and Romanticism. 'My art is not urban, nor is it romantic' Long says (R. Fuchs, 236). Looking at *A Line in Iceland*, a line of boulders in a wilderness space, shot against a brooding sky and a backdrop of snowbound mountains, one can see the affinities with the High Romanticism of Wordsworth's poeticizing of the Lake District, Turner and his watercolours of Snowdonia or the Alps, or Ruskin and his evocation of the Sublime.[1] True, *Red Slate Circle,* in the Fogg Art Museum in Boston, or *Sandstone Spiral* in the National Gallery of Canada, or the *Pine Tree Bark Circle* in Lyon, or *Bushwood Circle* in the National Gallery of Victoria, Melbourne, are set on museum floors, in the clean, sparse gallery environment, and look Minimal.

What concerns Richard Long is that '[e]ach work is appropriate to its place and context', and the wilderness works and the museum pieces are 'equal and complementary'. What counts, Long says, is the feelings that the work, whether inside or outside, arouses: 'my ambition is basically with the emotional power of the work, in both idea and image.'[2] Walking, nature and the landscape are at the heart of Long's work,[3] but Long knows, as any professional artist must know, that the art world conducts its business indoors. The slate, stick and wood circles look like late 20th century art-works, not 'Romantic', but Minimal, Conceptual and Arte Povera, like Carl Andre's copper and zinc plates. They have a coolness and clarity that one associates with Flavin, Morris, Smith and LeWitt. Long's stone circles make sense to the viewer partly because of a grounding in the discourses of postwar art. Without a grounding in the circularity of signs that flow around postwar art, one might not know how to make full sense of Long's circles. True, the circle as a shape has been around for eons, but only in the postwar era have circles been made out of bits of the landscape, in galleries and in landscape settings in this particular way.

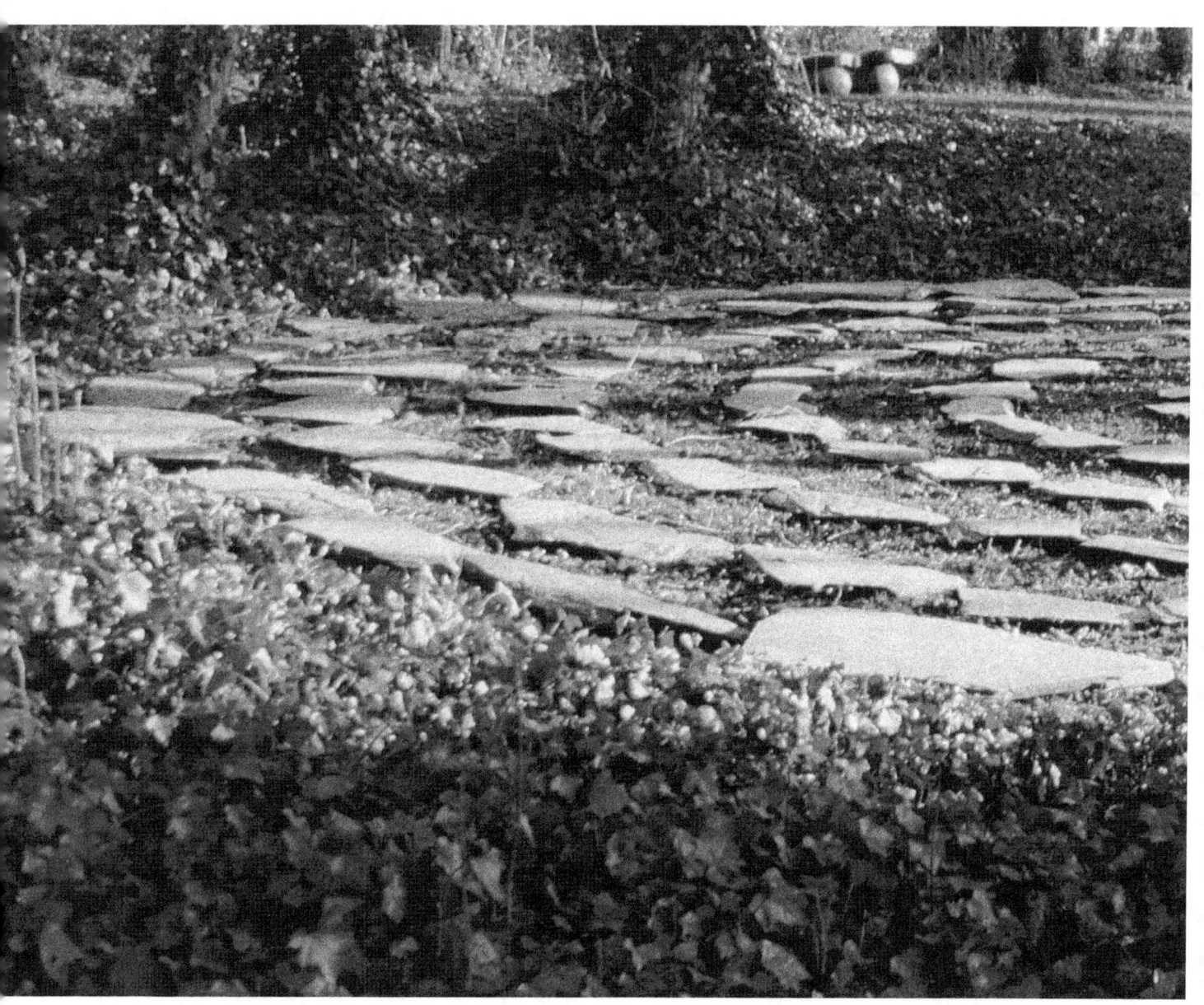

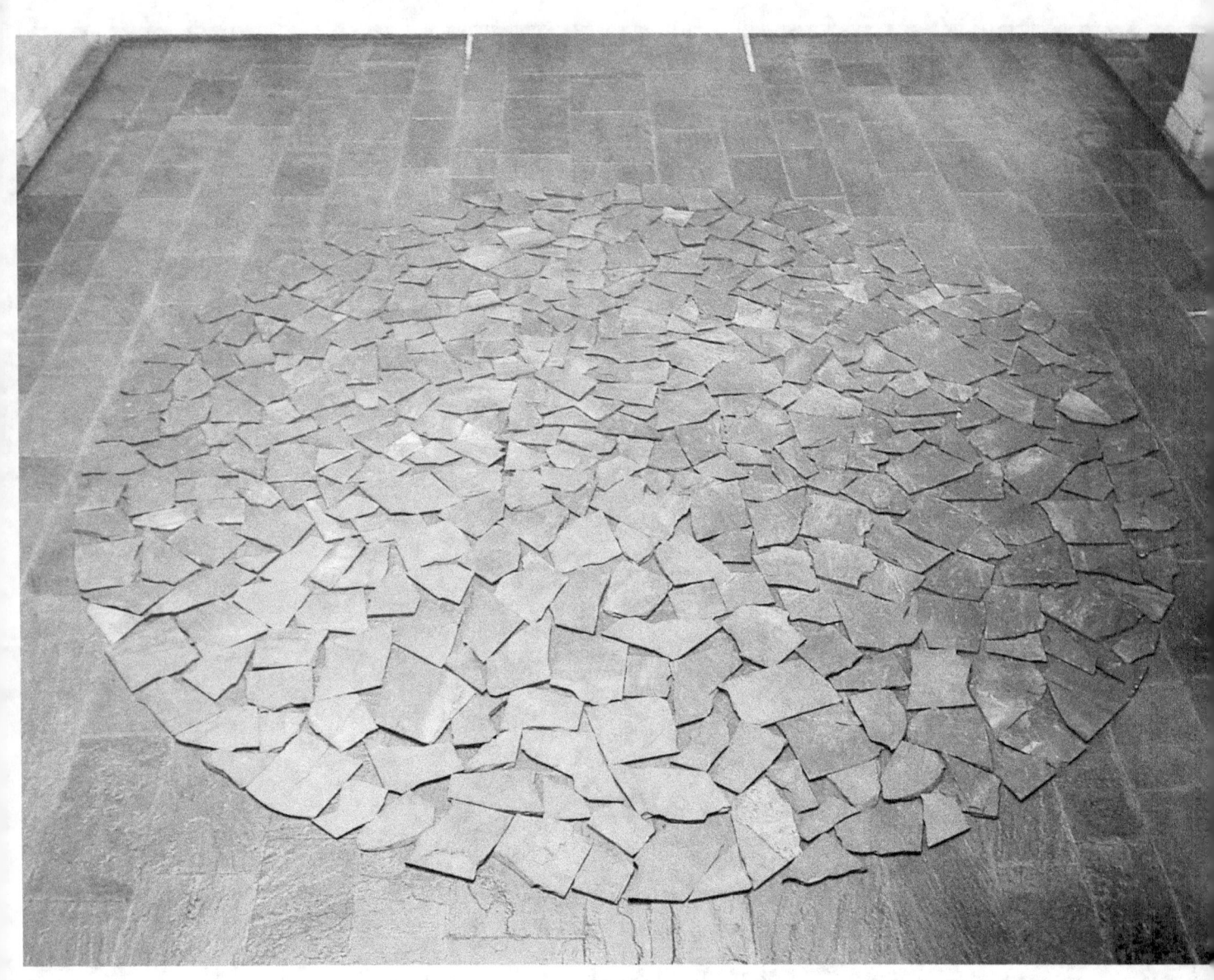

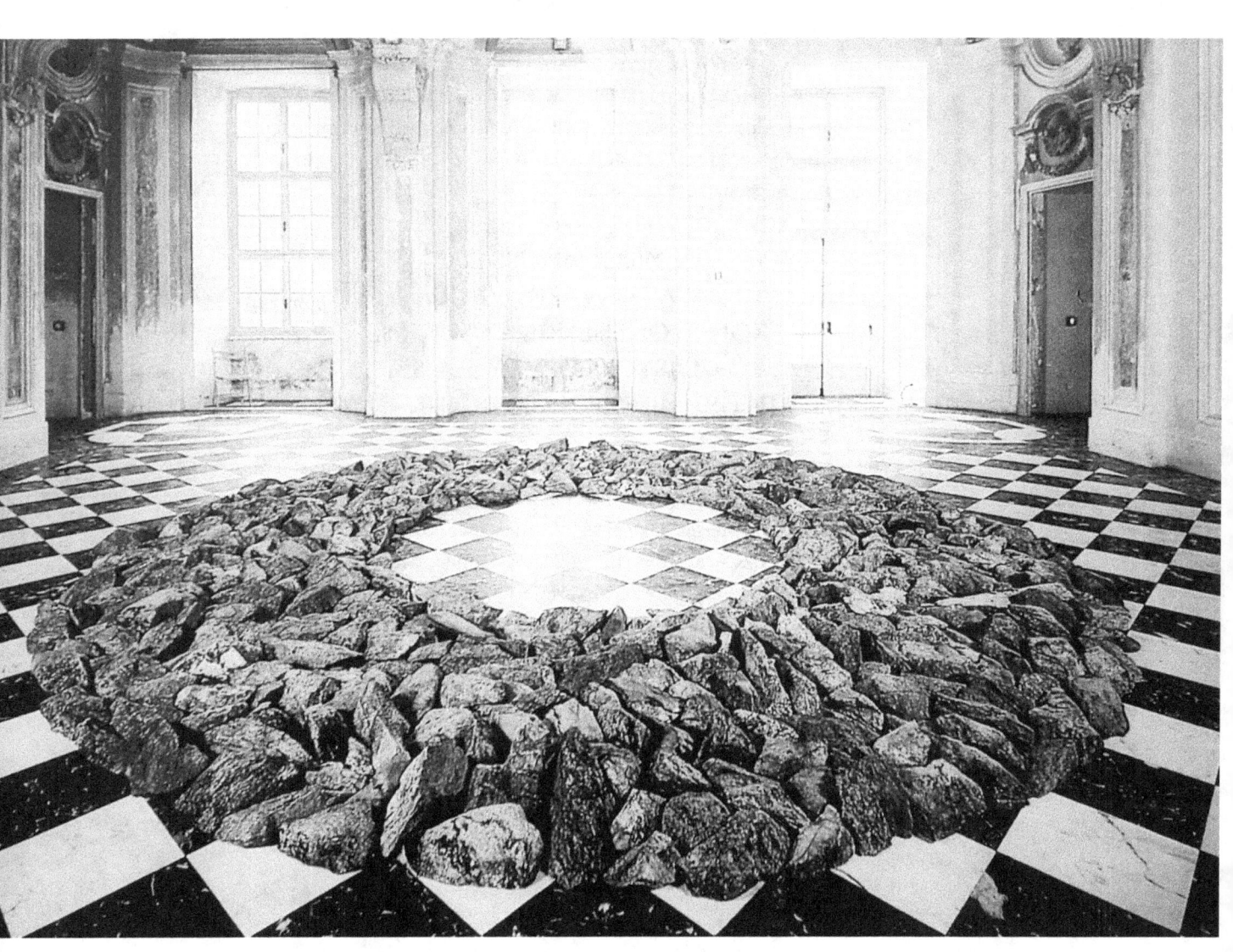

RICHARD LONG: *ON MIDSUMMER'S DAY*

Locations such as Silbury Hill and Glastonbury have long been revered by people as holy sites, 'places of power' as they are called. Land artists capitalize on the mystery of such places. One of Richard Long's works is a walk between two prime magical centres of Britain, Stonehenge and Glastonbury, both deeply associated with prehistoric astronomy, ancient priesthoods, Arthurian legend, Merlin the Magician, the Age of Aquarius, ley lines, Druids, geomancy, and so on:

ON MIDSUMMER'S DAY
A WESTWARD WALK
FROM STONEHENGE AT SUNRISE
TO GLASTONBURY BY SUNSET
FORTY FIVE MILES FOLLOWING THE DAY[1]

The photograph that goes with this text is the sort of picture postcard view one finds in newsagents and heritage centres around the UK: Glastonbury Tor at sunset. Like St Paul's, the Tower of London, Big Ben, Buckingham Palace, Beefeaters, the changing of the guard, red buses and telephone boxes, this is one of the archetypal images of Britain. And, typically, it is Glastonbury Tor that Long chooses to photograph, not the shops nearby, the electric pylons, the rubbish tips behind the trunk roads, the rows of garages, the housing estates.

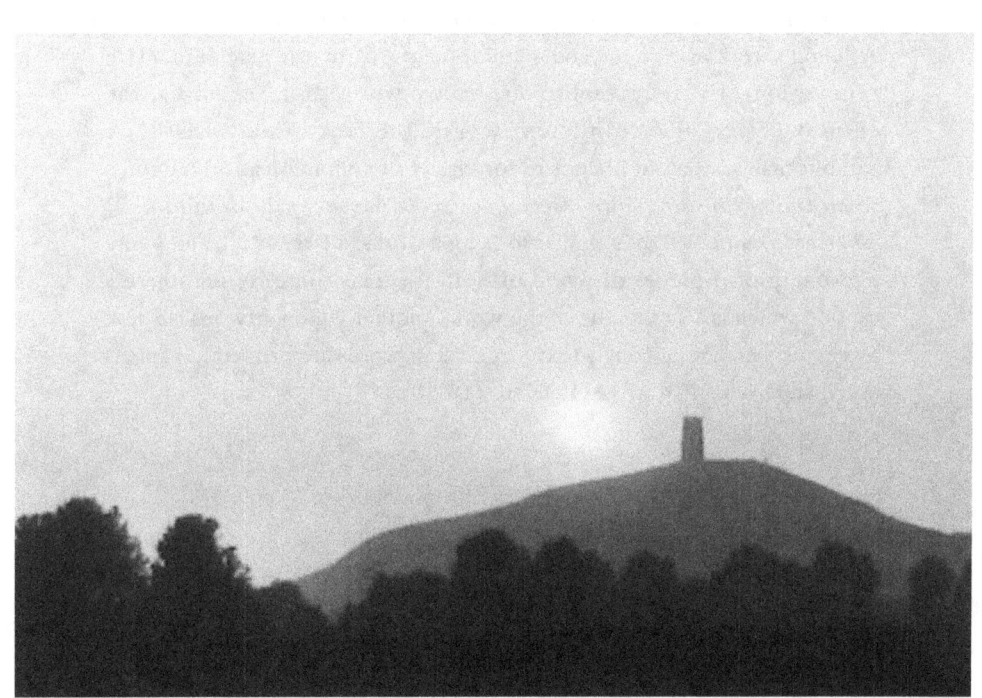

HAMISH FULTON: *ROCK FALL ECHO DUST*

Hamish Fulton is Richard Long's contemporary (he was born a year later than Long). Fulton is a companion of Long's many journeys and walks (and works). Fulton writes: '[m]y work is about the experience of walking' (echoing Long's ethics). Fulton continues: '[t]he framed artwork is about a state of mind – it cannot convey the experience of the walk.' What counts in Fulton's work may be the communication of a particular state of mind (in Zen fashion). The reduction to one or two words, like Zen *haiku*, the unfussy design of Fulton's text works, the lack of extra æsthetic paraphernalia, attest to his desire for clarity of communication. Fulton's *Seven Days (Whistling Elk): a seven day walk in the Rocky Mountains of Alberta Canada* (1978) is similar to Long's works: a large black and white photograph (of pieces of wood on soil, it seems to be) is set above a caption which is also the title of the work. Another Fulton artwork is a text piece, just like one of Long's text pieces: four words are printed in capitals in red and black: 'ROCK/ FALL/ ECHO/ DUST'.

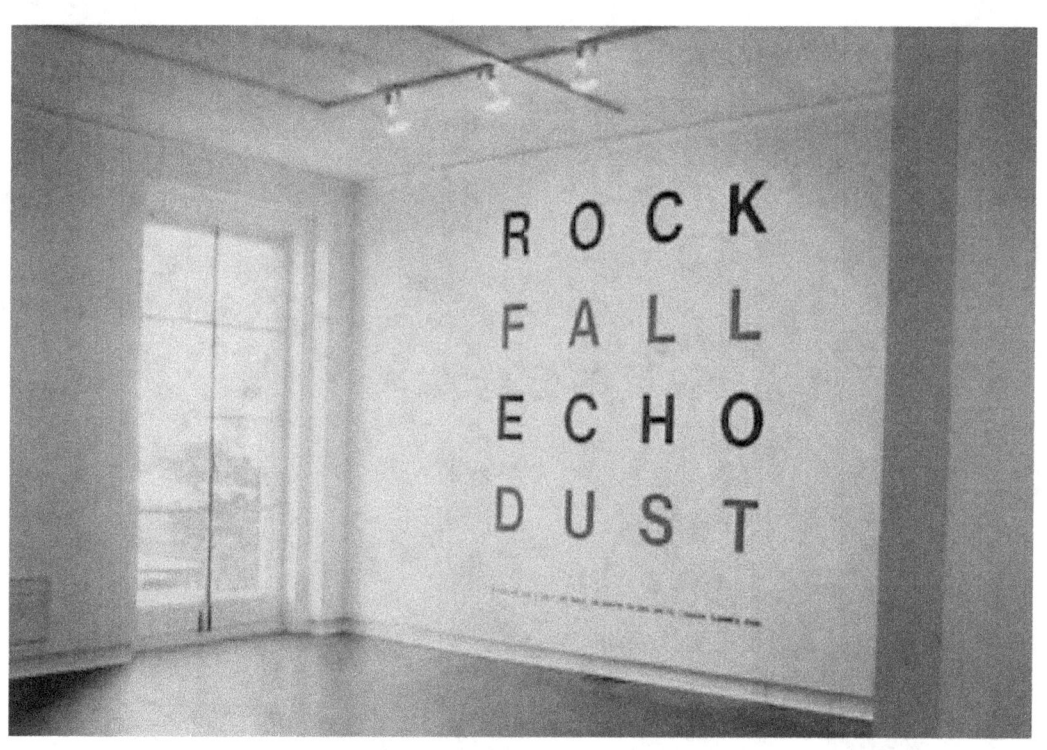

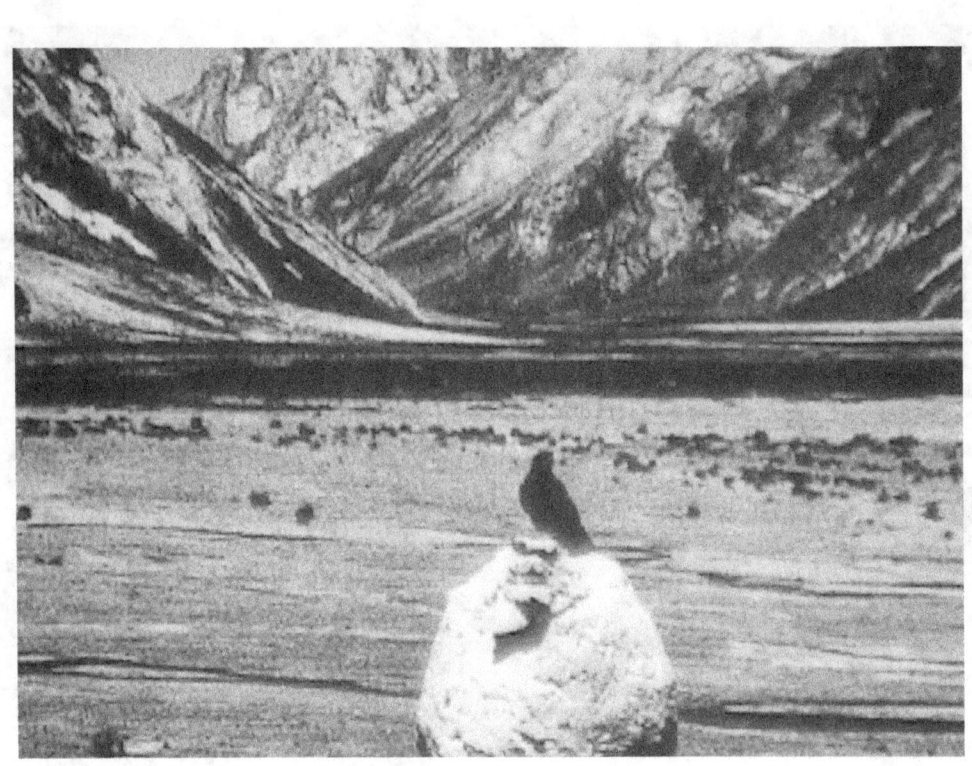

NO TALKING
FOR SEVEN DAYS

TALKING FOR SEVEN DAYS IN A WOOD JANUARY FULL MOON CAIRNGORMS SCOT

ALAN SONFIST

Some environmental/ action/ conceptual artworks had a built-in imperm-
anence, such as Allan Kaprow's *Fluids*, large structures made from blocks
of ice, which were left to melt. In "Natural Phenomena as Public Monuments" (1968), land artist Alan Sonfist suggested building 'museums of air'
in cities, which would 'recapture the smells of earth, trees and vegetation
different seasons and at different historical times, so that people would be
able to experience what has been lost' (1978). Sonfist also suggested
monumentalizing the natural world with sounds: '[c]ontinuous loops of
natural sounds at the natural level of volume can be placed on historic sites'
(ibid.).

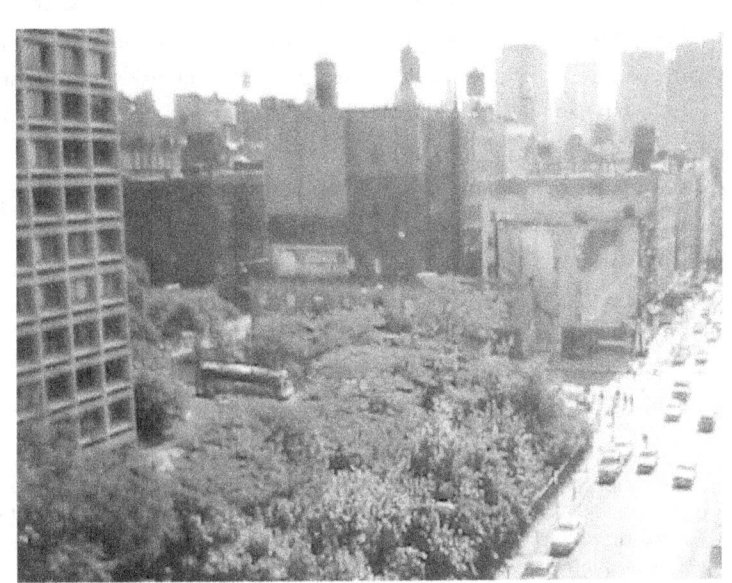

WOLFGANG LAIB

Wolfgang Laib dusts the Earth with pollen, to form an enormous square layer of brilliant yellow. The delicacy – and potency – of the sculpture is immediately apparent. This is the sort of sculpture that exerts a syn-æsthetic power over the gallery goer: the pollen affects not only the visual sense with its incandescent hues, but also affects smell, taste and touch. Another of Laib's installations is *The Passageway* (1988-93), made up of huge panels of beeswax. 'I believe that the impossible, the invisible and visions can become reality if one really wants to make the effort' said Laib.[1]

In the Japanese Zen garden, colours are carefully orchestrated, so that a single leaf can set off a vast acreage of predominantly green or ochre. In the Japanese garden, notions of *feng shui* control how a landscape is shaped by humans. In the system of *feng shui*, the elements of a garden or a building must be in harmony with the natural forces of air, water and earth. Get it wrong and you mess up your creation. The Zen or Taoist harmonizing approach is very much that of land art. In the manner of the Greenpeace/ecological follower, land artists speak of wanting to be in harmony with nature. Land artists, are seen as ecological artists, artists committed to ecological issues. Robert Rosenblum writes:

> There's a German artist Wolfgang Laib who does something of this sort too. He spends a lot of time in the woods gathering such things as pollen and collecting it and forming minimal geometric patterns out of gossamer and natural materials such as honey or dust of various kinds. It is some kind of ecological last gasp of communion with some pure beautiful stuff of nature. I guess this attitude is expiring even though it may, as in the case of Richard Long, still produce some marvellous artists.[2]

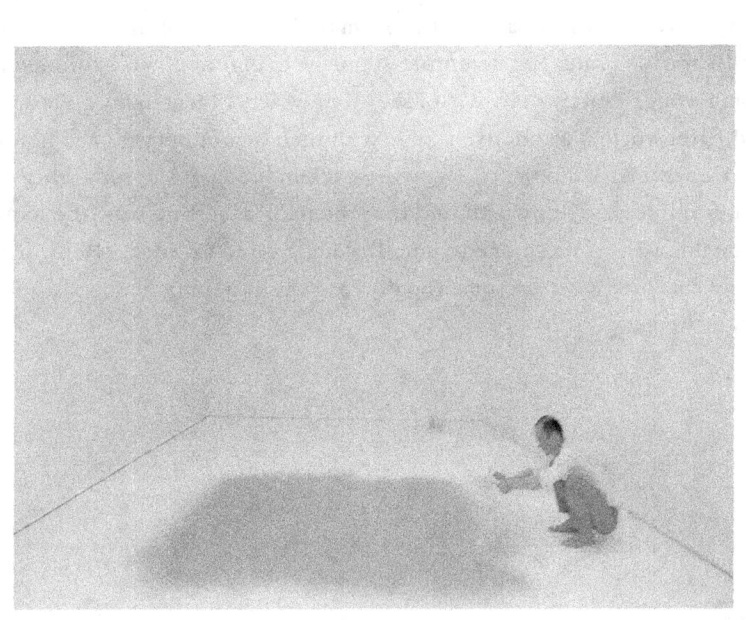

BARBARA HEPWORTH

Barbara Hepworth's organic forms, as with Constantin Brancusi's, hover between subjectivity and objectivity, between natural form and æsthetic abstraction (as in her *Two Forms*, for example). Like Brancusi, Hepworth maintained that she always returned to nature, and took her inspiration from nature. For her, nature meant the (Cornish) landscape, and the human body. 'We return always to the human form - the human form in landscape' she said. Her sculpture stems from emotion and expression, from feeling: 'I rarely draw what I see - I draw what I feel in my body' she said.[1] Hepworth's distinctive forms, with their smooth curves and holes, are clearly sensual objects. Hepworth acknowledged the sensuality of sculptural forms. Hepworth said that the natural setting was 'the most tremendously inspiring one to me'. Driving around Cornwall, Hepworth found that it was her personal (bodily) response to particular landscapes that mattered.[2]

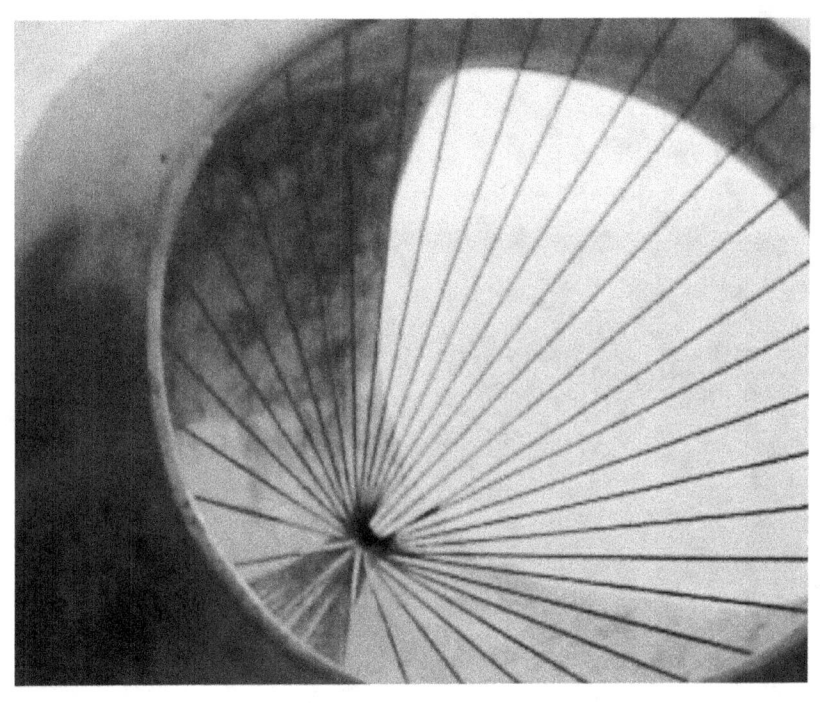

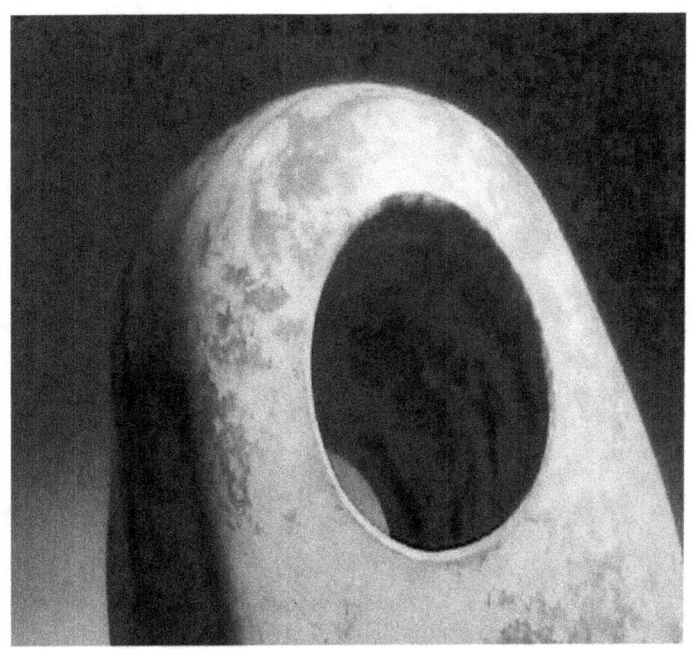

SOME MORE EXAMPLES
OF LAND ART

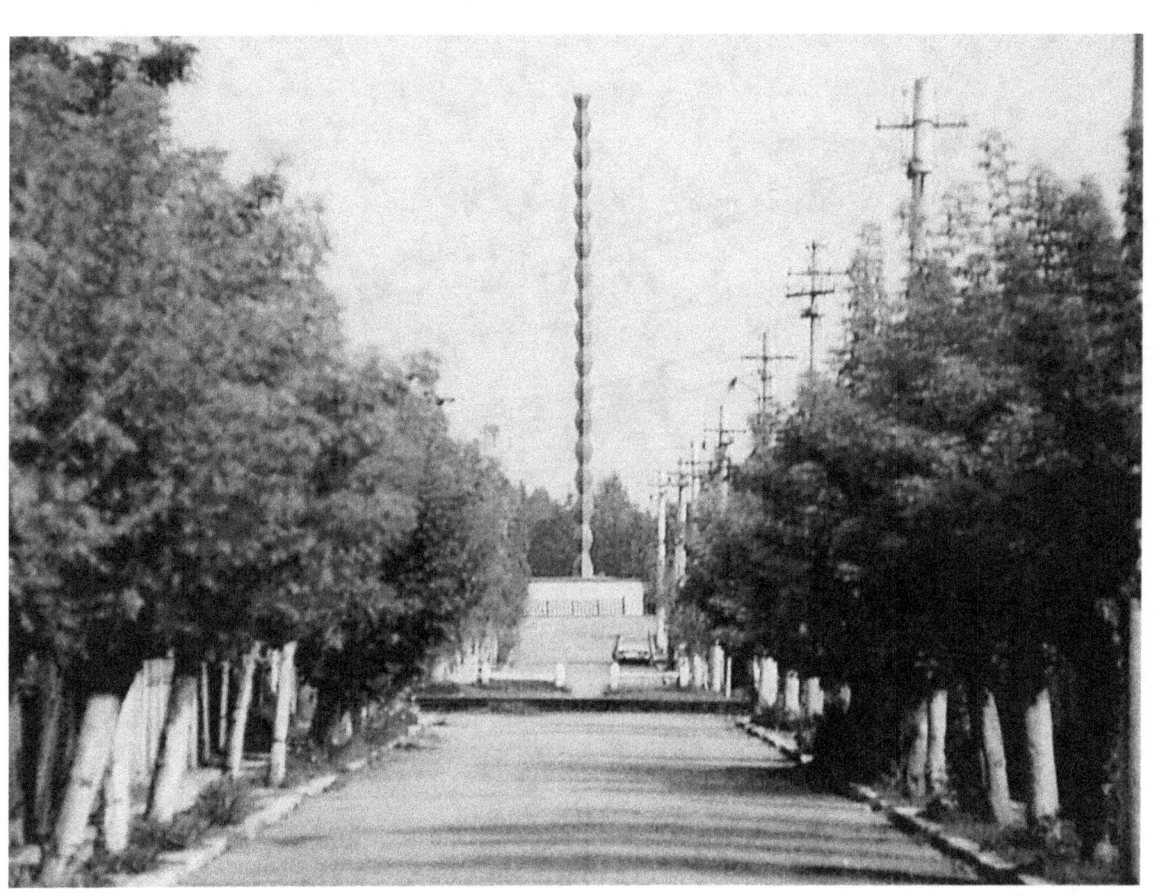

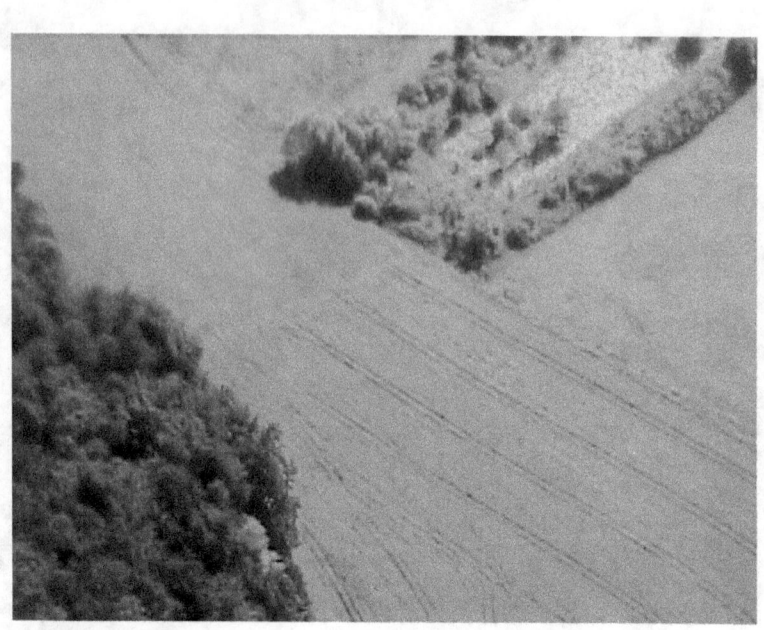

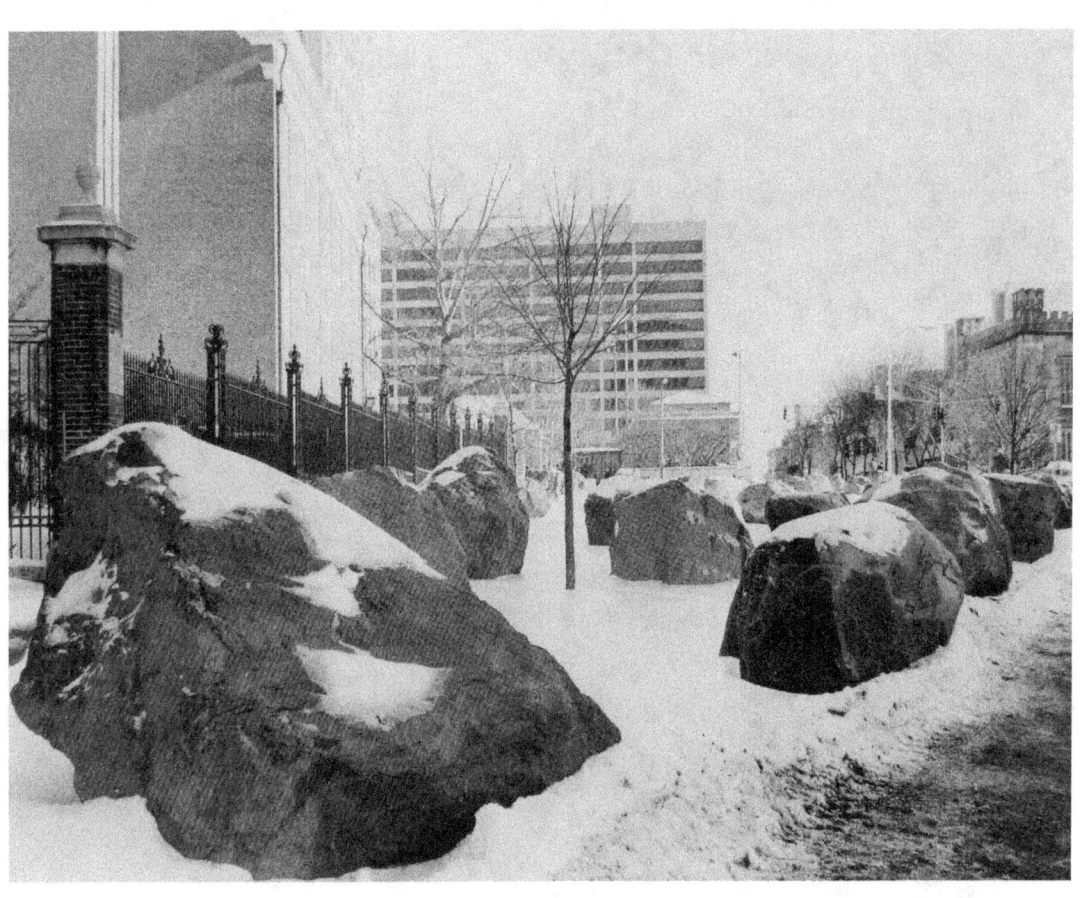

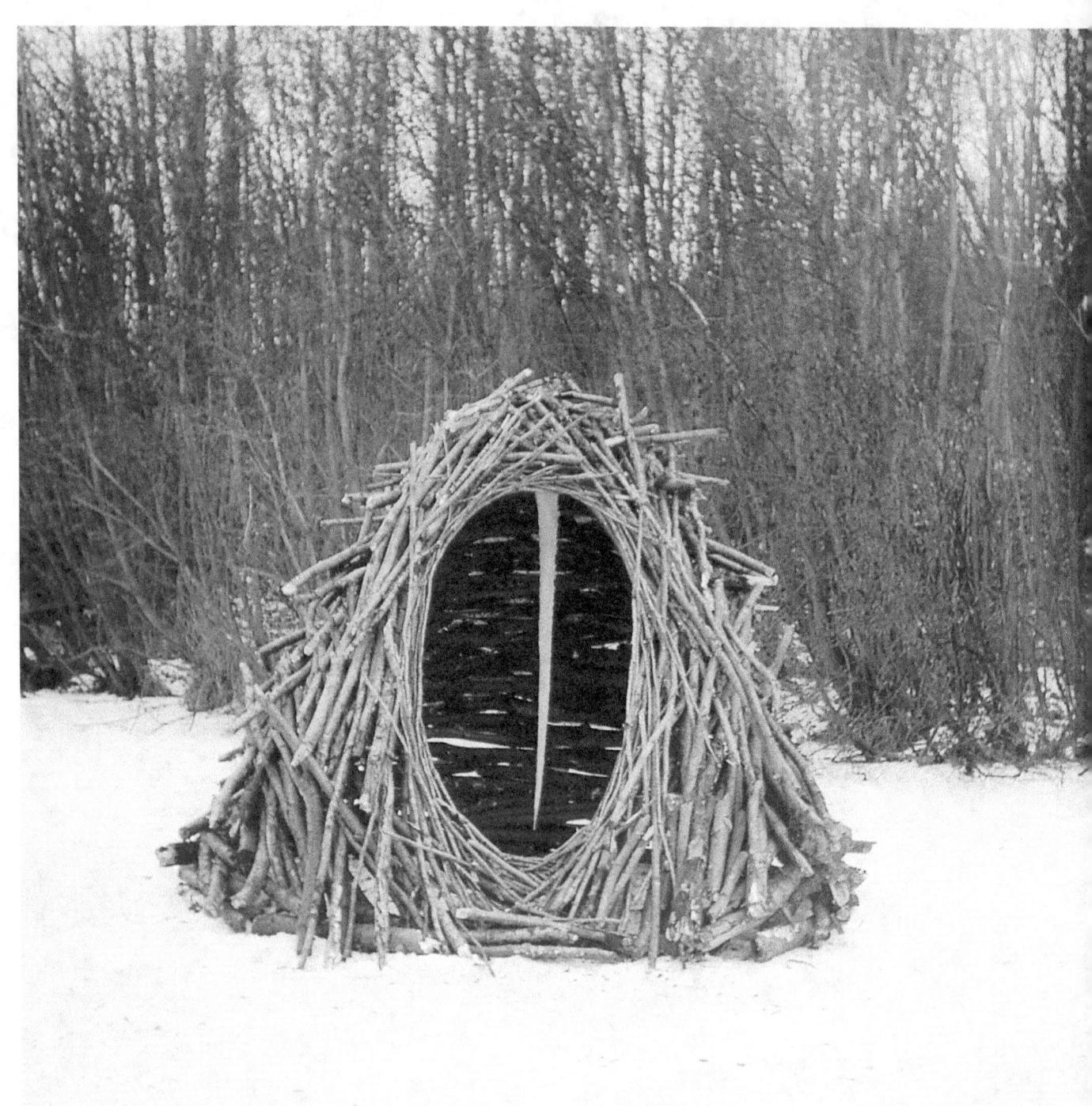

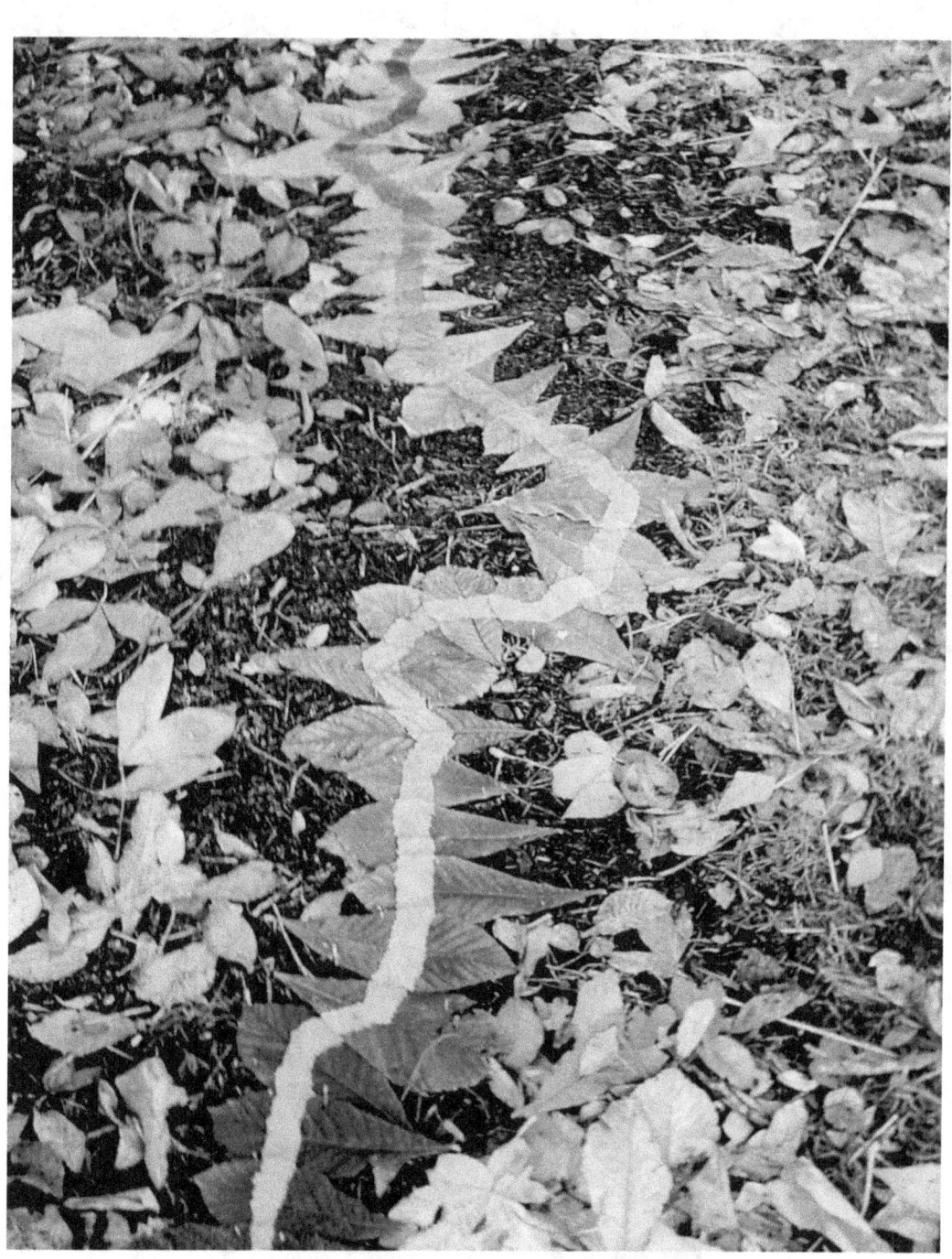

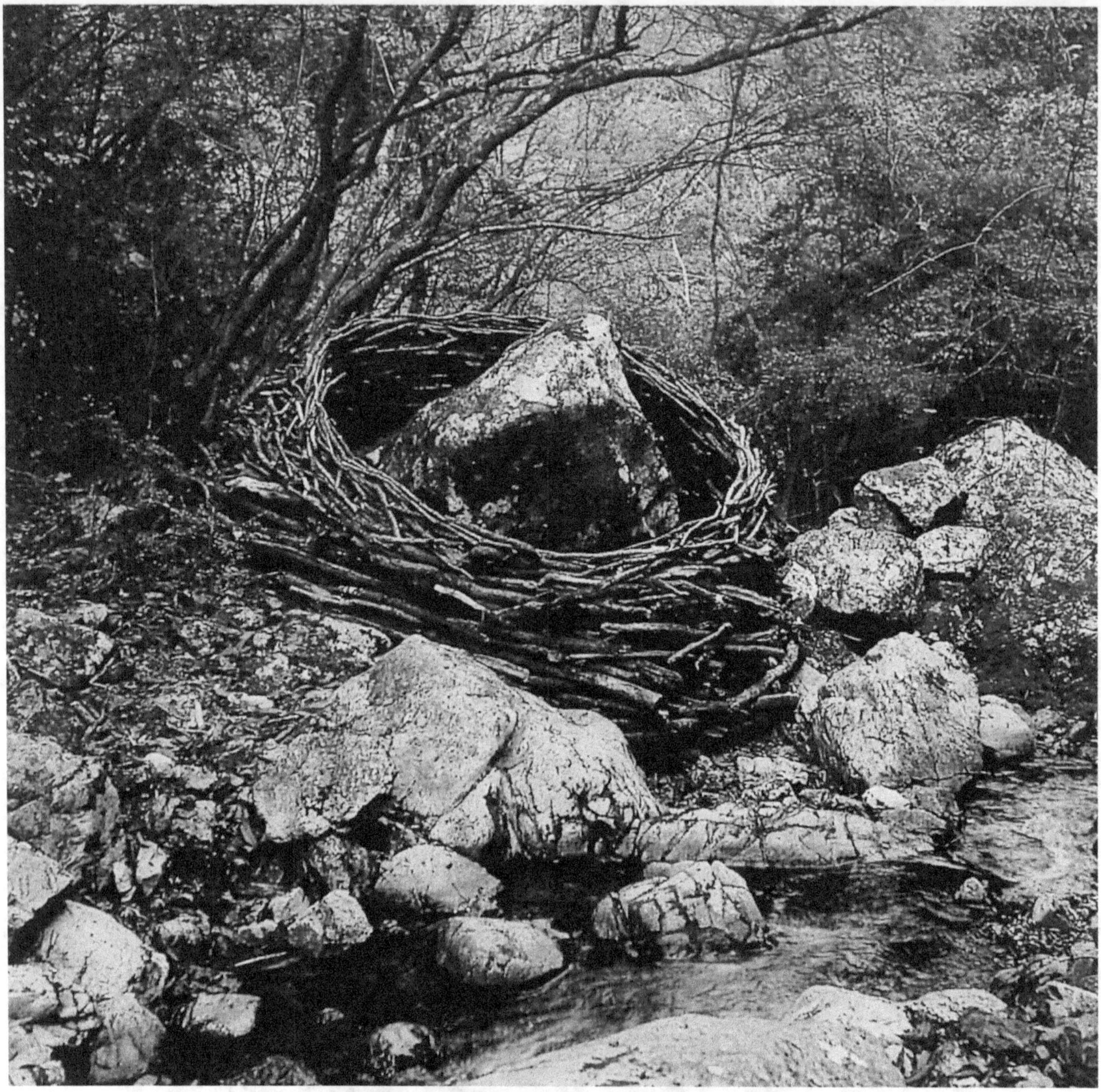

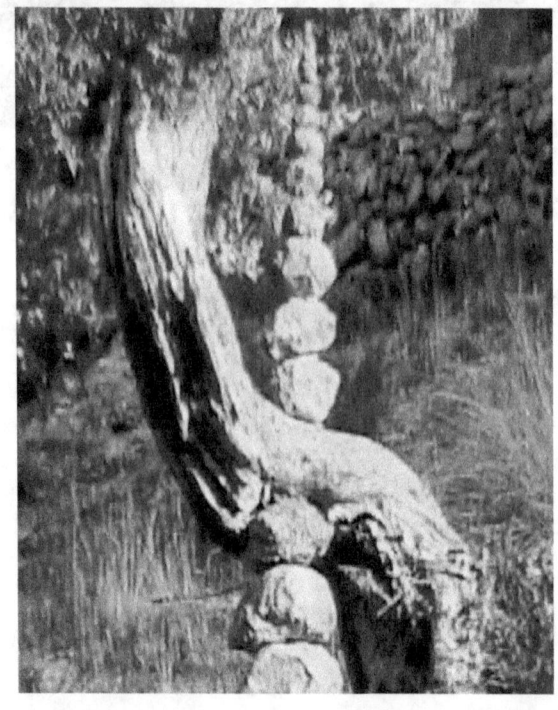

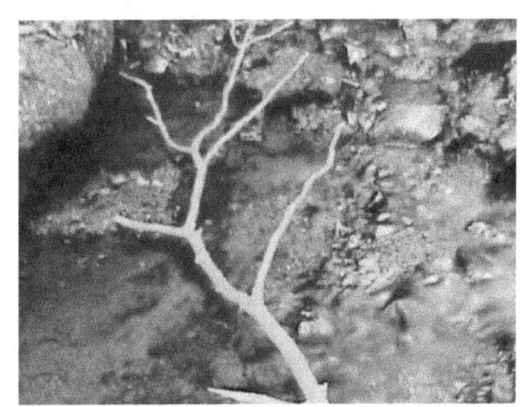

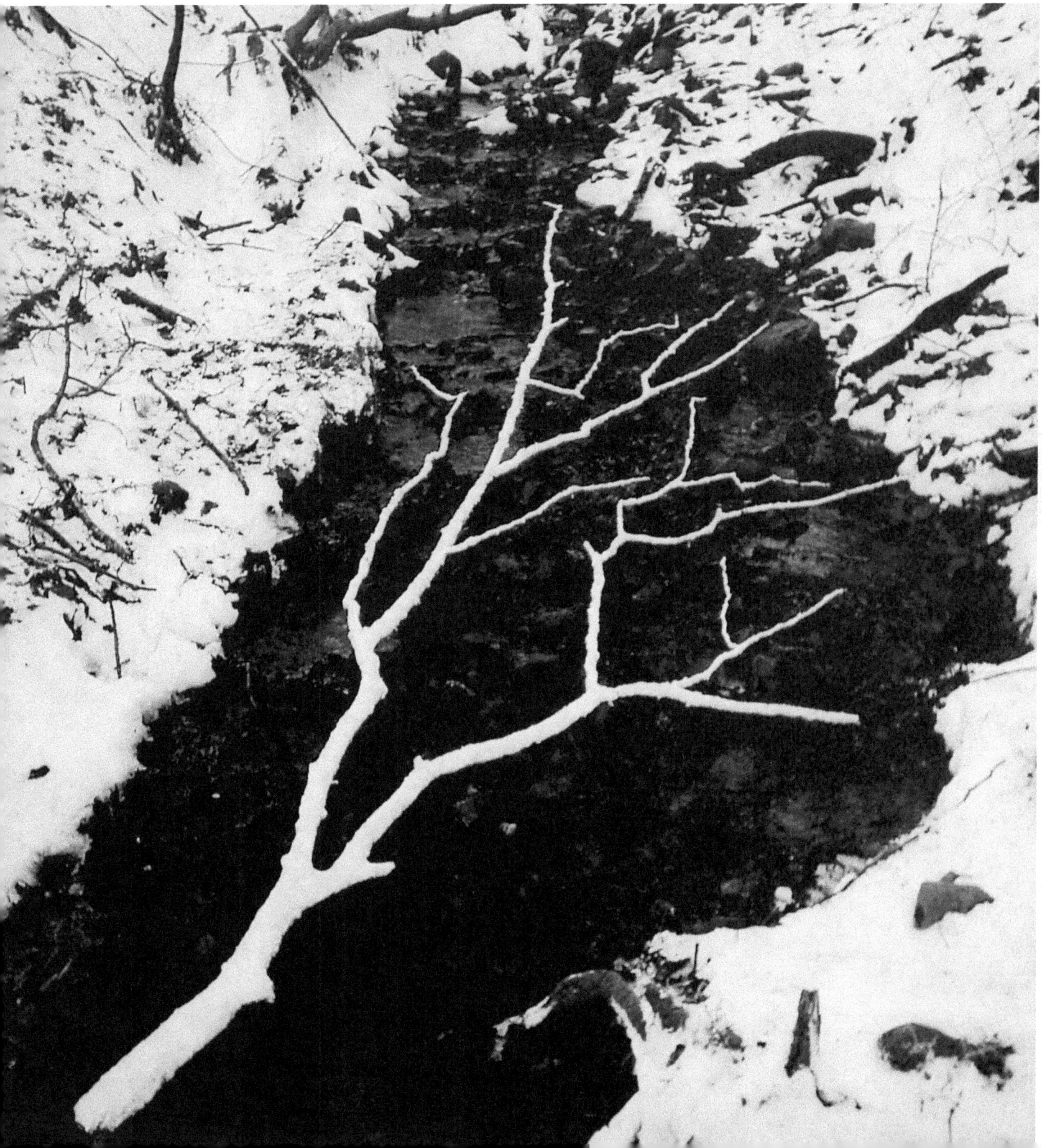

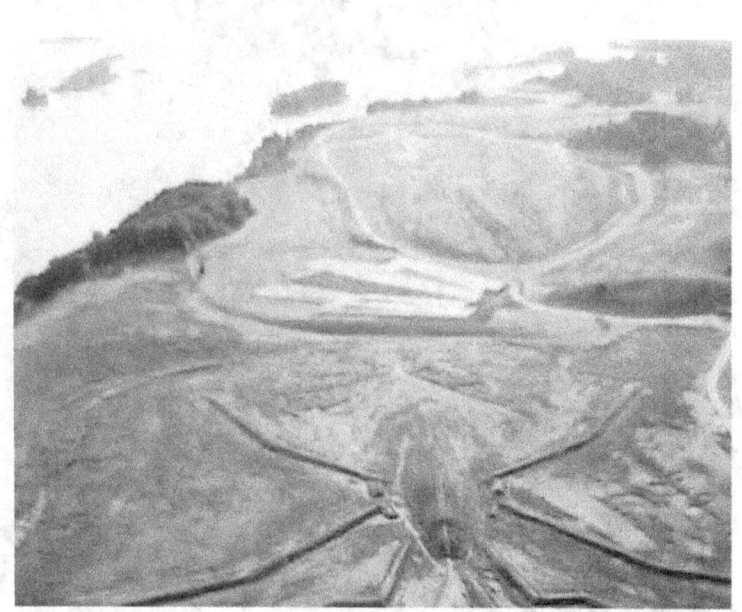

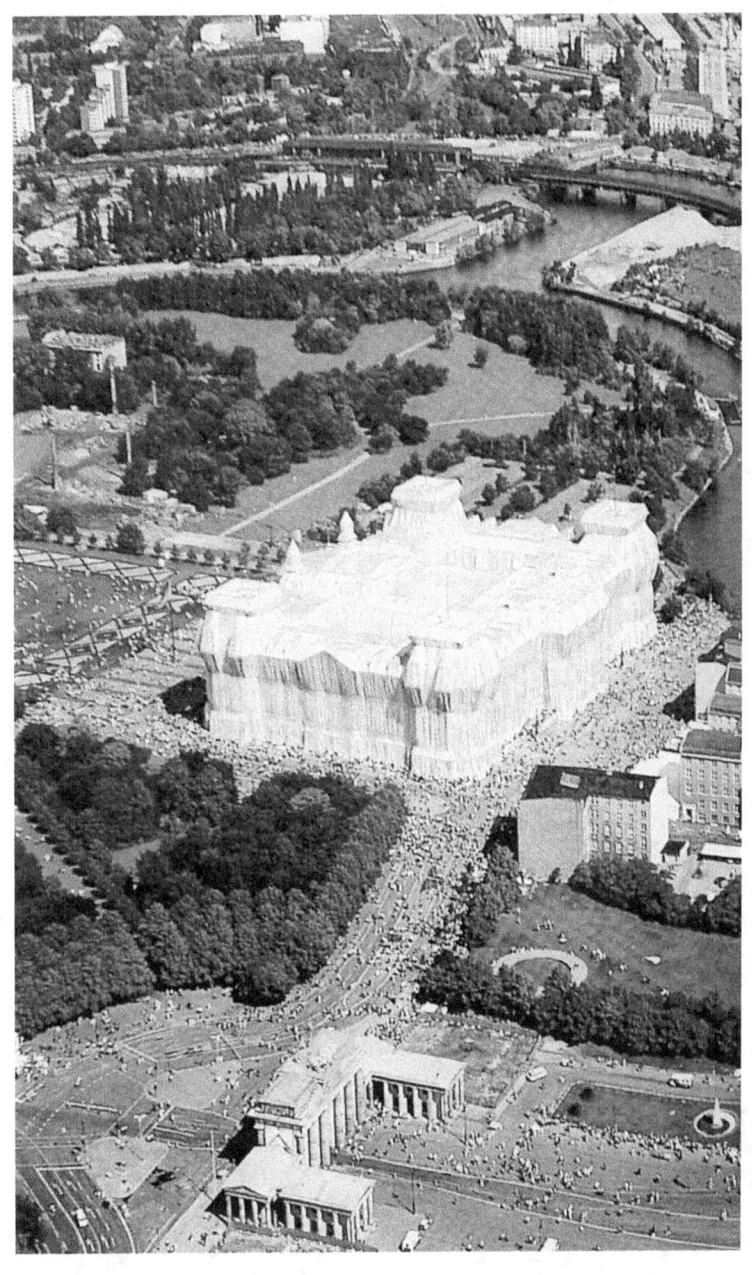

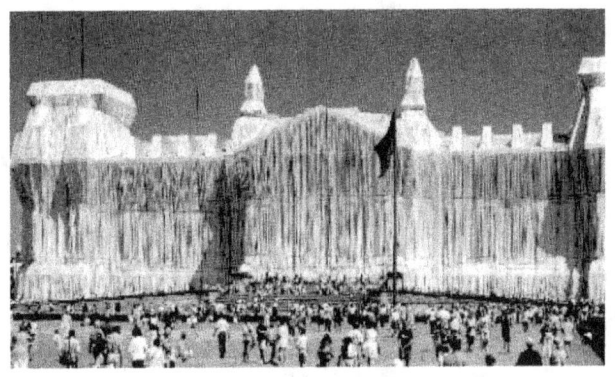

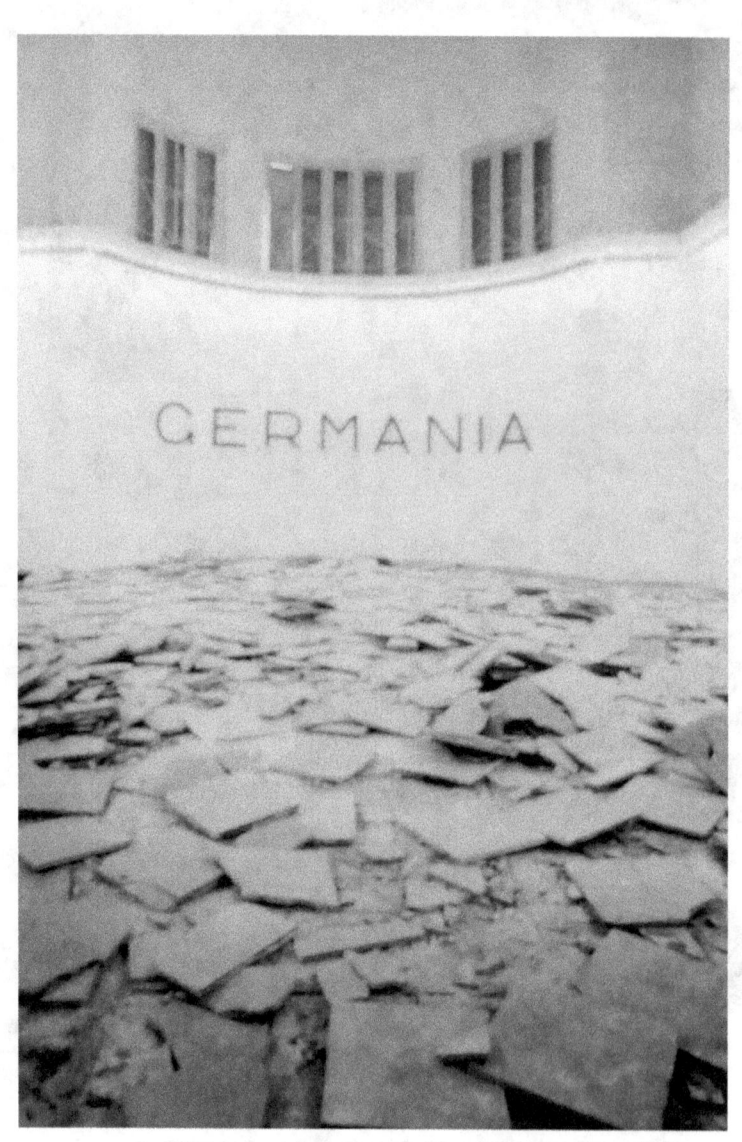

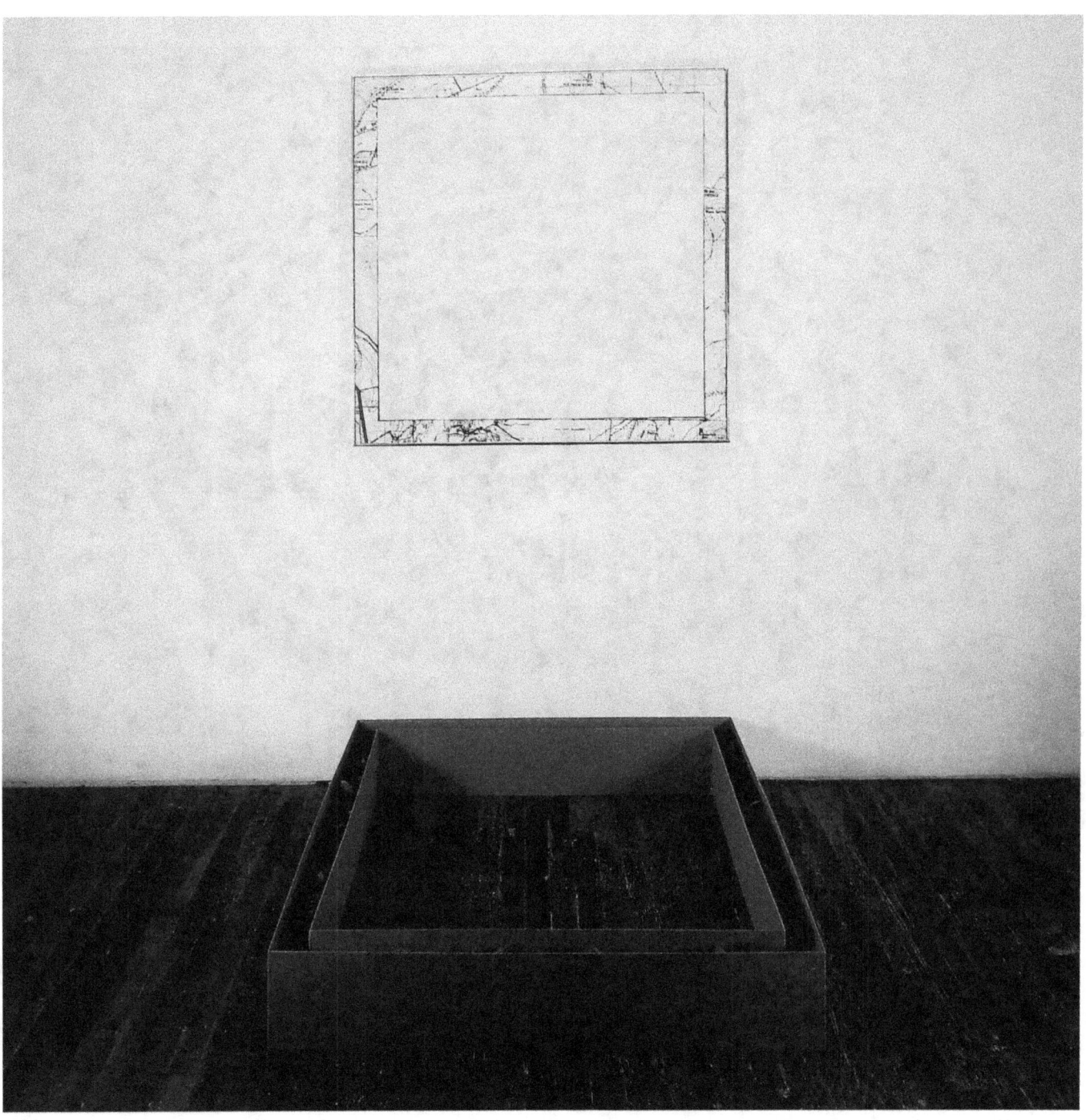

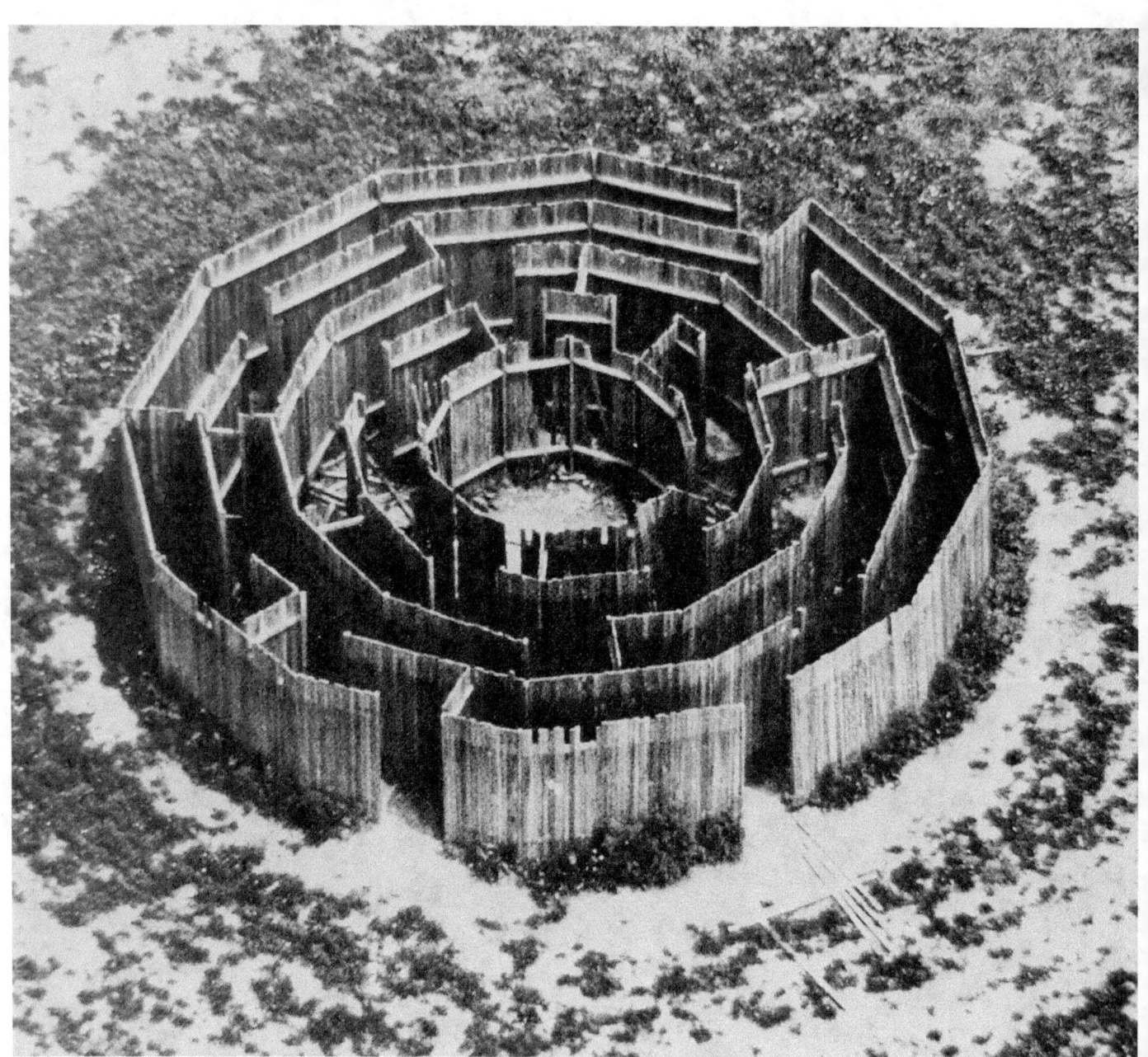

Notes

INTRODUCTION

1. In B. Redhead, 22.
2. S. Ross, 1993, 161.
3. C. Greenberg, "Abstract, Representational, and so forth", in 1961, 133.
4. Quoted in Norbert Lynton, introduction to *Tony Cragg*, Fifth Triennale India, British Council, 1982, 2.
5. Mircea Eliade, "The Sacred and the Modern Artist", *Criterion*, 4, 1965, and in M. Eliade, 1985.
6. A. Henri, *Total Art*, 81-82.
7. R. Long, quoted in Suzi Gablik, *Has Modernism Failed?*, Thames & Hudson, London, 1984, 44.
8. "Mel Bochner on Malevich", interview with John Coplans, *Artforum*, June, 1974, 62.
9. B. Flanagan, "Sculpture Made Visible", *Studio International*, 178, 915, Oct, 1969.
10. J. Beuys, in *Documenta* 7, 2, Documenta, Kassel, 1982.
11. Simon Mills, "Special Kaye [Tony Kaye]", *Sunday Times Magazine*, 12 June, 1994, 55.
12. Jan Dibbets, in L. Bear & W. Sharp, "DIBBETTS", *Avalanche*, 1, Autumn, 1970.
13. Robert Smithson reckons that a 'work of art when placed in a gallery loses its charge and becomes a portable object or surface disengaged from the outside world.' (*Robert Smithson: Writings*, 132).
14. Lawrence Weiner, in *Avalanche*, Spring, 1972, 67.
15. In M. Heizer, 1970.
16. Quoted in Lucy Lippard, "Tony Smith", *Art International*, Summer, 1967, 26.
17. '900...? That's an amazing fact I did not know' (Long, letter to the author, 11 July, 1994).

ROBERT SMITHSON: *SPIRAL JETTY*

1. *Writings*, 1979, 20.
2. *Writings*, 1979, 19.
3. See Marija Gimbutas; *The Language of the Goddess*, Thames & Hudson, London, 1989.
4. R. Smithson, "The Spiral Jetty", unpublished MS, quoted in Krauss, 282. See Hobbs, 1981.
5. I. Sandler, 1990, 60).

ROBERT SMITHSON: *SPIRAL JETTY*

1. *Writings*, 1979, 37.

ROBERT SMITHSON: *NON-SITE WORKS*

1. C. Robins, 1984, 82.
2. *Writings*, 1979, 115.
3. In L. Lippard, 1973, 88.

ROBERT SMITHSON: *BROKEN CIRCLE*

1. in R. Hobbs, 212.

ROBERT SMITHSON: *AMARILLO RAMP*

1. John Coplans, "Robert Smithson: The Amarillo Ramp", in R. Hobbs, 53.

LAWRENCE WEINER: *BILLOWING CLOUDS*

1. Lawrence Weiner, in E. Lucie-Smith, 1987, 117.
2. L. Weiner, *Billowing Clouds...*, 1986, 86.2 x 17.5 in, Anthony d'Offay Gallery, London.
3. *Richard Long: In Conversation* 2, 24.

ROBERT MORRIS: *OBSERVATORY*

1. R. Morris, quoted in M. Fried, 1967, in G. Battock, 1995, 126.

ROBERT MORRIS: *UNTITLED*

1. J. Haldane, 1997, 56.

JAMES TURRELL: *RODEN CRATER PROJECT*

1. *Complete Writings*, 200f.
2. In A. Benjamin, 47.
3. "Donald Judd", *The New York Times*, 1 Apl, 1977, C20.

CARL ANDRE: 37 *PIECES OF WORK*

1. D. Bourdon, 1978, 56.

CARL ANDRE: *EQUIVALENT VIII*

1. D. Bourdon, in G. Battock, 1968, 107.
2. M. Bochner, in G. Battock, 1968, 94.
3. Tomkins, 1989, 155.

WALTER DE MARIA: *LIGHTNING FIELD*

1. See D. Bourdon, 1968, 39-43, 72, M. Winton, 1970, 18-19; R. Smith, 1978, 102-5.
2. See Peter Redgrove, *The Black Goddess and the Sixth Sense*, Bloomsbury, 1987; *The Cyclopean Mistress*, Bloodaxe, 1993. (De Maria himself thinks that a lightning strike is a 'false climax' to the work, which really needs to be seen over a period of time to appreciate its qualities).
3. H. Smagula, 290.

CHRIS DRURY: *MEDICINE WHEEL*

1. C. Drury, M. Gooding & W. Furlong. *Song of the Earth,* Thames and Hudson, London, 2002, 91.
2. C. Drury, 2002, 72, 76.

MICHAEL HEIZER: *DOUBLE NEGATIVE*

1. See A. Sonfist, 1983; J. Beardsley, 1984.
2. Sol LeWitt was sceptical of enormity: '[i]f it's so big that you can't really comprehend it except by its emotive force then I don't want it' (in F. Colpitt, 77). And Robert Morris wrote that 'beyond a certain size the object can overwhelm and the gigantic scale becomes the loaded term' (1966, 21).
3. M. Heizer, quoted in H. Smagula, 1983, 286.
4. See J. Brown, 1984; G. Muller, 42-45.
5. M. Heizer, in Jane Bell, "Positive and Negative", *Arts Magazine*, Nov, 1974, 55.
6. R. Hughes, 1997, 571.

MICHAEL HEIZER: *COMPLEX ONE*

1. Robert Hughes, 1991, 386.

NANCY HOLT: *SUN TUNNELS*

1. See N. Holt, 1975, 1977; T. Castle, 1982.

NANCY HOLT: *STONE ENCLOSURE: ROCK RINGS*

1. C. Robins, 1984, 104.

MARY MISS: *PERIMETERS/ PAVILION/ DECOYS*

1. R. Onoratio, "Illusive Spaces: The Art of Mary Miss", *Artforum*, Dec, 1978, 32; see also K. Linker, "Mary Miss", *Mary Miss*, ICA, 1983.
2. See L. Anderson, 1973; *M. Miss,* 1981.

LAWRENCE WEINER: *BILLOWING CLOUDS*

1. Lawrence Weiner, in E. Lucie-Smith, 1987, 117.
2. L. Weiner, *Billowing Clouds...,* 1986, 86.2 x 17.5 in, Anthony d'Offay Gallery, London.
3. *Richard Long: In Conversation 2,* 24.

HANS HAACKE: *GRASS GROWS*

1. H. Haacke, in J. Burnham, 1967.
2. H. Haacke, in ib.

CONSTANTIN BRANCUSI: *ENDLESS COLUMN*

1. In D. Waldman, 1970, 19.

2. B. Flanagan, quoted in the catalogue of *Entre el Objeto y la Imagen: Escultura britanica contemporanea*, Palacio de Velasquez, Madrid, 1986, 233.

CHRISTO: *RUNNING FENCE*

1. See Werner Spies, *The Running Fence Project, Christo*, Abrams, New York, NY, 1977.
2. In A. Haden-Guest, 40.

CHRISTO: *VALLEY CURTAIN*

1. Christo, quoted in E. Johnson, 1982, 198.

CHRISTO: *WRAPPED MUSEUM OF CONTEMPORARY ART, CHICAGO*

1. Jan van der Marck, *Wrapped Museum*, Museum of Contemporary Art, Chicago, 1969.

DENNIS OPPENHEIM: *ANNUAL RINGS*

1. In M. Heizer, 1970.
2. D. Oppenheim, in M. Heizer, 1970.
3. In D. Oppenheim, 1978.

PETER HUTCHINSON

1. B. Nemitz, 78.

ANDY GOLDWORTHY: *LEAFWORKS*

1. Goldsworthy, quoted in Paul Nesbit: "Leafworks", in *Hand to Earth*, 108.

ANDY GOLDSWORTHY: *STONE CAIRNS*

1. In Y. Baginsky, "Sculptor for whom success snowballs", *Scotland on Sunday*, Jan 15, 1989.

ANDY GOLDSWORTHY: *THROWS AND SPLASHES*

1. A. Goldsworthy, sketchbook no. 19, Feb, 1988. HE, 150.
2. A. Goldsworthy, *Rain sun snow hail mist calm*, 4.
3. A. Goldsworthy, *Third Ear*, BBC Radio 3, June 30, 1989, in HE, 168.

DAVID NASH: *SLATE STOVE*

1. See A. McPherson, 1978; H. Adams, 1979; David Nash, 1980.

DAVID NASH: *WOOD SCULPTURE*

1. In A. McPherson, 30.

RICHARD LONG: *STONE CIRCLES*

1. In R. Fuchs, 236.

RICHARD LONG: *CIRCLES*

1. 'Working out there in nature, then, Long is a performer in the open-air theatre of the sublime' (David Sylvester, *About Modern Art*, Chatto & Windus, London, 1996).
2. *An Interview with Richard Long*, Neery Melkonian, Center for Contemporary Arts, Santa Fe, New Mexico, 1993-94
3. Interview with G. Lobacheff, 1994.

RICHARD LONG: *ON MIDSUMMER'S DAY*

1. R. Long, 1972, in *Fragments of a Conversation I-VI*, in *Walking in Circles*, 38.

WOLFGANG LAIB

1. In A. Benjamin, 91.
2. R. Rosenblum, 1988, 11.

BARBARA HEPWORTH

1. In A. Hammacher, op.cit., 98.
2. B. Hepworth, in W. Forma, 1965.

Bibliography

L.S. Adams. *A History of Western Art*, Abrams, New York, NY, 1994

S. Adams & A. Robins, eds. *Gendering Landscape Art*, Manchester University Press, Manchester, 2000

C. Adcock. *James Turrell*, University of California Press, Berkeley, CA, 1990

W. C. Agee. *Don Judd*, Whitney Museum of American Art, New York, NY, 1968

—. "Unit, Series, Site: A Judd Lexicon", *Art in America*, May, 1975

—. *The Sculpture of Donald Judd*, Art Museum of South Texas, Corpus Christi, TX, 1977

L. Aldrich. *Cool Art: 1967*, Museum of Contemporary Art, 1968

L. Alloway. "The American Sublime", *Living Arts*, 1, 2, June, 1963

—. *Systematic Painting*, New York, NY, 1966

—. *Christo*, Abrams, New York, NY, 1969

—. "Robert Smithson", *Artforum*, 11, Nov, 1972

—. "Residual Sign Systems in Abstract Expressionism", *Artforum*, Nov, 1973

W. Andersen. *American Sculpture in Process, 1930/ 1970*, New York Graphics Society, Boston, MA, 1975

L. Anderson. "Mary Miss", *Artforum*, Nov, 1973

C. Andre. "Frank Stella: Preface to Stripe Painting", in D. Miller, 1959

—. "An Interview with Carl Andre", P. Tuchman, *Artforum*, 8, 10, June, 1970

—. *Carl Andre, Sculpture, 1958-1974*, Kunsthalle, Bern, 1975

—. "Object vs Phenomenon", *Sculpture Today*, The International Sculpture Center, Toronto, 1978

—. *Carl Andre: Sculpture*, State University of New York Press, Albany, NY, 1984

—. *Carl-Andre: works on land*, Exhibitions International, 2001

J. Andrews. *The Sculpture of David Nash*, Lund Humphries, London, 1999

M. Andrews. *Landscape and Western Art*, Oxford Paperbacks, Oxford, 1999

E. de Antonio & M. Tuchman. *Painters Painting*, Abbeville Press, New York, NY, 1984

M. Archer. "A Walk In the Endless Summer From Duncansby Head To the Place of the Camel Droppinh", *Art Monthly*, Sept, 1991

—. *Art Since 1960*, Thames & Hudson, London, 1997

D. Ashton. *Modern American Sculpture*, Abrams, New York, NY, 1968

—. *American Art Since 1945*, Thames & Hudson, London, 1982

M. Auping. *Common Ground*, John and Mable Ringling Museum of Art, Sarasota, 1982

—. "Hamish Fulton", *Art in America*, 71, Feb, 1983

A. Aycock. "Work", "Maze", 1975, in A. Sondheim, 1977

J. Baal-Teshuva, ed. *Christo: The Reichstag and Urban Projects,* Prestel Verlag, Munich, 1993

E. Baker: "Judd the Obscure", *Art News*, 67, 2, 1968

K. Baker. "Andre in Retrospect", *Art in America*, Apl, 1980a

—. "Reckoning with Notation: The Drawings of Pollock, Newman, and Louis", *Artforum*, 18, 10, Summer, 1980b

—. *Minimalism: Art of Circumstance*, Abbeville, New York, NY, 1988

S. Bann & W. Allen, eds. *Interpreting Contemporary Art*, Reaktion Books, London, 1991

—. "Shrines, Gardens, Utopias", *New Literary History*, 24, 4, Autumn, 1994a

—. "The Map As Index of the Real: Land Art and the Authentication of Travel",

Imago Mundi, 46, British Library, London, 1994b

G. Baro. "Toward Speculation in Pure Form", *Art International*, Summer, 1967

—. "American Sculpture", *Studio International*, 172, 896, 1968

C. Barrett. *Op Art*, Viking, New York, NY, 1970

G. Battock, ed. *The New Art*, Dutton, New York, NY, 1966

—. *Idea Art*, Dutton, New York, NY, 1973

—. "Art in America: Confusions", *Domus*, Mch, 1975

—. ed. *New Artists Video*, Dutton, New York, NY, 1978

—. ed. *The Art of Performance*, Dutton, New York, NY, 1984

—. ed. *Minimal Art: A Critical Anthology*, University of California Press, Berkeley, CA, 1995

G. Beal. "Richard Long: "the simplicity of walking, the simplicity of stones"", in T. Neff, 1987

—. ed. *Art In the Landscape*, Chinati Foundation, Texas, 2000

J. Beardsley. *Probing the Earth: Contemporary Land Projects,* Smithsonian Press, Washington, DC, 1977

—. *Art in Public Spaces*, Partners For Liveable Places, Washington, DC, 1981

—. *Earthworks and Beyond: Contemporary Art in the Landscape*, Abbeville Press, New York, NY, 1984/ 1998

M.R. Beaumont. "Romantic Sculpture", in A. Papadakis, 1988

—. "Andy Goldsworthy", *Arts Review*, July 14, 1989

M. Beeren. *Century in Sculpture*, Stedelijk Museum, Amsterdam, 1992

D. Belgrad. *The Culture of Spontaneity: Improvisation and the Arts in Postwar America*, University of Chicago Press, Chicago, IL, 1998

A. Benjamin, ed. *Installation Art, Art & Design*, 30, 1993

L. Bennett. *The Life and Work of Andy Goldsworthy*, Heinemann, London, 2005

N. Bennett, ed. *The British Art Show: Old Allegiances and New Directions, 1979-1984*, Arts Council/ Orbis, London, 1984

M. Berger. *Labyrinths: Robert Morris, Minimalism, and the 1960s*, Harper & Row, New York, NY, 1989

F. Berthier. *Reading Zen in the Rocks: The Japanese Dry Landscape Garden*, University of Chicago Press, Chicago, IL, 2000

L. Biggs: *Between Object and Image*, British Council, London, 1986

M. Bloem, ed. *Lawrence Weiner*, Stedelijk Museum, Amsterdam, 1989

K.C. Bloomert & C.W. Moore. *Body, Memory and Architecture*, New Haven, 1977

M. Bochner. "Art in Process - Structures", *Arts Magazine*, 40, 9, 1966a

—. "Primary Structures", *Arts*, June, 1966b

—. "Systematic", *Arts Magazine*, 41, 1, Nov, 1966c

—. "Serial Art Systems: Solipsism", *Arts Magazine*, 41, 8, Summer, 1967

—. "Mel Bochner on Malevich", interview with J. Coplans, *Artforum*, June, 1974

S. Boettger. *Earthworks*, University of California Press, Berkeley, CA, 2002

Y. Bois. *Donald Judd*, Galerie Lelong, Paris, 1991

D. Bonetti, David. "Facing Eden: 100 years of landscape art in the Bay Area, is a show that limns a strong tradition", *San Francisco Examiner*, June 25, 1995

D. Bourdon. "The Razed Sites of Carl Andre", *Artforum*, 5, 2, Oct, 1966

—. "Walter de Maria: The Singular Experience", *Art International*, Dec 20, 1968

—"The Mini-Conceptual Age", *Village Voice*, Oct 17, 1974

—. "You Can't Tell a Painter By His Colors", *Village Voice*, Mch 24, 1975

—. *Carl Andre: Sculpture, 1959-1977*, Jaap Rietman, New York, NY, 1978

C. Brown. "Natural arts", *The Magazine*, July, 1987

D. Brown. "New British sculpture in Normandy", *Arts Review*, Feb 10, 1989

J. Brown *et al*. *Michael Heizer: Sculpture in Reverse*, see M. Heizer, 1984

—. ed. *Occluding Front: James Turrell*, Lapis Press, Larkspur Landing, CA, 1985

D. Bruckner. "Earth works", *New York Times Book Review*, Jan, 1996

J. Burnham. *Beyond Modern Sculpture*, Braziller, New York, NY, 1968

—. "A Dan Flavin Retrospective in Ottawa", *Artforum*, 8, 4, Dec, 1969

—. "Robert Morris", *Artforum*, 8, 7, 1970

—. "Haacke's Cancelled Show at the Guggenheim", *Artforum*, June, 1971

—. *Great Western Salt Works*, Brazillier, New York, NY, 1974

—. "Hans Haacke: Wind and Water Sculpture", 1967, in A. Sonfist, 1983

K. Bussman & F. Matzner, eds. *Hans Haacke*, Cantz, Stuttgart, 1993

J. Butterfield. *The Art of Light and Space*, Abbeville Press, New York, NY, 1993

D. Cameron. "When is a door not a door?", *XLIII esposizione Internazionale d'Arte La Biennale di Venezia*, Edizioni La Biennale, Venice, 1988

—. "Art for the new year: who's worth catching?", *Art & Auction*, Jan, 1994

J. Campbell. *The Power of Myth*, with B. Moyers, ed. B.S. Flowers, Doubleday, New York, NY, 1988

—. *The Hero With a Thousand Faces,* Paladin, London, 1988

—. *An Open Life*, Larson Publications, New York, NY, 1988

—. *The Hero's Journey: Joseph Campbell On his Life and Work,* ed. P. Cousineau, Harper & Row, San Francisco, CA, 1990

P. Carlson. "Donald Judd's Equivocal Objects", *Art in America*, Jan, 1984

T. Castle. "Nancy Holt, Siteseer", *Art in America*, Mch, 1982

A. Causey. "Space and Time in British Land Art", *Studio International*, 193, 98, Feb, 1977

—. *Nature as Material: An Exhibition of Sculpture and Photographs Purchased For the Arts Council Collection,* Arts Council, London, 1980

—. "Environmental Sculptures", in Goldsworthy, *Hand to Earth*, 1990

—. *Sculpture Since 1945*, Oxford University Press, Oxford, 1998

G. Celant. "Introduction", *Arte Povera*, Praeger, New York, NY, 1969

—. *Conceptual Art, Arte Povera, Land Art*, Galeria Civica d'Arte Moderna, Turin, 1970

—. "Tony Cragg and Industrial Platonism", *Artforum*, 20, 3, Nov, 1981

—. *Dennis Oppenheim*, Edizioni Charta Srl, 1997

A. Chave: "Minimalism and the Rhetoric of Power", *Arts*, Jan, 1990

H.B. Chipp, ed. *Theories of Modern Art,* University Press of California, LA, CA, 1968

M. Church. "A shower of stones, a flash in the river", *Sunday Telegraph*, 10 April, 1994, 6

F. Colpitt. *Minimal Art: The Critical Perspective,* University of Washington Press, Seattle, WA, 1990

B. Commoner. *The Closing Circle: Nature, Man and Technology*, Knopf, New York, NY, 1975

M. Compton. *Some Notes on the Work of Richard Long*, British Council, London, 1976

—. & D. Sylvester. *Robert Morris*, Tate Gallery, London, 1971

Concept Art, Minimal Art, Land Art, Edition Cantz, Stuttgart, 1990

L. Cooke. "Richard Long replies to a critic", *Art Monthly*, 68, July, 1983

—. *Alison Wilding*, Serpentine Gallery, London, 1985

J. Coplans. "Serial Imagery", *Artforum*, 7, 2, Oct, 1968

—. *Donald Judd*, Pasadena Art Museum, CA, 1971

—. "Robert Smithson", *Artforum,* Apl, 1974

D. Cosgrove, ed. *Mappings*, London, 1999

T. Cragg. *Writings*, Editions Isy Brachot, Brussels, 1992

—. *Sculptures on the Page*, Henry Moore Institute, Leeds, Yorkshire, 1997

M. Craig-Martin. *Minimalism*, Tate Gallery, Liverpool, 1989

D. Crane. *The Transformation of the Avant Garde: The New York Art World, 1940-1985*, University of Chicago Press, Chicago, IL, 1987

P. Crowther, ed. *The Contemporary Sublime, Art & Design,* 40, 1995

P. Curtis. *Modern British Sculpture from the Collection*, Tate Gallery, Liverpool, 1988

A. Davies. "Richard Long and Hamish Fulton", *Art Monthly*, 25, April, 1979

H. Davies *et al. Blurring the Boundaries: Installation Art 1969-1996*, Museum of Contemporary Art, San Diego, CA, 1997

R. Davies & T. Knipe, eds. *A Sense of Place: Sculpture in Landscape*, London, 1984

W. de Maria. "The Lightning Field", *Artforum,* 18, 8, Apl, 1980

P. de Monchaux, *et al*, eds. *The Sculpture Show*, Arts Council of Great Britain, London, 1983

N. de Oliveira *et al. Installation Art*, Thames & Hudson, London, 1994

—. *et al*, eds. *Installation Art in the New Millennium*, Thames & Hudson, London, 2003

R. Deutsche *et al. Hans Haacke*, MIT Press, Cambridge, MA, 1986

E. Develing. *Carl Andre*, Gemeentenmeuseum, The Hague, 1969

—. & L. Lippard. *Minimal Art*, Stadtische Kunsthalle, Dusseldorf, 1969

J. Dibbets, in L. Bear & W. Sharp. "DIBBETTS", *Avalanche*, 1, Autumn, 1970.

R. Donnell. *Double Vision: Perspectives On Gender and the Visual Arts*, Farleigh Dickinson University Press, Rutherford, NJ, 1995

L. Dougherty. "Art in nature: a new site for sculpture in Denmark", *Maquette*, Sept, 1994

C. Drury. *Shelters and Baskets*, Orchard Gallery, 1988

—. *Vessel: Sculpture 1990-95*, Towner Art Gallery, 1995

—. *Stones and Bundles*, Rebecca Hossack Gallery, London, 1995

—. *Silent Spaces*, Thames & Hudson, London, 1998/ 2004

—. *Journeys On Paper*, Stephen Lacey Gallery, London, 2000

—. interview with W. Furlong, in M. Gooding, 2002

—. *Defying Gravity*, North Carolina Museum of Art, NC, 2003

—. *Heart of Stone*, Aberystwyth Art Gallery, Wales, 2003

M. Duncan. "On site: straddling the great divide", *Art in America.* 83, 3, Mch, 1995

—. "Live from the Getty", *Art in America,* 86, 5, May, 1998

L. Durrell. *Justine*, Faber, London, 1963

—. *Spirit of Place*, Faber, London, 1971

A. Dyson. *Richard Long: Sao Paulo Biennial 1994,* The British Council, 1994

J.C. Eade, ed. *Projecting the Landscape*, Humanities Research Centre, Canberra, 1987

M. Eliade. *Patterns in Comparative Religion*, Sheed & Ward, London, 1958

—. *Shamanism: Archaic Techniques of Ecstasy*, Princeton University Press, Princeton, NJ, 1972

—. *Myths, Dreams and Mysteries*, Harper & Row, New York, NY, 1975

—. *From Primitives to Zen: A Sourcebook*, Collins, London, 1977

—*A History of Religious Ideas*, I, Collins, London, 1979

—. *Ordeal by Labyrinth*, University of Chicago Press, Chicago, IL, 1984

—*Symbolism, the Sacred and the Arts*, Crossroad, New York, NY, 1988

G. Evans. "Sculpture and Reality", *Studio International*, 177, 908, Feb, 1969

J. Fabricus. *Alchemy: The Medieval Alchemists and Their Royal Art*, Aquarian Press, Northants, 1989

D. Factor. "Los Angeles", *Artforum*, 4, 9, May, 1966

S. Farr. "Andy Goldsworthy: stone works in America", *Reflex*, 8, 6, Dec, 1995

R. Ferguson *et al*, eds. *Discourses: Conversations in Postmodern Art and Culture*, MIT Press, Cambridge, MA, 1990

S. Field. "Touching the Earth", *Art and Artists*, 8, Apl, 1973

J. Fineberg: "Robert Morris Looking Back", *Arts Magazine*, 55, 1, 1980

—. *Art Since 1940: Strategies of Being*, Laurence King, London, 1995

A. Fisher & G. Gerster. *The Art of the Maze*, Weidenfeld & Nicholson, London, 1990

—. & J. Saward. *The British Maze Guide*, Minotaur Designs, London, 1991

—. & D. Kingham. *Mazes*, Shire Punlications, London, 1991

J. Fisher. "Richard Long", *Aspects*, 14, Spring, 1981

B. Flanagan. "Sculpture made visible: Barry Flanagan in discussion with Gene Baro", *Studio International*, 178, 915, Oct, 1969

S. Foley. *Unitary Forms: Minimal Structures by Carl Andre, Donald Judd, John McCracken, Tony Smith*, Museum of Modern Art, San Francisco, CA, 1970

N. Foote. "Long Walks", *Artforum*, 18, Summer, 1980

W. Forma. *Five British Sculptors*, New York, NY, 1965

M. Fried. "Shape as Form: Frank Stella's New Paintings", *Artforum*, 5, 3, Nov, 1966

—. "Art and Objecthood", *Artforum*, 5, Summer, 1967

M. Friedman. "Robert Morris: Polemics and Cubes", *Art International*, 10, 10, Dec, 1966

—. *14 Sculptors*, Walker Art Center, Minneapolis, MN, 1969

E. Fry. *Alice Aycock*, University of South Florida Art Galleries, Tampa, FL, 1981

—. "The Poetic Machines of Alice Aycock", *Portfolio*, Nov, 1981

—. *et al. Robert Morris*, Museum of Contemporary Art, Chicago, IL, 1986

R.H. Fuchs. "Memories of Passing: A Note on Richard Long", *Studio International*, 187, 965, Apl, 1974

—. *Carl Andre*, Van Abenmuseum, Eindhoven, 1978

—. *Richard Long*, text, in R. Long, 1986

P. Fuller. *Peter Fuller's Modern Painters: Reflections on British Art*, ed. J. McDonald, Methuen, London, 1993

H. Fulton. *Hamish Fulton: Selected Walks, 1969-89*, Albright-Knox Art Gallery, Buffalo, New York, NY, 1990

—. *Richard Long,* Thames & Hudson, London, 1991

—. *One Hundred Walks*, Haags Gemeetemuseum, The Hague, 1991

—. "Into a Walk Into Nature", *Thirty One Horrors*, Lenbachhaus, Munich, 1995

—. *Walking Artist*, Annely Juda, London, 1998

—. *Walking Through*, Stour Valley Art Project, Challock, Kent, 1999

—. *Wild Life*, Pocketbooks, Edinburgh, 2000

—. *Walking Artist*, Richter Verlag, Düsseldorf, 2001

—. "Specific Places and Particular Events", in B. Tufnell, 2002

S. Gardiner. "Their medium is nature", *Landscape Architecture*, 80, Feb, 1990

M. Garlake. "Andy Goldsworthy", *Art Monthly*, 93, Feb, 1986

J. Gear. "Andy Goldsworthy", *Review*, Dec. 1, 1996

L. Gendron. "Le sculpteur d'éphémère", *L'actualité*, 22, 12, Aug, 1997

J. Gibson. *The Senses Considered as a Perceptual System*, Houghton Mifflin, Boston, MA, 1966

J. Giovannini. *Mary Miss*, Architectural Association, London, 1987

T. Godfrey. "Richard Wilson's watertable, Andy Goldsworthy", *Burlington Magazine*, 136, 1096, July, 1994

—. *Conceptual Art*, Phaidon, London, 1998

E. Goheen. *Wrapped Walk Ways*, Abrams, New York, NY, 1978

R. Goldberg. *Performance: Live Art Since the 60s*, Thames & Hudson, London, 1998

A. Goldsworthy. *Andy Goldsworthy, Alan Rankle, Nigel Jepson*, Brampton Banks, Cumbria, 1982

—. *Rain sun snow hail mist calm: Photoworks by Andy Goldsworthy*, Henry Moore Centre for the Study of Sculpture, Leeds, Yorkshire, 1985

—. *Land Matters*, Blackfriars Arts Centre, Reed Press, 1986

—. & J. Fowles. *Winter Harvest*, Scottish Arts Council, 1987

—. *Mountain and Coast: Autumn Into Winter: Japan 1987*, Art Data, 1988

—. *Parkland*, Yorkshire Sculpture Park, West Bretton, 1988

—. *Touching North*, Fabian Carlsson, London, 1989

—. *Snowballs in Summer Installation*, Old Museum of Transport, Glasgow, 1989

—. *Leaves*, Common Ground, London, 1989

—. *Andy Goldsworthy*, Viking, London, 1990

—. *Hand to Earth: Andy Goldsworthy, Sculpture, 1976-1990*, Henry Moore Centre for Sculpture, Leeds, Yorkshire, 1990

—. interview, *Third Ear*, BBC Radio 3, June 30, 1989, in 1990

—. "Geometry and Nature", interview, *Art & Design*, in A. Papadakis, 1991

—. *Sand Leaves*, Arts Club of Chicago, IL, 1991

—. *Ice and Snow Drawings*, Fruitmarket Gallery, Edinburgh, 1992

—. *Andy Goldsworthy: Breakdown*, Rose Art Museum, 1992

—. *Stone*, Viking, London, 1994

—. *Black Stones, Red Pools*, Pro Arte Foundation, 1995

—. *Wood*, Viking, London, 1996

—. *Sheepfolds*, Michael Hue-Williams Gallery, London, 1996

—. *Végètal*, Ballet Atlantique-Regine Chopinot, La Rochelle, France, 1996

—. *Alaska Works*, Anchorage Museum of History and Art, Anchorage, AK, 1996

—. *Andy Goldsworthy: A Collaboration With Nature*, Abrams, NY, 1996

—. *Andy Goldsworthy: Jack's Fold*, ed. Judy Glasman, University of Hertfordshire, 1996

—. *Hand to Earth: Andy Goldsworthy Sculpture*, T. Friedman, Thames and Hudson, London, 1997 & 2004

—. *Cairns*, Musée departemental de Digne, Reserve Geologique de haute Provence, 1997

—. *Andy Goldsworthy*, Musée d'art contemporain de Montréal, 1998

—. *Arch*, with D. Craig, Thames & Hudson, London, 1999

—. *Wall*, intr. K. Baker, Thames & Hudson, London, 2000

—. *Time*, Thames & Hudson, London, 2000

—. *Midsummer Snowballs*, intr. J. Collins, Abrams, New York, NY, 2001

—. *Andy Goldsworthy - Réfuges D'Art*, Editions Artha, 2002

—. *Passage*, Thames & Hudson, London, 2004

A. Goldstein, ed. *Reconsidering the Object of Art: 1965-1975*, Museum of Contemporary Art, L.A., CA, 1995

M. Gooding & W. Furlong. *Song of the Earth*, Thames and Hudson, London, 2002

A. Gopnik. "Basic Stuff: Robert Smithson, Myth, Science and Primitivism", *Art Magazine*, Mch, 1983

J. Grande. *Balance: art and nature*, Black Rose Books, Montréal, 1994

—. "Back to nature?", *Sculpture*, 13, 4, July/ Aug, 1994

—. *Art Nature Dialogues*, State University of New York Press, NY, 2004

N. Graydon. "Magic in the field", *Ritz*, 133, 1989

B. Graziani. "Robert Smithson's Picturable Situation", *Critical Inquiry*, 20, 3, Spring, 1994

C. Greenberg. *Art and Culture*, Beacon Press, Boston, MA, 1961

G. Greig. "Circular Tours In the Name of Art", *Sunday Times*, June 16, 1991

H. Gresty & D. Reason. *Landscape*, Kettle's Yard, Cambridge, 1986

—. *Bare: Alison Wilding: Sculptures, 1982-1993*, Newlyn Art Gallery, Cornwall, 1993

H. Haacke. *Framing and Being Framed*, New York University Press, New York, NY, 1975

A. Haden-Guest. "The King of Wrap", *Sunday Times Magazine*, Jan, 1994

O. Hahn & P. Restany. *Christo*, Editioni Apollinaire, Milan, 1966

J. Haldane. *A Road From the Past To the Future*, Crawford Arts Centre, St Andrews, 1997

—. "Images After the Fact", *Modern Painters*, 11, 3, Fall, 1998

—. "Back To the Land", *Art Monthly*, June, 1999

C. Hall. "Shared earth", *Arts Review*, 43, June 14, 1991

—. "Site lines", *Arts Review*, 46, Oct, 1994

A.M. Hammacher. *The Sculpture of Barbara Hepworth*, Abrams, New York, NY, 1968

C. Harrison. "Barry Flanagan's Sculpture", *Studio International*, 175, 900, May, 1968

—. "Sculpture's Recent Past", in T. Neff, 1987

B. Haskell. *BLAM! The Explosion of Pop, Minimalism, and Performance, 1958-64*, Whitney Museum of American Art, New York, NY, 1984

—. *Donald Judd*, Whitney Museum of American Art, New York, NY, 1988

N. Hedges. "Growth, decay and the movement of change", *World Magazine*, 45, Jan, 1991

M. Heizer, D. Oppenheim & R. Smithson. "Discussion", *Avalanche*, 1, Autumn, 1970

—. *Sculpture in Reverse*, Museum of Contemporary Art, LA, CA, 1984

A. Henri. *Environments and Happenings*, Thames & Hudson, London, 1974

—. *Total Art*, Praeger, New York, NY, 1974

A. Hess. "Technology Exposed", *Landscape Architecture*, May, 1992

T. Hess. *Barnett Newman*, Walker, New York, NY, 1969

—. & L. Nochlin. *Woman as Sex Object: Studies in Erotic Art*, Newsweek, New York, NY, 1972

—. & E. Baker. *Art and Sexual Politics*, Art New Series, Macmillan, New York, NY, 1973

Galerie Max Hetzler. *Carl Andre, Gunther Forg, Hubert Kiecol, Richard Long, Meuser, Reinhard Mucha, Bruce Nauman and Ulrich Ruckreim*, Cologne, 1985

G. Hilty. *Recent British Sculpture*, Arts Council, London, 1993

—. *Alison Wilding: Immersion/ Exposure*, Tate Gallery, Liverpool, 1991

R. Hobbs. *Robert Smithson: Sculpture*, Cornell University Press, Ithaca, NY, 1981

—. "Earthworks", *Art Journal*, 42, Fall, 1982

N. Hodges ed. *Art and the Natural Environment*, Art & Design, 36, 1994

—. ed. *The Contemporary Sublime*, Art & Design, 40, 1995

N. Holt. "Amarillo Ramp", *Avalanche*, Fall, 1973

—. "Hydra's Head", *Arts Magazine,* Jan, 1975

—. "Sun Tunnels", *Artforum*, Apl, 1977

P. Hovdenakk. *Christo: Complete Editions*, Schellman & Klüser, Munich, 1982

S. Hubbard, intr. *Sculpture At Goodwood: A VIsion For 21st Century British Sculpture*, Sculpture At Goodwood, Sussex, 2002

R. Hughes. *Nothing If Not Critical: Selected Essays on Art and Artists*, Collins Harvill, London, 1990

—. *The Shock of the New*, Thames & Hudson, London, 1991

—. *American Visions: The Epic History of Art In America*, Knopf, New York, NY, 1997

T. Hughes. *Poetry in the Making*, Faber, 1969

H.E. Hugo, ed. *The Portable Romantic Reader,* Viking Press, New York, NY, 1957

S. Hunter, ed. *An American Renaissance: Painting and Sculpture Since 1940*, Abbeville Press, New York, NY, 1986

L. Iizawa. "Earth work", *Studio Voice*, Mch, 1988

P. Inch. "Andy Goldsworthy", *Arts Review*, 42, July 13, 1990

R. Ingleby. "Visual arts: Andy Goldsworthy", *The Independent*, Nov 8, 1996

In Praise of Trees, Salisbury Festival, Wilts., 2002

G. Jeppson. *Richard Long*, Harvard College, Cambridge, MA, 1980

E.H. Johnson. *Modern Art and the Object*, Harper & Row, New York, NY, 1976

—. ed. *American Artist on Art*, Harper & Row, New York, NY, 1982

W. Johnson. *Riding the Ox Home: A History of Meditation from Shamanism to Science*, Rider, London, 1982

B. Jones. "A New Wave in Sculpture", *Artscribe*, 8, Sept, 1977

J. Jones. "Something nasty in the woods", *The Guardian*, Mch 4, 2000

D. Joselit. *American Art Since 1945*, Thames & Hudson, Londo, 2003

D. Judd. "Frank Stella", *Arts Magazine,* 36, Sept, 1962

—. "In the Galleries", *Arts Magazine*, 37, 10, Sept, 1963

—. "Local History", *Arts Yearbook 7*, 1964

—. "Black, White and Gray", *Arts Magazine*, 38, 6, Mch, 1964

—. "Specific Objects", *Arts Yearbook*, 8, Art Digest, New York, NY, 1965

—. "Barnett Newman", *Studio International*, 179, 919, Feb, 1970

—. *Complete Writings, 1959-1975*, Nova Scotia College of Art and Design, Halifax, Canada, 1975

—. *Complete Writings, 1975-1986*, Van Abbemuseum, Netherlands, 1987

E. Juncosa. "Landscape as experience", *Lapiz*, 61 Oct, 1989

D. Karshan. *Conceptual Art and Conceptual Aspects*, Farleigh Dickinson University, 1970

J. Kastner, ed. *Land and Environmental Art*, Phaidon, London, 1998

R. Katz. *Naked By the Window: The Fatal Marriage of Carl Andre and Ana Mendieta*, Atlantic Monthly Press, New York, NY, 1990

B. Kedar & R. Werblowsky, eds. *Sacred Space: Shrine, City, Land,* New York University Press, Albany, NY, 1998

S. Kemal & I. Gaskell, eds. *Landscape, natural beauty and the arts,* Cambridge University Press, Cambridge, 1993

G. Kepes, ed. *Arts of the Environment*, Brazillier, New York, NY, 1972

P. King *et al.* "Colour in Sculpture", *Studio International*, 177, 907, 1969

M. Kirby. *Happenings*, Dutton, New York, NY, 1966

C. Knight. *Art of the Sixties and Seventies: The Panza Collection*, Rizzoli, New York, NY, 1987

N. Konstam. *Sculpture: The Art and the Practice*, Collins, London, 1984

R. Kostelanetz. *The Theatre of Mixed Means*, Dial, New York, NY, 1968

—. *On Innovative Performance(s)*, McFarland, Jefferson, NC, 1994

R.E. Krauss. "Richard Serra: Sculpture Redrawn", *Artforum*, May, 1972

—. "Sense and Sensibility: Reflection on Post '60s Sculpture", *Artforum*, 12, Nov, 1973

—. *Passages in Modern Sculpture,* Thames & Hudson, London, 1977

—. "Sculpture in the Expanded Field", *October*, 8, Spring, 1979

—. *Eva Hesse*, Whitechapel Art Gallery, London, 1979

—. *et al. Robert Morris*, Abrams, New York, NY, 1994

Z. Kraus, ed. *From Nature to Art, From Art to Nature*, Venice Biennale, Milan, 1978

D. Kuspitt. "Sol LeWitt", *Art in America*, 63, 5, 1975

—. "Authoritarian Abstraction", *Journal of Aesthetics and Art Criticism*, 36, 1, Autumn, 1977

—. "Robert Smithson's Drunken Boat", *Arts Magazine*, Oct, 1981

—. "Aycock's Dream Houses", *Art in America*, Sept, 1985

—. "Donald Judd", *Artforum*, 23, 5, Feb, 1985

J. Kutner. "Brice Marden, David Novros, Mark Rothko: The Urge to Communicate through Non-Imagistic Painting", *Arts Magazine*, 50, 1, Sept, 1975

I. Lamaitre. "Interview with Tony Cragg", *Artefactum*, 2, Dec, 1985

T. Lang. "News from the imagination", *Issues in Architecture, Art & Design,* 3, 1, 1993

Land Marks, Edith C. Blum Art Institute, Bard College, Annadale-on-Hudson, 1984

D. Laporte. *Christo*, Pantheon Books, New York, NY, 1985

B. Laws. "Where Art and Nature Meet", *The Telegraph Weekly*, Nov 12, 1988

D. Lee. "Serial Rights", *Art News*, 66, 8, Dec, 1967

—. "London Ecology Centre, Exhibit", *Arts Review*, 38, Jan 17, 1986

—. "Great art of the outdoors: bio-degrading sculptures", *Country Life*, 181, 35, Aug 27, 1987

—. "Pure, ephemeral spires", *The Times*, June 26, 1989

—. "Opinion: Richard Long and Hamish Fulton", *Arts Review*, July 26, 1991

—. "In profile: Goldsworthy", *Arts Review*, 47, Feb 1995

A. Legg, ed. *Sol LeWitt*, Museum of Modern Art, New York, NY, 1978

P. Leider. "Literalism and Abstraction: Frank Stella's Retrospective at the Modern", *Artforum*, 8, Apl, 1970

—. "For Robert Smithson", *Art in America*, Nov, 1973

—. *Stella Since 1970*, Fort Worth Art Museum, TX, 1978

K. Levin. "Robert Smithson", *Art News*, Sept, 1982

—. "Reflections on Robert Smithson's *Spiral Jetty*", *Arts Magazine*, May, 1978

F. Licht. *Sculpture, 19th and 20th Centuries*, Michael Joseph, London, 1967

—. "Dan Flavin", *Artscanada*, Dec, 1968

L. Lippard. "New York Letter: Apl-June, 1965", *Art International*, 9, 6, 1965

—. "New York Letter: Recent Sculpture as Escape", *Art International*, Feb, 1966a

—. "An Impure Situation", *Art International*, May 20, 1966b

—. *Ad Reinhardt*, Jewish Museum, New York, NY, 1966c

—. *Pop Art*, Oxford University Press, New York, NY, 1966d

—. "The Silent Art", *Art in America*, 55, 1, Jan-Feb, 1967a

—. "Sol LeWitt: Non-Visual Structures", *Artforum*, Apl, 1967b

—. "Tony Smith", *Art International*, Summer, 1967c

—. "Rebelliously Romantic?", *New York Times*, June 4, 1967d

—. "Escalataion in Washington", *Art International*, 12, 1, Jan, 1968

—. ed. *Surrealists on Art*, Prentice-Hall, Englewood Cliffs, NJ, 1970

—. *Tony Smith*, Thames & Hudson, London, 1972a

—. *Grids*, Philadelphia Institute of Contemporary Art, PA, 1972b

—. *Six Years: The Dematerialization of the Art Object from 1966 to 1972*, Praeger, New York, NY, 1973

—. *From the Center: feminist essays on women's art*, Dutton, New York, NY, 1976

—. *Eva Hesse*, New York University Press, New York, NY, 1976

—. et al. *Sol LeWitt*, Museum of Modern Art, New York, NY, 1978

—. "Complexities: Architectural Sculpture in Nature", *Art in America*, Feb, 1979

—. "Dinner Party", *Art in America*, Apl, 1980

—. *Ad Reinhardt*, Abrams, New York, NY, 1981

—. *Overlay*, Pantheon, New York, NY, 1983

C. Loeffier, ed. *Performance Anthology*, Contemporary Art Press, San Francisco, CA, 1979

R. Long. *Touchstones*, Arnolfini, Bristol, 1983

—. *Richard Long: In Conversation*, Parts 1 & 2, MW Press, Noordwijk, Holland, 1985-86

—. *Richard Long*, text by R.H. Fuchs, Thames & Hudson, London, 1986

—. *Old World New World*, Anthony d'Offay, London, 1988

—. *Richard Long: Walking in Circles,* Hayward Gallery/ Thames & Hudson, London, 1992

—. *Kicking Stones,* Anthony d'Offay Gallery, London, 1990

—. *Richard Long: Mountains and Water*, Anthony d'Offay, London, 1992

—. *Circles, Cycles, Mud*, D. Friis-Hansen, Contemporary Arts Museum, 1996

—. *From Time to Time*, DAP, 1997

—. *Richard Long*, Hatje Cantz, Stuttgart, 1997

—. *A Walk Across England*, Thames & Hudson, London, 1997

—. *Mirage*, Phaidon, London, 1998

—. *Selected Walks, 1979-1996*, Morning Star Press, 1999

—. *Richard Long: a Moving World,* Tate Publishing, London, 2002

—. *Richard Long – Walking the Line,* Thames and Hudson, London, 2002

E. Lucie-Smith: *Sculpture Since 1945*, Phaidon, Oxford, 1987

R. Lund. "Why Isn't Minimal Art Boring?", *Journal of Aesthetics and Art Criticism*, 45, 2, Winter, 1986

N. Lynton. introduction to *Tony Cragg*, Fifth Triennale India, British Council, 1982

—. *David Nash: Sculpture, 1971-90*, Serpentine Gallery, London, 1990

R. Mabey. "Art and ecology", *Modern Painters*, 3, 4, Winter, 1990

D. Macmillan. "David Nash: Brancusi Joins the Garden Gang", *Art Monthly*, 65, Apl, 1983

L. MacRitchie. "Ancient Egypt", *Financial Times*, Dec 12, 1994

—. "Residency on earth", *Art in America*, 83, 4, Apl, 1995

S. Madoff. "Andy Goldsworthy", *Garden Design*, 13, June, 1994

W. Malpas. *Richard Long: The Art of Walking*, Crescent Moon, 1995/ 1998

—. *Andy Goldsworthy*, Crescent Moon, 1996/ 1998

—. *The Art of Andy Goldsworthy*, Crescent Moon, 1998/ 2004

J. van der Marck. *Wrapped Museum*, Museum of Contemporary Art, Chicago, IL, 1969

—. *Herbert Bayer*, Dartmouth College Museum, Hanover, NH, 1977

M. Marmer. "James Turrell", *Art in America*, 69, May, 1981

R. Martin. *The Sculpted Forest: Sculpture in the Forest of Dean*, Redcliff, Bristol,

1990

B. Matilsky. *Fragile Economies*, Rizzoli, New York, NY, 1992

J. May. "Landscape Fired by Ice", *Landscape*, Dec, 1987

D. Mayhall: *The Minimal Tradition*, The Aldrich Museum of Contemporary Art, Ridgefield, CT, 1979

B. McAvera. "Public art: site sensitivities", *Art Monthly*, 215, Apl, 1998

D. McKinney. *Yves Klein, Brice Marden, Sigmar Polke*, Hirschl & Alder Modern, New York, NY, 1989

A. McPherson. "David Nash: interviewed by Allan McPherson", *Artscribe*, 12, June, 1978

K. McShine. *Primary Structures*, Jewish Museum, New York, NY, 1966

—. *Information*, Museum of Modern Art, New York, NY, 1970

—. *An International Survey of Recent Painting and Sculpture*, MOMA, New York, NY, 1984

J. Meyer, ed. *Minimalism*, Phaidon, London, 2000

U. Meyer. *Conceptual Art*, Dutton, New York, NY, 1972

D.C. Miller, ed. *Sixteen Americans*, Museum of Modern Art, New York, NY, 1959

M. Miller. *The Garden as an Art*, State University of New York Press, Albany, NY, 1993

M. Miss. *Mary Miss: Interior Works*, Bell Gallery, University of Rhode Island, Autumn, 1981

J. Morland. *New Milestones: Sculpture, Community and the Land*, Common Ground, 1988

H. Morphy & M. Boles, eds. *Art from the Land*, University of Washington Press, 2000

R. Morris. "Notes on Sculpture", *Artforum,* Feb, 1966; Oct, 1966; June, 1967; Apl, 1969

—. "Aligned with Nazca", *Artforum*, Oct, 1975

—. *Robert Morris: Mirror Works, 1961-1978*, Leo Castelli Gallery, New York, NY, 1979

—. *et al. Earthworks*, Seattle Art Museum, Seattle, WA, 1979

—. *Selected Works*, Contemporary Arts Museum, Houston, TX, 1981

—. *Continuous Project Altered Daily*, MIT Press, Cambridge, MA, 1993

J. Morland. *New Milestones: Sculpture, Community and the Land*, Common Ground, London, 1988

H. Morphy & M. Boles, eds. *Art from the Land*, University of Washington Press, 2000

J. Morrison. "Landmatters", *British Journal of Photography*, 133, June 6, 1986

A. Morgan. "Maze and labyrinth", *Sculpture*, 14, 4, July/ Aug, 1995

R.C. Morgan. "Richard Long's Poststructural Encounters", *Arts*, 61, 6, Feb, 1987

—. *Art Into Ideas*, Cambridge, 1996

D. Morse. "At Runnymede Farm, the crop is sculptures", *San Francisco Examiner*, May 2, 1997

M. Mosser & G. Teyssot, eds. *The History of Garden Design*, Thames & Hudson, London, 1991

G. Müller. "Michael Heizer", *Arts Magazine*, Dec, 1969

—. "The Earth, Subjected To Cataclysms, Is a Cruel Master", *Arts Magazine*, Nov, 1971

S. Nairne & N. Serota. *British Sculpture in the Twentieth Century*, Whitechapel Art Gallery, London, 1981

H. Nakamura. "Andy Goldsworthy and Anthony Green", *Ikebana Ryusei*, 38, Apl,

1988

D. Nash. *Fletched Over Ash*, AIR Gallery, 1978

—. "David Nash", *Aspects*, 10, Spring, 1980

—. *Stoves and Hearths*, Duke Street Gallery, London, 1982

T.A. Neff, ed. *A Quiet Revolution: British Sculpture Since 1965*, Thames & Hudson, London, 1987

B. Nemitz. *Trans Plant: Living Vegetation in Contemporary Art*, Hatje Cantz, Stuttgart, 2000

C. Nemser. "An interview with Eva Hesse", *Artforum*, May, 1970

—. "My Memories of Eva Hesse", *Feminist Art Journal*, Winter, 1973

P. Nesbitt. "At Home with Nature: Andy Goldsworthy in Scotland", *Alba*, Spring, 1989

—. "A Landscape Touched by Gold", in G. Hughes, 1990

B. Newman. *Selected Writings*, Knopf, New York, NY, 1990

M. Newman. "New Sculpture in Britain", *Art in America*, Sept, 1982

I. Noguchi. *A Sculptor's World*, Harper & Row, New York, NY, 1968

J. Norrie. "Andy Goldsworthy", *Arts Review*, 3 July, 1987

B. Oakes, ed. *Sculpting the Environment*, Van Nostrand Reinhold, New York, NY, 1995

P. Oakes. "The Incomparable Andy Goldsworthy", *Country Living*, 48, Dec, 1989

R. Onoratio. "Illusive Spaces: The Art of Mary Miss", *Artforum*, Dec, 1978

—. *Mary Miss - Perimeters/ Pavilions/ Decoys*, Nassau County Museum, 1979

D. Oppenheim. *Dennis Oppenheim*, Musée d'Art Contemporain, Montréal, 1978

—. *Selected Works, 1967-1990*, Abrams, New York, NY, 1992

P. Osborne, ed. *Conceptual Art*, Phaidon, London, 2002

E. Osaka. *Andy Goldsworthy: Mountain and Coast: Autumn Into Winter*, Gallery Takagi, Nagoya, 1987

W. Packer. "Andy Goldsworthy's Transient Touch", *Sculpture*, July, 1989

—. "Sculpture from the countryside", *Financial Times*, July 7, 1987

T. Padon. "New York, New York", *Sculpture*, 13, 1, Jan/ Feb, 1994

E. Panofsky: *Studies in Iconology*, Harper & Row, New York, NY, 1972

A.C. Papadakis, ed. *British and American Art: The Uneasy Dialectic, Art & Design*, 3, 9/1, Academy Group, London, 1987

—. ed. *Abstract Art and the Rediscovery of the Spiritual, Art & Design*, 3, 5/6, Academy Group, London, 1987

—. ed. *The New Romantics, Art & Design*, 4, 11/12, Academy Group, 1988

—. *et al,* eds. *New Art*, Academy Group, London, 1991

R. Parker & G. Pollock. *Old Mistresses: Women, Art an Ideology*, Routledge & Kegan Paul, London, 1981

—. *Framing Feminism*, Pandora Press, London, 1987

D. Parr. "City focus: St. Louis: 'a different kind of energy'", *Art News,* 95, 3, Mch, 1996

J. Partridge. "Forest work", *Craft*, 81, July/ Aug, 1986

A. Patrizio. "Cube garden: sculpture at the Edinburgh Festival 1990", *Arts Review*, 42, July 27, 1990

P. Patton. "Robert Morris and the Fire Next Time", *Art News,* 82, 10, Dec, 1983

E. Pavese, ed. *Christo: Surrounded Islands*, Abrams, New York, NY, 1986

N. Pennick. *Mazes and Labyrinths*, Hale, London, 1990

J. Perreault. "A Minimal Future? Union-Made: Report on a Phenomenon", *Arts Magazine,* 41, Mch, 1967

J. Perrone. "Seeing Through Boxes", *Artforum*, 15, Nov, 1976

K. Petersen & J.J. Wilson: *Women Artists: Recognition and Reappraisal from the Early Middle Ages to the Twentieth Century,* Women's Press, London, 1978

R. Pincus-Witten. "Systematic Painting", *Artforum*, 5, 3, Nov, 1966

—. "Ryman, Marden, Manzoni: Theory, Sensibility, Mediation", *Artforum*, 10, 10, June, 1972

—. "Sol LeWitt", *Artforum*, 11, 6, Feb, 1973

—. *Postminimalism*, Out of London Press, New York, NY, 1977

—. *Entries: Maximalism*, Out of London Press, London, 1983

—. *Post-Minimalism into Maximalism*, UMI Research Press, Ann Arbor, MI, 1987

J. Poetter. *Donald Judd*, Cantz, Stuttgart, 1989

G. Pollock: *Vision and Difference: femininity, feminism and histories of art*, Routledge, London, 1988

L. Ponti. "Tony Cragg", *Domus*, 611, Nov, 1980

F. Popper. *Art, Action and Participation*, New York University Press, New York, NY, 1975

J.C. Powys. *Maiden Castle,* Cassell, London, 1937

—. *A Glastonbury Romance*, Macdonald, London, 1955

—. *Wolf Solent*, Penguin, London, 1964

—. *Autobiography*, Macdonald, London, 1967

A. Price. "A Conversation With Alice Aycock", *Architectural Design*, Apl, 1980

G. Prince. "With mud on their hands, growth, decay and the movement of change", *World Magazine,* Jan, 1991

J. Prinz. *Art Discourse*, Rutgers University Press, New Brunswick, NJ, 1991

S. Prokopoff. *A Romantic Minimalism*, Institute of Contemporary Art, Philadelphia, PA, 1967

J. Prown *et al. Discovered Lands, Invented Pasts*, Yale University Press, New Haven, CT, 1992

E. Rankin. "Popularising public sculpture in Britain: from landscape gardens to forest trails", *de Arte*, 53, Apl, 1996

C. Ratcliff. *In the Realm of the Monochrome*, Renaissance Society, University of Chicago, Chicago, IL, 1979

—. "The Compleat Smithson", *Art in America*, Jan, 1980

B. Redhead. *The Inspiration of Landscape: Artists in National Parks*, Phaidon, Oxford, 1989

W. Reh & C. Steenbergen. *Architecture and Landscape,* Prestel Publishing, 1996

C. Riley II. *Color Codes: Modern Theories in Color in Philosophy, Painting and Architecture, Literature, Music and Psychology*, University Press of New England, Hanover, NH, 1995

H. Risatti. "The Sculpture of Alice Aycock", *Woman's Art Journal*, Summer, 1985

J. Roberts. *Postmodernism, Politics and Art,* Manchester University Press, Manchester, 1990

C. Robins. "Object, Structure or Sculpture: Where Are We?", *Arts Magazine*, 40, 9, 1966

—. *The Pluralist Era: American Art, 1968-1981*, Harper & Row, New York, NY, 1984

P. Rodaway. *Sensuous Geographies*, Routledge, London, 1994

W. Romey. "The artist as geographer: Richard Long's Earth Art", *Professional Geographer*, 39, 4, 1987

B. Rose. "New York Letter", *Art International*, Feb 15, 1964

—. "Looking at American Sculpture", *Artforum*, 3, Feb, 1965a

—. "ABC Art", *Art in America*, 53, 5, Nov, 1965b

—. *A New Aesthetic*, Washington Gallery of Modern Art, Washington, DC, 1967

—. *American Art Since 1900*, Thames & Hudson, London, 1967

—. *Robert Morris*, Corcoran Gallery, Washington, DC, 1990

H. Rosenberg. *The De-Definition of Art*, Horizon Press, New York, NY, 1972

R. Rosenblum. "Notes on Sol LeWitt", in A. Legg, 1978

—. *Modern Painting and the Northern Romantic Tradition*, Thames & Hudson, London, 1978

—. *Jasper Johns' Paintings and Sculptures, 1954-1974,* Ann Arbor, Michigan, MI, 1985

—. "Romanticism and Retrospective: An Interview with Robert Rosenblum", in A. Papadakis, 1988

C. Ross. *Star Axis*, University of New Mexico Press, Albuqerque, NM, 1992

S. Ross. "Gardens, earthworks, and environmental art", in S. Kemal, 1993

—. *What Gardens Mean*, University of Chicago Press, Chicago, IL, 1998

M. Roth. "Robert Smithson on Duchamp", *Artforum*, Oct, 1969

—. ed. *The Amazing Decade: Women and Performance Art in America 1970-80*, Astro Artz, Los Angeles, CA, 1983

L. Rubin. *Frank Stella Paintings: 1958-1965*, New York, NY, 1986

W.S. Rubin. *Frank Stella*, New York Graphic Society, Greenwich, CT., 1970

—. *Frank Stella: 1970-1987*, Museum of Modern Art, New York, NY, 1987

M. Ryan, ed. *Gravity and Grace: The Changing Condition of Sculpture, 1965-1975*, Hayward Gallery, London, 1993

A. Saalfield. *Mary Miss*, Fogg Art Museum, Cambridge, MA, 1980

I. Sandler. *The Triumph of American Painting*, Harper & Row, New York, NY, 1970

—. *American Art of the 1960s*, Harper & Row, New York, NY, 1988

—. *Art of the Postmodern Era: From the 1960s to the Early 1990s*, Harper-Collins, London, 1997

H. Sayre, ed. *Happening and Fluxus*, Kölnischer Kunstverein, Cologne, 1970

D. Schaff. "British Art Now, at the Guggenheim and Beyond", *Art International*, Mch, 1980

M. Schinz. *Visions of Paradise: Themes and Variations on the Garden*, Thames & Hudson, London, 1985

P. Schjeldahl. *Art in Our Time: The Saatchi Collection*, Lund Humphries, London, 1984

P. Schuck. "Interview: Earth, Water, Wind", *Contemporanea*, Apl, 1990

D. Schwartz. *Lawrence Weiner*, König, Cologne, 1989

W. Seitz. *The Art of Assemblage*, MOMA, New York, NY, 1961

P. Selz. *Directions in Kinetic Sculpture*, University of California Press, Berkeley, CA, 1966

—. *Art in Our Times: A Pictorial History 1890-1980*, Thames & Hudson, London, 1982

H. Senie. *Contemporary Public Sculpture*, Oxford University Press, Oxford, 1983

—. & S. Webster, eds. *Critical Issues in Public Art*, Smithsonian Institution Press, Washington, DC, 1998

N. Serota, ed. *Donald Judd*, Tate Publishing, London, 2003

A. Seymour. *The New Art*, Hayward Gallery, London, 1972

—. "Walking in Circles", in R. Long, *Walking in Circles*

—. "Old World New World", in R. Long, *Old World New World*

E. Shanes. *Constantin Brancusi*, Abbeville, New York, NY, 1989

G. Shapiro. *Earthworks: Robert Smithson and After Babel*, University of

California Press, Berkeley, CA, 1995

W. Sharp *et al. Earth Art*, Andrew Dickson White Museum of Art, Cornell University, Ithaca, NY, 1969

—. "Structure and Sensibility", *Avalanche*, 5, Summer, 1972

N. Shulman. "Monday at the North Pole", *Arts Review*, June 2, 1989

N. Sinden. "Interview: Art in Nature: Andy Goldsworthy", *Resurgence*, 129, Aug, 1988

H. Singerman, ed. *Individuals: A Selected History of Contemporary Art, 1945-1986*, Museum of Contemporary Art, Los Angeles, CA, 1986

H.J. Smagula. *Currents: Contemporary Directions in the Visual Arts*, Prentice-Hall, Englewood Cliffs, NJ, 1983

B. Smith. *Fluorescent Light, etc, from Dan Flavin*, National Gallery of Canada, Ottawa, 1969

—. *Donald Judd*, National Gallery of Canada, Ottawa, 1975

D. Smith. *Sculpture and Drawings*, ed. J. Merkert, Prestel-Verlag, Munich, 1986

R. Smith. "Sol LeWitt", *Artforum*, Jan, 1975

—. "Review", *Artforum*, Dec, 1975

—. "De Maria: Elements", *Art in America*, May, 1978

R. Smithson. "Entropy and the New Monuments", *Artforum*, 4, 10, June, 1966

—. "Incidents of Mirror-Travel in the Yucatan", *Artforum*, Sept, 1967

—. The Monuments of Passaic", *Artforum*, Dec, 1967

—. "Toward the Development of an Air Terminal Site", *Artforum*, Summer, 1967

—. "A Museum of Language in the Vicinity of Art", *Art International*, 12, 3, Mch, 1968

—. *The Writings of Robert Smithson*, ed. N. Holt, New York University Press, New York, NY, 1979

—. *Robert Smithson*, ed. J. Flam, University of California Press, Berkeley, CA, 1996

—. *Robert Smithson: A Collection of Writings*, Pierogi Galery New York, NY, 1997

T. Sokolowski *et al. Robert Morris*, New York University Press, New York, NY, 1989

A. Sondheim, ed. *Post-Movement Art in America*, Dutton, New York, NY, 1977

A. Sonfist. *Alan Sonfist*, Neuberger Museum, New York, NY, 1978

—. ed. *Art in the Land: A Critical Anthology of Environmental Art*, Dutton, New York, NY, 1983

W. Spies. *The Running Fence Project, Christo*, Abrams, New York, NY, 1977

A. Staniszewski. *The Power of Display: A History of Exhibitions At the Museum of Modern Art*, MIT Press, Cambridge, MA, 1999

N. Stangos, ed. *Concepts of Modern Art*, Thames & Hudson, London, 1981

J. Stathatos. "Andy Goldsworthy's Evidences", *Creative Camera*, 255, Mch, 1986

F. Stella. *Working Space*, Harvard University Press, Cambridge, MA, 1986

—. *Frank Stella*, Madrid, 1995

N. Stewart. "Richard Long, Lines of Thought: A Conversation with Nick Stewart", *Circa*, Nov, 1984

K. Stiles & P. Selz, eds. *Theories & Documents of Contemporary Art: A Sourcebook of Artists' Writings*, University of California Press, Berkeley, CA, 1996

S.L. Stoops. *Andy Goldsworthy: Breakdown*, Rose Art Museum, 1992

W.J. Strachan. *Towards Sculpture: Maquettes and Sketches from Rodin to Oldenburg*, Thames & Hudson, London, 1976

—. *Open Air Sculpture in Britain*, Zwemmer, London, 1984

E. Suderburg, ed. *Space, Site, Intervention*, University of Minnesota Press,

Minneapolis, MN, 2000

T. Sultan. *Inability To Endure or Deny the World: Representation and Text In the Work of Robert Morris,* Corcoran Gallery, Washington, DC, 1990

G. Sutton. "Land art", *Landskab,* Dec, 1989

D. Sylvester. "Interview", *Jasper Johns Drawings,* Museum of Modern Art, Oxford, 1974

—. *About Modern Art,* Chatto & Windus, London, 1996

J. Taylor *et al. Robert Rauschenberg,* Smithsonian Institute, Washington, DC, 1976

C. Thacker. *The History of Gardens,* University of California Press, Berkeley, CA, 1979

G. Tiberghien. *Land Art*, Art Data, London, 1995

S. Tillim. "Earthworks and the New Picturesque", *Artforum,* Dec, 1968

C. Tomkins. *The Scene: Reports on Postmodern Art,* Viking, New York, NY, 1976

—. *Off the Wall: Robert Rauschenberg and the Art World of Our Time,* Doubleday, New York, NY, 1980

—. "Profiles", *New Yorker,* Sept, 1984

—. *Post- to Neo-: The Art World of the 1980s,* Penguin, London, 1989

M. Treib. "Frame, moment and sequence: the photographic book and the designed landscape", *Journal of Garden History,* 15, 2, Summer, 1995

E. Tsai. *Robert Smithson Unearthed,* Columbia University Press, New York, NY, 1991

M. Tuchman. *American Sculpture of the Sixties,* Los Angeles County Museum of Art, CA, 1967

—. *The Spiritual in Art: Abstract Painting 1880-1985,* Los Angeles County Museum of Art/ Abbeville Press, New York, NY, 1986

P. Tuchman. "Minimalism and Critical Response", *Artforum,* 15, 9, May, 1977

—. "Background of a Minimalist: Carl Andre", *Artforum,* Mch, 1978

—. "Minimalism", *Three Decades: The Oliver-Hoffmann Collection,* Museum of Contemporary Art, Chicago, IL, 1988

M. Tucker. *Robert Morris,* New York, NY, 1970

W. Tucker. *The Language of Sculpture,* Thames & Hudson, London, 1974

B. Tufnell & A. Wilson. *Hamish Fulton: Walking Journey,* Tate Publishing, London, 2002

J. Turrell. *Mapping Spaces,* Peter Blum, New York, NY, 1987.

—. interview, in B. Oakes, 1995

G. de Vries, ed. *On Art: Artists' Writings on the Changed Notion of Art After 1965,* Cologne, 1974

A.M. Wagner. *Three Artists (Three Women): Modernism and the Art of Hesse, Krasner and O'Keeffe,* University of California Press, Berkeley, CA, 1996

D. Waldman. "Samaras", *Art News,* Oct, 1966

—. *Carl Andre,* Guggenheim Museum, New York, NY, 1970a

—. "Holding the Floor", *Art News,* Oct, 1970b

J. Walker. *Art & Outrage: Provocation, Controversy and the Visual Arts,* Pluto Press, London, 1999

—. *Art and Celebrity,* Pluto Press, London, 2003

J. Watkins. "In the artist's studio: Andy Goldsworthy: Touching North", *Art International,* 9 Winter, 1989

M. Webster. "Andy Goldsworthy at San Jose Museum of Art", *ArtWeek,* 26, 4, Apl, 1995

U. Weilacher *et al. Between Landscape Architecture and Land Art,* Birkhauser

Verlag AG, 1999

L. Weiner. *Lawrence Weiner, Works,* Anatol AV und Film-produktion Hamburg, 1977

L. Weintraub. *The Maximal Implications of the Minimalist Line*, Edith C. Blum Art Institute, New York, NY, 1985

Welsh Sculpture Trust. *Sculpture in a Country Park*, Welsh Sculpture Trust, 1983

C. West. "From genesis to box", *Modern Painters*, 5, 4, Winter, 1992

D. Wheeler. *Art Since Mid-Century: 1945 to the Present*, Thames & Hudson, London, 1991

J. White. *The Birth and Rebirth of Pictorial Space*, Faber, London, 1981

O. Wick *et al*. *James Turrell*, Turske & Turske Gallery, Zurich, 1990

A. Wildermuth. *Richard Long*, Galerie Buchmann, Basel, 1985

A. Wilding: *Alison Wilding*, with M. Tooby, Tate Gallery, St Ives, Cornwall, 1994

R. Williams. *After Modern Sculpture: Art in the United States and Europe 1965-70*, Manchester University Press, Manchester, 2000

A. Windsor, ed. *British Sculptors of the 20th Century*, Ashgate, Aldershot, Hants., 2003

C. van Winkel. "The Crooked Path, Patterns of Kinetic Energy", *Parkett*, 33, 1992

M. Winton. "Sculptures That Blow Away", *Ark*, Spring, 1970

G. Woods *et al*, eds. *Art Without Boundaries*, Thames & Hudson, London, 1972

M. Wortz. *Light and Space*, Whitney Museum of American Art, New York, NY, 1980

S. Wrede & W. Adams. *Denatured Visions: Landscape and Culture in the 20th Century*, Abrams, New York, NY, 1991

S. Yard. *Christo: Oceanfront*, Princeton University Press, Princeton, NJ, 1975

—. *Sitings*, La Jolla Museum of Contemporary Art, La Jolla, CA, 1986

M. Yule. "Andy Goldsworthy, a Lake District photowork", *National Art-Collections Fund Review*, 88, 1992

L. Zelevansky. "Richard Long", *Art News*, 83, 8, Oct, 1984

WEBSITES

Christo <www.christojeanneclaude.net>
Walter de Maria <www.lightningfield.org>
Chris Drury <www.chrisdrury.co.uk>
Hamish Fulton <www.hamish-fulton.com>
Andy Goldsworthy, Sheepfolds site: <www.sheepfolds.org>
Andy Goldsworthy, *Rivers and Tides* DVD <www.skyline.uk.com/riversandtides>
Donald Judd <www.chinati.org>
Richard Long <www.richardlong.org>
Richard Long Newsletter <therichardlongnewsletter.org>
Mary Miss <www.marymiss.com>
Robert Smithson <www.robertsmithson.com>
James Turrell <www.rodencrater.org>

Earthworks <www.earthworks.org>
The Artists: <www.the-artists.org>
Sculpture at Goodwood, CASS: <www.sculpture.org.uk>
Crescent Moon Publishing: <www.crescentmoon.org.uk>

THE ART OF ANDY GOLDSWORTHY

COMPLETE WORKS: SPECIAL EDITION
(PAPERBACK and HARDBACK)

by William Malpas

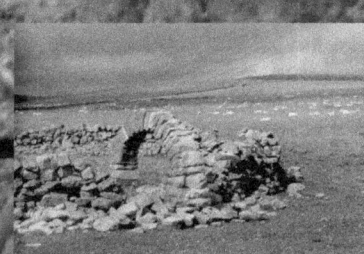

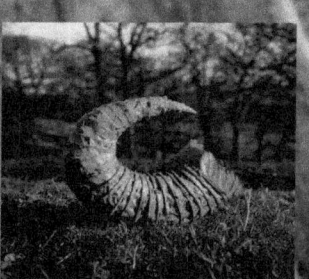

A new, special edition of the study of the contemporary British sculptor, Andy Goldsworthy, including a new introduction, new bibliography and many new illustrations.

This is the most comprehensive, up-to-date, well-researched and in-depth account of Goldsworthy's art available anywhere.

Andy Goldsworthy makes land art. His sculpture is a sensitive, intuitive response to nature, light, time, growth, the seasons and the earth. Goldsworthy's environmental art is becoming ever more popular: 1993's art book *Stone* was a bestseller; the press raved about Goldsworthy taking over a number of London West End art galleries in 1994; during 1995 Goldsworthy designed a set of Royal Mail stamps and had a show at the British Museum. Malpas surveys all of Goldsworthy's art, and analyzes his relation with other land artists such as Robert Smithson, Walter de Maria, Richard Long and David Nash, and his place in the contemporary British art scene.

The Art of Andy Goldsworthy discusses all of Goldsworthy's important and recent exhibitions and books, including the *Sheepfolds* project; the TV documentaries; *Wood* (1996); the New York Holocaust memorial (2003); and Goldsworthy's collaboration on a dance performance.

Illustrations: 70 b/w, 1 colour. 330 pages. New, special, 2nd edition.
Publisher: Crescent Moon Publishing. Distributor: Gardners Books.

ISBN 1-86171-059-3 (9781861710598) (Paperback) £25.00 / $44.00

ISBN 1-86171-080-1 (9781861710802) (Hardback) £60.00 / $105.00

ANDY GOLDSWORTHY IN CLOSE-UP

SPECIAL EDITION (HARDBACK and PAPERBACK)

by William Malpas

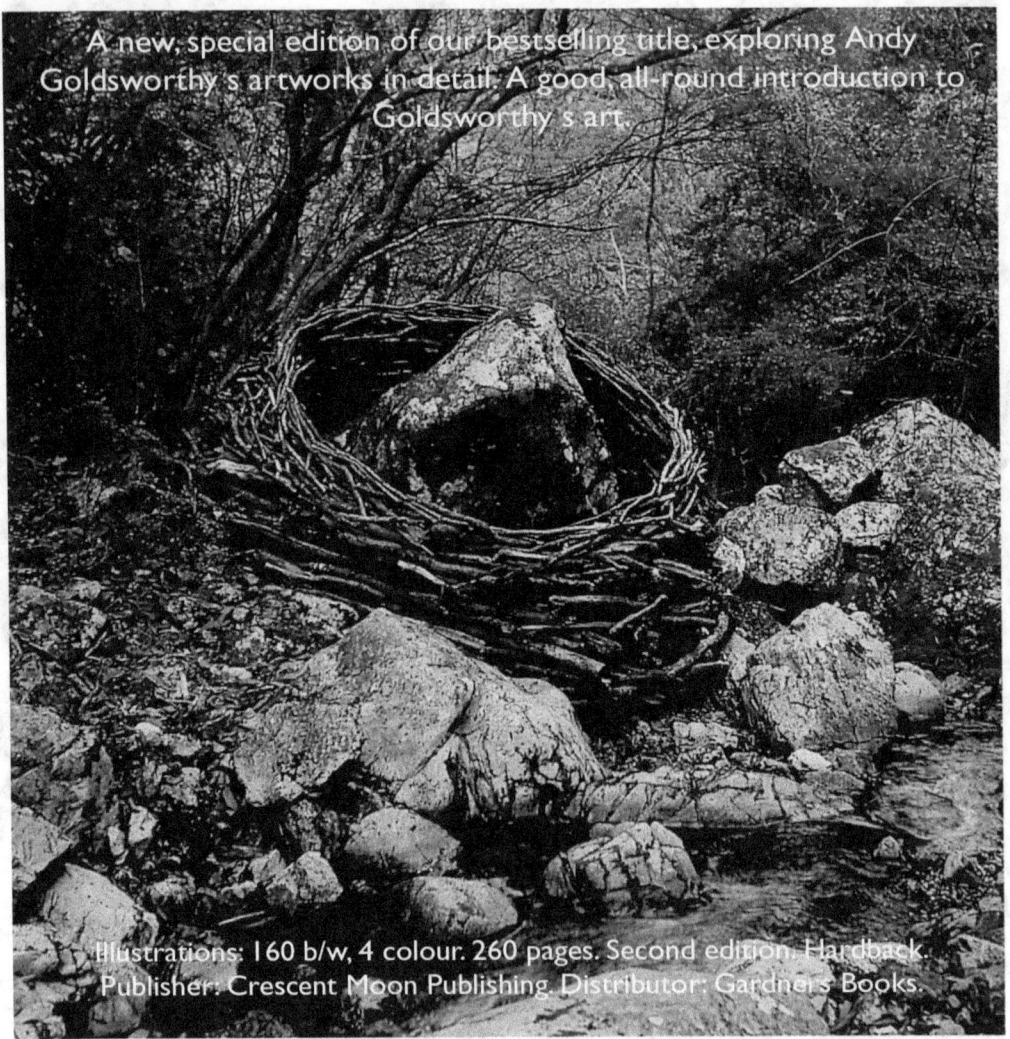

A new, special edition of our bestselling title, exploring Andy Goldsworthy's artworks in detail. A good, all-round introduction to Goldsworthy's art.

Illustrations: 160 b/w, 4 colour. 260 pages. Second edition. Hardback.
Publisher: Crescent Moon Publishing. Distributor: Gardner's Books.

ISBN 1-86171-094-1 (9781861710949) (Hbk) £60.00 / $105.00

ISBN 1-86171-091-7 (9781861710919) (Pbk) £25.00 / $44.00

Available from bookstores. amazon.com, play.com, tesco.com, and other web-sites.
In the United States from Baker & Taylor, (800) 7753760 or (800) 7751100
or (908) 5417062. electser@btol.com or btinfo@btol.com.

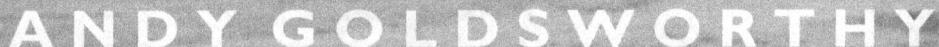

ANDY GOLDSWORTHY

TOUCHING NATURE:
SPECIAL EDITION

(PAPERBACK and HARDBACK)

by William Malpas

A new, special and updated edition of our bestselling title, providing
an excellent general introduction to the art of Andy Goldsworthy.

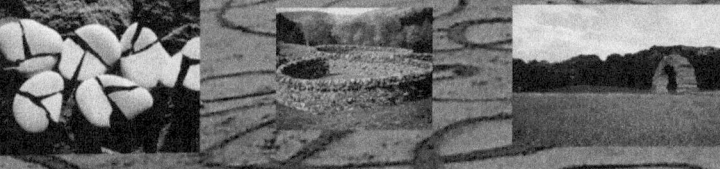

Illustrations: 75 b/w, 2 colour. 354 pages. Third edition. Paperback.

Publisher: Crescent Moon Publishing. Distributor: Gardners Books.

ISBN 1-86171-056-9 (9781861717) (Paperback) £25.00 / $44.00

ISBN 1-86171-087-9 (9781861710871) (Hardback) £60.00 / $105.00

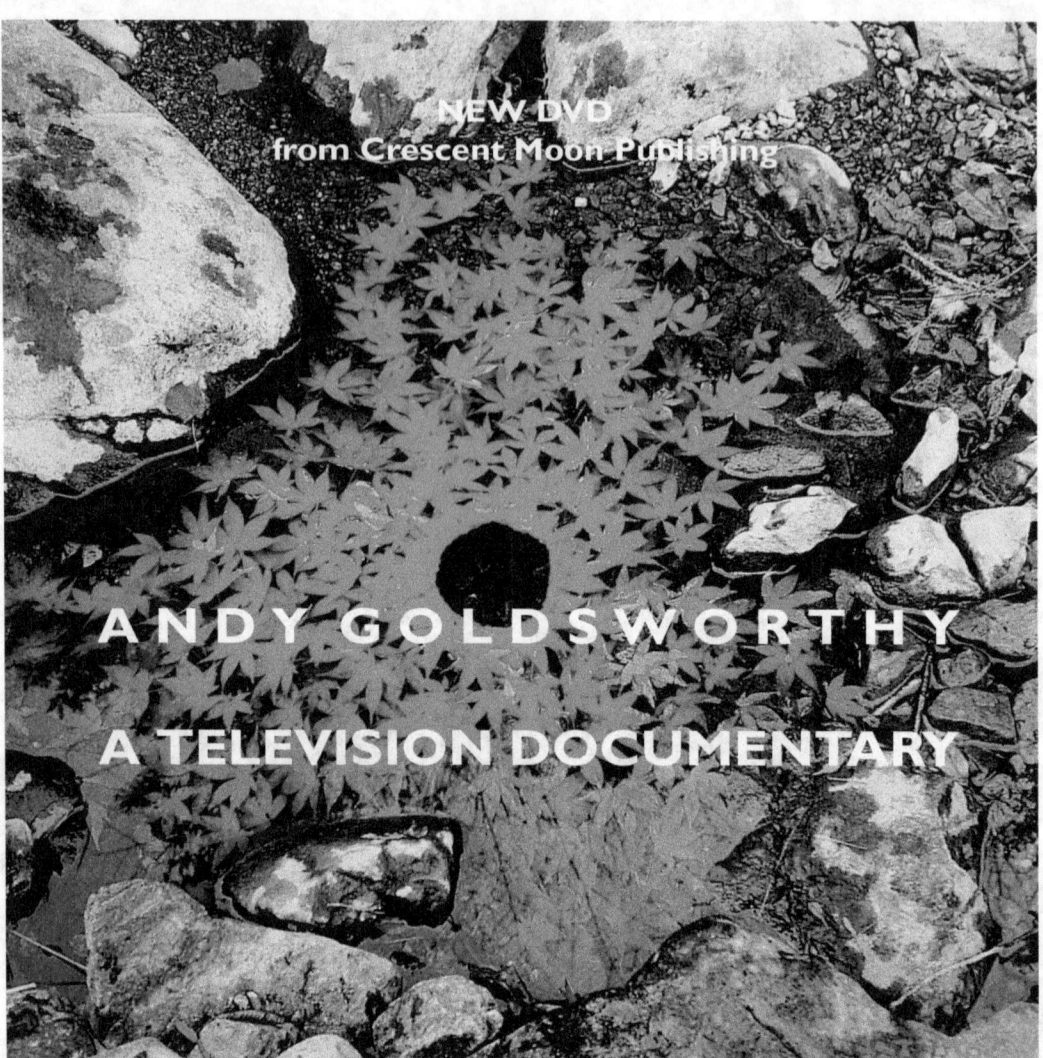

NEW DVD
from Crescent Moon Publishing

ANDY GOLDSWORTHY

A TELEVISION DOCUMENTARY

Andy Goldsworthy makes land art. His sculpture is a sensitive, intuitive response to nature, light, time, growth, the seasons and the earth. Goldsworthy's environmental art is becoming ever more popular: his art books are bestsellers; he has exhibited around the world; important and recent exhibitions include the Sheepfolds project; the Washington installation (2005); Passage (2004); the New York Holocaust memorial (2003); and a collaboration on a dance performance.

This video documentary surveys every aspect of Andy Goldsworthy's art, and all of his major works. It also discusses his relation with other land artists such as Robert Smithson, Walter de Maria, Richard Long and David Nash, and his place in the contemporary art scene in the UK.

This is the only TV documentary of its kind available on DVD and video.

EXTRAS

Resources: further reading; complete bibliography of Andy Goldsworthy, and life and work (on DVD-ROM); and weblinks.
Photo library of land artworks.
Extra footage.

55 minutes.   PAL and NTSC.   Colour.   DVD.   Multi-region.   VHS video.
Stereo.   E (Exempt from classification)

LAND ART

A COMPLETE GUIDE TO LANDSCAPE, ENVIRONMENTAL, EARTHWORKS, NATURE, SCULPTURE AND INSTALLATION ART

by William Malpas

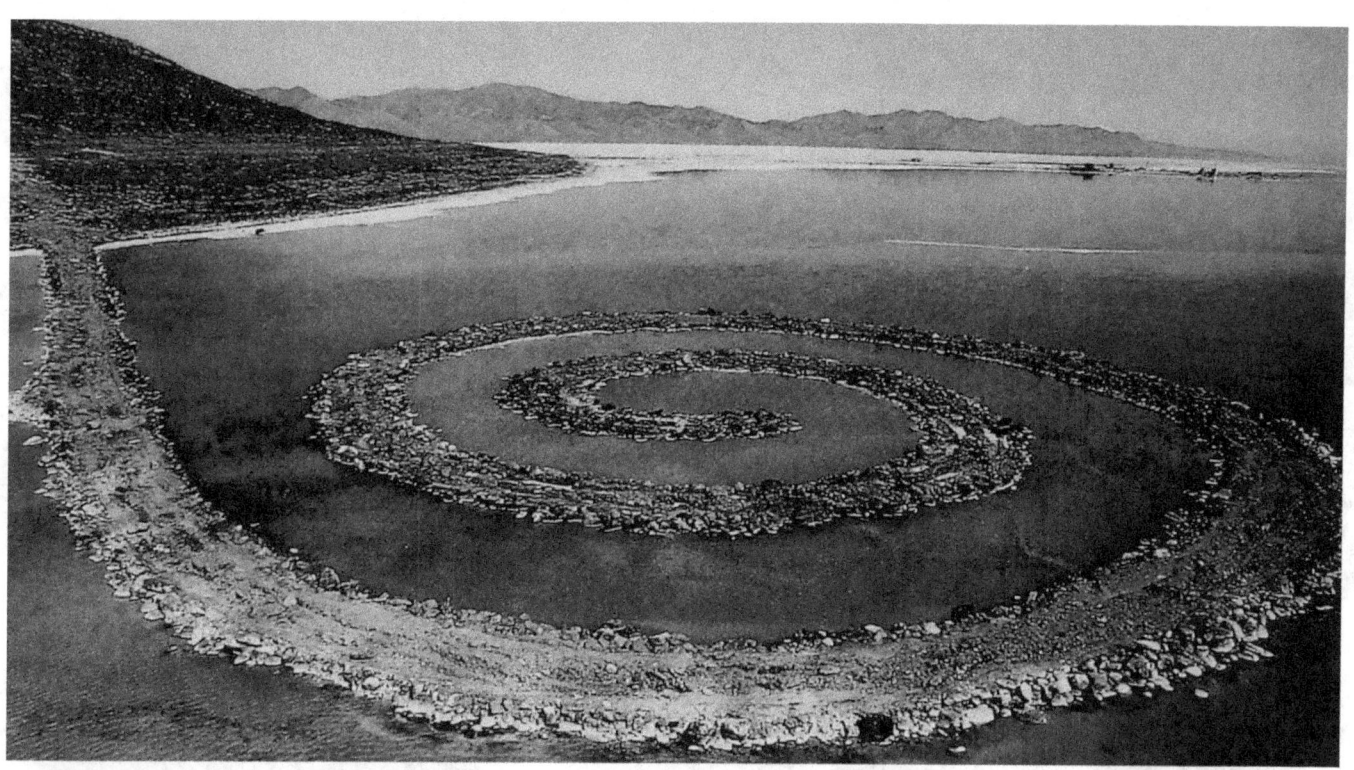

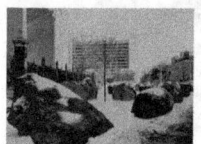 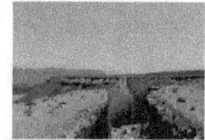 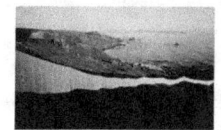 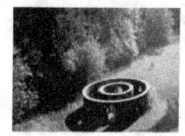 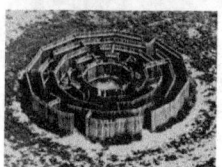

A new, special edition of our popular book on land art.
Chapters on land artists such as Robert Smithson, Walter de Maria, Christo,
Michael Heizer, Richard Long and Andy Goldsworthy.

Illustrations: 35 b/w, 2 colour. 314 pages. First edition. Paperback.

Publisher: Crescent Moon Publishing. Distributor: Gardners Books.

ISBN 1-86171-062-3 (9781861710628) £25.00 / $44.00

LAND ART IN CLOSE-UP

SPECIAL EDITION (PAPERBACK)

by William Malpas

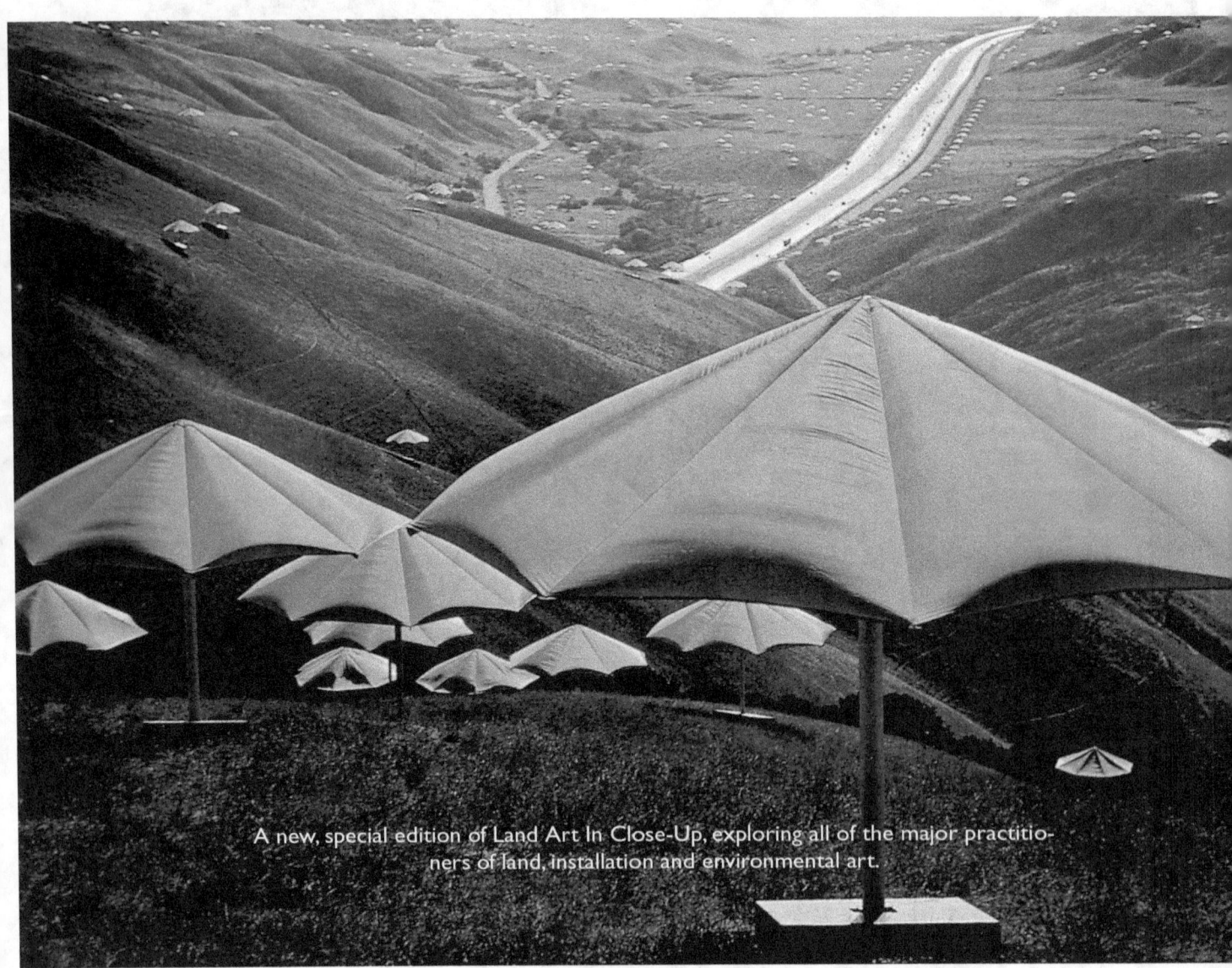

A new, special edition of Land Art In Close-Up, exploring all of the major practitioners of land, installation and environmental art.

Illustrations: 161 b/w, 2 colour. 248 pages. Second edition. Paperback.

Publisher: Crescent Moon Publishing. Distributor: Gardners Books.

ISBN 1-86171-092-5 (9781861710925) £25.00 / $44.00

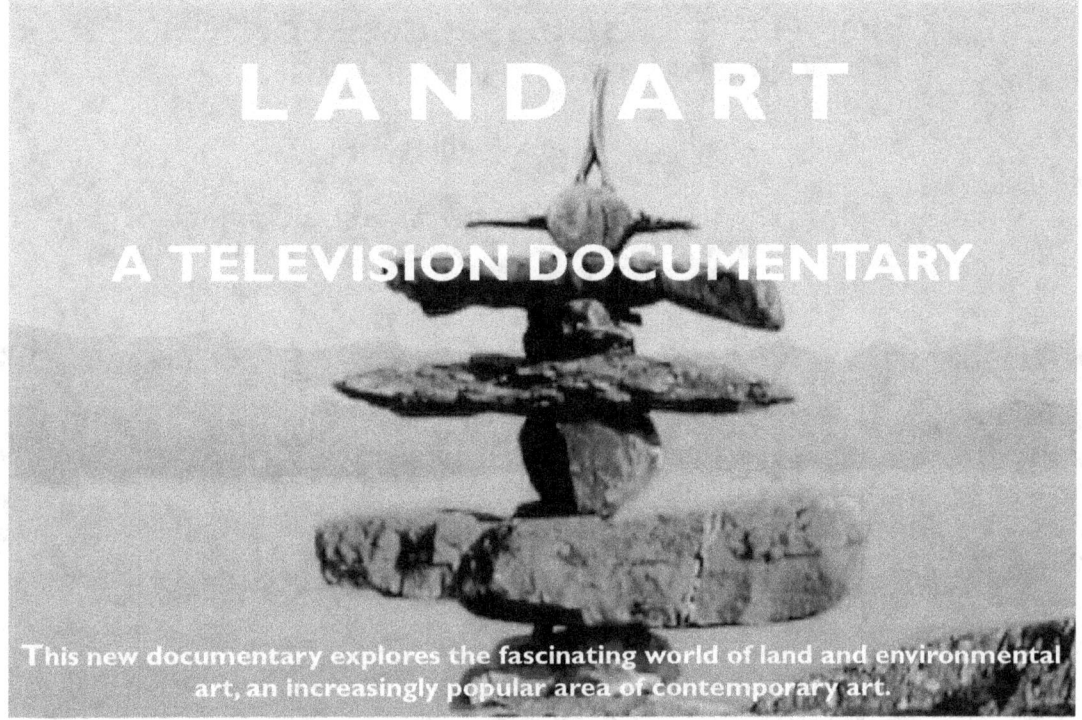

LAND ART

A TELEVISION DOCUMENTARY

This new documentary explores the fascinating world of land and environmental art, an increasingly popular area of contemporary art.

For the land artist, the whole planet is an artist's studio. The land artist ranges over the whole globe. A desert, a beach, a field, a forest becomes a studio, a place of creative activity. Land art is a world of towers and tunnels, stars and scars, pools and pipes, circles and chasms, maps and mazes, stones and cones. This documentary explores all of the major land, environmental and earthwork artists of the past 40 years, including James Turrell and his vast volcano site in Arizona, Michael Heizer's Nevada desert structures, Robert Smithson and his giant spiral, entropic earthworks, Christo's wrapped buildings and islands, Robert Morris's environments, Walter de Maria's Romantic Lightning Field, Hamish Fulton's walks and words, Richard Long and his art of walking, Andy Goldsworthy's natural, spontaneous sculptures, Alice Aycock's mysterious underground mazes, Mary Miss's sunken pools and pavilions, and Nancy Holt and her observatory sculptures.

This is the only TV documentary of its kind available on DVD and video.

EXTRAS

Resources (further reading; complete bibliography of land art (on DVD-ROM); and weblinks).
Photo library of land artworks.

60 minutes. PAL and NTSC. Colour. DVD. Multi-region. VHS video. Stereo. E (Exempt from classification)

Directed by Jeremy Robinson. Presented by Siena Lloyd.

Producer: Ocean Magic Entertainment. Publisher: Crescent Moon Publishing.

ISBN 1-86171-082-8 (9781861710826) £15.00 / $24.50

THE ART OF RICHARD LONG

COMPLETE WORKS : SPECIAL EDITION
(HARDBACK and PAPERBACK)

by William Malpas

A new study of the British artist Richard Long, an important contemporary international artist. The most detailed, in-depth exploration of Richard Long's art currently available.

Illustrations: 48 b/w, 2 colour. 439 pages.
First edition. Hardback and paperback editions.

Publisher: Crescent Moon Publishing. Distributor: Gardners Books.

ISBN 1-86171-079-8 (9781861710796) (Hardback) £60.00 / $105.00

ISBN 1-86171-081-X (9781861710819) (Paperback) £25.00 / $44.00

MINIMAL ART AND ARTISTS

FROM THE 1960S AND AFTER

by Laura Garrard

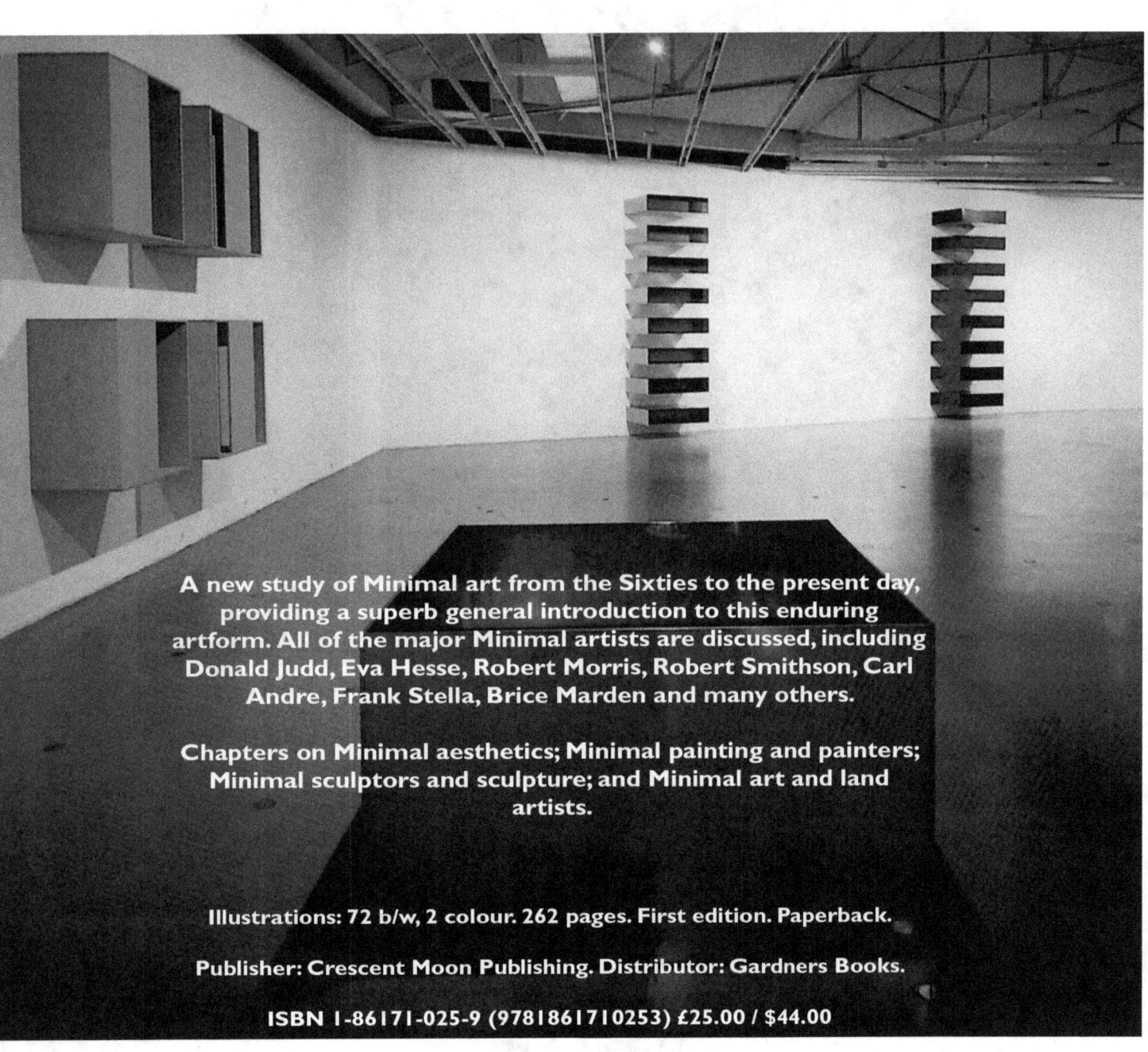

A new study of Minimal art from the Sixties to the present day, providing a superb general introduction to this enduring artform. All of the major Minimal artists are discussed, including Donald Judd, Eva Hesse, Robert Morris, Robert Smithson, Carl Andre, Frank Stella, Brice Marden and many others.

Chapters on Minimal aesthetics; Minimal painting and painters; Minimal sculptors and sculpture; and Minimal art and land artists.

Illustrations: 72 b/w, 2 colour. 262 pages. First edition. Paperback.

Publisher: Crescent Moon Publishing. Distributor: Gardners Books.

ISBN 1-86171-025-9 (9781861710253) £25.00 / $44.00

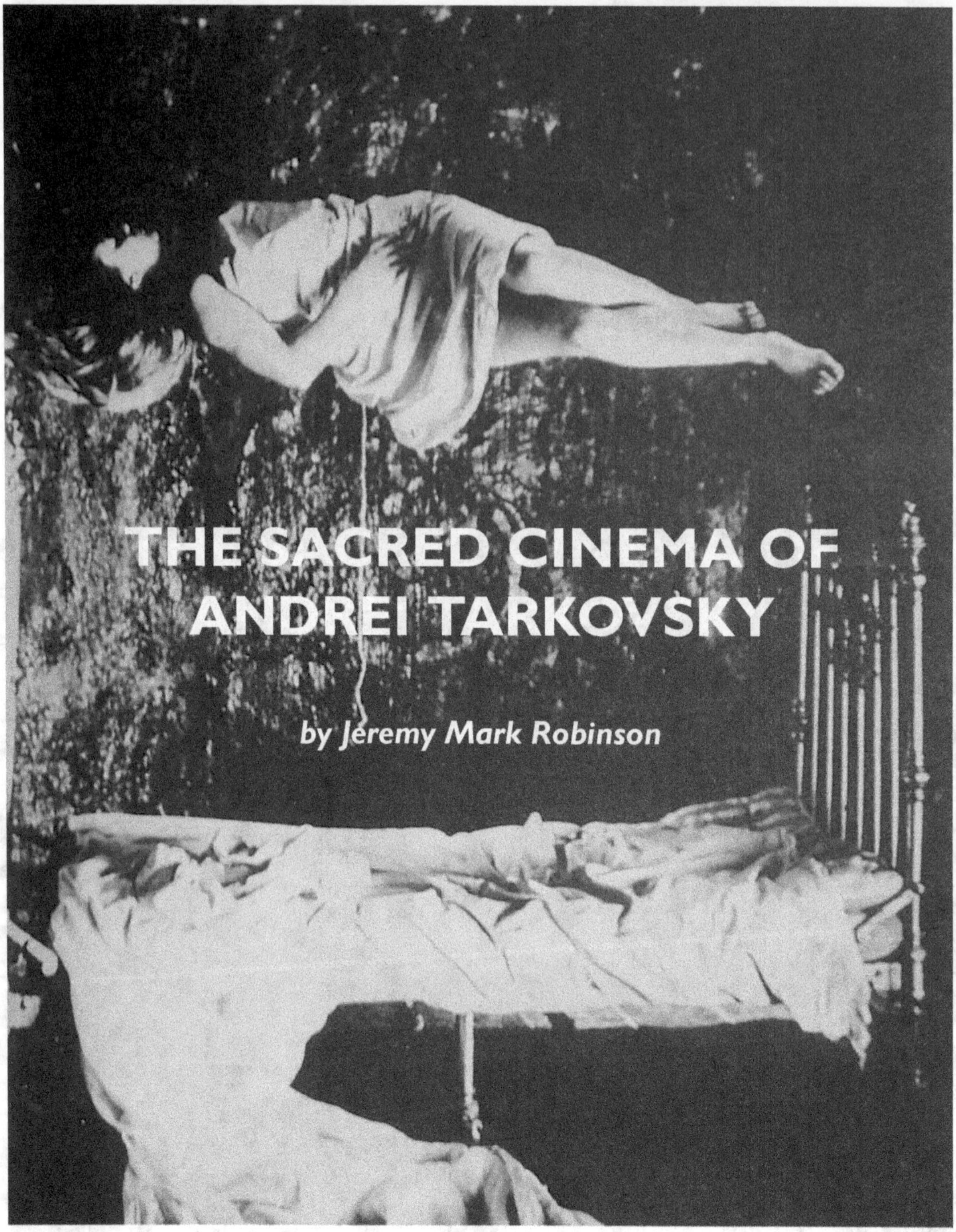

THE SACRED CINEMA OF
ANDREI TARKOVSKY

by Jeremy Mark Robinson

A new study of the Russian filmmaker Andrei Tarkovsky (1932-1986), director of seven feature films, including *Andrei Roublyov, Mirror, Solaris, Stalker* and *The Sacrifice*.
This is one of the most comprehensive and detailed studies of Tarkovsky's cinema available. Every film is explored in depth, with scene-by-scene analyses. All aspects of Tarkovsky's output are critiqued, including editing, camera, staging, script, budget, collaborations, production, sound, music, performance and spirituality. Tarkovsky is placed with a European New Wave tradition of filmmaking, alongside directors like Ingmar Bergman, Carl Theodor Dreyer, Pier Paolo Pasolini and Robert Bresson.
An essential addition to film studies.

Illustrations: 150 b/w, 4 colour. 682 pages. First edition. Hardback.

Publisher: Crescent Moon Publishing. Distributor: Gardners Books.

ISBN 1-86171-096-8 (9781861710963) £60.00 / $105.00

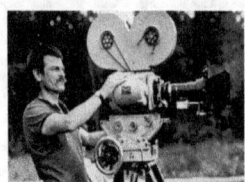

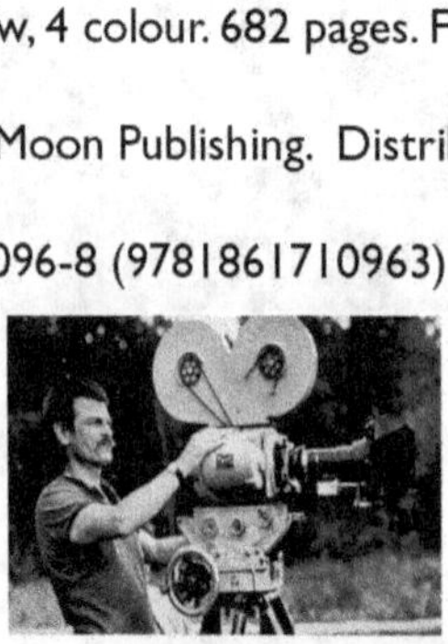

CRESCENT MOON PUBLISHING

ARTS, PAINTING, SCULPTURE

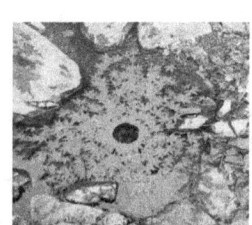

The Art of Andy Goldsworthy: Complete Works(Pbk)
The Art of Andy Goldsworthy: Complete Works (Hbk)
Andy Goldsworthy in Close-Up (Pbk)
Andy Goldsworthy in Close-Up (Hbk)
Land Art: A Complete Guide
Richard Long: The Art of Walking
The Art of Richard Long: Complete Works (Pbk)

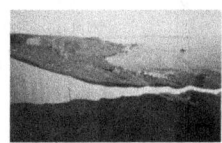

The Art of Richard Long: Complete Works (Hbk)
Richard Long in Close-Up
Land Art In the UK
Land Art in Close-Up
Installation Art in Close-Up

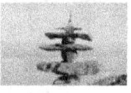

Minimal Art and Artists In the 1960s and After
Colourfield Painting
Land Art DVD, TV documentary
Andy Goldsworthy DVD, TV documentary
The Erotic Object: Sexuality in Sculpture From Prehistory to the Present Day
Sex in Art: Pornography and Pleasure in Painting and Sculpture
Postwar Art
Sacred Gardens: The Garden in Myth, Religion and Art
Glorification: Religious Abstraction in Renaissance and 20th Century Art
Early Netherlandish Painting

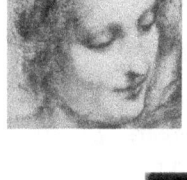

Leonardo da Vinci
Piero della Francesca
Giovanni Bellini
Fra Angelico: Art and Religion in the Renaissance
Mark Rothko: The Art of Transcendence
Frank Stella: American Abstract Artist

Jasper Johns: Painting By Numbers
Brice Marden
Alison Wilding: The Embrace of Sculpture
Vincent van Gogh: Visionary Landscapes
Eric Gill: Nuptials of God
Constantin Brancusi: Sculpting the Essence of Things
Max Beckmann
Egon Schiele: Sex and Death In Purple Stockings

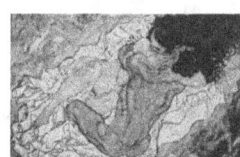

Delizioso Fotografico Fervore: Works In Process 1
Sacro Cuore: Works In Process 2
The Light Eternal: J.M.W. Turner
The Madonna Glorified: Karen Arthurs

LITERATURE

J.R.R. Tolkien: The Books, The Films, The Whole Cultural Phenomenon
Harry Potter
Sexing Hardy: Thomas Hardy and Feminism
Thomas Hardy's *Tess of the d'Urbervilles*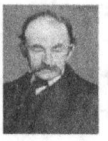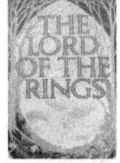
Thomas Hardy's *Jude the Obscure*
Thomas Hardy: The Tragic Novels
Love and Tragedy: Thomas Hardy
The Poetry of Landscape in Hardy
Wessex Revisited: Thomas Hardy and John Cowper Powys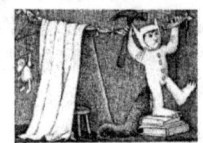
Wolfgang Iser: Essays
Petrarch, Dante and the Troubadours
Maurice Sendak and the Art of Children's Book Illustration
Andrea Dworkin
Cixous, Irigaray, Kristeva: The *Jouissance* of French Feminism
Julia Kristeva: Art, Love, Melancholy, Philosophy, Semiotics and Psychoanalysis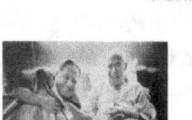
Hélene Cixous I Love You: The *Jouissance* of Writing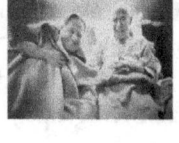
Luce Irigaray: Lips, Kissing, and the Politics of Sexual Difference
Peter Redgrove: Here Comes the Flood
Peter Redgrove: Sex-Magic-Poetry-Cornwall
Lawrence Durrell: Between Love and Death, East and West
Love, Culture & Poetry: Lawrence Durrell
Cavafy: Anatomy of a Soul
German Romantic Poetry: Goethe, Novalis, Heine, Hölderlin, Schlegel, Schiller
Feminism and Shakespeare
Shakespeare: Selected Sonnets
Shakespeare: Love, Poetry & Magic
The Passion of D.H. Lawrence
D.H. Lawrence: Symbolic Landscapes
D.H. Lawrence: Infinite Sensual Violence
Rimbaud: Arthur Rimbaud and the Magic of Poetry
The Ecstasies of John Cowper Powys
Sensualism and Mythology: The Wessex Novels of John Cowper Powys
Amorous Life: John Cowper Powys and the Manifestation of Affectivity (H.W. Fawkner)
Postmodern Powys: New Essays on John Cowper Powys (Joe Boulter)
Rethinking Powys: Critical Essays on John Cowper Powys
Paul Bowles & Bernardo Bertolucci
Rainer Maria Rilke
In the Dim Void: Samuel Beckett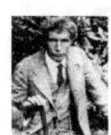
Samuel Beckett Goes into the Silence
André Gide: Fiction and Fervour
Jackie Collins and the Blockbuster Novel
Blinded By Her Light: The Love-Poetry of Robert Graves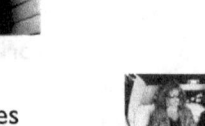
The Passion of Colours: Travels In Mediterranean Lands
Poetic Forms
The Dolphin-Boy

POETRY

The Best of Peter Redgrove's Poetry
Peter Redgrove: Here Comes The Flood
Peter Redgrove: Sex-Magic-Poetry-Cornwall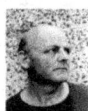
Ursula Le Guin: Walking In Cornwall
Dante: Selections From the Vita Nuova
Petrarch, Dante and the Troubadours
William Shakespeare: Selected Sonnets
Blinded By Her Light: The Love-Poetry of Robert Graves
Emily Dickinson: Selected Poems
Emily Brontë: Poems
Thomas Hardy: Selected Poems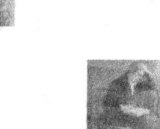
Percy Bysshe Shelley: Poems
John Keats: Selected Poems
D.H. Lawrence: Selected Poems
Edmund Spenser: Poems
John Donne: Poems
Henry Vaughan: Poems
Sir Thomas Wyatt: Poems
Robert Herrick: Selected Poems
Rilke: Space, Essence and Angels in the Poetry of Rainer Maria Rilke
Rainer Maria Rilke: Selected Poems
Friedrich Hölderlin: Selected Poems
Arseny Tarkovsky: Selected Poems
Arthur Rimbaud: Selected Poems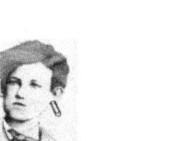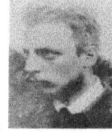
Arthur Rimbaud: A Season in Hell
Arthur Rimbaud and the Magic of Poetry
D.J. Enright: By-Blows
Jeremy Reed: Brigitte's Blue Heart
Jeremy Reed: Claudia Schiffer's Red Shoes
Gorgeous Little Orpheus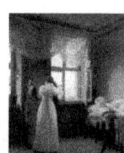
Radiance: New Poems
Crescent Moon Book of Nature Poetry
Crescent Moon Book of Love Poetry
Crescent Moon Book of Mystical Poetry
Crescent Moon Book of Elizabethan Love Poetry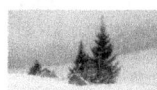
Crescent Moon Book of Metaphysical Poetry
Crescent Moon Book of Romantic Poetry
Pagan America: New American Poetry

MEDIA, CINEMA, FEMINISM and CULTURAL STUDIES

J.R.R. Tolkien: The Books, The Films, The Whole Cultural Phenomenon
Harry Potter
Cixous, Irigaray, Kristeva: The *Jouissance* of French Feminism
Julia Kristeva: Art, Love, Melancholy, Philosophy, Semiotics and   Psychoanalysis
Luce Irigaray: Lips, Kissing, and the Politics of Sexual Difference
Hélene Cixous I Love You: The *Jouissance* of Writing
Andrea Dworkin
'Cosmo Woman': The World of Women's Magazines
Women in Pop Music
Discovering the Goddess (Geoffrey Ashe)
The Poetry of Cinema
The Sacred Cinema of Andrei Tarkovsky (Pbk and Hbk)
Paul Bowles & Bernardo Bertolucci
Media Hell: Radio, TV and the Press
An Open Letter to the BBC
Detonation Britain: Nuclear War in the UK
Feminism and Shakespeare
Wild Zones: Pornography, Art and Feminism
Sex in Art: Pornography and Pleasure in Painting and Sculpture
Sexing Hardy: Thomas Hardy and Feminism

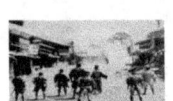
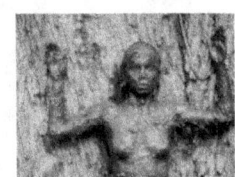
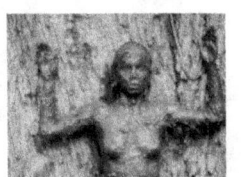
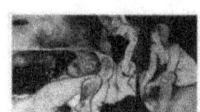

In my view *The Light Eternal* is among the very best of all the material I read on Turner. (Douglas Graham, director of the Turner Museum, Denver, Colorado)

The Light Eternal is a model monograph, an exemplary job. The subject matter of the book is beautifully organised and dead on beam. (Lawrence Durrell)

It is amazing for me to see my work treated with such passion and respect. (Andrea Dworkin)

Sex-Magic-Poetry-Cornwall is a very rich essay... It is like a brightly-lighted box. (Peter Redgrove)

CRESCENT MOON PUBLISHING
P.O. Box 393, Maidstone, Kent, ME14 5XU, United Kingdom.
01622-729593 (UK) 01144-1622-729593 (US) 0044-1622-729593 (other territories)
cresmopub@yahoo.co.uk   www.crescentmoon.org.uk